POLITICAL STAGES:

PLAYS THAT SHAPED
A CENTURY

Edited by

Emily Mann
and
David Roessel

APPLAUSE
THEATRE & CINEMA BOOKS

Political Stages: An Anthology of American Plays
Copyright ©2002 by Applause Theatre & Cinema Books
All Rights Reserved
ISBN 1-55783-490-3

Library of Congress Cataloging-in-Publication Data:

Political Stages: an anthology of plays / edited by Emily Mann & David Roessel,
    p. cm.
    ISBN 1-55783-490-3
    1. Political plays, American. 2. American Drama--20th Century. I. Mann, Emily.
II. Roessel, David E. (David Ernest), 1954-

PS627.P65 P65 2001
812'.5080358--dc21

        2001056092

APPLAUSE
THEATRE & CINEMA BOOKS
151 West 46th Street
New York, NY 10036
Phone: 212-575-9265
Fax: 646-562-5852
email: info@applausepub.com

SALES & DISTRIBUTION

NORTH AMERICA:	UK:
HAL LEONARD CORP.	COMBINED BOOK SERVICES LTD.
7777 West Bluemound Road	Units I/K, Paddock Wood Distribution Centre
P. O. Box 13819	Paddock Wood, Tonbridge, Kent TN12 6UU
Milwaukee, WI 53213	Phone: (44) 01892 837171
Phone: 1-414-774-3630	Fax: (44) 01892 837272
Fax: 1-414-774-3259	United Kingdom
email: halinfo@halleonard.com	
internet: www.halleonard.com	

TABLE OF CONTENTS

For Grace Shackney

PREFACE

by Emily Mann

From Aeschylus, Sophocles, and Shakespeare to Kushner, Marc Wolf, and Adrienne Kennedy—from poetic drama to documentary theatre—the great plays of an age are invariably the political plays of the age.

From the question of rational justice versus revenge in *The Oresteia* to the legacy of hate in *Romeo and Juliet*, from the disenfranchisement of women in *Trifles* to the failure of American race relations in *Mulatto*, from the attempt to hide from political horrors in *The Film Society* to facing the brutal horrors of violence in *Not About Nightingales*, these plays and playwrights looked at the world around them and asked the big questions of their day. They ask the audience to witness these stories and wrestle with the hard and essential questions these stories engender. The plays in this book tell the story of twentieth century America. We ask you, the reader, to bear witness.

INTRODUCTION

by David Roessel

The original concept behind this volume was to collect political plays spanning what has been called the "American Century," to reflect upon the place of the American theatre in our public sphere as we begin to explore where we have been and where we are going in this new millennium. Our choices serve as signposts to the interconnected relationship between politics and theatre in this country, and we hope will point the reader towards reading or producing the many other extraordinary political dramas we did not have space to include in this volume.

The framework is designed to promote comparison and discussion on several levels. For example, several plays evolved from journalistic techniques. *Trifles* evolved out of Susan Glaspell's notes from her work as a reporter in an Iowa courtroom covering a trial in which a woman killed her husband for strangling her bird. Clifford Odets's *Waiting for Lefty*, Emily Mann's *Execution of Justice* and Marc Wolf's *Another American: Asking and Telling* grew out of trial transcript, public record, and tape recorded testimony as they interviewed people concerning a taxi strike in New York in 1935, the murders of George Moscone and Harvey Milk in San Francisco in 1979, and the issue of gays in the military in the present day. Five of the plays, *Mulatto*, *Dutchman*, *Funnyhouse of a Negro*, *Open Admissions*, and *Film Society*, deal practically and symbolically with race. Although these five widely diverse plays span eight decades, our hope is that the reader will see the relationships among them. All of these plays, including Tony Kushner's *Slavs!* and Tennessee Williams's *Not About Nightingales*, raise questions about where America seems to be heading and offers suggestions about what directions it should take.

We wanted to offer diverse perspectives on the plays. We were fortunate to have had playwrights such as Moises Kaufman, Adrienne Kennedy, and Romulus Linney provide comments along with directors Oskar Eustis, Daniel Sullivan, and Michael Kahn. Expanding the discussion, we have included several notable scholars such as Kimberly Benston, Michael Cadden, Arnold Rampersad, and Alan Wald as well as the perspective of Janice Paran, a dramaturg and theatre professional.

One criteria central to choosing these plays is that each one had to be "playable" on the stage—we were interested in plays that had not only political and social impact but were also successful performance pieces. The exception to this rule might seem to be Langston Hughes's *Mulatto*, which has not yet entered the nation's theatrical repertoire. We think that it should, and to that end have helped to arrange a reading of the play sponsored by the National Portrait Gallery and The Shakespeare Theatre in Washington arranged by Jewell Robinson and Michael Kahn. We have also included a previously unpublished and unproduced Tennessee Williams one-act, *And Tell Sad Stories of the Deaths of Queens*, an extraordinary addition to the Williams canon, which just had a successful reading at the Shakespeare Theatre, arranged by Michael Kahn and directed by P. J. Paparelli, on December 10, 2001.

So how do we want readers to experience this book? Imagine, if you would, a three-day festival of American political theatre, where you could see these plays on the stage successively, each play speaking individually to the reader, but interconnecting, one writer answering another. Perhaps we could even envision the writers themselves—Susan Glaspell in the courthouse taking notes, Tennessee Williams examining articles about a prison strike in Pennsylvania, and Emily Mann and Marc Wolf with their tape recorders—all of the writers in this volume at work, excavating an aspect of the American Century.

FILM SOCIETY

JON ROBIN BAITZ

Originally Produced in English by the
Los Angeles Actors' Theatre,
Los Angeles Theatre Center,
Bill Bushnell, Artistic Producing Director

"Original New York Production by the
Second Stage Theatre July, 1988"

Film Society
by Jon Robin Baitz
Copyright ©1989 by Jon Robin Baitz
Reprinted by permission of William Morris Agency, Inc., on behalf of the
author.

INTRODUCTION

by Daniel Sullivan

Jon Robin Baitz writes about apartheid-era Durban with a divided eye. Unlike Athol Fugard, who has written his country's agony in the urgent voice of the front-line soldier, Baitz was, by circumstance, both participant and removed observer of this most violent and deluded period of South African history. His father, an American executive for a multi-national food corporation, was posted to South Africa when his son was ten years old and young Baitz attended a school very like the one in which *The Film Society* takes place. Coming of age in Durban, within the manicured and fated white society that was only now beginning to sense the inevitability of what was to come, Baitz would take a tentative place in his new world, as all uprooted children must, but he would also remain a foreigner, as puzzled by the animosity between the Afrikaaners and the English as he was by the unknowable life of the Zulu maid who lived in the servants' quarters behind his house. Learning to be a white South African during a time when the rules were. becoming less and less clear must have been deeply unsettling. His older brother could jump quickly into the turbulent stream of anti-apartheid political and social life but Jon Robin was relegated to watch, in his short pants and school jacket, from the sidelines. What he saw from there were the myriad ways in which supposedly like-minded people differ from one another in response to political upheaval.

The power of the forces at work outside the walls of Blenheim School are painfully apparent to each character in *The Film Society*, and yet that power is rarely addressed directly. Only Terry Sinclair, the play's nominal lefty, argues for the cause, but his invitation to a black man, Reverend Elias Bazewo, to speak at the school's Centenary Day, precipitating a near riot and the arrival of the police, carries with it the whiff of prankish self-importance. His wife, Nan, is "tired of being angry" and lives in fear of her husband's willfulness. Her response to the pressure is to insist that they destroy their banned books and avoid house-arrest. She is protector of the hearth. "We're schoolteachers," she reminds her husband, suggesting that they stand humbly outside the shifting ground of politics. The old order, represented by Neville Sutter and Hamish Fox, responds to the pressure like the South African government did: they tighten discipline and cleanse their institution of any "lefty nonsense." The play's unlikely protagonist, Jonathon Balton, lives by the credo "don't provoke them. Just let it all die down."

Jonathon has created the Film Society as an elective course to help humanize the "boys." To make them "look out at the world and feel a certain something about their place in it." Even though the Society is now under attack by parents as a potential politically subversive influence, one suspects that Jonathon has created it as a means of escape, an imaginative flight from reality. Like Tom in *The Glass Menagerie*, he's hiding in the dark from a world "lit by lightning." But when you are forced to come out of the darkness and face the world, how do you behave? Jonathon has been best friends with Terry and Nan since childhood and they have taken his good-heartedness and generosity for granted. The dark figure behind the action of the play, Mrs. Balton, Jonathon's mother, moves her son up through the ranks of the school by her continued patronage and creates a surprising endgame by feeding more and more power to her son. "You realize," says Mrs. Balton, "that survival is not automatic in this life, right?" And though she is talking about her spineless son, she is also talking about the Fortress Britannica, the island of tradition and comfort that she sees as her birthright. Jonathon feels no pressure because he has no power. The answer is simple: get him some.

The play spares no one. The Leftist is left rootless, the Orthodoxy is corrupt, the moderate is fearful and self-interested. And behind it all, moving the world relentlessly on, whatever the political will, lies money. Money talks, and it's interesting to note that, despite the sea change in South African society, the money that talks there is still White.

A few years after his father had been reassigned and the family returned to the U.S., Baitz wrote *The Film Society*. A remarkable work on its own, it becomes even more remarkable when one considers it is written, not only by a man in his early 20's, but by someone who so recently emerged from the circumstances he has chosen as his subject. Understandable, certainly, if this were a work of journalistic reportage, but we have, instead, a subtle and unflinching work of a mature dramatic imagination. If, through the tangle of adolescent obsessions and bewilderment, he was able pull the thread of this play, it is most certainly due to his status as an outsider.

It would have been hard, I think, for a South African to have written this play, to have seen the contradictions as clearly: British South African culture being kept alive in an increasingly hostile environment through the rigors of cricket and the terrors of caning. And in times of political unrest one seeks absolutes: qualifications lead to inaction. One needs clear heroes and villains.

And most South African drama of the apartheid period provided them. Jonathon Balton is most decidedly not among them. If he takes power in the world, it is simply to protect his right to ignore the world. It would have taken an outsider to understand Jonathon Balton. Or even to have noticed him.

I write this a month after the WTC attack startled America awake and added dread to the complicated list of modern anxieties that have become our daily lot. I notice that my television viewing habit has developed an interesting idiosyncrasy: as I jump from channel to channel to audit the most recent outrage, I find myself pausing more frequently at the American Movie Channel, instantly comforted by the bright sheen of the black and white images, the big-shouldered confident swagger of the heroes and heroines of an easy and innocent world. Jonathon Balton is not, I think, so difficult to understand.

CHARACTERS

JONATHON BALTON, in his 40s.

NAN SINCLAIR, in her 40s.

TERRY SINCLAIR, in his 40s,

MRS. BALTON (SYLVIA), in her 60s.

NEVILLE SUTTER, close to 70.

HAMISH FOX, in his 70s.

TIME: *1970.*

PLACE: *Durban, Natal Providence, South Africa.*

ACT I

Scene One

JONATHON's *classroom.* JONATHON *sits in the dark, watching the last moments of "Touch of Evil."*

MAN (V.O):   "Well. Hank was a great detective all right."

WOMAN (V.O.):   "And a lousy cop."

[*The door is flung open and* HAMISH FOX *enters.*]

FOX: What the bloody hell is going on in here! Turn on the lights!

BALTON: [*Turns off the projector.*] Just watching a film, is all, Hamish! [*He turns on the lights.*]

FOX: What do you mean 'watching a film'? Where are they?

BALTON: The boys? They didn't—It's not really film society now, I was just watching it again, you see.

FOX: Not the boys! Nan and Terry Sinclair!

BALTON: Not here. I don't know, really, with all the fuss and all, when it was over, I just came in here, you see, and—

FOX: You have anything to do with this fiasco, Balton?

BALTON: Really, I was … no! I was in charge of the iced-tea, I didn't have anything to do with it.

FOX: Well, they're your friends! You're always giggling together, it's always no good from you lot!

BALTON: No! That's not fair, is it?

FOX: Why're you sitting about in the dark watching a film at a time like this, when we've got policemen all over the place, hey?

BALTON: I don't know why it's such a bother, it's not like we were invaded, Hamish. Terry brought up one African speaker, I don't see why you had to call the entire Durban military out.

[*Pause.* FOX *stares incredulously at* JONATHON.]

FOX: That's very good! You defend them, then, and we'll see what happens when we're overrun! This is not some commie-summer-camp! It's Blenheim! The nerve! Bloody outrageous!

BALTON: I had nothing to do with it, don't shout at me!

[NEVILLE SUTTER *enters.*]

SUTTER: Any sign of the Sinclairs?

FOX: They're hiding.

SUTTER: Calm down, Hammy.

FOX: Don't tell me to calm down. There's been alot of lefty nonsense going on here lately …

SUTTER: Jonathon, I expect you didn't have anything to do with this business, did you? I've just spent the past hour with a roomful of angry parents, and it's an awful bore.

BALTON: No, I didn't at all! Because, you see, I had iced-tea and merangues and all to organize for after the speeches and prizes, and then, in all the fuss and all, I just came back here, because you see, I had ordered "Touch of Mink" but they sent "Touch of Evil" … which I quite liked.

SUTTER: —Jonathon, it's all right, you needn't—

BALTON: —and I wanted to see it again, because the boys didn't quite get it. It was all about Mexicans, and corruption.

FOX: Stop going on about your film society this second!

SUTTER: [*Sighs.*] Jonathon, if any of the parents come looking for me, or the Sinclairs for that matter—

FOX: —Not, bloody likely. They're retreating to Moscow—

SUTTER: Tell the Sinclairs, I want to see them up at my house. Joyce tripped over a chair during the commotion. [*He starts to exit.*] Come along, Hammy, we'd better finish up with the parents.

FOX: [*Following* SUTTER.] I told you not to put Sinclair in charge of Centenary day, but you refused to listen, well, all I can say, is …

SUTTER: [*To* FOX, *off.*] Tell the girl to bring the parents a drink in my office, and some ice for Joyce's leg, would you? There's a good chap.

> [*Pause.* BALTON *sighs. Looks outside after them. Turns off the lights, and turns on the projector. Watches the remaining moments of the film.*]

MAN: Is that all you have to say for him?

> [*Pianolla theme on soundtrack.*]

WOMAN: He was some kind of man. What does it matter what you say about people?

MAN: Goodbye, Tanya.

WOMAN: Adios.

> [*Pianolla theme on soundtrack. The door opens.* NAN *enters as the film credits begin.*]

NAN: Jonathon? Jonathon? Where's Terry?

BALTON: Get in here! They're looking all over for you and they're mad as hornets!

NAN: Terry's not here? God, he just disappeared.

BALTON: He went down to Durban jail to see if he could bail out that black priest you two brought up to the podium.

NAN: Me? Christ, I had nothing to do with it! You think I'd allow a stupid gesture like that? He got this man arrested! I had nothing to do with it!

BALTON: You'll have to tell Neville and Hamish that, and then it'll all die down, I'm sure. If you explain that … as for Terry, well. My. My. You know?

NAN: Jonathon, he's done us in! They're going to sack us this time! It's over.

BALTON: No they won't! Just tell them how terribly sorry you both are and start to cry for a bit, and it'll all be fine. Just like all the other little—episodes.

NAN: He's been so furtive, like one of the boys, I knew something was up! Damn it!

BALTON: I have a bit of whisky, you know!

NAN: Oh hell, sure.

[JONATHON *takes two teacups and a bottle of scotch out of his desk, pours.*]

BALTON: Yes, this'll calm you down. I was quite rattled by the whole business myself, I must admit. But it'll all blow over, don't you worry. Storm in a tea-thingie, eh?

NAN: But you know what this town is like! If they fire us, we'll be dead as cold mutton! I can't stand it anymore, he lies, goes off to these ludicrous little meetings, comes back with new words and books and it's all so childish.

BALTON: You'd have thought he'd have learnt his lesson after the parents went mad when he brought in those colored hippy fellows with the guitars and the big hair. My God.

[TERRY *enters, smiling.*]

TERRY: Well. Quite a day, eh?

NAN: Terry, you are an idiot!

TERRY: No! I know exactly what I'm doing. Give me a drink.

BALTON: [*Pouring whisky for* TERRY.] They're quite upset, I think, actually. They want you up at Neville's house, 'cause you somehow managed to trip his wife when you brought that native up. But I wouldn't go for a bit, I'd let it all die down.

NAN: What happened to that man you brought up? Who is he? They dragged him off …

TERRY: Reverend Elias Bazewo, and he's been arrested before, I followed him down there—they'll let him go tonight—it's nothing, it's happened before to him, he's fine.

NAN: Don't stand there smiling! How do you think it feels? Being dragged into this?

TERRY: Oh, it's wonderful. Both of you! This place has got to change, and we all know it, and someone has to do something. They all listened to him! Until Fox called the cops on him—

NAN: They were not listening! They just saw this black man and started screaming, I could have told you what was going to happen.

BALTON: I may not have understood it all, but the general effect was pretty scary. All those pink faces melting in the sun, tea cakes and merangues sticking to their laps. All they asked you to do was put together a nice dull little centenary day thingie, and it was meant to be nice and sweet and dull, deathly dull hopefully, like last year when they had the choir sing "The Halleluiah Chorus" for six hours straight.

NAN: It's supposed to be a celebration of a hundred years of Blenheim, Terry, that's all!

TERRY: Well, they got one. I can't stand the stagnation anymore. He talked about the blessings of education! Not armed revolution!

NAN: I don't care! If you had told me what you were up to I might feel differently but it's the childish plotting. You jump on these bandwagons, Terry, without really thinking. Do you think these boys give a damn about politics?

BALTON: It's true, Terry. They only like sports. And besides, you forget what it was like when we were boys here! All forced marches and military history and all that navigating by the stars and gutting wildebeasts every morning, ... much better now! Yes it is!

TERRY: How? Both of you are being so narrow minded. I'm amazed.

NAN: Where do you think you are? University of Natal debate club? This is Blenheim School for Boys!

BALTON: It's true! Let me give you an example of how things're better, as I see it. My film society, for one.

TERRY: Oh, Jonathon, please. The other day you told me that you loved film society because it was a bit of a rest for you. It's not some cultural institution. What'd you show them last week?

BALTON: "Passport to Pimlico," Terry: see. Perfectly wonderful story, and the boys loved it, and this week we had "Touch of Evil."

TERRY: That's not so bad.

BALTON: Actually I had ordered "Touch of Mink," you see I'm trying to go through it alphabetically …

NAN: Terry, I'm sick of it. I'm a schoolteacher, not an activist, and nor are you. It's one thing to have boys over to listen to your new Bob Dylan album and let them smoke on the verandah, and to refuse to cane 'em, fine. Treat them like human beings, but not these antagonistic little jabs—you just brought that man here to get attention for yourself.

BALTON: You've always been—when we were boys, Nan, he used to—

TERRY: Are you both honestly so furious at me? [*Pause.*] Please don't be angry. Think how it might've been. If instead of calling the police, Hamish Fox had sat there listening. [*He smiles. Goes on calmly.*] Elias Bazewo has been teaching black children at a school in Kwamashu for thirty years. He's a man of peace, with a great deal of experience, and a perspective on education that I thought, would remind all of us how privileged we are. How bad would that have been? I guess it wasn't possible. [*Pause.*]

NAN: Well, it didn't come off that way, did it? I just don't want to be misled by you. Is that reasonable?

TERRY: [*After a moment.*] It's just that sometimes, you're so clear-headed and practical, and pragmatic, that we do nothing.

BALTON: Please don't fight. [*Beat.*]

TERRY: Perhaps taking action requires a certain amount of stupid faith. I am sorry about not telling you, I don't like keeping things from you.

BALTON: He's sorry, Nan. He didn't mean anything bad to happen, you know that Nan. It just didn't work out. Like Gilerakis and his pen-pal society. Only one boy joined and he ended up sending postcards to his niece in Hong-Kong, and she never wrote back, so that was a bust … [*He smiles.*] Not to mention Viltonian.

NAN: Please, Jonathon. Stop it.

BALTON: He had his lizard boys.

TERRY: [*Laughing.*] It was reptile society, and you know it.

BALTON: Right, reptile society, all I know was one little bugger was bitten on the nose and the entire thing packed up, so. Not to mention the horror of "Sea Shell Club". Boys lollying about the beachfront all day. Sutter went mad, I remember. I was one of 'em. Takes a long time for things to work here at Blennies. Maybe if you started a political society … ?

TERRY: Jonathon. You miss the point. Why do you always miss the point?

BALTON: I'm just saying it's all getting more reasonable, slowly, if you don't force it. Just apologize to Sutter and Fox, and keep it very simple and all, in the classroom.

NAN: Jonathon!

BALTON: Yes, Nan! Really. I've yet to open a text book once this year. In history, I just showed them that Michael Caine film where ten men wipe out the entire Zulu army, no one suffers so much as a scratch, everybody gets a Victoria cross at the end, and the boys're pleased as punch, and then you rush 'em all off to see the native dancers, give 'em a bloody great quiz, and there you have it. South African history in a nutshell.

TERRY: Look, let's go down to the beachfront, and have some dinner. I'll buy you both dinner, and you can shout at me a bit more if you like, and we'll sort it all out, like adults, okay? Please?

BALTON: [*Begins to exit.*] I can't, I'm sorry. I booked a ticket, you see, it's the last night. I've got to go now so as not to miss the short. They're showing a film at the library. All about an un-conventional lady in America and her boy, and all the troubles … Auntie … thingie …

TERRY: Auntie thingie? It may be all orchid shows and cricket finals down here at Blennies but the rest of the word, my boy, is not exactly quiet.

BALTON: [*Stops.*] No, it's not. Is it? Well. Look. Don't provoke them. Just let it all die down, will you? Please? I don't want anything to happen. Politics, Terry. I'm the last person to talk to about politics. I can't even get a print of "Touch of Mink."

[*He exits.* NAN *looks at* TERRY, *sighs.*]

NAN: Well, we better think of something to say to Sutter and Fox.

TERRY: Oh don't worry. They like having me here. To turn about, to prove utterly wrong. Eh? [*Beat.*] Let's go see 'em now. [*Lights down.*]

Scene Two

JONATHON's *classroom. The next day. He is at his desk, wading unhappily through a pile of essays.*

BALTON: [*Reading incredulously.*] "The Panama Canal … links … Africa and America … ?" God. *God.* How do they get into this school? [*He reaches into his desk, takes out a cigar, unwraps and cuts, but does not light it. Puts it in his mouth. Sighs. Thinks. Then, he writes.*] "Cleasby. Uh … Don't you know this is 1970? Look at the world a bit more closely, thank you. Pass. But watch it." Odd.

> [JONATHON *looks up at the ceiling, notices something and stands on top of the desk, and does not notice when* NEVILLE SUTTER *enters.*]

Very odd.

SUTTER: Jonathon?

BALTON: Neville!

SUTTER: Here late aren't you?

BALTON: So're you!

SUTTER: Yes, but I live here, don't I?

BALTON: Well there you are. Rather lot of dust up here. Looks like one of those sea thingies.

SUTTER: Jonathon, get down at once, you're giving me vertigo.

JONATHON: I think I shall teach from here from now on. It's rather majestic.

SUTTER: Terribly cold for September.

BALTON: Oh but warm in here, isn't it?

SUTTER: Better in than out.

BALTON: They say—I read somewhere—there's something tricky going on with the polar ice-thingies.

SUTTER: Yes. They're melting. Be underwater any day now. Ice-caps and penguins.

BALTON: Was just thinking. Don't like the school uniform.

SUTTER: Perfectly fine uniform.

BALTON: Oh no it's not. In fact, when I was a boy, I asked you why we didn't
have long trousers. "This is Africa. Got to be tough."

SUTTER: Excuse me?

BALTON: Your reply. I said "well it's cold here, sir, long trousers would be much
better." And that was your answer. "Africa. Gotta be tough." Do you still think
so? 'Cause, you know, when I'm asked the same question, know what I say?

SUTTER: Africa, gotta be tough?

BALTON: No, no, no. I say "Headmaster Sutter feels, this being Africa and all,
you boys best toughen yourselves up!" And they laugh like hell, you know, 'cause
they're pretty fuckin' tough already, these little shits.

SUTTER: Oh please. Let's not be gutter. I'm not in the mood.

BALTON: I'm sorry, It's just that when one is with children all day, and then an
adult happens to wander in, it makes one a bit giddy.

SUTTER: Yes, I know. Confiscated a yo-yo yesterday and found myself playing
with it for hours. So. Did you have your film society today?

BALTON: [*Instantly suspicious.*] Why're you asking?

SUTTER: What'd you mean "why?" I'm headmaster—take an interest in the various projects going on.

BALTON: [*Scornful.*] Right. Like reptile society and seashell club?

SUTTER: Oh don't remind me. Well? Did you?

BALTON: Actually, no. And I'm quite upset. McNally just forced—literally
marched in here and took them off on some sort of arsonists training decathalon
or twenty mile marathon, I mean—came right in, Neville! Stole my—*conscripted*
my boys! This has never happened before, Nev?

SUTTER: Showing nice films, then?

BALTON: Nice? Yes, had a wonderful program scheduled today. *Top Hats*.

SUTTER: The boys benefit? An exposure to culture?

BALTON: That's my point. Exposure to culture.

SUTTER: Have you shown any travel films? [*Beat.*]

BALTON: Tr-*travel* films?

SUTTER: Exactly. Say, Malaysia, Australia, Ohio, and Greece?

BALTON: Ohio and *Greece*?

SUTTER: Or—even better really—closer to home; say Cape Town, Kimberly ...?

BALTON: Who the hell wants to see bloody Kimberly? I'd have a room full of empty boys—of empty desks, I mean.

SUTTER: I've got a marvelous collection of photographs that Joyce shot on her trips 'round the country.

BALTON: Oh, why not call it "little slide-show society?" You said I could have absolute free reign with film society. [*Beat.*] This is totally unacceptable, Neville.

SUTTER: I know I did. I know what I *said*.

BALTON: So ... You ... You let McNally take my boys.

SUTTER: We have had, thanks to Terry, four boys so far pulling out as of next week. All going to Durban High.

BALTON: Good! Let 'em go. What's it to do with film society?

SUTTER: Plenty. They give us money. We need money. Jonathon. Terry's guest of honor has died of a heart-attack in his cell. I got a call from the police. It will be in the newspaper tomorrow.

BALTON: Good God? A heart-attack? But ... why'd they hold him anyway? You'd think they'd just let him go ... a priest and all ... But, Neville. It's hardly our fault, is it?

SUTTER: No, but think of this as one of the shockwaves emanating from Centenary Day, and you'll have some idea of what I'm saying regarding film society.

BALTON: [*Sitting down.*] Wait. I'm utterly lost ... there's no connection here ...

I had nothing to do with … I mean … why?

SUTTER: Why? The parents. They've become very suspicious, very frightened.—they're forming a parents' committee, and when that happens, it's
hell. Believe me. Putsches, Coups d'Etat, purges. You see; moods change. And
the parents've been fairly passive until bloody Terry had to turn Centenary
Day into a commie fest. Now they think this is some sort of terribly Bohemian
institution.

BALTON: Blenheim? Are they mad?

SUTTER: You don't understand. There's to be a New Blenheim. The parents
want—total discipline. And no more nonsense.

BALTON: How *dare* they!

SUTTER: And you're going to feel the pinch too.

BALTON: Go on.

SUTTER: Parents are wondering what's going on in the dark here—in the middle of the day, middle of the week. What're these boys watching? What are
they doing? That sort of thing.

BALTON: Tell them to take their boys! They can all go to Durban High or hell
for that matter. We don't care, do we? Tell them to fuck off! Fuck 'em! Just
tell them really to go and fuck themselves, Neville!

SUTTER: I would never be so socially unattractive. We do care is the point. Can't
have classrooms without boys.

BALTON: What a bloody marvelous idea. Look, Nev. You admitted, didn't you,
that there had to be something besides cricket, rugger, and all the drudgery
that builds up? The thing that seperates Blenheim from Durban High is that
our boys come out of here with imagination. We've always encouraged the boys
to look out at the world and feel a certain something about their place in it.
No? Yes!

SUTTER: I really wish you wouldn't argue with me. I am the headmaster. I know
what I'm doing. I do own the school. Remember? Sometimes, I swear to God,
it seems everyone forgets.

BALTON: Well, I'll speak to the parents. They know me. I'm a Balton, for
Christ's sake. Leave my film society out of your New Blenheim, Neville,

alright?

SUTTER: But, my dear boy, this is one of those gruesome periods of re-adjust-
ment, and no compromise, no discipline, means no parents support, no
Blenheim, and no film society.

[*Beat.* JONATHON *nods.*]

BALTON: It's Terry. I've warned him a million times, he's making it harder for
all of us.

[*Beat.* SUTTER *nods.*]

SUTTER: Yes. Unfortunately.

BALTON: Oh God.

SUTTER: The thing is, we think we're going to have to let them both go, you
see.

BALTON: That would be a stupid, stupid mistake! Who runs this place?

SUTTER: Haven't you listened to a word I've told you? Hasn't he brought it upon
himself? How many times has he skirted this? The colored folk singers at assembly? The excursion to worker-housing at the sugar refinery? Eh? The constant
attacks on the government in senior history class?

BALTON: Yes, yes, yes. I know all about it. Little scandles ... Look. Shout at the
man a bit. I don't know. And Nan? Why must you drag her into this? She had
nothing to do with any of it.

SUTTER: They're *married*! How could she not?

BALTON: [*Laughs bitterly.*] Well she didn't. You've known Terry for thirty-some
years—is he not a sly man when he wants to be?

SUTTER: Yes! Exactly! That's why he has to go!

BALTON: He's also the only one here with any brains. And as for the ludicrous
notion of firing Nan, you and I both know that she's been the best thing for
this place. Lively, funny—it's like a morgue in the teacher's lounge without
her.

SUTTER: The parents are a bit suspicious of her.

BALTON: Tell them that she has no interest in Terry's political thingies. She indulges him, as we do.

SUTTER: I do honestly hate to let the parents push us about quite so much.

BALTON: That's my point exactly. [*Pause.*]

SUTTER: Well, we shall have to see.

SUTTER: Have you glasses?

BALTON: Tea-cups, top-right. [*Points to desk.*]

SUTTER: Yes. One's spirits tend to flagg at about half-past six.

BALTON: Blood sugar dropping.

> [SUTTER *hands* JONATHON *his drink*, SUTTER *taking a drink before speaking*.]

SUTTER: How'd you like to be assistant-headmaster?

BALTON: What?

SUTTER: Hamish Fox has spinal cancer.

BALTON: Spinal … ? How ghastly. I thought it was just the flu. Good God. Oh, poor man. My God.

SUTTER: And on top of that—on top of everything else, my eyes continue to go out on me.

BALTON: Well, there's eyes for you.

SUTTER: So. If you were to pass it up, I'd have to go to McNally, you see.

BALTON: Good Bloody Christ in Heaven!

SUTTER: My point exactly.

BALTON: This place is turning into hell suddenly. What's going on?

SUTTER: No, it's been building, it's just that you've had a quiet time of it until now. You never come to staff meetings, you never listen. You just think it all lurches foreward unremarkably. Well, let me tell you, Jonathon, when you become assistant head, you lose your invisibility. And you find yourself becoming more of the representative. And you've got to acknowledge what it is you're representing. Fox, McNally, parents' committees, rugger-teams, marching boys, all of it. Understand? [*Pause.*]

BALTON: What you're saying is … "Time for a change." Eh?

SUTTER: Precisely.

BALTON: Assistant head, eh? Well. Then McNally would leave me alone … and … mother'd be pleased. Finally. About something. Look. I'll tell you what. If we must have a change, how'd it be if I showed a travel short once a week?

SUTTER: A harmless exposure to culture that the parents will appreciate. A film on monkeys. On photosynthesis and pollination, that sort of thing.

BALTON: Alright, but leave Nan alone, and tell McNally to keep away from my boys. They're not all marathonists.

SUTTER: Agreed. Good. See how we can circumvent the problems if we work together? Exactly. I'm exhausted. Well, how 'bout a little toast?

BALTON: Smashing.

SUTTER: Er. Let's see. A toast … to …

[*Both men stand still for a moment,* JONATHON *watching* NEVILLE *attentively. Finally,* NEVILLE *merely shrugs and downs his drink.* JONATHON *follows suit, as lights fade.*]

Scene Three

NAN & TERRY's *flat. Early evening. They both enter. He has on a dark suit, she, a dark dress.*

TERRY: [*Quietly.*] Do you want a drink, love?

NAN: Yes, please, I … [*She sits down. Rubs her eyes.*]

TERRY: Do they think we're all morons? People stopped believing fucking "heart attack in his cell" fifteen years ago, at least go for "fell on his head while falling." A bit of imagination. Right — I wonder if Jackson left any supper; did you speak to him before we left?

NAN: No.

> [TERRY *goes off for a moment, returns with a plate of sandwiches, puts them next to* NAN.]

TERRY: God bless Jackson and his little cucumber sandwiches.

NAN: Did you see them taking photographs?

TERRY: [*Pouring two drinks.*] Yes. It was probably the Bureau of State Security, I imagine. They do that at funerals. [*Pause.*]

NAN: Are they—are they going to come here, do you think?

TERRY: I don't think so. They know my family, they'll leave us alone. That's my estimate, at any rate. I don't know, perhaps they're not impressed by old names. They pulled Bazewo off the podium and they killed him, and I can't even get bloody arrested. [*Phone rings.*]

TERRY: [*Answering.*] Hello, Jonathon? Um, look, sorry I can't talk now, I'll call you back. Goodbye. [*He hangs up. Pause.*] I think our phone's bugged.

NAN: How can you tell?

TERRY: Very telling little click. There's some little fuck with a Sony down at police headquarters. I could almost smell their heavy Vortrecker breathing.

NAN: Our book shelves are filled with banned books, Terry.

TERRY: Yes, I know.

NAN: I think we ought to do something about them.

TERRY: What? Burn them?

NAN: You're surrounded by a lot of misery right now, Terry, and I think you should listen to me. We've just come from a pathetic funeral in the middle of a dusty cemetery in the middle of nowhere, twenty silly people singing "we shall overcome" having their pictures snapped by the police, so, perhaps you should burn your books, yes.

TERRY: [*Nods.*] Yes. It was a stupid funeral, wasn't it?

NAN: Well, I haven't been to very many happy ones, love, have you?

TERRY: Listen, if you're this angry at me, then please tell me what you want me to say, and I'll say it, because I'm—

NAN: Angry? Oh, I've been angry for days. I'm tired to death of being angry. Tell me what you intend to do. No more silence. No more sneaking. They fired you, Terry, and Bazewo is dead, so I want to know what you want to do. [*She gets up, looks outside.*] God. You should've known. They arrested Julius Baskin the day he graduated from bloody medical school! You saw what they did to him! He's been under house-arrest since '67! What? Are you jealous? How many people does he get to save sitting about at home? We're schoolteachers and you're probably going to be unhireable after this.

TERRY: While you were at school this morning, about a dozen parents called to tell me that they admired what I tried to do, and they were furious I was sacked.

NAN: Oh God, Terry …

TERRY: Not that it matters anymore, I mean, just to fold up like this, after twelve years? Especially after this man has died …

NAN: No, Whatever you're thinking it won't work. There's a parents' committee being formed, and they're much stronger than the few families that're behind you, Terry. You'll just make it worse.

TERRY: Doesn't it make you sick? Look at this beachfront—little amusement park, rust and booze and sunken garden filled with cops. It's like I said to Bazewo Elias, "old mate, Blenheim is a broadminded, reasonable place." Well I didn't know how wrong I was. You think it was attention-getting on my part, and perhaps it was, but please don't lord over me with your beachfront Jesuit agony. [*Beat.*]

NAN: What will end up happening, actually, is very simple. I shall be fired as well, instantly, at the first sign of trouble from you.

TERRY: No you won't. I had calls from the DeVilliers, the Dixons, the Mellons, Templeton, Soltair—the list goes on—incensed that I was fired, and offering to call Neville.

NAN: Well, Fox will be very receptive, won't he? I agree that firing you was un—

TERRY: Yes, well Fox is dying and that's just fine, because nobody could be that brutal for so many years without developing a fatal illness. The whole place is in the midst of this phenomenal earthquake and I'm part of it.

NAN: Terry. Listen to yourself. [*Pause.*]

TERRY: If they won't have me back, and you're left there, spinning in the wind, if I cannot get another job here, if it's all so pointless and miserable, then perhaps we should just pack it in and leave.

NAN: Leave.

TERRY: We've talked about it before.

NAN: Idly, Terry. Idly.

TERRY: This is not out of the blue. Are you afraid to leave?

NAN: I'm afraid for you!

TERRY: Oh, God, Nan, I'm fine. Please, don't sit there looking at me like that.

NAN: I have parents here. They haven't got a lot of time left, I'm not going to leave them. Think about it. Think about me, for a change. Do you think leaving is the answer?

TERRY: I don't know …

NAN: [*Almost in tears.*] But you—you would—are you saying you would go without me? God, is that it? Is that how—we're—you can't just dictate to me—your terms! I love you. I want to share this with you, what you're in—don't threaten me—please. Please. [*Pause.*]

TERRY: I don't know.

NAN: I almost have to laugh. We have … what, five hundred rand in the bank. Not exactly a fortune. God, listen to me being practical, I'm gonna die from practical one of these days.

TERRY: Well I could see my parents at the farm. I'm sure they'd be relieved to give me something to finally see me off, having foresaken a tenth of one of the better sugarcane outfits in Natal.

NAN: Your parents? Terry, you don't even speak to them and you'd take their money. Terry, I … am exhausted. We just watched them put a man under and I feel, for my part, somehow responsible. Isn't that odd? I don't want to discuss this anymore tonight. I want another drink in fact, I want a booze-up, and a cold shower, and frankly, a break from you for a few hours.

TERRY: Nan, I see us wasting away here, forever. Before we drove to that ridiculous sham of a funeral, I shared Jackson's rice and beans with him, and we sat on the verandah. I suggested to him that the beans might be a bit softer and he started to cry. Isn't that something? There we were, about to go off to Bazewo's funeral and there was Jackson, the only homosexual Zulu servant in all of Durban, weeping over his beans. And it was all suddenly very clear to me—shudderingly clear; you and me, politely wasting away in old khakis with bad teeth, craving new books, and new causes, all of us, weighted down effectively, forever by this great entropy down here. I just can not abide the feeling of being utterly defeated, and paunchy. [*Pause.*]

NAN: Yes, well, in the meantime, would you do something about those books? Because when they come in here with a warrant, none of it will make any sense, or matter in the slightest.

TERRY: My passport. It's expired.

[*She exits, leaving him standing alone, looking out over the Durban beach front.*]

Scene Four

Lights up on MRS. BALTON's *flat. Exudes a faded, Edwardian air of decayed elegance.* MRS. B. *has on an absurd African Kaaftan, is clutching a whisky and a cigarette, and both are surrounded by a number of men's suits.*

BALTON: Oh look, I know you're excited, but really, I find the entire subject utterly incomprehensible, mother. Accountants? Might as well be speaking. Balinese.

MRS. BALTON: No, it's very simple! You're doing so splendidly, all I'm asking is for you to be the slightest bit attentive when they come by. Listen to what they're saying, engage with them a bit.

BALTON: You've managed fine without me for centuries, darling. I don't understand the problem.

MRS. BALTON: The issue is where all the accounts are and how to keep track of 'em.

BALTON: Then get a secretary-thingie or something, some service that does figures and numbers and all that business.

MRS. BALTON: No, you don't understand. It seems the accounts in Cape Town were transferred to Salisbury for some reason, and then London, and now, they tell me they've found a bit in Zurich; all of which your father never bothered telling anyone about. And I don't want you to muddle about—an assistant head cannot afford to be ignorant of his monies.

BALTON: Not ignorant, mother. Just not interested, and besides, what's it got to do with being assistant head—they're totally unrelated.

MRS. BALTON: Oh love. I'm only trying to help. You've realized that survival is not automatic in this life, right?

BALTON: What's not automatic?

MRS. BALTON: Was not the farm a tangled bush of savagery before your father planted sugarcane? And did we not have to bum it back constantly?

BALTON: Yes, I'll say. Snakes and cats and all, quite a business, and-

MRS. BALTON: [*Cuts him off.*] A business, exactly! Just like being involved with

25

the accountants.

BALTON: Well, darling. Wouldn't you say it's useless to talk to me about business at this late date? Just when I've become so busy being assistant head? And may I just say, I mean, really, the way you go on about the farm and the bush, it's as dull as dirty dishwater. We haven't owned it since I was a boy, right? And it's your only frame of reference, these days. It's so provincial. I mean, can't we just be adults here?

[*Pause. He stares at her knowingly. She stares back.*]

MRS. BALTON: All I'm saying is I've bought you these marvelous suits, and wouldn't it be nice if you were to take on some corresponding responsibilities? That's the only thing I'm saying. Aren't they lovely?

BALTON: Quite a world. The world of clothes, eh?

MRS. BALTON: And to succeed in your field? A marvel. That's all I'm saying.

BALTON: And then one has one's suits, eh?

MRS. BALTON: Why not try on the yellow?

BALTON: [*Begins undressing.*] If you like. You know, just thinking; after we moved to the city from the farm, and I went off to Blennies, I was bloody worried 'bout managing, remember? All rashes and coughs, eh? But you know what? It turns out, it doesn't seem to make the slightest bit of difference. I've done fine without the least bit of managing. One worries. One frets. And in the end they go and make you assistant head.

MRS. BALTON: The point is, you're assuming your natural leadership tendencies.

BALTON: But that's the point! I don't have any! You know that! It's a joke!

MRS. BALTON: Well perhaps you might if you wore better undies: There's a bloody great hole the size of a kruger rand in your backside.

BALTON: Well, nobody ever sees the damn things, mother, unfortunately. Quite a world. The world of … the suit. [*He puts on the yellow linen jacket.*] How do I look?

MRS. BALTON: Like your father. An aristocrat in his linen suits! Where's nanny? Where is she? She's got to see this, she won't believe it—you look just like him!

Where is she? [*She rings furiously.*]

BALTON: Going as deaf as a bat is where she is, love.

MRS. BALTON: I know. [*She rings again.*]

BALTON: Well leave her alone. You run her ragged, poor dear, probably in a coma. [*Beat.*] I do like the lapel, though.

MRS. BALTON: Oh it's true. Just like Christopher, you look.

BALTON: Well then. I suppose we've made a success of it, eh? [*He stands for a moment.*] It's interesting, what a new suit does, isn't it? [*Beat.*] I have plans, you know, mother. I have plans.

MRS. BALTON: Tell me!

BALTON: [*Quiet, almost a reverie.*] Oh it's fairly mundane, really, more of a spirit of growth, let people like Gilerakis and his pen-pal boys thrive, bring in some more women teachers—you know how stuffy it gets in the faculty lounge, all cigars and sports talk and off color little jokes. We haven't had a dramatics society since I was a boy, Terry and I did panto at Christmas … remember?

MRS. BALTON: Yes, I remember.

BALTON: I feel so old sometimes, mother. I feel old today. Isn't that odd?

MRS. BALTON: We're all getting on, nanny stumbling about, love, and me, well, look at me …

BALTON: You? Nonsense, you'll out live us all, darling … no, I walked into my classroom today. My classroom. Hah! Who would've thought. It's a pity doing radio drama didn't work out. That was the life I was meant for, that was the life for me. Sitting about, chatting with the other show-people, going on about the new styles, the new scripts and all … pots of tea and glasses of whisky and cigarettes, there was nothing better, nothing like it. [*Beat.*] No use reminiscing, eh? None at all.

MRS. BALTON: Let's have a drink, shall we love, before dinner?

TERRY: [*Entering.*] Hello? … You know, I've told you, you can't leave your door wide open anymore. Lots of angry natives milling about these days, eh … hello …

MRS. BALTON: Hello Terry, come in, Terry, darling.

[*He kisses her.*]

Sit down. I'm sure you'd know more about all that then we would, eh? Let's give him a drink shall we, Jon-Jon?

TERRY: Not for me, thanks, no. I know you wanted to talk to me.

BALTON: Terry, I'm glad you're here, I was going to call you again. I would like to go with you to your friend's funeral, I think, I …

MRS. BALTON: What a sweet idea. How lovely …

TERRY: [*Serious.*] I'm sorry, Jonathon, but it was yesterday, you see.

MRS. BALTON: Oh dear. What a ghastly time it's been for you, dear.

BALTON: I didn't know. There wasn't a word in the papers.

TERRY: Really, it's all right, it wasn't expected of you. There were plenty of people there. His children had a marvelous time of it.

BALTON: Terry, I know you must be angry at all of us—this whole business.

TERRY: No, I have nothing to be angry at. Is that why you wanted to see me?

BALTON: No, no, no. Please. I know you. I know how you think, and I'm sorry, I must ask you, please do not try anything. Not now.

TERRY: Really, Jonathon. I'm done. You needn't worry.

BALTON: Yes, but I'm worried. You must understand, Nan is just barely hanging on. And if you provoked them, if you tried anything, there'd be nothing I could do, Terry. It would be out of my hands, they'd fire her in a shot. [*Beat.*]

TERRY: [*Nods. Softens.*] Yes. Nan said the same thing.

BALTON: So you understand this?

TERRY: No, quite. [*Beat.*] I must re-think everything.

BALTON: If they let her go, there'd be no-one left for me. I'd be all alone, those people hardly say a word to me, they never even smile at me. It has just been the three of us, and I don't want to … endanger Nan. With you gone, I've got to do all of it on my own, I've no support and I don't know what to do.

TERRY: Well … it turns out, I seem to have some people on my side.

BALTON: What?

TERRY: … Yes. Parents calling me up since I was sacked … [*Pause.*]

BALTON: Who?

TERRY: [*Looks at* JONATHON. *Sighs. Thinks a moment before replying.*] Well, there was the Neams, the Travis's, the Lawsons, the Chases … about … a dozen, really. [*Pause.*]

BALTON: I … I wonder if … If perhaps those—those parents—perhaps they should be on the parents' committee …

TERRY: [*Doubtful.*] Well, if you could get them on … yes, I suppose. They might be able to dilute some of Fox's hard liners a bit …

MRS. BALTON: Travis's? Neams? All of those people? Yes, well, those are all pretty much scholarship names. Everyone knows that. Not quite the same league as the parents' thingie, is it?

TERRY: [*Smiles.*] There we are, Sylvia. You can not but fail to give yourself away every time.

BALTON: You two, please.

MRS. BALTON: But I think Jonathon is quite right, you really should keep away from it all, now. Why don't you think about going back to the farm, love?

BALTON: Mother.

TERRY: [*Still smiling, exhausted.*] Ah, the farm, yes, it's always the farm with you, isn't it? Well, that business is all over with now, Sylvia.

MRS. BALTON: Is it really? I remember even as a boy of ten, you were quick with a whip. You had the natives thrashed to a raw and bloody pulp if you didn't get fresh cream in the morning. You loved it all. Horses, guns, all of it. Interesting. Blood always being shed by you, Terry.

TERRY: Times change, Sylvia.

MRS. BALTON: Do they? Still blood being shed by you. Pity.

TERRY: It is what makes you happy, right? Bloodshed?

BALTON: That's enough! God, I'm tired of it all! God, you have no idea how tired of it all I am, both of you. Damn it, I'm asking for help, because I have no idea what I'm doing! I became a schoolteacher because it's quiet and there was no work to be had as a radio actor in Durban. [*Pause.*] I just want a bit of peace, damn it, and I'm sure dinner is destroyed. [*He exits.*]

MRS. BALTON: Are you eating with us, love? It's just like when you were a boy, you'd come by, causing all sorts of trouble, driving everyone mad. Do you remember the time you were sick into the swimming pool?

TERRY: No.

[*She remains seated. Lights down.*]

Scene Five

BALTON's *classroom*. HAMISH FOX, NEVILLE, *and* JONATHON.

FOX: And why do I see Terry Sinclair's name here? On this agenda?

BALTON: Well, if you let me explain; what it finally—it was more a matter of the senior matriculation tutorials. Not a staff position at all. Just a situation wherein he might come by once a week to coach the seniors. And I've certainly not broached the subject with him, so you needn't worry, Hamish. But the point is, we used to have a ninety-six percent pass rate—the highest. And thanks mostly due to ... Terry. So, you see, that's why I ... see?

SUTTER: Yes. Quite. There is that to be considered. Exactly. There is that, isn't there. No, that is true, yes.

FOX: It would not be appropriate, would it, headmaster? [*Pause.*] I didn't think it would. Bloody outrageous!

SUTTER: Steady on, Hamish. You've only just this second come from chemotherapy.

BALTON: [*Taking out a list.*] And I do think perhaps these people should be included on the parents' committee. They've been very good friends to Blenheim.

FOX: [*Takes list and looks at it.*] Humph. Well, this lot won't be much good to us, will they. Hum. And perhaps, Jonathon, you might inquire as to Mr. Fidel Castro's availability next?

BALTON: Fidel Cas ... Ah! Hah! Yes. No. No.

FOX: I wonder if perhaps I don't have doubts as to your readiness to be assistant-headmaster.

BALTON: Well I can listen to your doubts, Hamish.

SUTTER: Nobody has any doubts, Jonathon. Hamish, honestly, you mustn't get excited. But Jonathon, what Hamish is trying to say is, I think it's not dis-similar to when we were in the foreign service. One often wanted to accomodate friends. Not unlike any position of choice, eh, Hammy?

FOX: [*After a pause.*] In Kenya, they found my sister-in-law tied up to a tree in her garden, with a Mau-Mau's spear inserted through the anus, up the rectum, and into the intestines.

SUTTER: Perhaps we might talk about Jonathon's duties.

FOX: Of course, but it's all in the interests of clarity. One becomes concerned that there might be a shift; we might become like one of those cafes where they go on about bizarre ideologies all night. The battles of two-hundred years ago have not been concluded, have they? No. Mr. Amin is hanging above our heads, grinning down on us, waiting, waiting! Who's to win? The savage, drum-beating white-hating-Stalin-worshiping natives, with the Terry Sinclairs of the world urging them on?

SUTTER: Well of course, exactly the point. First on the agenda is sports practice and seniors. Do they get time off to study or do they buckle down and have sports as well?

FOX: Do you know, when I saw the mad kaffir with the priest's collar up on the podium, I had to smile? There it was, the genesis of decay and rot of our Africa, having spread down the continent, like, dare I say it, the cancer in my own spine. [*Pause.*]

SUTTER: Indeed. Yes. Very interesting, Hamish. [*Beat.*] I say we give 'em time to study and sports be damned. Also, up to you, Jon, to make sure the field's kept trimmed for cricket practice. They're losing balls in the grass, it seems.

FOX: Then there is the small matter of caning, which you have to take over as I can no longer swing my arm.

SUTTER: But mostly just making sure the algae doesn't get too thick in the pool, my boy.

FOX: Also, keeping an eye on the boys' changing room, as the African staff has a tendency to go through the boys' pockets while they're playing sports. Oh it is a battle, I'm telling you, it is a war …

SUTTER: Invitations to parents' day tea, smiles, phone calls about little Evan and Timothy. The usual. Oh, and actually, one job I rather enjoyed; the retaining walls are swarming with lizards, and I like to fill up the holes with dry-ice and take the pellet gun and get 'em. Nothing like seeing a gecko dashing about in one's sights.

FOX: And Neville and I feel quite strongly that as part of the New Blenheim, it would be very clever to revive yachting club.

BALTON: Yachting club?

FOX: Perfectly fine dinghy in the shed, hasn't seen water in a quarter of a century.

BALTON: I see.

FOX: Your responsibility.

BALTON: Me.

SUTTER: Lovely on the bay in December.

FOX: Which won't leave much time for your cinema society, will it?

BALTON: My film society?

FOX: Exactly! Film society. New conditions. Neville and I agree that it's far too—

SUTTER: [*Cutting him off.*] Yes, well that's quite enough for one day, Hamish. You must be exhausted. We'll continue tomorrow at lunch, perhaps?

BALTON: [*Gets up to exit.*] I—I have some boys waiting, if I may … ? [*He exits rapidly.*]

SUTTER: Honestly, Hamish.

FOX: I've just got two things to say.

SUTTER: [*Sighing.*] Go ahead.

FOX: Not at all like his father. Or mother.

SUTTER: No. A blessing, as I see it. And the other.

FOX: Name the new hall the Christopher and Sylvia Balton Hall, put up a plaque, have a ceremony, and proceed forth, eh? You follow me? Considering our current … depletion.

SUTTER: [*An exhausted whisper.*] Yes. That's my point. Isn't it? Exactly.

[*Lights down.*]

Scene Six

BALTON's *classroom*.

BALTON: Well the fact of it is, that instead of meeting thrice weekly as anticipated, we'll be having these screenings only on Thursday afternoons at half-
past three. And you'd best bring with you a sports excuse. Thursday is, of course,
junior rugby and third cricket practice, and it seems that to be in film society
now, you must have a sports excuse. That is the way it goes. And … boys on
detention are no longer permitted to come to film society in order to work off
detention time. [*Pause*.] I shouldn't worry too much … you can't work off detention time on sports time either, so it's at least somewhat democratic. If you are
on detention, you must either remain to work off the detention time at a rate
of one point per hour, or else you could, as an alternative, erase the detention
altogether by being caned twice for each point. The choice is yours. [*Pause*.]
Mind you, detention boys, if you do decide to get caned instead of detention
itself, you would then have time to come to film society. Unless the reason for
the punishment is not going to sports practice, in which case, perhaps we'll see
you here next term if you have a more agreeable schedule. [*Pause*.] Yes, I
know. It's all a bit complicated, but what's one to do? [*Pause*.] For those of you
joining us here for the first time, what happens here is that I show films, no
quiz, no tests … Occasionally the odd bit of post-film discussion, and say …
if some famous film star happened to be in Durban, well, one of the benefits
of the film society is that you might get to meet him. You know, I used to be
a radio actor … which is quite different from films. [*Pause*.] We used to sit in
the studio, in fact, the Old Radio Natal studio near the beachfront and one would
just lose oneself, really. It was all that one had … the rest of the world of no
consequence … and … one might find that coming out … coming out into
the street from the studio, you might be dazed … in the sunlight. It would all
seem translucent, shimmering. And my thought was that coming out after film
society … [*Pause*.] Might be just a bit like that. [*Pause*.] One finds that after
Blenheim, the world. [*Pause*.] The world. We have a wonderful film about rep-
tiles today.

> [JONATHON *stands quite still, looking out, and then he slowly moves
> his hand to the projector, and switches it on*.]

Blackout.

ACT TWO

[*Two months later, November.* JONATHON, *wearing one of his new suits, angrily slams into the classroom, goes straight to his desk, stops, looks out for a moment before pulling a bottle of Scotch from his drawer. He pours a little into a teacup, and waits ...* NAN *rushes in.*]

NAN: Jonathon!

BALTON: I don't bloody want to discuss it!

NAN: I only wanted to thank you for putting an end to that ghastly meeting.

BALTON: I get so angry. I totally humiliated myself.

NAN: No, really, it wasn't that bad. I've always wanted to tell McNally to go fuck himself.

BALTON: I mean, I'm trying to help them! And they sit there laughing at me. McNally, this great big, sweaty huge smelly fat redfaced baboon, sits there snickering at me? Oh, Christ, and if he doesn't stop going on and on about his regiment and Angola and his rifle, I'll ... [*He stops.*] I can't let them upset me.

NAN: You did make rather a dramatic sort of exit. And that was a hell of a speech you gave.

BALTON: Don't flatter me. You liked it? Totally off the top of my head, just ... said what came to mind, really.

NAN: I think it's about time someone said those things, you're right about it all, pulling together, and the future and cleaning the floors were very true. But you did go on for half an hour about ... plasterwork.

BALTON: Did I? I know it's boring but nobody does anything about it except me. And I'm doing it all, is the problem! Did you know there are bats—A herd of bats living in the mango trees, attacking boys of the junior school? The eucalyptus grove has termites the size of landrovers scurrying about. At any minute we could have a tree come crashing down wiping out the entire first form. Have you seen the swimming pool lately? It looks like a science experiment—boys go in, have to send a team to find 'em. We had a monkey come out of the mangrove at cricket practice last week and swipe a ball. The only one we had. And Fox blamed me, I mean—God knows why he's still here, the man's meant to be in bed but he keeps patrolling like some sort of military zombie—so Fox proceeds to tell me the story of why the British lost the battle of Islan-Dwana, because they didn't have hammers or something. I don't know—couldn't open the ammo boxes, nails rusting in the humidity, they all died. I have no idea what it had to do with monkeys swiping cricket balls, but still ...

NAN: [*Trying not to laugh.*] It's mad! They're all bloody mad! I'm in charge of fingernail inspection. Yes, they stick out their grubby little digits and wave 'em in front of my eyes.

BALTON: [*Begins to laugh.*] Well that's nothing, because let me tell you first bloody thing this morning, I get a note from Neville. [*A la* SUTTER.] Jonathon, in strolling past the junior school toilets. I was assailed by the most unimaginable stench ... please investigate. Best. Nev.

NAN: Well get out your scuba gear, love. Oh, God, give me a drink, would you?

BALTON: [*Pouring her a drink.*] So, I go down there, right? It's like the seventh circle of hell. The man is absolutely bloody on target. Water—everywhere. Sort of ... brown, unfortunately. With little bits offal floating towards the showers, all of which are sending out huge primeval great mists of ... steam. I just stood there, hypnotized. The windows have a gruel like film over them, and instead of toilet paper, instead of toilet paper—there are tiny little shreds of ... newspaper—all over the stalls. Like a hamsters cage. [*Beat.*] I swear. The bowel movements of the very young are a total mystery to me, [*Beat.*]

NAN: Nobody goes in there to clean? What about Malcom and Montgomery?

BALTON: [*Picks up a cane, swings it, continues rather sadly.*] Ah, it turns out they've not set foot in there since Fox took ill. Had to fire 'em both. Not the great pleasure it's cracked up to be, but not the horror either.

NAN: Oh, Jonathon, it's all changing, eh?

BALTON: You know something? My dad, horrid as he was, was easily able to delegate authority. I'm going to have to be a bit rough with those pricks in the staff room, for a bit.

NAN: Getting into the spirit of the New Blenheim, are we?

BALTON: I just want them to behave well. Be helpful. Less selfish. I never dreamt this job was just one huge campaign. [*Beat.*] How does one think, Nan, when thinking has not been necessary?

NAN: If you could tell me—when has it not been necessary, love?

BALTON: They're all watching me. The way I see it, first, I get rid of the bats and the termites and the mildew, and then, we can try and do away with the damn parents' committee, and finally, McNally. Let's drink to that shall we?

NAN: [*After a drink.*] You know, I meant to ask you, did I see you shooting at lizards this morning?

BALTON: Oh no. No, just trying to scare them, really. They … you know lizards. Boys see 'em, go mad, can't get 'em back in the classroom. I've had to post-pone film society three times in a row. So typical. I said to Nev, at lunch, "the trouble with the world, is that nobody has any imagination anymore." And he thought, and said. "Yes. A blessing really." [*Pause.*] Nobody, that is, except you. Remember we used to go sailing? Wasn't that nice?

NAN: You hated sailing.

BALTON: Did not.

NAN: Please! It was always Ter who did all the work, you were too busy being ill or whining constantly about the waves and capsizing.

BALTON: But *you* enjoyed sailing, didn't you?

NAN: Actually, yes. Jonathon. Why're we talking about sailing?

BALTON: They've been going on for the past two months about wanting me to take on sailing.

NAN: We don't have sailing.

BALTON: [*Sighs, not happy.*] I'm to help with the Durban Yacht Club Junior Races.

NAN: But what for?

BALTON: Neville seems to think that if a team from Blenies won, we'd attract a new sort. Nautical boys, you know …

NAN: I mean … *absurd*. Please! That's not the way to get boys!

BALTON: Oh I don't know about that. Makes sense from a P.R. standpoint. Could be prestigious.

NAN: Typical. But why you, of all people?

BALTON: Neville recalled that the three of us had that dinghie-thingie and I was hoping you might take it on, as I haven't a clue.

NAN: Quite impossible, and you know it. I'm teaching all of Terry's classes and half of Fox's. It's hard enough as it is.

BALTON: I understand. But you'd look awfully good to the parents' committee if you took on the damn yachting. They're not very keen on you, still.

NAN: Honestly. Do you think I give a damn about that?

BALTON: It's lovely on the bay in December.

NAN: I've got too much to do as it is, and I'm not going to take time away from Terry. And you've stopped calling him …

BALTON: That's not fair—he doesn't want to talk to me—you know I've tried.

NAN: Look, I didn't want to tell you, we're having a very bad time. [*Beat.*] We've no money left. We were like some sort of package here, two for one. On my wages alone, we're sinking.

BALTON: I had no idea.

NAN: They want us out of the flat. We haven't paid the rent. All our accounts at the shops are shut down. Last week he charged three hundred rands at the book-shop—gave dictionaries out at the school where Bazewo taught. Sat there weeping, passing out books, so really, yachting? Fuck it.

BALTON: Nan, you should've said something to me earlier, because this is the one area where I can help with no problem at all.

[JONATHON *takes a checkbook out of his jacket.*]

NAN: He went out to see his parents in Zululand, they wouldn't talk to him. What're you doing?

BALTON: [*Writing.*] I'm giving you a check for five thousand rand.

NAN: No, stop it. I'm not going to take your money, please, Jonathon, put it away. I don't want a loan.

BALTON: Don't argue with me, it makes no difference to me, I just want you to be happy, I can't sit about and let you—

NAN: [Cuts him off.] I want a raise. [Beat.]

BALTON: A raise? Nan, there's no money for plastering, love, let alone raises. Look, just take the check, for Christ's sake. I have this money, my father left it sitting about in boxes!

NAN: No, I can't. You see, we really are leaving. I can't.

BALTON: What do you mean? Leaving? You're not leaving.

NAN: Terry has nothing here. We decided …

BALTON: Just take this check, and we'll see how you all feel in a few months—

NAN: No! I can't. Look, we're leaving, I'm not going to take five thousand rand from you and bugger off! I want to save something up over six months—and if Blenheim paid me what I deserved, we might be able to.

BALTON: I tried leaving, didn't I? When I went to London, I never told you. I took our stupid, idiotic Lux Radio Theatre tapes. This stupid idea of getting a job in radio drama at the BBC? Insane. Simply insane. And I ended up, you know where? In the bloody isolation ward of some hospital in Chelsea, with spinal menengitis. Tapes just lay next to me on the bed.

NAN: Well, if we stay here, Terry'll end up worse off than that!

BALTON: It's ancient, ghastly Paki-doctors with shaking hands! That's leaving! It's spinal taps missing the spine, that's leaving! It's a hospital room with wood soap and a clock!

NAN: Oh please, Jonathon, try not to take this as abandoning you—

BALTON: Overseas is vastly over-rated! You won't know what to do and you'll be despised, let me tell you, I know it! You'll be all by yourselves! And nobody will help you.

NAN: Well my husband seems to be asphyxiating and nobody here is helping him.

BALTON: Well just be sure, if you're at some fucking pub in fucking Earl's Court, you tell them, when they ask, that you're from fucking Sydney. [*Beat.*] Damn it, no! I'll be alone, I'll have no-one! Please!

NAN: Jonathon, we must—all of us, try and build something as best we can.

BALTON: Right, I shall get you an extra two fifty a week, starting today, all right?

NAN: Jonathon, can you do that? Because, you'd be literally saving our lives and—

BALTON: Providing, of course, you were to take on the yachting, starting tomorrow.

NAN: Pardon me? What is this, Jonathon?

BALTON: It's a condition, Nan. A condition. Well. I still have Faber pencils and blotting paper to order. Lots of work still. [*Smiles at a stunned* NAN, *and looks out the window.*] There goes the cricket team. Aren't they super. Super. [*He looks at her, as lights fade down.*]

Scene Two

NAN *and* TERRY'*s flat. That night.* TERRY *is sitting, quite still, in his corner chair, as* NAN *is heard, letting herself in, holding a small bag of groceries and a bag of Chinese food.*

TERRY: Well. Good. See me, sitting here? Like an odd and patient breed of dog, oh?

> [NAN *braces herself, smiles.*]

NAN: A long and bad, stupid day, Terry. So we'll give it a rest, for tonight, right?

TERRY: [*Pause.* TERRY *looks at the bag.*] They actually let you take merchandise out of there? I mean, I have to shout for a lamb chop.

NAN: He's not so bad.

TERRY: He is a little Indian racist, and I don't think we should be giving him our business.

NAN: [*As calm as* TERRY.] ... And why now, suddenly?

TERRY: [*Shrugs, smiling.*] He wouldn't sell me my smokes.

NAN: [*Taking a package of cigarettes from the bag.*] As long as there's a social context, for your boycott ...

> [*Pause. She sighs and crosses to him.*]

TERRY: There's no such thing as a social context. It's all just chemical, you know. I've been wrong all along. It's all about mommy, daddy, genes, and neurons or something.

NAN: I've brought Chinese.

TERRY: Chinese, what a joke. Honorary whites. I wonder, is that all 60 billion of them or just the ones living here. And what on earth would possess a China-man to come to South Africa, eh? So. What? Why so late? Watching a flick with old Jonathon? A musical?

> [*Pause.*]

NAN: Ah, I see.

TERRY: [*Laughs a bit.*] Ah? You see?

NAN: The 'ah' of recognition. As in "Ah, he's just spent the day in some sort of rage." [*Pause.* TERRY *nods.*]

TERRY: [*Looks at the bag of groceries, picks out a tin of tea.*] Please, must you buy this cheap kaffir tea? I mean, I don't expect, like, Fortnum's Russian Caravan, exactly, but something other than "twin roses." Something that gives one the illusion that there's something mysterious to look forward to.

NAN: What I should do is stop myself, rather soon, if I were you, love. Don't you think?

TERRY: The bug is off the phone.

NAN: … Really? How—how can you tell?

TERRY: 'Cause they shut the phone off. You never paid them. I actually like this kind of little ironic victory.

NAN: I'll have it on tomorrow.

TERRY: Needn't bother. It's only you, or Jonathon—stuttering.

NAN: *What is wrong?* [*Pause.*]

TERRY: Jackson was arrested.

NAN: What for?

TERRY: What for? What do you think? You couldn't possibly imagine him out agitating, could you? He was violating the pass-laws.

NAN: You … you got him out, Ter?

TERRY: [*Calm, but utterly exhausted.*] That was interesting. My family name still carries. I think of myself as some sort of pariah, an outcast? But do the Bantu Affairs Police know me? They're busy with their own usual array of murky, oblique affairs. So. I got dressed, very carefully, and I went down to their little corner of hell with its stench of burning rubber reality, and I said to the warrant officer, "Listen mate, that is my bloody servant you've got there, and my servant has windows to wash, and toilets to clean, and a lot to learn, so just hand him over to me, and I'll smack him." [*Pause.*] And there was this hesitation. The suspicion of my Afrikaaner brethren is boundless. So, I stood there, and looked him in the eye, rather contemptuously, and addressed him in Afrikaans: "Hey, bloke. My grandfather *ran* your lousy outfit. I deserve a bit of respect and a lot of lee-way" … and he nods. [*Pause.*] This man has never heard of Blenheim. [*Pause.*] And he hands me Jackson.

NAN: So—he's alright?

TERRY: Oh, fine.

NAN: Jesus, it's endless.

TERRY: Isn't it? Of course, you've just come from a "long, bad, and stupid day" yourself.

NAN: Actually, I have come from a pretty shoddy bit of manipulation and humiliation, and it has left me feeling pretty stupid, so Christ knows, I don't need to walk in here and be insulted by you.

TERRY: [*Picks up letter from the table beside the chair.*] Please don't tell me about your lousy day at Blenheim and your humiliations. Please. Not now. [*Pause.*] Because I have just received a letter from Victor Frame offering a job at the Esquella Americana in Rio de Janeiro, and I can't take it, because we don't have enough money to get out!

NAN: Victor Frame? Let me see …

TERRY: Blenheim. Class of '61. Was on the cricket team when I was captain. Worshipped me.

NAN: Well, let's start again. Look. I've got a raise, so if we put some money away, we could go, in about six months … [*Pause.*]

TERRY: Oh please, you must be joking. What pack of lies did they feed you? A raise? It's impossible. They're on the verge of shutting down by now, and I did it to them.

NAN: Wait a second. I'm telling you, Jonathon's got me a raise. Look, we can get out, it's all you talk about, come on.

TERRY: Jonathon … got you … a raise. Something's wrong here, Nan. It doesn't make sense. Come on, you're smart, what do you mean? Have you seen the place? It looks like a Moorish ruin. Jonathon? Raise? What? He could show you a double feature, but a raise … it's a lie, it's one of those things they say

... [*Beat.*] I mean, don't be naive.

NAN: No, no, no. You don't understand. It was a very specific transaction, Terry. He made me take on yachting in return for the raise.

TERRY: Yachting, oh now we're into sheer fantasy. Yachting my dear, you couldn't put up a spinacker if there was one sticking out your bum. Don't be absurd. These boys'd kill you out there! You want to end up floating face down in Durban harbour, with half the school dancing on the prow? It's a con job! Yachting.

NAN: Hey. You sit about here all day, doing God knows what. I mean, I have no idea. You say you can't read anymore, you can't think, so what? I'm telling you, Terry, I'm tired to death of it, now, it makes up for what we've been losing. All you talk about is leaving, now we can do it. Write back to Victor Frame, and ask him to give you some time, I don't know. Brazil sounds lovely, anything, Terry.

TERRY: Two-fifty? Well, seeing as you got a raise, why don't you get Jackson back? [*Beat.*]

NAN: What do you mean?

TERRY: Do you know, I spent our last cent getting him sprung? Yes. I let him go, Nan. I sent the man packing.

NAN: I don't understand. Are you trying to tell me you've fired Jackson?

TERRY: Yes, I fired Jackson. Yes!

NAN: Jesus, what the hell is the matter with you? Where the hell do you think the man's going to go? Do you know how long he'll last out there? He has nothing! He has nowhere!

TERRY: [*Vicious, snaps back.*] Yes, and we have no money! And Christ, it's enough of this crap, people padding about furtivly, making little plans, this miasma, and I'm so sick of it, I don't care anymore! Waiting for the dusty green Kaffir bus—you should've seen him—I stood here, watching him from this window. Bus after bus, he stood there, couldn't move! Weeping! I mean, finally, I couldn't watch any more. Goodbye Jackson, this stick figure, frozen, terrified, I hate it.

NAN: Oh, Terry, how far do you want to fall? How much ... pain do you think you can inflict? I don't think I can take much more.

TERRY: Even with your raise, we're trapped. How much can we save? We owe money all over town! It'll take a year to pay all the bills, and I'm not going to run out on every little shopkeeper in this town. If that's what you expect. Save? We're in the blackhole of Calcutta.

NAN: No. I understand. [*She sits down.*] I've really been so stupid, it's so clear to me now. Here I've been thinking, it'll be okay, once we leave. But the fact of it is, you really don't want to go anywhere, do you? Except a little walk along the beachfront now and then.

TERRY: Pardon?

NAN: Oh, don't. "Pardon?" Please. I mean, it's all very easy. Jackson's not the frozen and terrified one, really.

TERRY: Let me tell you, I'm being practical, you come in talking about a raise like it's the answer to all our problems, big deal. And that school-mistress tone may work with your home-fucking economics class, but don't ever bring it in here.

NAN: No. Talk to me, don't—

TERRY: [*Shouting, cuts her off.*] Then don't you play at Freud! Don't play at amateur ladies charity tea-shrink-contest-runner up! God, none of your pat little answers and—and the kind of sympathy you reserve for a—

NAN: —how dare you? I mean, all you do is, is take these positions, I mean, talk about clothing yourself in stances, please. At first it's funny, this man rushing out to buy the Beatles, fine, funny, rush out to smoke dope, hipper, always, than all of us. [*Beat.*] But the thing is, you really love it all. Blenheim, this beachfront, this small world here. It's just this fading of honesty, Terry. I'm sorry. Just stop lying to me! I don't care about you changing your mind, Christ knows I don't want to pack up and move to bloody Brazil. It's the posing. Do you understand? You don't have to do that, we've been married long enough. Just say "I want to stay." Because I want you to understand, this whole … wretched … business has been breaking my heart. [*Long pause.*]

TERRY: Not much else to say, eh? It's … you know, the times I—I go for a walk, pass Blenheim, and I'll just stop, remembering what it was like to be a boy there. Holding my cricket kit. In the same spot, fifteen years ago. So happy, so amazed, a boyhood could be so perfect. I just stand there, here I am, in my thirties, and reduced to memory, already. [*Beat.*] Well tell me what I should do then? I mean, I don't ... I don't know where I belong, is the thing, I thought as kid "I'm a gentleman farmer, fine." And then, Oh, "I'm an academic" and I detest the academics—so fine, radical. I'm a radical, right, great. Make a little radical gesture, hope to join that club, and someone's dead, so—I don't know what to do ... I would go back. I would go back and teach. I mean, finally, I only belong at Blenheim, just like Jonathon. I let it ... destroy me. Is it so bad? To want to go back? Is it such a ... defeat?

NAN: No, of course not. No. It hasn't destroyed you. [*She holds him.*]

TERRY: [*Closes his eyes. Shakes his head.*] I would've ... liked to have shown you the Amazon, because you know, it's going. It's the mining. [*Beat.*] It's ... [*Lights fade down. He gasps, reaches for her.*] a whole other world ...

Scene Three

MRS. BALTON'S *flat.* SUTTER *and* MRS. BALTON. *Late afternoon.*

MRS. BALTON: You see, if you look out over the verandah—that little red thingie in the water?

SUTTER: I can't possibly see that far anymore, Sylvia.

MRS. BALTON: Shark-net buoy. Swim past there and they'll eat you up like they did that girl a few months ago.

SUTTER: Never cared for the water myself.

MRS. BALTON: Christopher and I used to swim out for miles.

SUTTER: Extraordinary.

MRS. BALTON: How's the farm?

SUTTER: Haven't been for ages. Joyce has shingles again.

MRS. BALTON: You did the right thing, holding on to it.

SUTTER: It's just the house and some acres—had to sell some more this term, in fact.

MRS. BALTON: City is becoming harder to bear, daily. Like Bombay and Cairo.

SUTTER: I knew we'd end up on the farm one day. Still have the same herd boy. Ninety-one. Isn't doing much now—lives in the same shack. Bring him his tea and biscuit myself when I'm there. Sheds a tear every time. You'll come for Christmas, as usual, of course.

MRS. BALTON: Very upsetting seeing my old farm just across from yours. In the country, one can still smell old Africa. Clean, English sort of Africa, hint of something else out of range. India.

SUTTER: Well, that's all gone now. Here in the city as well.

MRS. BALTON: But one doesn't want to end one's days in the city. Remember what this town used to be like? Banquets at the Oyster Box Hotel?

SUTTER: The old beachfront. Three Monkeys coffeehouse? Remember?

MRS. BALTON: The old Durban, the old style. Indian waiters with sashes about their waists and bright red thinges on their heads.

SUTTER: Jonathon is doing a remarkable job, Sylvia.

MRS. BALTON: And you're surprised?

SUTTER: A bit, yes. So soon.

MRS. BALTON: It shouldn't surprise you; he's Christopher's and my son.

SUTTER: True, but at Blenheim one sees many sons. Even Hamish Fox is happy.

MRS. BALTON: Hamish Fox's happiness could not be of less consequence.

SUTTER: Yes, well it is to me. My heavy, eh? Syl, love. We need that rather large push we've all been talking about, right now, and of course, we're asking certain families to help.

MRS. BALTON: Nev, love. The point is this—Blenheim needs more than a mere push. You are on the verge of bankruptcy, are you not?

SUTTER: Exactly where we are, yes.

MRS. BALTON: You've continued to lose old boy support, have you not?

SUTTER: That's true, yes.

MRS. BALTON: And the new families have formed some sort of parents' committee, have they not?

SUTTER: Sylvia, must we negotiate like Jews? Tell me your terms. I'll tell you if they can be met.

MRS. BALTON: I am prepared to make a permanent endowment.

SUTTER: Please go on.

MRS. BALTON: You must retire within twelve months and Jonathon must be made headmaster.

SUTTER: I thought it might be something like that, dear.

MRS. BALTON: Or I could take my money and go off and buy some little farm somewhere, which would leave very little for endowments. I'll need to ask the accountant, Mr. Schorr.

SUTTER: Jonathon, as headmaster. May I remind you, when I bought Blenheim, your husband lent me the money?

MRS. BALTON: A lot. With no qualms, and no interest.

SUTTER: Exactly. And I thought I could build a gentleman's sort of place, with a rigorous approach to education, and yet at the same time, be rather humane. Wasn't that the oddest youthful presumption?

MRS. BALTON: I used to find sugarcane farming romantic. One learns perspective, Neville. Jonathon is the only way.

SUTTER: And when I purchased Blenheim from McFarquire, it really was rather nightmarish. 1936. So primitive, floggings day and night, forced marches into the bush, barefoot, smell of rotten wood rising up to one's nostrils at every turn. Boys with infections and bleeding welts from beatings, and fully one-third of them with broken limbs from rugby against the Afrikaaner school. Which they never lost. And the staff, Syliva? You and Christopher never really knew them, you never mingled with the hoi-poloi, did you?

MRS. BALTON: I'm sure they were most remarkable men, Neville.

SUTTER: The original Blenheim staff?. They came with the place when I bought it. Religious hysterics exiled from England by their families—fat rejects with quivering, bluish lips, breathing heavily after the little boys, shell-shocked great-war fodder, re-living the trenches in the classroom … the flotsam and jetsam of the empire, but you know—the truly mind-boggling thing is that Blenheim has never been as popular as it was then! And I gradually replaced that clutch of barnyard animals with a more reasonable lot. And felt so proud when Jonathon and Terry came on. It seemed the final dissolution of the old Blenheim. And look where it's got me.

MRS. BALTON: I shouldn't punish myself quite so hard, Nev. Could always pack it in, close the doors. Turn it into a nursing home. I'm told those do rather well.

SUTTER: Ah, yes. There you are. Built something, got to defend it. Jonathon'll be head, of course, Sylvia. But don't ask me for a date; he's not ready yet.

MRS. BALTON: I do think next year is sufficient, actually. And I should like, if I may, to have something in writing. [*Pause.*]

SUTTER: I beg your pardon?

MRS. BALTON: A simple contract, Neville. It's business, Neville. Business. [*Pause.*]

SUTTER: Look, at who we are. And look, Sylvia, at what we are, and tell me when a handshake has not been utterly sufficient. [*Beat.*]

MRS. BALTON: But, Neville, it is precisely because of who we are and what we are, that I *do* want a contract. [*Pause.*]

SUTTER: I see.

[SYLVIA *offers him her pen, as the lights fade down.*]

Scene Four

NAN: [*Addressing her class.*] When I asked for essays on the Zulus, I wasn't looking for detailed accounts of native laziness in your father's factory, Cleasby.
Nor am I interested in your examination of native killing techniques. It's
tired, and I'm tired of it. It's as if your Africa were some kind of Atlantis, with
drums and spears. It's not the one we're in. [*Pause.*] I thought we might, then,
try these essays again? Somehow de-mythologyzed, okay? I was thinking—as
I was reading them—I was thinking back, remembering, because my family had
a number of maids as I was growing up. And there was a blur, a period of faces,
names—I can't connect, but there was Edna. And she had been with us for some
years—this good-natured, virtually invisible friend. Whose life was actually far
more complicated than ours. My father did nothing really. There was a vast-
ness of leisure time, a morass. [*Pause.*] And Edna had this husband who worked
in the mines, whom she saw with less and less frequency over the years. My
mother found his presence—his dusty, coarse skin—upsetting, even if he was
only to spend the night in the little room in the back. He was never actually
forbidden; it was a kind of subtle discouragement. And—it was the same with
her children—who had been cast out to the grandmother's little squash-patch
and mud-hut in Zululand … somewhere where everyone might be re-united
at Christmas for a couple of days or so. Eventually, the circumstances of this
thwarted, enslaved life, all the wretchedness, made functioning as a human being
harder and harder. [*Pause.*] And of course, as it becomes harder to function as
a human being, it makes being a good servant pretty much an impossibility.
[*Pause.*] She became moody. Forgetting to bathe, becoming, finally, something
of a darkness in our home. And as Edna's personality became that of a toast-
burning hag, I started to develop an intense dislike for her. There was a point
where my family's main source of bored, wintry amusement—the height of mor-
bidity, finally, was to, over dinner, discuss the decline of Edna, discuss it, in
fact, as she served. [*Pause.*] And, of course, she began to sour. Her human-ness
became overwhelming, like meat left out far too long. And when the dimension of her life overtook our own, she was finally, simply sent away. [*Pause.*]
And the next week, it began again, with a new servant. So really, I mean, this
kind of Atlantis you describe, it hardly does credit to the real one, which has
its own violence, its own terrors, quite independent of Fox's Africa of guns and
war. That Africa—denies what we are. Our own brand of callousness. Surely
there have been lives that have meant something to you? And I would very much

like to know about that. Do you understand this?

[HAMISH FOX *has entered moments before, stood in the doorway.*]

FOX: Ergh.

NAN: Oh! Hello … ? Class, please stand up.

FOX: Sit. I just came to fetch some items, if you don't mind, Mrs. Sinclair. I'd like to have my goodbyes with the boys, please.

NAN: [*Starting to exit.*] Yes, of course. Please. Go ahead.

FOX: Many years of rubbish collected in here. You'll be amazed, Mrs. Sinclair, when you come and fetch it all.

NAN: Yes. I expect I will. [*She exits.*]

FOX: [*To class.*] When writing an essay, every thought must be crystal clear. Picture the sentence before you. Does it look correct. The comma in the right place? Spelling accurate? And the thought itself. How is that? Your penmanship must not waver, because when it does, it weakens the idea. And of equal importance, is that you do not let an ink-blot foul the paper. Nothing is so damaging as an ink-blot, like some vile black stain, occluding the light, breaking clarity. Make certain that the ink is running smoothly through the body of the pen, to the nib, which must never be bent. The nib must be as clean as the surgeon's scalpel—as vital an instrument. Imprint of the manufacturer must always be visible on the nib, or blots will occur. Do not put red ink into a pen which has had blue or black. Rather, keep three pens. If you cannot afford three pens, then you must wash the one thoroughly before putting in the new colour of ink. From the blue book, learn three new words a day. You must be able to convey the clarity of your intent, under fire, in the office, on the field; clarity of expression equals success. Your privilege is this education which separates you from the savage, and in the years ahead, this will be a most formidable weapon. [*Pause.*] I would also say, if I may be a bit more personal for a moment, that I would prefer it if nobody visited me in hospital—a strain on all parties that is best avoided. So, without further rigmarole, rigmarole, I shall see you, I'm certain, after Boxing Day, when I shall tell you about the idiocy of the Maginot Line. And Douglas Bader, the war hero with no legs.

[FOX *exits slowly, as lights fade down.*]

Scene Six

BALTON's *classroom.* BALTON *and* SUTTER.

SUTTER: You must understand, this is very upsetting.

BALTON: Oh dear.

SUTTER: What the hell's the matter with her?

BALTON: Well now, we don't know exactly what went on, do we?

SUTTER: Hamish Fox—Hamish Fox comes in and tells me of some sort of mad-woman speech in social bloody history class?

BALTON: Yes. This from a man who's less evolved than the creature for which he's named.

SUTTER: Don't be clever, Jonathon. The Mowatts, the Ashburnhams and the Halliwells have all decided to withdraw their boys at end of term if nothing is done.

BALTON: Look, if Blenheim is to move forward, don't you think we should be permitted to do so without the constant terrorization of our staff by hysterics? Don't you agree, Nev?

SUTTER: Of course I fucking agree! But the point is, that Mowatt woman is the most fertile female in Natal. I was looking forward to another four boys at least! I mean, the whole business has gone way, way too far!

BALTON: Sometimes boys come back, don't they?

SUTTER: [*Scornful.*] Oh, thank you. [*He stumbles over a chair.*] Christ—I can't see! She must've known that with things the way they are, this would cost her her damn job!

BALTON: I was expecting something like that—are you serious?

SUTTER: Deadly serious. I'm too tired of it. Why the hell should we be destroyed over this? We've all seen fine boys come out of here—I'm not going to just sit here and watch the whole place eroding. The parents' committee may be repulsive, but they're absolutely correct; we need a purge—a blood-letting—

their words exactly!

BALTON: Well, then I have the right idea—fire McNally, hell, I'll do it! Let's be bloody aggressive about it—bring back Terry! And if—if you stand there, telling me that he's a fucking communist, I'll be out the door myself, old man, I swear it!

[*Pause.* SUTTER *raises his eyebrows, regards* JONATHON.]

SUTTER: I know he's not a communist. But that's not the point. He could be a cross between Aristotle and Jesus Christ for all I care. He's not coming back. I've got to have surgery on my eyes, or I shall end up being led about by a water-spaniel. I'm going to Capetown for surgery, and I'm leaving you in charge, and I have decided, Jonathon, that it is to be your responsibility to end this business. She's to have her last day on Friday. And be gone after lunch.

BALTON: It is just giving in to those dull horrors who drop their kids off here every morning! Why? Why, Neville?

SUTTER: It is not for further discussion. I'm exhausted. It has been decided.

BALTON: But why must I do it, then?

SUTTER: [*Icy.*] Because I, Jonathon, am going blind.

BALTON: But I can't even—I can't do it—

SUTTER: [*Thundering.*] No discussion! I am dead from discussion! And diplomacy! It ... is ... over. And I want new septic tanks, please, Jonathon, by the time I return. The smell of offal around here is overwhelming. Joyce can't entertain the parents' committee.

BALTON: [*After a pause.*] I ask you this. One question, Neville. What is left? [*Pause.*]

SUTTER: What is left, Jonathon, is Blenheim.

[*Lights fade down.*]

Scene Seven

Early evening. The bench by the wall. TERRY *is sitting alone. He is clean-shaven, calm and well-dressed, in khaki-twills, a striped shirt and sweater.*

BALTON: Terry.

TERRY: It's very lovely, isn't it, when it's this quiet?

BALTON: [*Entering, his jacket carried over his shoulder, a cigar in his teeth.*] My favourite times; early morning, and in the evening, after the little buggers have left. When it's empty. Good to see you, Ter.

TERRY: Yes. You look well. This is all agreeing with you, eh? [*Pause.*]

BALTON: [*Quietly.*] Yes it is. I showed myself a film just now. Mr. Blandings builds his ... dream house. Very sad, funny. Sort of. Hmn.

TERRY: [*Leaning over, picks up a stone.*] You know, once when I was a boy, I found a spear-head here.

BALTON: I remember. But I think, in fact, it was planted by Fox. [*Pause.*] Are you well? You look better.

TERRY: [*Shrugs, embarrassed.*] I think. Yes. Been a hell of a time ... I ... [*Pause.*] They're building Balton Hall?

BALTON: A brilliant and aggressive move on Neville's part. Sort of cross between Versailles and Walter Gropius. Daring. He's gone off. Left me in charge. They're doing something to his corneas.

TERRY: Yes. And left you to do as you will?

BALTON: ... I suppose ... Yes. He has.

TERRY: Jon—I had an interview, ah, at the University of Natal. But the poor old head of English, and Speech and Drama, just a tired, fucked old bloke— they've got half his Faculty gone—whispered in my ear, "Love to take you on, Ter. But it's just not on, old boy." [*Pause.*] "Can't ... take any chances now," he said.

BALTON: Ah.

TERRY: Yes. They have their own troubles. A Jesuit in the Law School arrested.

BALTON: Yes. I read it. Look up there, up the hill—they're burning sugarcane … smell it?

TERRY: [*Looking off left.*] I know—I was thinking before you came, watching it. It's like the huge, roaring wall of flame between us and the rest of the world. How do you ever get through it? The firey wall of mythology? McNally's stories of Negroes descending en masse from Harlem, Fox's Pakis and Arabs taking over London … look at that fire. It's growing and growing. The hatred for the rest of the world. And how do you find passage through it?

BALTON: I wonder. You were trying, weren't you? Somehow. To connect … at the centenary? It's one of the things I love in the cinema—the movies. [*Pause.*] That thing, heroism in unexpected places. Look. Give this to Nan, will you? I missed her this afternoon, meeting Sutter. Her raise—first cheque.

[JONATHON *reaches into his pocket and hands* TERRY *a cheque.*]

TERRY: They've got you signing cheques now, eh?

BALTON: Yes. A heady feeling indeed.

TERRY: Not much more to give you then, is there?

BALTON: It all seems to be working out, somehow, for once, I think.

TERRY: [*Embarrassed.*] I have uhm … [*He stands up.*] God. I should just say this, I'd like to come back. I grew up here, I don't really know where else to go. I know you've got some lee-way now. [*He looks away. Thinks.*] I miss you. I miss the place. I miss being liked by certain boys. The ones who … can make you laugh. The ones who're worth it. I miss 'em. I'm standing here now, it's the only place I feel comfortable. [*Beat.*] It'll be very quiet. I don't like doing this to you, but I've always helped you, Jonathon, I've never really, not that I can remember, asked you for very much. You know, when you moved here from the farm, you asked if I would come too. So now, I'm asking you, bring me back. This is the only place I know how to fight that fire. [*Long pause.*]

BALTON: [*Quiet.*] Yes, good. You can start in the new year.

[*Lights fade down.*]

Scene Eight

A cemetery by the Indian Ocean. It stretches off—a pastoral green, under an intense sun. In the distance, there is the crashing sound of waves hitting rocks. BALTON *and* SUTTER *enter, the latter with a patch over one eye.*

BALTON: Neville. Do you think you should rest? You've only just got off an aeroplane.

SUTTER: No. I shall rest tomorrow, at the farm. [*He pulls his flask out of his blazer.*] Drink?

BALTON: Yes. Thank you.

SUTTER: Huge cemetery, isn't it?

BALTON: Never been in here.

SUTTER: [*Pointing off.*] The old Durban faces—all out. Seems the only time we see one another is when one of us dies. Was a time, when instead of a grave, we met at the cricket finals. I do wish more of the old boys had shown. To say goodbye to Hamish. This saddens.

BALTON: You didn't see them! The Mowatts, the Cleasbys.

SUTTER: Must be my eyes.

BALTON: How was the aeroplane?

SUTTER: Joyce was bilious and broke out in shingles. A spell of bad luck, eh? Her shingles. My eyes, spending money madly …

BALTON: But it should turn about in the spring.

SUTTER: Wish I had a biscuit with my whisky. This eye treatment? They use a laser, burns a hole, you can hear the eye sizzling like bacon. They insist it's painless, but really, it's hell.

BALTON: But useful, eh?

SUTTER: You did a remarkable job, making Hamish's funeral arrangements and all.

BALTON: Yes. And I've put a nice Christmas tree in Assembly Hall.

SUTTER: You know, I looked at my body in the mirror before the funeral. I'm all white, all soft. Little veins, like a tea-doily under the white. Like a map. An old and tattered map. Up my left leg is a vein that looks remarkably like the Blue Nile. Been up 'em both.

BALTON: Ah.

SUTTER: Quite interesting, seeing the old crowd here, out to bury Hamish. Because I looked at them, and they're white and veiny too. Cumberland told me that he had little capillaries exploding all over his left side. Showed me. Looked like Ghana, from years and years, his doctor told him, of drinking cane spirits. Gotta stop drinking they tell him, and we had a bit of a laugh over that. I mean— what's the point, at this stage, eh? [*Pause.*] What a pathetic bunch of old men and their stray wives, standing about in a cemetery. A clutch of rheumy-eyed, sodden, yellow-toothed old gentlemen farmers and their distorted wives, all of us with nowhere to go. And yet, look out there—the sulphuric red-streaked mad sea. Pounding on the rocks. A dead-end for me. [*Pause.*] Not only have you not fired her, but you've given her a raise. I looked at the ledger before I came. Why?

BALTON: [*Sighing.*] I'm sorry. Well then, here we are. Should I pack my things?

SUTTER: Let's discuss it.

BALTON: Oh, let's not, Nev. Let's not be clever, shall we? Just fire me, if you're going to.

SUTTER: Jonathon. You needn't stand there like a fifth former about to get a hiding.

BALTON: But, Neville, you see, I've always been terrified of those who judge— always wanted to please authority. First father, then mother, Terry … and now, you.

SUTTER: I know.

[*Pause.* JONATHON *takes a deep breath.*]

BALTON: Neville. Do you honestly believe that I do not know why I was made assistant-head? All it took was the tiny bit of intuition I've got. Mother. It's shameful, Nev, to think I'd be so dull-witted as to not understand. And so, at the point of realization—the epiphany—one feels pretty dreadful, pretty damn ugly. Incapable, swindled. And for you to assume utter unquestioning on my part, the absolute certainty of my taking orders, makes me feel utterly pathetic.

SUTTER: Not my intent, Jonathon.

BALTON: So why not help my only friends? Two people who have had the best intentions—the most fairminded … you know why I am friends with Terry? Because since we were boys—he could always be good enough for the both of us. And, Nan—they're not like us. Why not help two such friends? [*Pause.*]

SUTTER: And what about politics, Jonathon?

BALTON: Politics?

SUTTER: Exactly.

BALTON: And after all this time, why is it … that *now* … I should suddenly find myself involved, in of all things, *your* … politics?

SUTTER: An education, isn't it?

BALTON: Because, if we're all to end up white, corroded bodies at the edge of the sea, I'd rather have the memory of my own cowardice, my own shrivelling-up. Anything, anything other than this exhaustion, this—depletion—this ceaseless, repulsive dignity.

SUTTER: I agree completely.

BALTON: And that is why I did not fire her.

SUTTER: Jonathon, lad. Listen, please.

BALTON: But you see, I think—I think … it's gone far enough. Let's stop, shall we? I've had quite enough.

SUTTER: No cinematic histrionics, please.

BALTON: Neville, you don't understand.

SUTTER: It is you again, who does not understand. Though it is refreshing to hear you make so much sense for once. Look. Your mother does help us. True. But your mother's money did not make you assistant headmaster. Though it is convenient for her to think that she protects you.

BALTON: Oh, yes it did.

SUTTER: No. It is you that I have thought of. Your well-being and Blenheim's. I have built and defended that place, and it's virtually killed me. It's more, ultimately, than just the dry bones of mere ritual. I could've found another way, if I thought you were wrong. You're far more interesting than either of your parents. Your mother is a viper. And your father was like a killer whale, gulping in air. So do me this favour. This thing. Fire Nan, and then you're headmaster of Blenheim.

BALTON: I won't do it to Nan.

SUTTER: It is your only chance, your only hope. There are, you must realize, very definite, very cogent reasons for this business. Do you remember what I told you when you took assistant-head? "You find yourself becoming more the representative. And you've got to acknowledge what it is you're representing."I need to know, now, what, and who it is, you are representing. You must let Nan go—then I'll know you're ready.

MRS. BALTON: [*Entering.*]That's very good, Neville. I think you're right. Please don't get up.

BALTON: Oh, mother. I'm not interested in discussing it with you. Look. Let me put it clearly: Just fire me.

MRS. BALTON: It's the coldest of worlds out there. I've told you many times. But you've not listened. If you left Blenheim, how would you spend your days? [*Pause.*] You know, don't you? You'd end up serving me tea on a tray, just like nanny, wasting away in her room. You think you are lonely now, but without Blenheim, the days will just stretch ahead of you, agonizingly, Jonathon. And you will find yourself an old man, with flail hands, outrageous scarves, in an oceanfront flat, eating pudding on a white plate. Absolutely—irredeemably isolated.

BALTON: That's not true!

MRS. BALTON: As if in a hole. And your pleasure? You will go to the cinema, alone, purchase your ticket, sit in the dark, and you'll walk out, a little closer to death.

BALTON: No.

MRS. BALTON: No. You can't do that anymore, can you, Jonathon? You have begun to enjoy this new experience. This power. Have you not? Your new suits? You are more careful in your bathing, in combing your hair. You have been admired, effective. And it would end.

BALTON: Listen to yourself, mother.

MRS. BALTON: I cannot allow this to happen. Because I won't be here to protect you. Be realistic.

BALTON: Like you? It doesn't interest me.

MRS. BALTON: You are destined to be lonely, Jonathon. It is only a matter of degree. The choice is yours. Life is such a trifle, such a small thing. And one is left with what little one has built.

BALTON: What have we built, mother?

MRS. BALTON: A relatively quiet, somewhat safe, permanently endowed home for my boy. Blenheim School for Boys.

BALTON: A home? With no friends. Like our home, mother.

MRS. BALTON: Do you know what would happen if Nan stayed on and you brought back Terry? Could you build the Blenheim you want? Nobody else wants it. And you didn't even have the stamina to sustain your film society. You would destroy yourself for two people who will live without you, and whom you can never have. [*Long pause.*]

BALTON: You are a brutal and savage woman, which you know. But what nobody has ever told you, is that actually, you are an extraordinarily shallow one as well.

[JONATHON *to exit.*]

SUTTER: Jonathon! [JONATHON *stops.*] Whatever you decide now—you are going to have to live with. Forever. There is no going back. Do you understand?

[JONATHON *walks off.*]

SUTTER: [*Pointing off.*] Look over the wall, Sylvia. The Hindus are burning their dead. Let's go and have a look, shall we?

[*Lights fade down.*]

Scene Nine

JONATHON's *classroom. A small Christmas tree stands in one corner.* JONATHON *is at his desk. On the blackboard is a note. "Classes dismissed in order to attend the funeral of* MR. FOX." TERRY *and* NAN *enter.*

TERRY: Jonathon.

BALTON: Ah, there you are. Nice funeral, wasn't it?

NAN: No. There was hardly anyone there for him. I mean—not to sentimental-ize him, but …

TERRY: He had nobody, really. God I need a drink. May I?

BALTON: Help yourself. Frightening, isn't it? And sad. Did you know that he shrunk to the size of a pygmy before he finally died?

NAN: Are you alright? You look pale.

BALTON: This was only my second funeral. My father's the only other. You were very fond of my father, weren't you, Terry? Horses, and all that. But you did-n't really know him. Did you?

TERRY: … No. I mean, the public version only. Right? You look like you could use a drink, Jonathon …

BALTON: No. Just tired out. I was thinking of the farm. Every Saturday night, father'd give one of the cows to the natives. A treat. Few farms did that. But actually, it was no sacrifice, just a small feeble animal. And yet, canecutters, herd boys, all of them … would look forward to Saturday night. The compound would come alive. That mad Zulu pop music on the Bantu radio. I'd sit in nanny's lap, watching. It was all very festive. [*Beat.*] I was mostly interested in the killing of the cow. Used to be, they used a knife, and that was vivid, very much a thing of the bush. To see the creature's dull eyes flashing, hooves scraping at the dirt as the knife was led across the throat—and the blood running into a gourd on the ground. But the part that fascinated me the most, was when it was dead. Its evisceration. The skin drawn slowly back, and the veins exposed, black blood clotting into the reddish dust of the compound, which would be dead quiet, sombre. Little ivory coloured and purple-hued sacks filled with bile and acid and urine. Balloons of undigested grass, bones cracked, and muscles pulsing gently, as a fire was readied, and the tongue, the great curled muscle, unravelled, cut out, and the teeth and jaw laid bare. [*Pause.*] But it is one Saturday in particular that I remember. It was my birthday, and I was given the honour of killing the cow. I was eleven. The knife was dispensed with, and my father gave me a pistol with tiny silver-tipped bullets. I was to blow out the brains from a little spot between the eyes, and this death had none of the ritual of the knife. It was an assassination and I believe the natives knew this. Unbearable to have this cow led to me, docile, and uncomplaining. She was tied to a post, with a little strand of rope, and I tried to do the thing very quickly. But you see, I did not do a proper job of it. And the bullet ricochetted off her skull and down into the jaw—this shattered pulp of bone and blood, through which she screamed, you see, as I recall it. And tore loose from her feebly tied rope. And there she was, with saliva, and plasma all about, bolting into the cane fields, everyone stunned. She was gone. And I stood there. Frozen. [*Pause.*] And I looked up, and saw my father standing on the verandah of the main house with my mother—and he said something to her, and went inside, and nanny came to me. And of course, by this time, I was crying. The natives staring at their feet— mortified. No laughter—which might have been preferable. [*Pause.*] And then my father came out of the house with his shotgun, got on his horse, and rode into the field, and there was a single muffled blast, and nanny put me to bed. A quiet supper that night, no singing or dancing, and of course, not long after, we moved into the city—my mother's idea. So I was just thinking about my father, and all. [*Pause.*]

TERRY: Funerals. It's death … that makes us think. Not life, usually, unfortunately. It's natural.

BALTON: Natural. No, it has nothing to do with nature, Terry. And also, after all is said and done, after all our reasoning, and … grasping, searching … nobody really … cares.

TERRY: Well I used to think that.

BALTON: No. You don't understand, Terry. You can't come back.

TERRY: What's happened?

BALTON: I've been made headmaster. And Nan, you are … fired.

NAN: Are you telling me—I don't understand. You just fired me?

TERRY: That's right. I understand. They've made you headmaster.

BALTON: No, you don't understand. At all. You've always said "there's something terribly odd about Jonathon. He's baffled by it all" … but you are wrong. I am not at all baffled by it all.

NAN: No. There's nothing you can say.

BALTON: Nan, remember when I asked you, "must you leave?" You said … "we must all of us … try and build something as best we can?" That is what I have done.

NAN: Yes, you have. Well, you will be alone, Jonathon.

BALTON: You see? I can not live with that anymore! These judgements. The echo of some whispered judgement on a verandah. All your talk, I have to say "no" to it. Your demands, your politics—the rightness of your politics I say no, and I will survive you have this idea. It is of change and the future, and hope, and prevailing. And you hand me a gun. [*Beat.*] It's so easy for you to judge me. You hand me a gun, point it at my head. And watch. [*Beat.*] No. Say whatever you like. [*Almost smiles, almost self-mocking.*] Say I am a monster. In this room, the projector gone, the true product of Blenheim. Blenheim's monster. Skipping, lurching down the halls, really. As a boy. And as a man. Say anything.

TERRY: [*After a moment. Shakes his head.*] Happy … New Year, Jonathon.

[*They look at him for a moment. He looks back. They exit.*]

BALTON: [*A whisper.*] Yes. It is.

[JONATHON *walks over to the desk. Picks up a box of Christmas tree decorations, and goes to the tree. He places a small star on the pinnacle. And then, from the box, a tin of artificial snow. Which he begins to spray all over the tree, and after a moment, slowly, straight up into the air, over his head And he lifts his hands to catch the white powder as it filters down upon him, swirling to the floor, a small storm.*]

END OF PLAY

TRIFLES

SUSAN GLASPELL

—————⇒⊰⊷⊱⊱⊰————

Originally performed in 1916

INTRODUCTION

by Janice Paran

"Without thinking too much about it in specific terms, I was showing the America I knew and observed to others who might not have noticed."
— Norman Rockwell

Trifles was written in 1916, the same year that a Norman Rockwell illustration first graced the cover of *The Saturday Evening Post* and Albert Einstein proposed the theory of relativity. Woodrow Wilson was in the White House, Charlie Chaplin was turning out two-reelers and Margaret Sanger opened the nation's first birth control clinic. The United States was a year away from being drawn into the First World War and four years from granting women the right to vote. For Susan Glaspell (1876-1948), an Iowa-bred newspaper reporter-turned-writer, it was a heady time, fueled by reformist impulses in politics and the arts, some homegrown, others emulating European movements, and ignited by the conviction that America's future was to be a collaborative effort.

Married in 1913 to George Cram Cook, a prominent figure among Davenport's liberal intelligentsia, Glaspell–who by this time had moved beyond her journalistic roots to become a novelist and short story writer–soon turned her attentions to the theatre. She and Cook moved East, dividing their time between New York City and Provincetown, Massachusetts in the company of like-minded artists and activists, and in 1915 they launched the Provincetown Players to seek out and produce new work, including their own. Eugene O'Neill was an early convert to their ranks, and Glaspell later said that when they first heard *Bound East for Cardiff* read aloud, "we knew what we were for."

What they were for was a new American drama, one rooted in psychological truth and created in opposition to the sensational fare, star vehicles and patently artificial stage decor that dominated the repertoire. The American drama critic Clayton Hamilton, writing in 1910, had this to say about the state of the American theatre: "Most of our American playwrights, like Juliet in the balcony scene, speak, yet they say nothing. They represent facts, but fail to reveal truths. What they lack is purpose. They collect, instead of meditating; they invent, instead of wondering; they are clever instead of being real." For the Provincetown Players, "being real" was the proper business of the stage, and though O'Neill's contributions have eclipsed Glaspell's in staying power, *Trifles* set the American theatre a new course in pursuit of that ideal.

Glaspell and Cook had been inspired by the work of the Abbey Theatre's Irish Players, seen on tour in Chicago, and by America's fledgling Little Theatre movement, modeled on European innovations and undertaken in opposition to The Syndicate, a consortium of producers whose star packages and monopolizing booking tactics had already turned the youthful, energetic and unruly American theatre into a primarily commercial venture. The simultaneous development of the new medium of film was a further blow to the self-esteem of the American theatre, which was still in search of its own identity.

The impulse for reform was two-fold, as it had been in the European independent theatre movement of the late 19th and early 20th centuries — to promote new scenic ideas radically different from the elaborate stock settings of the 19th century stage, and to cultivate adventurous new writers suited to such an enterprise. What André Antoine, Otto Brahm, Ibsen, Strindberg, Stanislavsky, Chekhov and Shaw, among others, had done for the theatre in Europe was a rallying cry for a handful of American artists and intellectuals out to invent a serious American theatre.

Trifles seems an unlikely harbinger of a theatrical revolution. Modestly produced in Provincetown in August of 1916, a month before the group met to announce their first New York season, the hastily written one-act, inspired by a famous murder case Glaspell had covered for the *Des Moines Daily News*, demonstrated the ensemble's commitment to a theatre where playwrights could see their work performed with simplicity and integrity. Though Glaspell went on to write several more plays for the company, including *The Verge* (1921), a fascinating expressionistic drama about a woman's descent into madness, *Trifles* remains her best known work.

A slight naturalistic play about two Iowa housewives biding their time in a farmhouse kitchen while their husbands — the town sheriff and a neighboring farmer — search elsewhere in the house for clues in a murder investigation, *Trifles* neither shocks nor proselytizes, nor does it attempt to be particularly dramatic in any conventional sense. The murder in question has already taken place — John Wright was found strangled in his bed the previous day, and his wife Minnie has been taken into custody — and neither victim nor suspect appear as characters. The women merely wait, and while they wait, their own observations of such domestic "trifles" as sloppy stitching on a quilt square and a broken hinge on a birdcage door begin to unsettle them, hinting at a story of abuse and retaliation. Unlike the active protagonists of a traditional murder mystery, Mrs. Hale and Mrs. Peters are unwitting detectives, content at first to leave the business at hand to the law, whose representatives are upstairs, pledging to go over the evidence "piece by piece." That is, of course, precisely what they fail to do, while the women reluctantly "piece" together the truth of Minnie's lonely life and her husband's death. By the time the men return, shaking their heads over the absence of any clear motive that would implicate Minnie Wright in her husband's murder, the women have, without really saying so, solved a mystery they resisted acknowledging, and in a furtive last-minute gesture of sympathy for and solidarity with the unhappy woman, they suppress the evidence that could convict her.

Often hailed as a feminist work, *Trifles* was certainly groundbreaking in the attention it paid to the details of women's lives and in the relative importance it assigned them, but it stops short of endowing its female characters with heroic sensitivity. Granted, the men in the play overlook the women's domestic and emotional affairs as a matter of course, but the women, too, are forced to acknowledge their complicity in Minnie Wright's fate. "I wish I had come over sometimes when *she* was here," Mrs. Hale says. "I stayed away because it weren't cheerful — and that's why I ought to have come." In the course of this brief play, whose dramatic action is almost entirely subtextual, facts give way to truths, and those truths to deeper ones, implicating not only a woman suspected of killing her husband, but the society that turned a blind eye to her suffering. The "scene of the crime," we are given to understand, cannot be reduced to the narrow confines of the traditional whodunit. The plot of *Trifles*, which inscribes a neat circle around an oppressed housewife, a dead songbird and a strangled husband, may seem rather tidily symbolic to us today, but the play's underlying political point still stings. Though the term "domestic drama" has long since become a pejorative, it is useful to remember that naturalism in the theatre, frequently accused of robbing the art form of its capacity to surprise and transform, was born out of an impulse for reform. "Here is what exists," proclaimed Zola in 1880. "Endeavor to repair it."

Glaspell and Cook parted company with the Provincetown Players in 1922, and though Glaspell didn't give up the theatre altogether–she won a Pulitzer in 1931 for *Alison's House*, a play loosely based on the life of Emily Dickinson, and served in the Midwest bureau of the Federal Theatre Project from 1936 to 1938 — the stage was never again her primary focus. That's always been something of a shame for the American theatre, because *Trifles*, and the subsequent plays Glaspell wrote in her six short years with the Provincetown Players, are the work of an ambitious and profoundly original writer with a journalist's zeal and a poet's instincts for interrogating the world around her and looking beneath its surfaces for motivating truths. Whether through circumstance or inclination, her early promise as a playwright failed to sustain her, but *Trifles*, for all its homespun simplicity, needs no apology, and time hasn't obscured its subversive inner life. Susan Glaspell knew and observed America, too, just not the same one captured on the cover of *The Saturday Evening Post*.

CHARACTERS

GEORGE HENDERSON, County Attorney
HENRY PETERS, Sheriff
LEWIS HALE, A Neighboring Farmer
MRS. PETERS
MRS. HALE

SCENE: *The kitchen in the now abandoned farmhouse of* JOHN WRIGHT, *a gloomy kitchen, and left without having been put in order—unwashed pans under the sink, a loaf of bread outside the breadbox, a dish towel on the table—other signs of incompleted work. At the rear the outer door opens and the* SHERIFF *comes in followed by the* COUNTY ATTORNEY *and* HALE. *The* SHERIFF *and* HALE *are men in middle life, the* COUNTY ATTORNEY *is a young man; all are much bundled up and go at once to the stove. They are followed by the two women—the* SHERIFF's *wife first; she is a slight wiry woman, a thin nervous face.* MRS. HALE *is larger and would ordinarily be called more comfortable looking, but she is disturbed now and looks fearfully about as she enters. The women have come in slowly, and stand close together near the door.*

COUNTY ATTORNEY: [*Rubbing his hands.*] This feels good. Come up to the fire, ladies.

MRS. PETERS: [*After taking a step forward.*] I'm not—cold.

SHERIFF: [*Unbuttoning his overcoat and stepping away from the stove as if to mark the beginning of official business.*] Now, Mr. Hale, before we move things about, you explain to Mr. Henderson just what you saw when you came here yesterday morning.

COUNTY ATTORNEY: By the way, has anything been moved? Are things just as you left them yesterday?

SHERIFF: [*Looking about.*] It's just the same. When it dropped below zero last night I thought I'd better send Frank out this morning to make a fire for us—no use getting pneumonia with a big case on, but I told him not to touch anything except the stove—and you know Frank.

COUNTY ATTORNEY: Somebody should have been left here yesterday.

SHERIFF: Oh—yesterday. When I had to send Frank to Morris Center for that man who went crazy—I want you to know I had my hands full yesterday, I knew you could get back from Omaha by today and as long as I went over everything here myself—

COUNTY ATTORNEY: Well, Mr. Hale, tell just what happened when you came here yesterday morning.

HALE: Harry and I had started to town with a load of potatoes. We came along the road from my place and as I got here I said, "I'm going to see if I can't get John Wright to go in with me on a party telephone." I spoke to Wright about it once before and he put me off, saying folks talked too much anyway, and all he asked was peace and quiet—I guess you know about how much he talked himself; but I thought maybe if I went to the house and talked about it before his wife, though I said to Harry that I didn't know as what his wife wanted made much difference to John—

COUNTY ATTORNEY: Let's talk about that later, Mr. Hale. I do want to talk about that, but tell now just what happened when you got to the house.

HALE: I didn't hear or see anything; I knocked at the door, and still it was all quiet inside. I knew they must be up, it was past eight o'clock. So I knocked again, and I thought I heard somebody say, "Come in." I wasn't sure, I'm not sure yet, but I opened the door—this door [*Indicating the door by which the two women are still standing.*] and there in that rocker [*Pointing to it.*] sat Mrs. Wright. [*They all look at the rocker.*]

COUNTY ATTORNEY: What—was she doing?

HALE: She was rockin' back and forth. She had her apron in her hand and was kind of—pleating it.

COUNTY ATTORNEY: And how did she—look?

HALE: Well, she looked queer.

COUNTY ATTORNEY: How do you mean—queer?

HALE: Well, as if she didn't know what she was going to do next. And kind of done up.

COUNTY ATTORNEY: How did she seem to feel about your coming?

HALE: Why, I don't think she minded—one way or other. She didn't pay much attention. I said, "How do, Mrs. Wright, it's cold, ain't it?" And she said, "Is it?"—and went on kind of pleating at her apron. Well, I was surprised; she didn't ask me to come up to the stove, or to set down, but just sat there, not even looking at me, so I said, "I want to see John." And then she—laughed. I guess you would call it a laugh. I thought of Harry and the team outside, so I said a little sharp: "Can't I see John?" ... "No," she says, kind o' dull like. "Ain't he home?" says I. "Yes," says she, "he's home." "Then why can't I see him?" I asked her, out of patience. "'Cause he's dead," says she. "Dead?" says I. She just nodded her head, not getting a bit excited, but rockin' back and forth. "Why—where is he?" says I, not knowing what to say. She just pointed upstairs—like that [*Himself pointing to the room above.*]. I got up, with the idea of going up there. I walked from there to here—then I says, "Why, what did he die of?" … "He died of a rope round his neck," says she, and just went on pleatin' at her apron. Well, I went out and called Harry. I thought I might—need help. We went upstairs and there he was lyin'—

COUNTY ATTORNEY: I think I'd rather have you go into that upstairs, where you can point it all out. Just go on now with the rest of the story.

HALE: Well, my first thought was to get that rope off. It looked … [*Stops, his face twitches.*] … but Harry, he went up to him, and he said, "No, he's dead all right, and we'd better not touch anything." So we went back downstairs. She was still sitting that same way. "Has anybody been notified?" I asked. "No," says she, unconcerned. "Who did this, Mrs. Wright?" said Harry. He said it businesslike—and she stopped pleatin' of her apron. "I don't know," she says. "You don't *know*?" says Harry. "No," says she. "Weren't you sleepin' in the bed with him?" says Harry. "Yes," says she, "but I was on the inside." "Somebody slipped a rope round his neck and strangled him and you didn't wake up?" says Harry. "I didn't wake up," she said after him. We must 'a looked as if we didn't see how that could be, for after a minute she said, "I sleep sound." Harry was going to ask her more questions but I said maybe we ought to let her tell her story first to the coroner, or the sheriff, so Harry went fast as he could to Rivers' place, where there's a telephone.

COUNTY ATTORNEY: And what did Mrs. Wright do when she knew that you had gone for the coroner?

HALE: She moved from that chair to this one over here [*Pointing to a small chair in the corner.*] and just sat there with her hands held together and looking down. I got a feeling that I ought to make some conversation, so I said I had come in to see if John wanted to put in a telephone, and at that she started to laugh, and then she stopped and looked at me—scared.

[*The* COUNTY ATTORNEY, *who has had his notebook out, makes a note.*]

I dunno, maybe it wasn't scared. I wouldn't like to say it was. Soon Harry got back, and then Dr. Lloyd came, and you, Mr. Peters, and so I guess that's all I know that you don't.

COUNTY ATTORNEY: [*Looking around.*] I guess we'll go upstairs first—and then out to the barn and around there. [*To the* SHERIFF.] You're convinced that there was nothing important here—nothing that would point to any motive.

SHERIFF: Nothing here but kitchen things.

[*The* COUNTY ATTORNEY, *after again looking around the kitchen, opens the door of a cupboard closet. He gets up on a chair and looks on a shelf. Pulls his hand away, sticky.*]

COUNTY ATTORNEY: Here's a nice mess.

[*The women draw nearer.*]

MRS. PETERS: [*To the other woman.*] Oh, her fruit; it did freeze. [*To the* COUNTY ATTORNEY.] She worried about that when it turned so cold. She said the fire'd go out and her jars would break.

SHERIFF: Well, can you beat the woman! Held for murder and worryin' about her preserves.

COUNTY ATTORNEY: I guess before we're through she may have something more serious than preserves to worry about.

HALE: Well, women are used to worrying over trifles.

[*The two women move a little closer together.*]

COUNTY ATTORNEY: [*With the gallantry of a young politician.*] And yet, for all their worries, what would we do without the ladies?

[*The women do not unbend. He goes to the sink, takes a dipperful of water from the pail and pouring it into a basin, washes his hands. Starts to wipe them on the roller towel, turns it for a cleaner place.*]

Dirty towels! [*Kicks his foot against the pans under the sink.*] Not much of a house-keeper, would you say, ladies?

MRS. HALE: [*Stiffly.*] There's a great deal of work to be done on a farm.

COUNTY ATTORNEY: To be sure. And yet [*With a little bow to her.*] I know there are some Dickson county farmhouses which do not have such roller towels. [*He gives it a pull to expose its full length again.*]

MRS. HALE: Those towels get dirty awful quick. Men's hands aren't always as clean as they might be.

COUNTY ATTORNEY: Ah, loyal to your sex, I see. But you and Mrs. Wright were neighbors. I suppose you were friends, too.

MRS. HALE: [*Shaking her head.*] I've not seen much of her of late years. I've not been in this house—it's more than a year.

COUNTY ATTORNEY: And why was that? You didn't like her?

MRS. HALE: I liked her all well enough. Farmers' wives have their hands full, Mr. Henderson. And then-

COUNTY ATTORNEY: Yes—?

MRS. HALE: [*Looking about.*] It never seemed a very cheerful place.

COUNTY ATTORNEY: No—it's not cheerful. I shouldn't say she had the home-making instinct.

MRS. HALE: Well, I don't know as Wright had, either.

COUNTY ATTORNEY: You mean that they didn't get on very well?

MRS. HALE: No, I don't mean anything. But I don't think a place'd be any cheer-fuller for John Wright's being in it.

COUNTY ATTORNEY: I'd like to talk more of that a little later. I want to get the lay of things upstairs now.[*He goes to the left, where three steps lead to a stair door.*]

SHERIFF: I suppose anything Mrs. Peters does'll be all right. She was to take in some clothes for her, you know, and a few little things. We left in such a hurry yesterday.

COUNTY ATTORNEY: Yes, but I would like to see what you take, Mrs. Peters, and keep an eye out for anything that might be of use to us.

MRS. PETERS: Yes, Mr. Henderson.

[*The women listen to the men's steps on the stairs, then look about the kitchen.*]

MRS. HALE: I'd hate to have men coming into my kitchen, snooping around and criticizing.

[*She arranges the pans under sink which the* COUNTY ATTORNEY *had shoved out of place.*]

MRS. PETERS: Of course it's no more than their duty.

MRS. HALE: Duty's all right, but I guess that deputy sheriff that came out to make the fire might have got a little of this on. [*Gives the roller towel a pull.*] Wish I'd thought of that sooner. Seems mean to talk about her for not having things slicked up when she had to come away in such a hurry.

MRS. PETERS: [*Who has gone to a small table in the left rear corner of the room, and lifted one end of a towel that covers a pan.*] She had bread set. [*Stands still.*]

MRS. HALE: [*Eyes fixed on a loaf of bread beside the breadbox, which is on a low shelf at the other side of the room. Moves slowly toward it.*] She was going to put this in there. [*Picks up loaf, then abruptly drops it. In a manner of returning to familiar things.*] It's a shame about her fruit. I wonder if it's all gone. [*Gets up on the chair and looks.*] I think there's some here that's all right, Mrs. Peters. Yes—here; [*Holding it toward the window.*] this is cherries, too. [*Looking again.*] I declare I believe that's the only one. [*Gets down, bottle in her hand. Goes to the sink and wipes it off on the outside.*] She'll feel awful bad after all her hard work in the hot weather. I remember the afternoon I put up my cherries last summer.

[*She puts the bottle on the big kitchen table, center of the room. With a sigh, is about to sit down in the rocking-chair. Before she is seated realizes what chair it is; with a slow look at it, steps back. The chair which she has touched rocks back and forth.*]

MRS. PETERS: Well, I must get those things from the front room closet. [*She goes to the door at the right, but after looking into the other room, steps back.*] You coming with me, Mrs. Hale? You could help me carry them.

[*They go in the other room; reappear,* MRS. PETERS *carrying a dress and skirt,* MRS. HALE *following with a pair of shoes.*]

MRS. PETERS: My, it's cold in there. [*She puts the clothes on the big table, and hurries to the stove.*]

MRS. HALE: [*Examining the skirt.*] Wright was close. I think maybe that's why she kept so much to herself. She didn't even belong to the Ladies Aid. I suppose she felt she couldn't do her part and then you don't enjoy things when you feel shabby. She used to wear pretty clothes and be lively, when she was Minnie Foster, one of the town girls singing in the choir. But that—oh, that was thirty years ago. This all you was to take in?

MRS. PETERS: She said she wanted an apron. Funny thing to want, for there isn't much to get you dirty in jail, goodness knows. But I suppose just to make her feel more natural. She said they was in the top drawer in this cupboard. Yes, here. And then her little shawl that always hung behind the door. [*Opens stair door and looks.*] Yes, here it is. [*Quickly shuts door leading upstairs.*]

MRS. HALE: [*Abruptly moving toward her.*] Mrs. Peters?

MRS. PETERS: Yes, Mrs. Hale?

MRS. HALE: Do you think she did it?

MRS. PETERS: [*In a frightened voice.*] Oh, I don't know.

MRS. HALE: Well, I don't think she did. Asking for an apron and her little shawl. Worrying about her fruit.

MRS. PETERS: [*Starts to speak, glances up, where footsteps are heard in the room above. In a low voice.*] Mr. Peters says it looks bad for her. Mr. Henderson is awful sarcastic in a speech and he'll make fun of her sayin' she didn't wake up.

MRS. HALE: Well, I guess John Wright didn't wake when they was slipping that rope under his neck.

MRS. PETERS: No, it's strange. It must have been done awful crafty and still. They say it was such a—funny way to kill a man, rigging it all up like that.

MRS. HALE: That's just what Mr. Hale said. There was a gun in the house. He says that's what he can't understand.

MRS. PETERS: Mr. Henderson said coming out that what was needed for the case was a motive; something to show anger, or—sudden feeling.

MRS. HALE: [*Who is standing by the table.*] Well, I don't see any signs of anger around here. [*She puts her hand on the dish towel which lies on the table, stands looking down at table, one half of which is clean, the other half messy.*] It's wiped to here. [*Makes a move as if to finish work, then turns and looks at loaf of bread outside the breadbox. Drops towel. In that voice of coming back to familiar things.*] Wonder how they are finding things upstairs. I hope she had it a little more red—up up there. You know, it seems kind of *sneaking*. Locking her up in town and then coming out here and trying to get her own house to turn against her!

MRS. PETERS: But Mrs. Hale, the law is the law.

MRS. HALE: I s'pose 'tis. [*Unbuttoning her coat.*] Better loosen up your things, Mrs. Peters. You won't feel them when you go out.

> [MRS. PETERS *takes off her fur tippet, goes to hang it on hook at back of room, stands looking at the underpart of the small corner table.*]

MRS. PETERS: She was piecing a quilt.

> [*She brings the large sewing basket and they look at the bright pieces.*]

MRS. HALE: It's log cabin pattern. Pretty, isn't it? I wonder if she was goin' to quilt it or just knot it?

> [*Footsteps have been heard coming down the stairs. The* SHERIFF *enters followed by* HALE *and the* COUNTY ATTORNEY.]

SHERIFF: They wonder if she was going to quilt it or just knot it!

> [*The men laugh; the women look abashed.*]

COUNTY ATTORNEY: [*Rubbing his hands over the stove.*] Frank's fire didn't do much up there, did it? Well, let's go out to the barn and get that cleared up.

> [*The men go outside.*]

MRS. HALE: [*Resentfully.*] I don't know as there's anything so strange, our takin' up our time with little things while we're waiting for them to get the evidence. [*She sits down at the big table smoothing out a block with decision.*] I don't see as it's anything to laugh about.

MRS. PETERS: [*Apologetically.*] Of course they've got awful important things on their minds. [*Pulls up a chair and joins* MRS. HALE *at the table.*]

MRS. HALE: [*Examining another block.*] Mrs. Peters, look at this one. Here, this is the one she was working on, and look at the sewing! All the rest of it has been so nice and even. And look at this! It's all over the place! Why, it looks as if she didn't know what she was about!

> [*After she has said this they look at each other, then start to glance back at the door. After an instant* MRS. HALE *has pulled at a knot and ripped the sewing.*]

MRS. PETERS: Oh, what are you doing, Mrs. Hale?

MRS. HALE: [*Mildly.*] Just pulling out a stitch or two that's not sewed very good. [*Threading a needle.*] Bad sewing always made me fidgety.

MRS. PETERS: [*Nervously.*] I don't think we ought to touch things.

MRS. HALE: I'll just finish up this end. [*Suddenly stopping and leaning forward.*] Mrs. Peters?

MRS. PETERS: Yes, Mrs. Hale?

MRS. HALE: What do you suppose she was so nervous about?

MRS. PETERS: Oh—I don't know. I don't know as she was nervous. I sometimes sew awful queer when I'm just tired.

> [MRS. HALE *starts to say something, looks at* MRS. PETERS, *then goes on sewing.*]

Well, I must get these things wrapped up. They may be through sooner than we think. [*Putting apron and other things together.*] I wonder where I can find a piece of paper, and string.

MRS. HALE: In that cupboard, maybe.

MRS. PETERS: [*Looking in cupboard.*] Why, here's a birdcage. [*Holds it up.*] Did she have a bird, Mrs. Hale?

MRS. HALE: Why, I don't know whether she did or not—I've not been here for so long. There was a man around last year selling canaries cheap, but I don't know as she took one; maybe she did. She used to sing real pretty herself.

MRS. PETERS: [*Glancing around.*] Seems funny to think of a bird here. But she must have had one, or why would she have a cage? I wonder what happened to it.

MRS. HALE: I s'pose maybe the cat got it.

MRS. PETERS: No, she didn't have a cat. She's got that feeling some people have about cats—being afraid of them. My cat got in her room and she was real upset and asked me to take it out.

MRS. HALE: My sister Bessie was like that. Queer, ain't it?

MRS. PETERS: [*Examining the cage.*] Why, look at this door. It's broke. One hinge is pulled apart.

MRS. HALE: [*Looking too.*] Looks as if someone must have been rough with it.

MRS. PETERS: Why, yes.

[*She brings the cage forward and puts it on the table.*]

MRS. HALE: I wish if they're going to find any evidence they'd be about it. I don't like this place.

MRS. PETERS: But I'm awful glad you came with me, Mrs. Hale. It would be lonesome for me sitting here alone.

MRS. HALE: It would, wouldn't it? [*Dropping her sewing.*] But I tell you what I do wish, Mrs. Peters. I wish I had come over sometimes when she was here. I— [*Looking around the room.*]—wish I had.

MRS. PETERS: But of course you were awful busy, Mrs. Hale—your house and your children.

MRS. HALE: I could've come. I stayed away because it weren't cheerful—and that's why I ought to have come. I—I've never liked this place. Maybe because it's down in a hollow and you don't see the road. I dunno what it is, but it's a lonesome place and always was. I wish I had come over to see Minnie Foster sometimes. I can see now—[*Shakes her head.*]

MRS. PETERS: Well, you mustn't reproach yourself, Mrs. Hale. Somehow we just don't see how it is with other folks until—something comes up.

MRS. HALE: Not having children makes less work—but it makes a quiet house, and Wright out to work all day, and no company when he did come in. Did you know John Wright, Mrs. Peters?

MRS. PETERS: Not to know him; I've seen him in town. They say he was a good man.

MRS. HALE: Yes—good; he didn't drink, and kept his word as well as most, I guess, and paid his debts. But he was a hard man, Mrs. Peters. Just to pass the time of day with him—[*Shivers.*] Like a raw wind that gets to the bone. [*Pauses, her eye falling on the cage.*] I should think she would 'a wanted a bird. But what do you suppose went with it?

MRS. PETERS: I don't know, unless it got sick and died.

[*She reaches over and swings the broken door, swings it again. Both women watch it.*]

MRS. HALE: You weren't raised 'round here, were you?

[MRS. PETERS *shakes her head.*]

You didn't know—her?

MRS. PETERS: Not till they brought her yesterday.

MRS. HALE: She—come to think of it, she was kind of like a bird herself—real sweet and pretty, but kind of timid and—fluttery. How—she—did—change.

[*Silence; then as if struck by a happy thought and relieved to get back to every day things.*]

Tell you what, Mrs. Peters, why don't you take the quilt in with you? It might take up her mind.

MRS. PETERS: Why, I think that's a real nice idea, Mrs. Hale. There couldn't possibly be any objection to it, could there? Now, just what would I take? I wonder if her patches are in here—and her things.

[*They look in the sewing basket.*]

MRS. HALE: Here's some red. I expect this has got sewing things in it. [*Brings out a fancy box.*] What a pretty box. Looks like something somebody would give you. Maybe her scissors are in here. [*Opens box. Suddenly puts her hand to her nose.*] Why—

[MRS. PETERS *bends nearer, then turns her face away.*]

There's something wrapped up in this piece of silk.

MRS. PETERS: Why, this isn't her scissors.

MRS. HALE: [*Lifting the silk.*] Oh, Mrs. Peters—its—

[*Mrs. Peters bends closer.*]

MRS. PETERS: It's the bird.

MRS. HALE: [*Jumping up.*] But, Mrs. Peters—look at it! Its neck! Look at its neck! It's all—other side *to.*

MRS. PETERS: Somebody—wrung—its—neck.

> [*Their eyes meet. A look of growing comprehension, of horror. Steps are heard outside.* MRS. HALE *slips box under quilt pieces, and sinks into her chair. Enter* SHERIFF *and* COUNTY ATTORNEY. MRS. PETERS *rises.*]

COUNTY ATTORNEY: [*As one turning from serious things to little pleasantries.*] Well, ladies, have you decided whether she was going to quilt it or knot it?

MRS. PETERS: We think she was going to—knot it.

COUNTY ATTORNEY: Well, that's interesting, I'm sure. [*Seeing the birdcage.*] Has the bird flown?

MRS. HALE: [*Putting more quilt pieces over the box.*] We think the—cat got it.

COUNTY ATTORNEY: [*Preoccupied.*] Is there a cat?

> [MRS. HALE *glances in a quick covert way at* MRS. PETERS.]

MRS. PETERS: Well, not now. They're superstitious, you know. They leave.

COUNTY ATTORNEY: [*To* SHERIFF PETERS, *continuing an interrupted conversation.*] No sign at all of anyone having come from the outside. Their own rope. Now let's go up again and go over it piece by piece.

> [*They start upstairs.*]

It would have to have been someone who knew just the—

> [MRS. PETERS *sits down. The two women sit there not looking at one another, but as if peering into something and at the same time holding back. When they talk now it is in the manner of feeling their way over strange ground, as if afraid of what they are saying, but as if they cannot help saying it.*]

MRS. HALE: She liked the bird. She was going to bury it in that pretty box.

MRS. PETERS: [*In a whisper.*] When I was a girl—my kitten—there was a boy took a hatchet, and before my eyes—and before I could get there—[*Covers her face an instant.*] If they hadn't held me back I would have—[*Catches herself, looks upstairs* *where steps are heard, falters weakly.*]—hurt him.

MRS. HALE: [*With a slow-look around her.*] I wonder how it would seem never to have had any children around. [*Pause.*] No, Wright wouldn't like the bird—a thing that sang. She used to sing. He killed that, too.

MRS. PETERS: [*Moving uneasily.*] We don't know who killed the bird.

MRS. HALE: I knew John Wright.

MRS. PETERS: It was an awful thing was done in this house that night, Mrs. Hale. Killing a man while he slept, slipping a rope around his neck that choked the life out of him.

MRS. HALE: His neck. Choked the life out of him. [*Her hand goes out and rests on the birdcage.*]

MRS. PETERS: [*With rising voice.*] We don't know who killed him. We don't know.

MRS. HALE: [*Her own feeling not interrupted.*] If there'd been years and years of nothing, then a bird to sing to you, it would be awful—still, after the bird was still.

MRS. PETERS: [*Something within her speaking.*] I know what stillness is. When we homesteaded in Dakota, and my first baby died—after he was two years old, and me with no other then—

MRS. HALE: [*Moving.*] How soon do you suppose they'll be through, looking for the evidence?

MRS. PETERS: I know what stillness is. [*Pulling herself back.*] The law has got to punish crime, Mrs. Hale.

MRS. HALE: [*Not as if answering that.*] I wish you'd seen Minnie Foster when she wore a white dress with blue ribbons and stood up there in the choir and sang. [*A look around the room.*] Oh, I wish I'd come over here once in a while! That was a crime! That was a crime! Who's going to punish that?

MRS. PETERS: [*Looking upstairs.*] We mustn't—take on.

MRS. HALE: I might have known she needed help! I know how things can be— for women. I tell you, it's queer, Mrs. Peters. We live close together and we live far apart. We all go through the same things—it's all just a different kind of the same thing. [*Brushes her eyes; noticing the bottle of fruit, reaches out for it.*]

If I was you I wouldn't tell her her fruit was gone. Tell her it *ain't*. Tell her it's all right. Take this in to prove it to her. She—she may never know whether it was broke or not.

MRS. PETERS: [*Takes the bottle, looks about for something to wrap it in; takes petticoat from the clothes brought from the other room, very nervously begins winding this around the bottle. In a false voice.*] My, it's a good thing the men couldn't hear us. Wouldn't they just laugh! Getting all stirred up over a little thing like a— dead canary. As if that could have anything to do with—with—wouldn't they *laugh*!

[*The men are heard coming down stairs.*]

MRS. HALE: [*Under her breath.*] Maybe they would—maybe they wouldn't.

COUNTY ATTORNEY: No, Peters, it's all perfectly clear except a reason for doing it. But you know juries when it comes to women. If there was some definite thing. Something to show—something to make a story about—a thing that would connect up with this strange way of doing it—

[*The women's eyes meet for an instant. Enter* HALE *from outer door.*]

HALE: Well, I've got the team around. Pretty cold out there.

COUNTY ATTORNEY: I'm going to stay here a while by myself [*To the* SHER-IFF.] You can send Frank out for me, can't you? I want to go over everything. I'm not satisfied that we can't do better.

SHERIFF: Do you want to see what Mrs. Peters is going to take in?

[*The* COUNTY ATTORNEY *goes to the table, picks up the apron, laughs.*]

COUNTY ATTORNEY: Oh, I guess they're not very dangerous things the ladies have picked out. [*Moves a few things about, disturbing the quilt pieces which cover the box. Steps back.*] No, Mrs. Peters doesn't need supervising. For that matter, a sheriff's wife is married to the law. Ever think of it that way, Mrs. Peters?

MRS. PETERS: Not—just that way.

SHERIFF: [*Chuckling.*] Married to the law. [*Moves toward the other room.*] I just want you to come in here a minute, George. We ought to take a look at these windows.

COUNTY ATTORNEY: [*Scoffingly.*] Oh, windows!

SHERIFF: We'll be right out, Mr. Hale.

[HALE *goes outside. The* SHERIFF *follows the* COUNTY ATTORNEY *into the other room. Then* MRS. HALE *rises, hands tight together, looking intensely at* MRS. PETERS, *whose eyes make a slow turn, finally meeting* MRS. HALE's. *A moment* MRS. HALE *holds her, then her own eyes point the way to where the box is concealed. Suddenly* MRS. PETERS *throws back quilt pieces and tries to put the box in the bag she is wearing. It is too big. She opens box, starts to take bird out, cannot touch it, goes to pieces, stands there helpless. Sound of a knob turning in the other room.* MRS. HALE *snatches the box and puts it in the pocket of her big coat. Enter* COUNTY ATTORNEY *and* SHERIFF.]

COUNTY ATTORNEY: [*Facetiously.*] Well, Henry, at least we found out that she was not going to quilt it. She was going to—what is it you call it, ladies?

MRS. HALE: [*Her hand against her pocket.*] We call it—knot it, Mr. Henderson.

CURTAIN

MULATTO:
A Tragedy of the Deep South

LANGSTON HUGHES

First production opening at the Vanderbilt Theatre,
New York, October, 1935

Produced by Martin Jones (who significantly changed the text),
and directed by Charles Erskine

INTRODUCTION

by Arnold Rampersad

On October 24, 1935, Langston Hughes's *Mulatto: A Play of the Deep South* had its Broadway premiere at the Vanderbilt Theatre in Manhattan. For an African-American playwright this should have been a triumphant occasion, but Hughes was not in the audience. After bitter exchanges with his producer, a wealthy young white man named Martin Jones, Hughes decided to boycott the opening. Acquiring rights to the play without Hughes's knowledge, Jones had boldly inserted various crude changes to make the plot even more sensational than Hughes had imagined it.

Mulatto is the story of a white Southern planter, Colonel Norwood; his long-suffering but devoted black "wife," Cora, who has no legal standing in the eyes of the law or of white society; and their children—especially their rebellious son Bert. Bert's insistence that his white father acknowledge him, and Norwood's obstinate refusal to do so, ends in Bert's slaying of his father and his own eventual lynching. To Hughes's original plot Martin Jones had added certain gory touches, including the rape of Bert's sister, to which Hughes strongly objected. Making matters worse was Jones's bigoted snubbing not only of Hughes but also of the sole black member of the cast, the acclaimed actress Rose McClendon, whose portrayal of Cora would win her the finest accolades in the press. In addition, Jones sought the major credit for writing the play even as he tried to pay Hughes as little as possible out of his profits. This experience left Hughes frustrated and embittered. Nevertheless, in part because of Jones's changes and his often shameless advertising, *Mulatto* would enjoy the longest run on Broadway of any play by an African-American playwright until the 1960s, when Lorraine Hansberry's *A Raisin in the Sun* (with its title taken from a Hughes poem) achieved its extraordinary success.

The basic theme of the play—the tragedy of racial mixing in a nation contemptuous of blacks—clearly appealed to Hughes as a writer. Although he himself was of mixed race, neither of his parents had been white. Instead, neglected by both—his father emigrated to Mexico, and his restless mother had flitted in and out of Langston's life—he had come to empathize to some extent with the classic mulatto of American racial legend. Spurned by his white father and by whites in general, but incapable of full identification with his mother's people, the mulatto struggles painfully toward an almost inevitable personal disaster. The "tragic mulatto" had been the theme of various popular novels and plays in the nineteenth century, and would be a feature of Faulkner's writing in works such as *Light in August* and *Absalom, Absalom!*

Like Faulkner, Hughes was also interested in the psychosexual aspects of American race relations. The themes of miscegenation and mulatto angst would inform his important dramatic poem of 1925; "Cross," ("My old man's a white old man / And my old mother's black") which Hughes included in his first book, *The Weary Blues* (1926). About three years later, the poem led to Hughes's first major attempt to write a play, when he started work on "Cross: A Play of the Deep South," later renamed *Mulatto*. Next, he rewrote the play as a substantial short story for his collection *The Ways of White Folks* (1934). Finally, *Mulatto* formed the basis of his opera *The Barrier*, with music by Jan Meyerowitz, which succeeded initially before failing on Broadway in 1950.

Although Hughes deliberately set his story in the South, its message and impact unquestionably applied to the whole nation. In part he drew loosely on his family history. His maternal grandfather, Charles Langston, had been the son of a white Virginian planter and an African-American mother with whom the planter had lived during slavery as man and wife. Clearly Hughes saw the tormented household in *Mulatto* as symbolic of the South's and the nation's tragic blindness in facing its past, as well as the mixture of desire and inhumanity in dealing with its black citizens. Unresolved, *Mulatto* declares, this blindness and inhumanity would surely lead to disaster for all concerned. The play is a jeremiad of authentic power. Whatever its limitations as a work of theatrical art, on stage *Mulatto* is capable of conveying a harrowing sense of the waste and horror of American race relations. It effectively dramatizes the idea that both the South and the nation as a whole are doomed unless Americans can move past their obsession with the notions of the supremacy of whites and the innate inferiority of blacks.

Most reviewers of the production, ignorant of Jones's tampering, lambasted Hughes for his shortcomings as a dramatist. Some also attacked him for what they perceived as his sardonic view of race relations in the South. Brooks Atkinson saw something of value: "After a season dedicated chiefly to trash it is a sobering sensation to sit in the presence of a playwright who is trying his best to tell what he has on his mind."

By 1935, Hughes had moved far to the left politically. During a year in the Soviet Union (1932-1933), when he published some of the most radical verse ever written by an American, he had been exposed to the rich range of Soviet theater, including agit-prop and other experimental productions. Little of this radicalism plays a part in the shaping of *Mulatto*; however, his Moscow experience served him well as he sought to develop his career as a playwright in the 1930s. Working mainly with the Gilpin Players at Karamu House in Cleveland, he wrote several comedies, at least one domestic drama, and a play about the Haitian revolution. These productions achieved only moderate, local success in general. After he returned home in 1938 following several months as a war correspondent in Spain, he quickly founded the Harlem Suitcase Theatre. He launched this company with his loosely structured but vigorously propagandistic drama *Don't You Want to be Free?*

Later, Hughes would be a prime figure in the development of the gospel play tradition, and he would take pride in his general contributions to the theater. For him, however, *Mulatto* was associated with the arrogance of Martin Jones and the humiliations visited by Jones on the young playwright. Nevertheless, it remains an integral part of his considerable literary legacy as well as a fascinating commentary on an aspect of the history of American race relations.

CHARACTERS

COLONEL THOMAS NORWOOD, Plantation owner, a still vigorous man of about sixty, nervous, refined, quick-tempered, and commanding; a widower who is the Father of four living mulatto children by his Negro housekeeper

CORA LEWIS, A brown woman in her forties who has kept the house and been the mistress of Colonel Norwood for some thirty years

WILLIAM LEWIS, The oldest son of Cora Lewis and the Colonel; a fat, easy-going, soft-looking mulatto of twenty-eight; married

SALLIE LEWIS, The seventeen-year-old daughter, very light with sandy hair and freckles, who could pass for white

ROBERT LEWIS, Eighteen, the youngest boy; strong and well-built; a light mulatto with ivory-yellow skin and proud thin features like his father's; as tall as the Colonel, with the same gray-blue eyes, but with curly black hair instead of brown; of a fiery, impetuous temper—immature and willful—resenting his blood and the circumstances of his birth

FRED HIGGINS, A close friend of Colonel Norwood's; a county politician; fat and elderly, conventionally Southern

SAM, An old Negro retainer, a personal servant of the Colonel

BILLY, The small son of William Lewis; a chubby brown kid about five

TALBOT, The overseer

MOSE, An elderly Negro, chauffeur for Mr. Higgins

A STOREKEEPER

AN UNDERTAKER

UNDERTAKER'S HELPER (Voice off-stage only)

THE MOB

TIME: *An afternoon in early fall.*

SETTING: *The living room of the Big House on a plantation in Georgia. Rear center of the room, a vestibule with double door leading to the porch; at each side of the doors, a large window with lace curtains and green shades; at left a broad flight of stairs leading to the second floor; near the stairs, downstage, a doorway leading to the dining room and kitchen; opposite, at right of stage, a door to the library. The room is furnished in the long out-dated horsehair and walnut style of the nineties; a crystal chandelier, a large old-fashioned rug, a marble-topped table, upholstered chairs. At the right there is a small cabinet. It is a very clean, but somewhat shabby and rather depressing room, dominated by a large oil painting of* NORWOOD's *wife of his youth on the center wall. The windows are raised. The afternoon sunlight streams in.*

ACTION: *As the curtain rises, the stage is empty. The door at the right opens and* COLONEL NORWOOD *enters, crossing the stage toward the stairs, his watch in his hand. Looking up, he shouts:*

NORWOOD: Cora! Oh, Cora!

CORA: [*Heard above.*] Yes, sir, Colonel Tom.

NORWOOD: I want to know if that child of yours means to leave here this afternoon?

CORA: [*At head of steps now.*] Yes, sir, she's goin' directly. I's gettin' her ready now, packin' up an' all. 'Course, she wants to tell you goodbye 'fore she leaves.

NORWOOD: Well, send her down here. Who's going to drive her to the railroad? The train leaves at three—and it's after two now. You ought to know you can't drive ten miles in no time.

CORA: [*Above.*] Her brother's gonna drive her. Bert. He ought to be back here most any time now with the Ford.

NORWOOD: [*Stopping on his way back to the library.*] Ought to be *back* here? Where's he gone?

CORA: [*Coming downstairs nervously.*] Why, he driv in town 'fore noon, Colonel Tom. Said he were lookin' for some tubes or somethin' 'nother by de mornin' mail for de radio he's been riggin' up out in de shed.

NORWOOD: Who gave him permission to be driving off in the middle of the morning? I bought that Ford to be used when I gave orders for it to be used, not …

CORA: Yes, sir, Colonel Tom, but …

NORWOOD: But what? [*Pausing. Then deliberately.*] Cora, if you want that hardheaded yellow son of yours to get along around here, he'd better listen to me. He's no more than any other black buck on this plantation—due to work like the rest of 'em. I don't take such a performance from nobody under me—driving off in the middle of the day to town, after I've told him to bend his back in that cotton. How's Talbot going to keep the rest of those darkies working right if that boy's allowed to set that kind of an example? Just because Bert's your son, and I've been damn fool enough to send him off to school for five or six years, he thinks he has a right to privileges, acting as if he owned this place since he's been back here this summer.

CORA: But, Colonel Tom …

NORWOOD: Yes, I know what you're going to say. I don't give a damn about him! There's no nigger-child of mine, yours, ours—no darkie—going to disobey me. I put him in that field to work, and he'll stay on this plantation till I get ready to let him go. I'll tell Talbot to use the whip on him, too, if he needs it. If it hadn't been that he's yours, he'd-a had a taste of it the other day. Talbot's a damn good overseer, and no saucy, lazy Nigras stay on this plantation and get away with it. [*To* CORA.] Go on back upstairs and see about getting Sallie out of here. Another word from you and I won't send your [*Sarcastically.*] pretty little half-white daughter anywhere, either. Schools for darkies! Huh! If you take that boy of yours for an example, they do 'em more harm than good. He's learned nothing in college but impudence, and he'll stay here on this place and work for me awhile before he gets back to any more schools. [*He starts across the room.*]

CORA: Yes, sir, Colonel Tom. [*Hesitating.*] But he's just young, sir. And he was mighty broke up when you said last week he couldn't go back to de campus.

[COLONEL NORWOOD *turns and looks at* CORA *commandingly. Understanding, she murmurs.*]

Yes, sir.

[*She starts upstairs, but turns back.*]

94

Can't I run and fix you a cool drink, Colonel Tom?

NORWOOD: No, damn you! Sam'll do it.

CORA: [*Sweetly.*] Go set down in de cool, then, Colonel. 'Taint good for you to be going on this way in de heat. I'll talk to Robert maself soon's he comes in. He don't mean nothing—just smart and young and kinder careless, Colonel Tom, like ma mother said you used to be when you was eighteen.

NORWOOD: Get on upstairs, Cora. Do I have to speak again? Get on! [*He pulls the cord of the servants' bell.*]

CORA: [*On the steps.*] Does you still be in the mind to tell Sallie good-bye?

NORWOOD: Send her down here as I told you. [*Impatiently.*] Where's Sam? Send him here first. [*Fuming.*] Looks like he takes his time to answer that bell. You colored folks are running the house to suit yourself nowadays.

CORA: [*Coming downstairs again and going toward door under the steps.*] I'll get Sam for you.

> [CORA *exits left.* NORWOOD *paces nervously across the floor. Goes to the window and looks out down the road. Takes a cigar from his pocket, sits in a chair with it unlighted, scowling. Rises, goes toward servants' bell and rings it again violently as* SAM *enters, out of breath.*]

NORWOOD: What the hell kind of a tortoise race is this? I suppose you were out in the sun somewhere sleeping?

SAM: No sah, Colonel Norwood. Just tryin' to get Miss Sallie's valises down to de yard so's we can put 'em in de Ford, sah.

NORWOOD: [*Out of patience.*] Huh! Darkies waiting on darkies! I can't get service in my own house. Very well. [*Loudly.*] Bring me some whiskey and soda, and ice in a glass. Is that damn Frigidaire working right? Or is Livonia still too thickheaded to know how to run it? Any ice cubes in the thing?

SAM: Yes, sah, Colonel, yes, sah. [*Backing toward door left.*] 'Scuse me, please sah, but

> [*As* NORWOOD *turns toward library.*]

Cora say for me to ask you is it all right to bring that big old trunk what you give Sallie down by de front steps. We ain't been able to tote it down them narrer little back steps, sah. Cora, say, can we bring it down de front way through here?

NORWOOD: No other way?

[*Sam shakes his head.*]

Then pack it on through to the back, quick. Don't let me catch you carrying any of Sallie's baggage out of that front door here. You all'll be wanting to go in and out the front way next. [*Turning away complaining to himself.*] Darkies have been getting mighty fresh in this part of the country since the war. The damn Germans should've … [*To* SAM.] Don't take that trunk out that front door.

SAM: [*Evilly, in a cunning voice.*] I's seen Robert usin' de front door—when you ain't here, and he comes up from de cabin to see his mammy.

[SALLIE, *the daughter, appears at the top of the stairs, but hesitates about coming down.*]

NORWOOD: Oh, you have, have you? Let me catch him and I'll break his young neck for him. [*Yelling at* SAM.] Didn't I tell you some whiskey and soda an hour ago?

[SAM *exits left.* SALLIE *comes shyly down the stairs and approaches her father. She is dressed in a little country-style coat-suit ready for traveling. Her features are Negroid, although her skin is very fair.* COLONEL NORWOOD *gazes down at her without saying a word as she comes meekly toward him, half-frightened.*]

SALLIE: I just wanted to tell you goodbye, Colonel Norwood, and thank you for letting me go back to school another year, and for letting me work here in the house all summer where mama is.

[NORWOOD *says nothing. The girl continues in a strained voice as if making a speech.*]

You mighty nice to us Colored folks certainly, and mama says you the best white man in Georgia.

[*Still* NORWOOD *says nothing. The girl continues.*]

You been mighty nice to your—I mean to us colored children, letting my sister and me go off to school. The principal says I'm doing pretty well and next year I can go to Normal and learn to be a teacher. [*Raising her eyes.*] You reckon I can, Colonel Tom?

NORWOOD: Stand up straight and let me see how you look. [*Backing away.*] Humm-m-m! Getting kinder grown, ain't you? Do they teach you in that school to have good manners, and not be afraid of work, *and to respect white folks?*

SALLIE: Yes, sir, I been taking up cooking and sewing, too.

NORWOOD: Well, that's good. As I recall it, that school turned your sister out a right smart cook. Cora tells me she's got a good job in some big hotel in Chicago. I'm thinking about you going on up North there with her in a year or two. You're getting too old to be around here, and too womanish. [*He puts his hands on her arms as if feeling her flesh.*]

SALLIE: [*Drawing back slightly.*] But I want to live down here with mama. I want to teach school in that there empty school house by the Cross Roads what hasn't had a teacher for five years.

[SAM *has been standing with the door cracked, overhearing the conversation. He enters with the drink and places it on the table, right.* NORWOOD *sits down, leaving the girl standing, as* SAM *pours out a drink.*]

NORWOOD: Don't get that into your head, now. There's been no teacher there for years—and there won't be any teacher there, either. Cotton teaches these pickaninnies enough around here. Some of 'em's too smart as it is. The only reason I did have a teacher there once was to get you young ones o' Cora's educated. I gave you all a chance and I hope you appreciate it. [*He takes a long drink.*] Don't know why I did it. No other white man in these parts ever did it, as I know of. [*To* SAM.] Get out of here!

[SAM *exits left.*]

Guess I couldn't stand to see Cora's kids working around here dumb as the rest of these no good darkies—need a dozen of 'em to chop one row of cotton, or to keep a house clean. Or maybe I didn't want to see Talbot eyeing you gals. [*Taking another drink.*] Anyhow, I'm glad you and Bertha turned out right well. Yes, hum-m-m! [*Straightening up.*] You know I tried to do something for those brothers of yours, too, but William's stupid as an ox—good for work, though—and that Robert's just an impudent, hardheaded, yellow young fool. I'm gonna break his damn neck for him if he don't watch out. Or else put Talbot on him.

SALLIE: [*Suddenly frightened.*] Please, sir, don't put the overseer on Bert, Colonel Tom. He was the smartest boy at school, Bert was. On the football team, too. Please, sir, Colonel Tom. Let brother work here in the house, or somewhere else where Talbot can't mistreat him. He ain't used …

NORWOOD: [*Rising.*] Telling me what to do, heh? [*Staring at her sternly.*] I'll use the back of my hand across your face if you don't hush. [*He takes another drink. The noise of a Ford is heard outside.*] That's Bert now, I reckon. He's to take you to the railroad line, and while you're riding with him, you better put some sense into his head. And tell him I want to see him as soon as he gets here.

[CORA *enters left with a bundle and an umbrella.* SAM *and* WILLIAM *come downstairs with a big square trunk, and exit huriedly, left.*]

SALLIE: Yes, sir, I'll tell him.

CORA: Colonel Tom, Sallie ain't got much time now. [*To the girl.*] Come on, chile. Bert's here. Yo' big brother and Sam and Livonia and everybody's all waiting at de back door to say goodbye. And your baggage is being packed in.

[*Noise of another car is heard outside.*]

Who else is that there coming up de drive? [CORA *looks out the window.*] Mr. Higgins' car, Colonel Tom. Reckon he's coming to see you … Hurry up out o' this front room, Sallie. Here, take these things of your'n [*Hands her the bundle and parasol.*] while I opens de door for Mr. Higgins. [*In a whisper.*] Hurry up, chile! Get out!

[NORWOOD *turns toward the front door as* CORA *goes to open it.*]

SALLIE: [*Shyly to her father.*] Goodbye, Colonel Tom.

NORWOOD: [*His eyes on the front door, scarcely noticing the departing* SALLIE, *he motions.*] Yes, yes, goodbye! Get on now!

[CORA *opens the front door as her daughter exits left.*]

Well, well! Howdy do, Fred. Come in, come in!

[CORA *holds the outer door of the vestibule wide as* FRED HIGGINS *enters with rheumatic dignity, supported on the arm of his chauffeur,* MOSE, *a very black Negro in a slouchy uniform.* CORA *closes the door and exits left hurriedly, following* SALLIE.]

NORWOOD: [*Smiling.*] How's the rheumatiz today? Women or licker or heat must've made it worse—from the looks of your speed!

HIGGINS: [*Testily, sitting down puffing and blowing in a big chair.*] I'm in no mood for fooling, Tom, not now. [*To* MOSE.] All right.

[*The* CHAUFFEUR *exits front.* HIGGINS *continues angrily.*]

Norwood, that damned yellow nigger buck of yours that drives that new Ford tried his best just now to push my car off the road, then got in front of me and blew dust in my face for the last mile coming down to your gate, trying to beat me in here—which he did. Such a deliberate piece of impudence I don't know if I've ever seen out of a nigger before in all the sixty years I've lived in this county.

[*The noise of the Ford is heard going out the drive, and the cries of the* NEGROES *shouting farewells to* SALLIE. HIGGINS *listens indignantly.*]

What kind of crazy coons have you got on your place, anyhow? Sounds like a black Baptist picnic to me. [*Pointing to the window with his cane.*] Tom, listen to that.

NORWOOD: [*Flushing.*] I apologize to you, Fred, for each and every one of my darkies.

[SAM *enters with more ice and another glass.*]

Permit me to offer you a drink. I realize I've got to tighten down here.

HIGGINS: Mose tells me that was Cora's boy in that Ford—and that young black fool is what I was coming here to talk to you about today. That boy! He's not gonna be around here long—not the way he's acting. The white folks in town'll see to that. Knowing he's one of your yard niggers, Norwood, I thought I ought to come and tell you. The white folks at the Junction aren't intending to put up with him much longer. And I don't know what good the jail would do him once he got in there.

NORWOOD: [*Tensely.*] What do you mean, Fred—jail? Don't I always take care of the folks on my plantation without any help from the Junction's police force? Talbot can do more with an unruly black buck than your marshal.

HIGGINS: Warn't lookin' at it that way, Tom. I was thinking how weak the doors to that jail is. They've broke 'em down and lynched four niggers to my memory since it's been built After what happened this morning, you better keep that yellow young fool out o' town from now on. It might not be safe for him around there—today, nor no other time.

NORWOOD: What the hell? [*Perturbed.*] He went in just now to take his sister to the depot. Damn it, I hope no ruffians'll break up my new Ford. What was it, Fred, about this morning?

HIGGINS: You haven't heard? Why, it's all over town already. He sassed out Miss Gray in the post office over a box of radio tubes that come by mail.

NORWOOD: He did, heh?

HIGGINS: Seems like the stuff was sent C. O. D. and got here all smashed up, so he wouldn't take it. Paid his money first before he saw the box was broke Then wanted the money order back. Seems like the post office can't give money orders back—rule against it. Your nigger started to argue, and the girl at the window—Miss Gray—got scared and yelled for some of the mail clerks. They threw Bert out of the office, that's all. But that's enough. Lucky nothing more didn't happen. [*Indignantly.*] That Bert needs a damn good beating—talking back to a white woman—and I'd like to give it to him myself, the way he kicked the dust up in my eyes all the way down the road coming out here. He was mad, I reckon. That's one yellow buck don't know his place, Tom, and it's your fault he don't—sending 'em off to be educated.

NORWOOD: Well, by God, I'll show him. I wish I'd have known it before he left here just now.

HIGGINS: Well, he's sure got mighty aggravating ways for a buck his color to have. Drives down the main street and don't stop for nobody, white or black. Comes in my store and if he ain't waited on as quick as the white folks are, he walks out and tells the clerk his money's as good as a white man's any day. Said last week standing out on my store front that he wasn't *all* nigger no how; said his name was Norwood—not Lewis, like the rest of his family—and part of your plantation here would be his when you passed out—and all that kind of stuff, boasting to the walleyed coons listening to him.

NORWOOD: [*Astounded.*] Well, I'll be damned!

HIGGINS: Now, Tom, you know that don't go 'round these parts o' Georgia, nor nowhere else in the South. A darkie's got to keep in his place down here. Ruinous to other niggers hearing that talk, too. All this postwar propaganda on the radio about freedom and democracy—why the niggers think it's meant for them! And that Eleanor Roosevelt, she ought to been muzzled. She's driving our niggers crazy—your boy included! Crazy! Talking about civil rights. Ain't been no race trouble in our country for three years—since the Deekin's lynching—but I'm telling you, Norwood, you better see that that buck of yours goes away from here. I'm speaking on the quiet, but I can see ahead. And what happened this morning about them radio tubes wasn't none too good.

NORWOOD: [*Beside himself with rage.*] A black ape! I—I …

HIGGINS: You been too decent to your darkies, Norwood. That's what's the matter with you. And then the whole county suffers from a lot of impudent bucks who take lessons from your crowd. Folks been kicking about that, too. Guess you know it. Maybe that's the reason you didn't get that nomination for committeeman a few years back.

NORWOOD: Maybe 'tis, Higgins. [*Rising and pacing the room.*] God damn niggers! [*Furiously.*] Everything turns on niggers, niggers, niggers! No wonder Yankees call this the Black Belt! [*He pours a large drink of whiskey.*]

HIGGINS: [*Soothingly.*] Well, let's change the subject. Hand me my glass, there, too.

NORWOOD: Pardon me, Fred. [*He puts ice in his friend's glass and passes him the bottle.*]

HIGGINS: Tom, you get excited too easy for warm weather … Don't ever show black folks they got you going, though. I think sometimes that's where you make your mistake. Keep calm, keep calm—and then you command. Best plantation manager I ever had never raised his voice to a nigger—and they were scared to death of him.

NORWOOD: Have a smoke. [*Pushes cigars toward* HIGGINS.]

HIGGINS: You ought've married again, Tom—brought a white woman out here on this damn place o' yours. A woman could help you run things. Women have soft ways, but they can keep things humming. Nothing but blacks in the house—a man gets soft like niggers are inside. [*Puffing at cigar.*] And living with a colored woman! Of course, I know we all have 'em—I didn't know you could make use of a white girl till I was past twenty. Thought too much o' white women for that—but I've given many a yellow gal a baby in my time. [*Long puff at cigar.*] But for a man's own house you need a wife, not a black woman.

NORWOOD: Reckon you're right, Fred, but it's too late to marry again now. [*Shrugging his shoulders.*] Let's get off of darkies and women for awhile. How's crops? [*Sitting down.*] How's politics going?

HIGGINS: Well, I guess you know the Republicans is trying to stir up trouble for us in Washington. I wish the South had more men like Bilbo and Rankin there. But, say, by the way, Lawyer Hotchkiss wants to see us both about that budget money next week. He's got some real Canadian stuff at his office, in his filing case, too—brought back from his vacation last summer. Taste better'n this old mountain juice we get around here. Not meaning to insult your drinks, Tom, but just remarking. I serve the same as you myself, label and all.

NORWOOD: [*Laughing.*] I'll have you know, sir, that this is prewar licker, sir!

HIGGINS: Hum-m-m! Well, it's got me feelin' better'n I did when I come in here—whatever it is. [*Puffs at his cigar.*] Say, how's your cotton this year?

NORWOOD: Doin' right well, specially down in the south field. Why not drive out that road when you leave and take a look at it? I'll ride down with you. I want to see Talbot, anyhow.

HIGGINS: Well, let's be starting. I got to be back at the Junction by four o'clock. Promised to let that boy of mine have the car to drive over to Thomasville for a dance tonight.

NORWOOD: One more shot before we go. [*He pours out drinks.*] The young ones must have their fling, I reckon. When you and I grew up down here it used to be a carriage and the best pair of black horses when you took the ladies out—now it's an automobile. That's a good lookin' new car of yours, too.

HIGGINS: Right nice.

NORWOOD: Been thinking about getting a new one myself, but money's been kinder tight this year, and conditions are none too good yet, either. Reckon that's why everybody's so restless. [*He walks toward stairs calling.*] Cora! Oh,

Cora! … If I didn't have a few thousand put away, I'd feel the pinch myself.

[*As* CORA *appears on the stairs.*]

Bring me my glasses up there by the side of my bed … Better whistle for Mose, hadn't I, Higgins? He's probably 'round back with some of his women. [*Winking.*] You know I got some nice black women in this yard.

HIGGINS: Oh, no, not Mose. I got my servants trained to stay in their places—right where I want 'em—while they're working for me. Just open the door and tell him to come in here and help me out.

[NORWOOD *goes to the door and calls the* CHAUFFEUR. MOSE *enters and assists his master out to the car.* CORA *appears with the glasses, goes to the vestibule and gets the* COLONEL's *hat and cane which she hands him.*]

NORWOOD: [*To* CORA.] I want to see that boy o' yours soon as I get back. That won't be long, either. And tell him to put up that Ford of mine and don't touch it again.

CORA: Yes, sir, I'll have him waiting here. [*In a whisper.*] It's hot weather, Colonel Tom. Too much of this licker makes your heart upset. It ain't good for you, you know.

[NORWOOD *pays her no attention as he exits toward the car. The noise of the departing motor is heard.* CORA *begins to tidy up the room. She takes a glass from a side table. She picks up a doily that was beneath the glass and looks at it long and lovingly. Suddenly she goes to the door left and calls toward the kitchen.*]

William, you William! Com'ere, I want to show you something. Make haste, son.

[*As* CORA *goes back toward the table, her eldest son,* WILLIAM, *enters carrying a five-year-old boy.*]

Look here at this purty doily yo' sister made this summer while she been here. She done learned all about sewing and making purty things at school. Ain't it nice, son?

WILLIAM: Sho' is. Sallie takes after you, I reckon. She's a smart little crittur, ma.

103

[*Sighs.*] De Lawd knows, I was dumb at school. [*To his child.*] Get down, Billy, you's too heavy. [*He puts the boy on the floor.*] This here sewin's really fine.

BILLY: [*Running toward the big upholstered chair, and jumping up and down on the spring seat.*] Gityap ! I's a mule driver. Haw! Gee!

CORA: You Billy, get out of that chair 'fore I skins you alive. Get on into de kitchen, sah.

BILLY: I'm playin' horsie, grandma. [*Jumps up in the chair.*] Horsie! Horsie!

CORA: Get! That's de Colonel's favorite chair. If he knows any little darkie's been jumpin' on it, he raise sand. Get on, now.

BILLY: Ole Colonel's ma grandpa, ain't he? Ain't he ma white grandpa?

WILLIAM: [*Snatching the child out of the chair.*] Boy, I'm gonna fan your hide if you don't hush!

CORA: Shs-ss-s! You Billy, hush yo' mouth! Chile, where you hear that? [*To her son.*] Some o' you all been talking too much in front o' this chile. [*To the boy.*] Honey, go on in de kitchen till yo' daddy come. Get a cookie from 'Vonia and set down off de back porch.

      [*Little* BILLY *exits left.*]

WILLIAM: Ma, you know it 'twarn't me told him. Bert's the one been goin' all over de plantation since he come back from Atlanta remindin' folks right out we's Colonel Norwood's chilluns.

CORA: [*Catching her breath.*] Huh!

WILLIAM: He comes down to my shack tellin' Billy and Marybell they got a white man for grandpa. He's gonna get my chilluns in trouble sho'—like he got himself in trouble when Colonel Tom whipped him.

CORA: Ten or 'leven years ago, warn't it?

WILLIAM: And Bert's *sho'* in trouble now. Can't go back to that college like he could-a if he'd-a had any sense. You can't fool with white folks—and de Colonel ain't never really liked Bert since that there first time he beat him, either.

CORA: No, he ain't. Leastwise, he ain't understood him. [*Musing sadly in a low voice.*] Time Bert was 'bout seven, warn't it? Just a little bigger'n yo' Billy.

WILLIAM: Yes.

CORA: Went runnin' up to Colonel Tom out in de horse stable when de Colonel was showin' off his horses—I 'members so well—to fine white company from town. Lawd, that boy's always been foolish! He went runnin' up and grabbed a-holt de Colonel and yelled right in front o' de white folks' faces, "O, papa, Cora say de dinner's ready, papa!" Ain't never called him papa before, and I don't know where he got it from. And Colonel Tom knocked him right backwards under de horse's feet.

WILLIAM: And when de company were gone, he beat that boy unmerciful.

CORA: I thought sho' he were gonna kill ma chile that day. And he were mad at me, too, for months. Said I was teaching you chilluns who they pappy were. Up till then Bert had been his favorite little colored child round here.

WILLIAM: Sho' had.

CORA: But he never liked him no more. That's why he sent him off to school so soon to stay, winter and summer, all these years. I had to beg and plead to have him home this summer—but I's sorry now I ever got that boy back here again.

WILLIAM: He's sho' growed more like de Colonel all de time, ain't he? Bert thinks he's a real white man hisself now. Look at de first thing he did when he come home, he ain't seen de Colonel in six years—and Bert sticks out his hand fo' to shake hands with him!

CORA: Lawd! That chile!

WILLIAM: Just like white folks! And de Colonel turns his back and walks off. Can't blame him. He ain't used to such doings from colored folks. God knows what's got into Bert since he come back. He's acting like a fool—just like he was a boss man round here. Won't even say "Yes, sir" and "No, sir"—no more to de white folks. Talbot asked him warn't he gonna work in de field this mornin'. Bert say "No!" and turn and walk away. White man so mad, I could see him nearly foam at de mouth. If he warn't yo' chile, ma, he'd been knocked in de head fo' now.

CORA: You's right.

WILLIAM: And you can't talk to him. I tried to tell him something the other day, but he just laughed at me, and said we's all just scared niggers on this plantation. Says he ain't no nigger, no how. He's a Norwood. He's half-white, and he's gonna act like it. [*In amazement at his brother's daring.*] And this is Georgia, too!

CORA: I's scared to death for de boy, William. I don't know what to do. De Colonel says he won't send him off to school no mo'. Says he's too sassy and impudent now than any nigger he ever seed. Bert never has been like you was, and de girls, quiet and sensible like you knowed you had to be. [*She sits down.*] De Colonel say he's gonna make Bert stay here now and work on this plantation like de rest of his niggers. He's gonna show him what color he is. Like that time when he beat him for callin' him "papa." He say he's gwine to teach him his place and make de boy know where he belongs. Seems like me or you can't show him. Colonel Tom has to take him in hand, or these white folks'll kill him around here and then—oh, My God!

WILLIAM: A nigger's just got to know his place in de South, that's all, ain't he, ma?

CORA: Yes, son. That's all, I reckon.

WILLIAM: And ma brother's one damn fool nigger. Don't seems like he knows nothin'. He's gonna ruin us all round here. Makin' it bad for everybody.

CORA: Oh, Lawd, have mercy! [*Beginning to cry.*] I don't know what to do. De way he's acting up can't go on. Way he's acting to de Colonel can't last. Somethin's gonna happen to ma chile. I had a bad dream last night, too, and I looked out and seed de moon all red with blood. I seed a path o' living blood across this house, I tell you, in my sleep. Oh, Lawd, have mercy! [*Sobbing.*] Oh, Lawd, help me in ma troubles.

[*The noise of the returning Ford is heard outside.* CORA *looks up, rises, and goes to the window.*]

There's de chile now, William. Run out to de back door and tell him I wants to see him. Bring him in here where Sam and Livonia and de rest of 'em won't hear ever'thing we's sayin'. I got to talk to ma boy. He's ma baby boy, and he don't know de way.

[*Exit* WILLIAM *through the door left.* CORA *is wiping her eyes and pulling herself together when the front door is flung open with a bang and* ROBERT *enters.*]

ROBERT: [*Running to his mother and hugging her teasingly.*] Hello, ma! Your daughter got off, and I've come back to keep you company in the parlor! Bring out the cookies and lemonade. Mister Norwood's here!

CORA: [*Beginning to sob anew.*] Take yo' hands off me, boy! Why don't you mind? Why don't you mind me?

ROBERT: [*Suddenly serious, backing away.*] Why, mamma, what's the matter? Did I scare you? Your eyes are all wet! Has somebody been telling you 'bout this morning?

CORA: [*Not heeding his words.*] Why don't you mind me, son? Ain't I told you and told you not to come in that front door, never? [*Suddenly angry.*] Will somebody have to beat it into you? What's got wrong with you when you was away at that school? What am I gonna do?

ROBERT: [*Carelessly.*] Oh, I knew that the Colonel wasn't here. I passed him and old man Higgins on the road down by the south patch. He wouldn't even look at me when I waved at him. [*Half playfully.*] Anyhow, isn't this my old man's house? Ain't I his son and heir? [*Grandly, strutting around.*] Am I not Mr. Norwood, Junior?

CORA: [*Utterly serious.*] I believes you goin' crazy, Bert. I believes you wants to get us all killed or run away or something awful like that. I believes …

[WILLIAM *enters left.*]

WILLIAM: Where's Bert? He ain't come round back. [*Seeing his brother in the room.*] How'd you get in here?

ROBERT: [*Grinning.*] Houses have front doors.

WILLIAM: Oh, usin' de front door like de white folks, heh? You gwine do that once too much.

ROBERT: Yes, like de white folks. What's a front door for, you rabbit-hearted coon?

WILLIAM: Rabbit-hearted coon's better'n a dead coon any day.

ROBERT: I wouldn't say so. Besides you and me's only half-coons, anyhow, big boy. And I'm gonna act like my white half, not my black half. Get me, kid?

WILLIAM: Well, you ain't gonna act like it long here in de middle o' Georgy. And you ain't gonna act like it when de Colonel's around, either.

ROBERT: Oh, no? My stay down here'll be short and sweet, boy, short and sweet. The old man won't send me away to college no more—so you think I'm gonna stick around and work in the fields? Like fun? I might stay here awhile and teach some o' you darkies to think like men, maybe—till it gets too much for the old Colonel—but no more bowing down to white folks for me—not Robert Norwood.

CORA: Hush, son!

ROBERT: Certainly not right on my own old man's plantation—Georgia or no Georgia.

WILLIAM: [*Scornfully.*] I hears you.

ROBERT: *You* can do it if you want to, but I'm ashamed of you. I've been away from here six years. [*Boasting.*] I've learned something, seen people in Atlanta, and Richmond, and Washington where the football team went—real colored people who don't have to take off their hats to white folks or let 'em go to bed with their sisters—like that young Higgins boy, asking me what night Sallie was comin' to town. A damn cracker! [*To* CORA.] 'Scuse me, ma. [*Continuing.*] Back here in these woods maybe Sam and Livonia and you and mama and everybody's got their places fixed for 'em, but not me. [*Seriously.*] Nobody's gonna fix a place for me. I'm old man Norwood's son. Nobody fixed a place for him. [*Playfully again.*] Look at me. I'm a 'fay boy. [*Pretends to shake his hair back.*] See these gray eyes? I got the right to everything everybody else has. [*Punching his brother in the belly.*] Don't talk to me, old slaverytime Uncle Tom.

WILLIAM: [*Resentfully.*] I ain't playin', boy. [*Pushes younger brother back with some force.*] I ain't playin' a-tall.

CORA: All right, chilluns, stop. Stop! And William, you take Billy and go on home. 'Vonia's got to get supper and she don't like no young-uns under her feet in de kitchen. I wants to talk to Bert in here now 'fore Colonel Tom gets back.

[*Exit* WILLIAM *left.* CORA *continues to* BERT.]

Sit down, child, right here a minute, and listen.

ROBERT: [*Sitting down.*] All right, ma.

CORA: Hard as I's worked and begged and humbled maself to get de Colonel to keep you chilluns in school, you comes home wid yo' head full o' stubbornness and yo' mouth full o' sass for me. an' de white folks an' everybody. You know can't no colored boy here talk like you's been doin' to no white folks, let alone to de Colonel and that old devil of a Talbot. They ain't gonna stand fo' yo' sass. Not only you, but I 'spects we's all gwine to pay fo' it, every colored soul on this place. I was scared to death today fo' yo' sister, Sallie, scared de Colonel warn't gwine to let her go back to school, neither, 'count o' yo' doins, but he did, thank Gawd—and then you come near makin' her miss de train. Did she have time to get her ticket and all?

ROBERT: Sure! Had to drive like sin to get there with her, though. I didn't mean to be late getting back here for her, ma, but I had a little run-in about them radio tubes in town.

CORA: [*Worried.*] What's that?

ROBERT: The tubes was smashed when I got 'em, and I had already made out my money order, so the woman in the post office wouldn't give the three dollars back to me. All I did was explain to her that we could send the tubes back— but she got hot because there were two or three white folks waiting behind me to get stamps, I guess. So she yells at me to move on and not give her any of my "educated nigger talk." So I said, "I'm going to finish showing you these tubes before I move on" —and then she screamed and called the mail clerk working in the back, and told him to throw me out. [*Boasting.*] He didn't do it by himself, though. Had to call all the white loafers out in the square to get me through that door.

CORA: [*Fearfully.*] Lawd have mercy!

ROBERT: Guess if I hadn't-a had the Ford then, they'd've beat me half-to-death, but when I saw how many crackers there was, I jumped in the car and, beat it on away.

CORA: Thank God for that!

ROBERT: Not even a football man [*Half-boasting.*] like me could tackle the whole junction. 'Bout a dozen colored guys standing around, too, and not one of 'em would help me—the dumb jiggaboos! They been telling me ever since I been here, [*Imitating darky talk.*] "You can't argue wid whut folks, man. You better stay out o' this Junction. You must ain't got no sense, nigger! You's a fool" … Maybe I am a fool, ma—but I didn't want to come back here nohow.

CORA: I's sorry I sent for you.

ROBERT: Besides you, there ain't nobody in this country but a lot of evil white folks and cowardly niggers. [*Earnestly.*] I'm no nigger, anyhow, am I, ma? I'm half-white. The Colonel's my father—the richest man in the county—and I'm not going to take a lot of stuff from nobody if I do have to stay here, not from the old man either. He thinks I ought to be out there in the sun working, with Talbot standing over me like I belonged in the chain gang. Well, he's got another thought coming! [*Stubbornly.*] I'm a Norwood—not a field-hand nigger.

CORA: You means you ain't workin' no mo'?

ROBERT: [*Flaring.*] No, I'm not going to work in the fields. What did he send me away to school for—just to come back here and be his servant, or pick his hills of cotton?

CORA: He sent you away to de school because *I* asked him and begged him, and got down on my knees to him, that's why. [*Quietly.*] And now I just wants to make you see some sense, if you can. I knows, honey, you reads in de books and de papers, and you knows a lot more'n I do. But, chile, you's in Georgy—and I don't see how it is you don't know where you's at. This ain't up North—and even up yonder where we hears it's so fine, yo' sister has to' pass for white to get along good.

ROBERT: [*Bitterly.*] I know it.

CORA: She ain't workin' in no hotel kitchen like de Colonel thinks. She's in a office typewriting. And Sallie's studyin' de typewriter, too, at de school, but yo' pappy don't know it. I knows we ain't s'posed to study nothin' but cookin' and hard workin' here in Georgy. That's all I ever done, or knowed about. I been workin' on this very place all ma life—even 'fore I come to live in this Big House. When de Colonel's wife died, I come here, and borned you chilluns And de Colonel's been real good to me in his way. Let you all sleep in this house with me when you was little, and sent you all off to school when you growed up. Ain't no white man in this county done that with his cullud chilluns before, far as I can know. But you—Robert, be awful, awful careful! When de Colonel comes back, in a few minutes, he wants to talk to you. Talk right to him, boy. Talk like you was colored, 'cause you ain't white.

ROBERT: [*Angrily.*] And I'm not black, either. Look at me, mama. [*Rising and throwing up his arms.*] Don't I look like my father? Ain't I light as he is? Ain't my eyes gray like his eyes are? [*The noise of a car is heard outside.*] Ain't this our house?

CORA: That's him now. [*Agitated.*] Hurry, chile, and let's we get out of this room. Come on through yonder to the kitchen. [*She starts toward the door left.*] And I'll tell him you're here.

ROBERT: I don't want to run into the kitchen. Isn't this our house?

[*As* CORA *crosses hurriedly left,* ROBERT *goes toward the front door.*]

The Ford is parked out in front, anyway.

CORA: [*At the door left to the rear of the house.*] Robert! Robert!

[*As* ROBERT *nears the front door,* COLONEL NORWOOD *enters, almost runs into the boy, stops at the threshold and stares unbelievingly at his son.* CORA *backs up against the door left.*]

NORWOOD: Get out of here! [*He points toward the door to rear of the house where* CORA *is standing.*]

ROBERT: [*Half-smiling.*] Didn't you want to talk to me?

NORWOOD: Get out of here!

ROBERT: Not that way.

[*The* COLONEL *raises his cane to strike the boy.* CORA *screams.* BERT *draws himself up to his full height, taller than the old man and looking very much like him, pale and proud. The man and the boy face each other.* NORWOOD *does not strike.*]

NORWOOD: [*In a hoarse whisper.*] Get out of here. [*His hand is trembling as he points.*]

CORA: Robert! Come on, son, come on! Oh, my God, come on. [*Opening the door left.*]

ROBERT: Not that way, ma.

[ROBERT *walks proudly out the front door.* NORWOOD, *in an impotent rage, crosses the room to a small cabinet right opens it nervously with a key from his pocket, takes out a pistol and starts toward the front door.* CORA *overtakes him, seizes his arm, stops him.*]

CORA: He's our son, Tom. [*She sinks slowly to her knees, holding his body.*] Remember, he's our son.

CURTAIN

ACT TWO

Scene One

TIME: *After supper. Sunset.*
SETTING: *The same.*
ACTION: *As the curtain rises, the stage is empty. Through the windows the late afternoon sun makes two bright paths toward the footlights.* SAM, *carrying a tray bearing a whiskey bottle and a bowl of ice, enters left and crosses toward the library. He stoops at the door right, listens a moment, knocks, then opens the door and goes in. In a moment* SAM *returns. As he leaves the library, he is heard replying to a request of* NORWOOD's.

SAM: Yes, sah, Colonel! Sho' will, sah! Right away, sah! Yes, sah, I'll tell him. [*He closes the door and crosses the stage muttering to himself.*] Six o'clock. Most nigh that now. Better tell Cora to get that boy right in here. Can't nobody else do nothin' with that fool Bert but Cora. [*He exits left. Can be heard calling.*] Cora! You, Cora …

        [*Again the stage is empty. Off stage, outside, the bark of a dog is heard, the sound of Negroes singing down the road, the cry of a child. The breeze moves the shadows of leaves and tree limbs across the sunlit paths from the windows. The door left opens and* CORA *enters, followed by* ROBERT.]

CORA: [*Softly to* ROBERT *behind her in the dining room.*] It's all right, son. He ain't come out yet, but it's nearly six, and that's when he said he wanted you, but I was afraid maybe you was gonna be late. I sent for you to come up here to de house and eat supper with me in de kitchen. Where'd you eat yo' vittuals at, chile?

ROBERT: Down at Willie's house, ma. After the old man tried to hit me you still want me to hang around and eat up here?

CORA: I wanted you to be here on time, honey, that's all. [*She is very nervous.*] I kinder likes to have you eat with me sometimes, too, but you ain't et up here more'n once this summer. But this evenin' I just wanted you to be here when de Colonel sent word for you, 'cause we's done had enough trouble today.

ROBERT: He's not here on time, himself, is he?

CORA: He's in de library. Sam couldn't get him to eat no supper tonight, and I atn't seen him a-tall.

ROBERT: Maybe he wants to see me in the library, then.

CORA: You know he don't 'low no colored folks in there 'mongst his books and things 'cept Sam. Some o' his white friends goes in there, but none o' us.

ROBERT: Maybe he wants to see *me* in there, though.

CORA: Can't you never talk sense, Robert? This ain't no time for foolin' and jokin.' Nearly thirty years in this house and I ain't never been in there myself, not once, 'mongst de Colonel's papers. [*The clock strikes six.*] Stand over yonder and wait till he comes out. I's gwine on upstairs now, so's he can talk to you. And don't aggravate him no mo' fo' God's sake. Agree to whatever he say. I's scared fo' you, chile, de way you been actin,' and de fool tricks you done today, and de trouble about de post office besides. Don't aggravate him. Fo' yo' sake, honey, 'cause I loves you—and fo' all de po' colored folks on this place what has such a hard time when his humors get on him—agree to whatever he say, will you, Bert?

ROBERT: All right, ma. [*Voice rising.*] But he better not start to hit me again.

CORA: Shs-ss-s! He'll hear you. He's right in there.

ROBERT: [*Sullenly.*] This was the day I ought to have started back to school—like my sister. I stayed my summer out here, didn't I? Why didn't he keep his promise to me? You said if I came home I could go back to college again.

CORA: Shs-ss-s! He'll be here now. Don't say nothin', chile. I's done all I could.

ROBERT: All right, ma.

CORA: [*Approaching the stairs.*] I'll be in ma room, honey, where I can hear you when you goes out. I'll come down to de back door and see you 'fore you goes back to de shack. Don't aggravate him, chile.

> [*She ascends the stairs. The boy sits down sullenly, left, and stares at the door opposite from which his father must enter. The clock strikes the quarter after six. The shadows of the window curtains have lengthened on*

the carpet. The sunshine has deepened to a pale orange, and the light paths grow less distinct across the floor. The boy sits up straight in his chair. He looks at the library door. It opens. NORWOOD *enters. He is bent and pale. He looks across the room and sees the boy. Suddenly he straightens up. The old commanding look comes into his face. He strides directly' across the room toward his son. The boy, half afraid, half defiant, yet sure of himself, rises. Now that* ROBERT *is standing, the white man turns, goes back to a chair near the table, right, and seats himself. He takes out a cigar, cuts off the end and lights it, and in a voice of mixed condescension and contempt, he speaks to his son.* ROBERT *remains standing near the chair.*]

NORWOOD: I don't want to have to beat you another time as I did when you were a child. The next time I might not be able to control myself. I might kill you if I touched you again. I been runnin' this plantation for thirty-five years, and I never had to beat a Nigra as old as you are. I never had to beat one of Cora's children either—but you. The rest of 'em had sense 'nough to keep out of my sight, and to speak to me like they should … I don't have any trouble with my colored folks. Never have trouble. They do what I say, or what Mr. Talbot says, and that's all there is to it. I give 'em a chance. If they turn in crops they get paid. If they're workin' for wages, they get paid. If they want to spend their money on licker, or buy an old car, or fix up their cabins, they can. Do what they choose long as they know their places and it don't hinder their work. And to Cora's young ones I give all the chances any colored folks ever had in these parts. More'n many a white child's had. I sent you all off to school. Let Bertha go on up North when she got grown and educated. Intend to let Sallie do the same. Gave your brother William that house he's living in when he got married, pay him for his work, help him out if he needs it. None of my darkies suffer. Sent you to college. Would have kept on, would have sent you back today, but I don't intend to pay for no darky, or white boy either if I had one, that acts the way you've been acting. And certainly for no black fool. Now I want to know what's wrong with you? I don't usually talk about what I'm going to do with anybody on this place. It's my habit to tell people *what to do*, not discuss it with 'em. But I want to know what's the matter with you—whether you're crazy or not. In that case, you'll have to be locked up. And if you aren't, you'll have to change your ways a damn sight or it won't be safe for you here, and you know it—venting your impudence on white women, parking the car in front of my door, driving like mad through the Junction, and going, everywhere, just as you please. Now, I'm going to let you talk to me, but I want you to talk right.

ROBERT: [*Still standing.*] What do you mean, "talk right?"

NORWOOD: I mean talk like a nigger should to a white man.

ROBERT: Oh! But I'm not a nigger, Colonel Tom. I'm your son.

NORWOOD: [*Testily.*] You're Cora's boy.

ROBERT: Women don't have children by themselves.

NORWOOD: Nigger women don't know the fathers. You're a bastard.

> [ROBERT *clenches his fist.* NORWOOD *turns toward the drawer where the pistol is, takes it out, and lays it on the table. The wind blows the lace curtains at the windows, and sweeps the shadows of falling leaves across the paths of sunlight on the floor.*]

ROBERT: I've heard that before. I've heard it from Negroes, and I've heard it from white folks. Now I hear it from you. [*Slowly.*] You're talking about my mother.

NORWOOD: I'm talking about Cora, yes. Her children are bastards.

ROBERT: [*Quickly.*] And you're their father. [*Angrily.*] How come I look like you, if you're not my father?

NORWOOD: Don't shout at me, boy. I can hear you. [*Half-smiling.*] How come your skin is yellow and your elbows rusty? How come they threw you out of the post office today for talking to a white woman? How come you're the crazy young buck you are?

ROBERT: They had no right to throw me out. I asked for my money back when I saw the broken tubes. Just as you had no right to raise that cane today when I was standing at the door of this house where you live, while I have to sleep in a shack down the road with the field hands. [*Slowly.*] But my mother sleeps with you.

NORWOOD: You don't like it?

ROBERT: No, I don't like it.

NORWOOD: What can you do about it?

116

ROBERT: [*After a pause.*] I'd like to kill all the white men in the world.

NORWOOD: [*Starting.*] Niggers like you are hung to trees.

ROBERT: I'm not a nigger.

NORWOOD: You don't like your own race?

      [ROBERT *is silent.*]

Yet you don't like white folks either?

ROBERT: [*Defiantly.*] You think I ought to?

NORWOOD: You evidently don't like me.

ROBERT: [*Boyishly.*] I used to like you, when I first knew you were my father, when I was a little kid, before that time you beat me under the feet of your horses. [*Slowly.*] I liked you until then.

NORWOOD: [*A little pleased.*] So you did, heh? [*Fingering his pistol.*] A pickaninny calling me "papa." I should've broken your young neck for that first time. I should've broken your head for you today, too—since I didn't then.

ROBERT: [*Laughing scornfully.*] You should've broken my head?

NORWOOD: Should've gotten rid of you before this. But you was Cora's child. I tried to help you. [*Aggrieved.*] I treated you decent, schooled you. Paid for it. But tonight you'll get the hell off this place and stay off. Get the hell out of this county. [*Suddenly furious.*] Get out of this state. Don't let me lay eyes on you again. Get out of here now. Talbot and the storekeeper are coming up here this evening to talk cotton with me. I'll tell Talbot to see that you go. That's all.

      [NORWOOD *motions toward the door, left.*]

Tell Sam to come in here when you go out. Tell him to make a light here.

ROBERT: [*Impudently.*] *Ring* for Sam—I'm not going through the kitchen. [*He starts toward the front door.*] I'm not your servant. You're not going to tell me what to do. You're not going to have Talbot run me off the place like a field hand you don't want to use any more.

NORWOOD: [*Springing between his son and the front door, pistol in hand.*] You black bastard!

[ROBERT *goes toward him calmly, grasps his father's arm and twists it until the gun falls to the floor. The older man bends backward in startled fury and pain.*]

Don't you dare put your ...

ROBERT: [*Laughing.*] Why don't you shoot, papa? [*Louder.*] Why don't you shoot?

NORWOOD: [*Gasping as he struggles, fighting back.*] ... black ... hands ... on . .. you ...

ROBERT: [*Hysterically, as he takes his father by the throat.*] Why don't you shoot, papa?

[NORWOOD's *hands claw the air helplessly.* ROBERT *chokes the struggling white man until his body grows limp.*]

Why don't you shoot! [*Laughing.*] Why don't you shoot? Huh? Why?

[CORA *appears at the top of the stairs, hearing the commotion. She screams.*]

CORA: Oh, my God!

[*She rushes down.* ROBERT *drops the body of his father at her feet in a path of flame from the setting sun.* CORA *starts and stares in horror.*]

ROBERT: [*Wildly.*] Why didn't he shoot, mama? He didn't want *me* to live. Why didn't he shoot? [*Laughing.*] He was the boss. Telling me what to do. Why didn't he shoot, then? He was the white man.

CORA: [*Falling on the body.*] Colonel Tom! Colonel Tom! Tom! Tom! [*Gazes across the corpse at her son.*] He's yo' father, Bert.

ROBERT: He's dead. The white man's dead. My father's dead. [*Laughing.*] I'm living.

CORA: Tom! Tom! Tom!

ROBERT: Niggers are living. He's dead. [*Picks up the pistol.*] This is what he wanted to kill me with, but he's dead. I can use it now. Use it on all the white men in the world, because they'll be coming looking for me now. [*Stuffs the pistol into his shirt.*] They'll want me now.

CORA: [*Rising and running toward her boy.*] Quick, chile, out that way, [*Pointing toward the front door.*] so they won't see you in de kitchen. Make for de swamp, honey. Cross de fields fo' de swamp. Go de crick way. In runnin' water, dogs can't smell no tracks. Hurry, chile!

ROBERT: Yes, mama. I can go out the front way now, easy. But if I see they gonna get me before I can reach the swamp, I'm coming back here, mama, and [*Proudly.*] let them take me out of my father's house—if they can. [*Pats the gun under his shirt.*] They're not going to string me up to some roadside tree for the crackers to laugh at.

CORA: [*Moaning aloud.*] Oh, O-o-o! Hurry! Hurry, chile!

ROBERT: I'm going, ma. [*He opens the door. The sunset streams in like a river of blood.*]

CORA: Run, chile!

ROBERT: Not out of my father's house. [*He exits slowly, tall and straight against the sun.*]

CORA: Fo' God's sake, hurry, chile! [*Glancing down the road.*] Lawd have mercy! There's Talbot and de storekeeper in de drive. They sees my boy! [*Moaning.*] They sees ma boy. [*Relieved.*] But thank God, they's passin' him!

[CORA *backs up against the wall in the vestibule. She stands as if petrified as* TALBOT *and the* STOREKEEPER *enter.*]

TALBOT: Hello, Cora. What's the matter with you? Where's that damn fool boy o' your'n goin', coming out the front door like he owned the house? What's the matter with you, woman? Can't you talk? Can't you talk? Where's Norwood? Let's have some light in this dark place.

[*He reaches behind the door and turns on the lights.* CORA *remains backed up against the wall, looking out into the twilight, watching* ROBERT *as he goes across the field.*]

Good God, Jim! Look at this!

[*The* TWO WHITE MEN *stop in horror before the sight of* NORWOOD'*s body on the floor.*]

STOREKEEPER: He's blue in the face. [*Bends over the body*.] That nigger we saw walking out the door! [*Rising excitedly*.] That nigger bastard of Cora's ... [*Stooping over the body again*.] Why the Colonel's dead!

TALBOT: That nigger! [*Rushes toward the door*.] He's running toward the swamp now ... We'll get him ... Telephone town—there, in the library. Telephone the sheriff. Get men, white men, after that nigger.

STOREKEEPER: [*Rushes into the library. He can be heard talking excitedly on the phone*.] Sheriff! Sheriff! Is this the sheriff? I'm calling from Norwood's plantation. That nigger, Bert, has just killed Norwood—and run, headed for the swamp. Notify the gas station at the crossroads! Tell the boys at the sawmill to head him off at the creek. Warn everybody to be on the lookout. Call your deputies! Yes! Yes! Spread a dragnet. Get out the dogs. Meanwhile we'll start after him. [*He slams the phone down and comes back into the room*.] Cora, where's Norwood's car? In the barn?

[CORA *does not answer*.]

TALBOT: Talk, you black bitch!

[*She remains silent*. TALBOT *runs, yelling and talking, out into the yard, followed by the* STOREKEEPER. *Sounds of excited shouting outside, and the roar of a motor rushing down the drive. In the sky the twilight deepens into early night.* CORA *stands looking into the darkness*.]

CORA: My boy can't get to de swamp now. They's telephoned the white folks down that way. So he'll come back home now. Maybe he'll turn into de crick and follow de branch home directly. [*Protectively*.] But they shan't get him. I'll make a place for to hide him. I'll make a place upstairs down under de floor, under ma bed. In a minute ma boy'll be runnin' from de white folks with their hounds and their ropes and their guns and everything they uses to kill po' colored folks with. [*Distressed*.] Ma boy'll be out there runnin'. [*Turning to the body on the floor*.] Colonel Tom, you hear me? Our boy, out there runnin'. [*Fiercely*.] *You* said he was ma boy—*ma* bastard boy. I heard you ... but he's yours too ... but yonder in de dark runnin'—runnin' from yo' people, from white people. [*Pleadingly*.] Why don't you get up and stop 'em? He's *your* boy. His eyes is gray—like your eyes. He's tall like you's tall. He's proud like you's proud. And he's runnin'—runnin' from po' white trash what ain't worth de little finger o' nobody what's got your blood in 'em, Tom. [*Demandingly*.] Why don't you get up from there and stop 'em, Colonel Tom? What's that you say? He ain't your chile? He's ma bastard chile? My yellow bastard chile? [*Proudly.*] Yes, he's mine. But don't call him that. Don't you touch him. Don't you put your white hands on him. You's beat him enough, and cussed him enough. Don't you touch him now. He *is* ma boy, and no white folks gonna touch him now. That's finished. I'm gonna make a place for him upstairs under ma bed. [*Backs away from the body toward the stairs.*] He's ma chile. Don't you come in ma bedroom while he's up there. Don't you come to my bed no mo'. I calls you to help me now, and you just lay's there. I calls you for to wake up, and you just lays there. Whenever you called me, in de night, I woke up. When you called for me to love, I always reached out ma arms fo' you. I borned you five chilluns and now one of 'em is out yonder in de dark runnin' from yo' people. Our youngest boy out yonder in de dark runnin'. [*Accusingly.*] He's runnin' from you, too. You said he warn't your'n—he's just Cora's po' little yellow bastard. But he *is* your'n, Colonel Tom. [*Sadly.*] And he's runnin' from you, You are out yonder in de dark, [*Points toward the door.*] runnin' our chile, with de hounds and de gun in yo' hand, and Talbot's followin' 'hind you with a rope to hang Robert with. [*Confidently.*] I been sleepin' with you too long, Colonel Tom, not to know that this ain't you layin' down there with yo' eyes shut on de floor. You can't fool me—you ain't never been so still like this before—you's out yonder run-nin' ma boy. [*Scornfully.*] Colonel Thomas Norwood, runnin' ma boy through de fields in de dark, runnin' ma poor little helpless Bert through de fields in de dark to lynch him ... Damn you, Colonel Norwood! [*Backing slowly up the stairs, staring at the rigid body below her.*] Damn you, Thomas Norwood! God damn you!

CURTAIN

Scene Two

TIME: *One hour later. Night.*

SETTING: *The same.*

ACTION: *As the curtain rises, the* UNDERTAKER *is talking to* SAM *at the outer door. All through this act the approaching cries of the man hunt are heard.*

UNDERTAKER: Reckon there won't be no orders to bring his corpse back out here, Sam. None of us ain't seen Talbot or Mr. Higgins, but I'm sure they'll be having the funeral in town. The coroner told us to bring the body into the Junction. Ain't nothin' but niggers left out here now.

SAM: [*Very frightened.*] Yes, sah! Yes, sah! You's right, sah! Nothin' but us niggers, sah!

UNDERTAKER: The Colonel didn't have no relatives far as you know, did he, Sam?

SAM: No, sah. Ain't had none. No, sah! You's right, sah!

UNDERTAKER: Well, you got everything o' his locked up around here, ain't you? Too bad there ain't no white folks about to look after the Colonel's stuff, but every white man that's able to walk's out with the posse. They'll have that young nigger swingin' before ten.

SAM: [*Trembling.*] Yes, sah, yes, sah! I 'spects so. Yes, sah!

UNDERTAKER: Say, where's that woman the Colonel's been living with— where's that black housekeeper, Cora, that murderin' bastard's mother?

SAM: She here, sah! She's up in her room.

UNDERTAKER: [*Curiously.*] I'd like to see how she looks. Get her down here. Say, how about a little drink before we start that ride back to town, for me and my partner out there with the body?

SAM: Cora got de keys to all de licker, sah!

UNDERTAKER: Well, get her down here then, double quick!

[SAM *goes up the stairs. The* UNDERTAKER *leans in the front doorway talking to his partner outside in the wagon.*]

Bad business, a white man having saucy nigger children on his hands, and his black woman living in his own house.

VOICE OUTSIDE: Damn right, Charlie.

UNDERTAKER: Norwood didn't have a gang o' yellow gals, though, like Higgins and some o' these other big bugs. Just this one bitch far's I know, livin' with him damn near like a wife. Didn't even have much company out here. And they tell me ain't been a white woman stayed here overnight since his wife died when I was a baby.

[SAM's *shuffle is heard on the stairs.*]

Here comes a drink, I reckon, boy. You needn't get down off the ambulance. I'll have Sam bring it out there to you.

[SAM *descends followed by* CORA *who comes down the stairs. She says nothing. The* UNDERTAKER *looks up grinning at* CORA.]

Well, so you're the Cora that's got these educated nigger children? Hum-m! Well, I guess you'll see one of 'em swinging full of bullet holes when you wake up in the morning. They'll probably hang him to that tree down here by the Colonel's gate—'cause they tell me he strutted right out the front gate past that tree after the murder. Or maybe they'll burn him. How'd you like to see him swinging there roasted in the morning when you wake up, girlie?

CORA: [*Calmly.*] Is that all you wanted to say to me?

UNDERTAKER: Don't get smart! Maybe you think there's nobody to boss you now. We gonna have a little drink before we go. Get out a bottle of rye.

CORA: I takes ma orders from Colonel Norwood, sir.

UNDERTAKER: Well, you'll take no more orders from him. He's dead out there in my wagon—so get along and get the bottle.

CORA: He's out yonder with de mob, not in your wagon.

UNDERTAKER: I tell you he's in my wagon!

CORA: He's out there with de mob.

UNDERTAKER: God damn! [*To his partner outside.*] I believe this black woman's gone crazy in here. [*To* CORA.] Get the keys out for that licker, and be quick about it!

[CORA *does not move.* SAM *looks from one to the other, frightened.*]

VOICE OUTSIDE: Aw, to hell with the licker, Charlie. Come on, let's start back to town. We want to get in on some of that excitement, too. They should've found that nigger by now—and I want to see 'em drag him out here.

UNDERTAKER: All right, Jim. [*To* CORA *and* SAM.] Don't you all go to bed until you see that bonfire. You niggers are getting besides yourselves around Polk County. We'll burn a few more of you if you don't be careful. [*He exits, and the noise of the dead-wagon going down the road is heard.*]

SAM: Oh, Lawd, hab mercy on me! I prays, Lawd hab mercy! O, ma Lawd, ma Lawd, ma Lawd! Cora, is you a fool? *Is* you a fool? Why didn't you give de mens de licker, riled as these white folks is? In ma old age is I gonna be burnt by de crackers? Lawd, is I sinned? Lawd, what has I done? [*Suddenly stops moaning and becomes schemingly calm.*] I don't have to stay here tonight, does I? I done locked up de Colonel's library and he can't be wantin' nothin'. No, ma Lawd, he won't want nothin' now. He's with Jesus—or with de devil, one. [*To* CORA.] I's gwine on away from here. Sam's gwine in town to his chilluns' house, and I ain't gwine by no road either. I gwine through de holler where I don't have to pass no white folks.

CORA: Yes, Samuel, you go on. De Colonel can get his own drinks when he comes back tonight.

[*Bucking his eyes in astonishment at* CORA.]

Lawd God Jesus!

[*He bolts out of the room as fast as his old legs will carry him.* CORA *comes down stairs, looks for a long moment out into the darkness, then closes the front door and draws the blinds. She looks down at the spot where the* COLONEL's *body lay.*]

CORA: All de colored folks are runnin' from you tonight. Po' Colonel Tom, you too old now to be out with de mob. You got no business goin', but you had to go, I reckon. I 'members that time they hung Luke Jordon, you sent yo' dogs out to hunt him. The next day you killed all de dogs. You were kinder soft-hearted. Said you didn't like that kind of sport. Told me in bed one night you could hear them dogs howlin' in yo' sleep. But de time they burnt de court-house when that po' little cullud boy was locked up in it cause they said he hugged a white girl, you was with 'em again. Said you had to go help 'em. Now you's out chasin' ma boy. [*As she stands at the window, she sees a passing figure.*] There goes yo' other woman, Colonel Tom, Livonia is runnin' from you too, now. She would've wanted you last night. Been wantin' you again ever since she got old and fat and you stopped layin' with her and put her in the kitchen to cook. Don't think I don't know, Colonel Tom. Don't think I don't remember them nights when you used to sleep in that cabin down by de spring. I knew 'Vonia was there with you. I ain't no fool, Colonel Tom. But she ain't bore you no chilluns. I'm de one that bore 'em. [*Musing.*] White mens, and colored wom-ens, and little bastard chilluns—that's de old way of de South—but it's end-ing now. Three of your yellow brothers yo' father had by Aunt Sallie Deal—what had to come and do your laundry to make her livin'—you got colored rela-tives scattered all over this county. Them de ways o' de South—mixtries, mix-tries.

[WILLIAM *enters left, silently, as his mother talks. She is sitting in a chair now. Without looking up.*]

Is that you, William?

WILLIAM: Yes, ma, it's me.

CORA: Is you runnin' from him, too?

WILLIAM: [*Hesitatingly.*] Well, ma, you see … don't you think kinder … well, I reckon I ought to take Libby and ma babies on down to de church house with Reverend Martin and them, or else get 'long to town if I can hitch up them mules. They's scared to be out here, my wife and her ma. All de folks done gone from de houses down yonder by de branch, and you can hear de hounds a bayin' off yonder by de swamp, and cars is tearin' up that road, and de white folks is yellin' and hollerin' and carryin' on somethin' terrible over toward de brook. I done told Robert 'bout his foolishness. They's gonna hang him sure. Don't you think you better be comin' with us, ma. That is, do you want to? 'Course we can go by ourselves, and maybe you wants to stay here and take care o' de big house. I don't want to leave you, ma, but I … I …

CORA: Yo' brother'll be back, son, then I won't be by myself.

WILLIAM: [*Bewildered by his mother's sureness.*] I thought Bert went … I thought he run … I thought …

CORA: No, honey. He went, but they ain't gonna get him out there. I sees him comin' back here now, to be with me. I's gwine to guard him 'till he can get away.

WILLIAM: Then de white folks'll come here, too.

CORA: Yes, de Colonel'll come back here sure.

[*The deep baying of the hounds is heard at a distance through the night.*]

Colonel Tom will come after his son.

WILLIAM: My God, ma! Come with us to town.

CORA: Go on, William, go on! Don't wait for them to get back. You never was much like neither one o' them—neither de Colonel or Bert—you's mo' like de field hands. Too much o' ma blood in you, I guess. You never liked Bert much, neither, and you always was afraid of de Colonel. Go on, son, and hide yo' wife and her ma and your chilluns. Ain't nothin' gonna hurt you. You never did go against nobody. Neither did I, till tonight. Tried to live right and not hurt a soul, white or colored. [*Addressing space.*] I tried to live right, Lord. [*Angrily.*] Tried to live right, Lord. [*Throws out her arms resentfully as if to say, "and this is what you give me."*] What's de matter, Lawd, you ain't with me?

[*The hounds are heard howling again.*]

WILLIAM: I'm gone, ma. [*He exits fearfully as his mother talks.*]

CORA: [*Bending over the spot on the floor where the* COLONEL *has lain. She calls.*] Colonel Tom! Colonel Tom! Colonel Tom! Look! Bertha and Sallie and William and Bert, all your chilluns, runnin' from you, and you layin' on de floor there, dead! [*Pointing.*] Out yonder with the mob, dead. And when you come home, upstairs in my bed on top of my body, dead. [*Goes to the window, returns, sits down, and begins to speak as if remembering a far-off dream.*] Colonel Thomas Norwood! I'm just poor Cora Lewis, Colonel Norwood. Little black Cora Lewis, Colonel Norwood. I'm just fifteen years old. Thirty years ago, you put your hands on me to feel my breasts, and you say, "You a pretty little piece of flesh, ain't you? Black and sweet, ain't you?" And I lift up ma face, and you pull me to you, and we laid down under the trees that night, and I wonder if your wife'll know when you go back up the road into the big house. And I wonder if my mama'll know it, when I go back to our cabin. Mama said she nursed you when you was a baby, just like she nursed me. And I loved you in the dark, down there under that tree by de gate, afraid of you and proud of you, feelin' your gray eyes lookin' at me in de dark. Then I cried and cried and told ma mother about it, but she didn't take it hard like I thought she'd take it. She said fine white mens like de young Colonel always took good care o' their colored womens. She said it was better than marryin' some black field hand and workin' all your life in de cotton and cane. Better even than havin' a job like ma had, takin' care o' de white chilluns. Takin' care o' you, Colonel Tom.

[As CORA speaks the sound of the approaching mob gradually grow louder and louder. Auto horns, the howling of dogs, the far-off shouts of men, full of malignant force and power, increase in volume.]

And I was happy because I liked you, 'cause you was tall and proud, 'cause you said I was sweet to you and called me purty. And when yo' wife died—de Mrs. Norwood [Scornfully.] that never bore you any chilluns, the pale beautiful Mrs. Norwood that was like a slender pine tree in de winter frost … I knowed you wanted me. I was full with child by you then—William, it was—our first boy. And ma mammy said go up there and keep de house for Colonel Tom, sweep de floors and make de beds, and by and by, you won't have to sweep de floors and make no beds. And what ma mammy said was right. It all come true. Stan and Rusus and 'Vonia and Lucy did de waitin' on you and me, and de washin' and de cleanin' and de cookin'. And all I did was a little sewin' now and then, and a little preservin' in de summer and a little makin' of pies and sweet cakes and things you like to eat on Christmas. And de years went by. And I was always ready for you then you come to me in de night. And we had them chilluns, your chilluns and mine, Tom Norwood, all of 'em! William, born dark like me, dumb like me, and then Baby John what died; then Bertha, white and smart like you; and then Bert with your eyes and your ways and your temper, and mighty nigh your color; then Sallie, nearly white, too, and smart, and purty. But Bert was yo' chile! He was always yo' child … Good-looking, and kind, and headstrong, and strange, and stubborn, and proud like you, and de one I could love most 'cause he needed de most lovin'. And he wanted to call you "papa," and I tried to teach him no, but he did it anyhow and [Sternly.] you beat him, Colonel Thomas Norwood. And he growed up with de beatin' in

127

his heart, and your eyes in his head, and your ways, and your pride. And this summer he looked like you that time I first knowed you down by de road under them trees, young and fiery and proud. There was no touchin' Bert, just like there was no touchin' you. I could only love him, like I loved you. I could only love him. But I couldn't talk to him, because he hated you. He had your ways—and you beat him! After you beat that chile, then you died, Colonel Norwood. You died here in this house, and you been living dead a long time. You lived dead. [*Her voice rises above the nearing sounds of the mob.*] And when I said this evenin', "Get up! Why don't you help me?" you'd done been dead a long time—a long time before you laid down on this floor, here, with the breath choked out o' you—and Bert standin' over you living, living, living. That's why you hated him. And you want to kill him. Always, you wanted to kill him. Out there with de hounds and de torches and de cars and de guns, you want to kill ma boy. But you won't kill him! He's comin' home first. He's comin' home to me. He's comin' home!

[*Outside the noise is tremendous now, the lights of autos flash on the window curtains, there are shouts and cries.* CORA *sits, tense, in the middle of the room.*]

He's comin' home!

A MAN'S VOICE: [*Outside.*] He's somewhere on this lot.

ANOTHER VOICE: Don't shoot, men. We want to get him alive.

VOICE: Close in on him. He must be in them bushes by the house.

FIRST VOICE: Porch! Porch! Porch! There he is yonder—running to the door!

[*Suddenly shots are heard. The door burst opens and* ROBERT *enters, firing back into the darkness. The shots are returned by the mob, breaking the windows. Flares, lights, voices, curses, screams.*]

VOICES: Nigger! Nigger! Nigger! Get the nigger!

[CORA *rushes toward the door and bolts it after her son's entrance.*]

CORA: [*Leaning against the door.*] I was waiting for you, honey. Yo' hiding place is all ready, upstairs, under ma bed, under de floor. I sawed a place there fo' you. They can't find you there. Hurry—before yo' father comes.

ROBERT: [*Panting.*] No time to hide, ma. They're at the door now. They'll be coming up the back way, too. [*Sounds of knocking and the breaking of glass.*] They'll be coming in the windows. They'll be coming in everywhere. And only one bullet left, ma. It's for me.

CORA: Yes, it's fo' you, chile. Save it. Go upstairs in mama's room. Lay on ma bed and rest.

ROBERT: [*Going slowly toward the stairs with the pistol in his hand.*] Goodnight, ma. I'm awful tired of running, ma. They been chasing me for hours.

CORA: Goodnight, son.

[CORA *follows him to the foot of the steps. The door begins to give at the forcing of the mob. As* ROBERT *disappears above, it bursts open. A great crowd of white men pour into the room with guns, ropes, clubs, flashlights, and knives.* CORA *turns on the stairs, facing them quietly.* TALBOT, *the leader of the mob, stops.*]

TALBOT: Be careful, men. He's armed. [*To* CORA.] Where is that yellow bastard of yours—upstairs?

CORA: Yes, he's going to sleep. Be quiet, you all. Wait. [*She bars the way with outspread arms.*]

TALBOT: [*Harshly.*] Wait, hell! Come on, boys, let's go!

[*A single shot is heard upstairs.*]

What's that?

CORA: [*Calmly.*] My boy ... is gone ... to sleep!

[TALBOT *and some of the men rush up the stairway,* CORA *makes a final gesture of love toward the room above. Yelling and shouting, through all the doors and windows, a great crowd pours into the room. The roar of the mob fills the house, the whole night, the whole world. Suddenly* TALBOT *returns at the top of the steps and a hush falls over the crowd.*]

TALBOT: Too late men. We're just a little too late.

[*A sigh of disappointment rises from the mob.* TALBOT *comes down the stairs, walks up to* CORA *and slaps her once across the face. She does not move. It is as though no human hand can touch her again.*]

CURTAIN

DUTCHMAN

LEROI JONES
(AMIRI BARAKA)

—⇒⊕⇐—

Dutchman was first presented at
The Cherry Lane Theatre, New York City
on March 24, 1964.

· INTRODUCTION

by Kimberly W. Benston

Dutchman: Theatrical Ghost of a Future Politics

Dutchman debuted at New York's Cherry Lane Theatre in early 1964, a moment of transition and anxiety in American cultural history. Its appearance was framed (as we can now see) by defining acts of social violence and insurgency: the assassinations of John Kennedy (November, 1963) and Malcolm X (January, 1965); the murders of four black children in a Birmingham, Alabama church bombing (September, 1963) and three young civil rights volunteers in Philadelphia, Mississippi (June, 1964); the collective assertions of the March on Washington (August, 1963) and the Watts Riot (August, 1965). Written, then, in an atmosphere of social ferment, Baraka's play provides an index of important shifts then underway in the related realms of political discourse, theatrical method, and authorial consciousness. For *Dutchman* registers simultaneously the confrontation of the Civil Rights Movement's pacifist integrationism with Black Power's militant separatism, social realism's encounter with mythic content and vernacular style, and self-professed "schwartze Bohemien" LeRoi Jones's imminent metamorphosis into "revolutionary" black nationalist Amiri Baraka. Emerging from such an atmosphere of communal upheaval and ideological conflict, *Dutchman* could not help but function as "political theatre," at least insofar as that vexed term designates a drama committed to transforming historical conditions in the service of individual and collective emancipation. Whether considered as social document or personal testament, *Dutchman* is a play forged at the crossroads of self-exploration and civic struggle, that intersection of private need and public value that traditionally lends political theatre its sense of urgent, unruly purpose.

And yet, when we look more closely at the specific conceptions that have helped shape our understanding of modern "political theatre"—whether as articulated (for example) by Erwin Piscator's "proletarian" pragmatism or Bertolt Brecht's "epic" didacticism, Living Theatre's "improvisational" transgression or Dario Fo's "carnivalesque" satire—*Dutchman* cannot be so easily assimilated to the blend of polemic, pedagogy, and provocation by which the genre of political drama has characteristically staked its claims to social significance. Rather, Baraka's play reimagines these and similar terms of topical engagement by rendering them more thematic problems confronted by its characters and audience than formal means guided by some presupposed conviction. That is to say, *Dutchman* not so much embodies as interrogates the idea of political theatre by pressuring each of its terms. Through the intersection of plot, language, and gesture, the play poses fundamental questions concerning *relations* between power and impersonation, history and action, cultural struggle and dramatic enactment. If *Dutchman* is a "political play," that is less because its characters and categories evoke recognizable social variables than because it explores the *politics of performance itself*. By thus truly "staging" politics, *Dutchman* forces reconsideration of theatre's own limits and possibilities as an instrument of radical aspiration.

Baraka's theatre manifesto, "The Revolutionary Theatre" (1964), offers a suggestive glossary for our reading of *Dutchman*'s particular vision of political drama:

> This should be a theatre [...] where the spirit can be
> shown to be the most competent force in the world. [...]
> The Revolutionary Theatre is shaped by the world, and
> moves to reshape the world [...] We are history and desire
> [...] we will change the drawing rooms into places where
> real things can be said about a real world [...] Our theatre
> will show victims so that their brothers in the audience
> will be better able to understand that they are the
> brothers of victims [...] And what we show must cause the
> blood to rush, so that pre-revolutionary temperaments
> will be bathed in this blood, and it will cause their deepest
> souls to move [...] We will scream and cry, run through the
> streets in agony, if it means some soul will be moved [...]
> —*Home*, 212-13

Baraka envisions here a theatre located at the intersections of morality and necessity, vision and experience, "desire" and the "real." Founding its "revolutionary" imperative on the fusion of spiritual intensity and corporeal immediacy, this theatre proposes the confluence of art and politics as a violent spectacle binding "victim" and "audience" in a drama of sacrifice. But rather than the sacrifice of conventional tragedy (the contrived ruin of "drawing room" stages), the Revolutionary Theatre thus conceived would shatter the walls of dramatic artifice, bursting the confines of traditional form and inherited meaning. Its ability to "change" and not just represent "the world" presumes a refusal of customary theatrical practice, that medium of artificial rather than genuine "agony" wherein dramatic imitation mirrors a social order upheld by rigid adherence to sanctioned scripts.

And yet, when we turn to *Dutchman* itself, what do we find but a game of mirrors, masks, and deceptions, those elemental ingredients of theatrical craft where "blood" is always dyed water and the catharsis it "moves" us to always ersatz and ephemeral? From the opening dumbshow, when Lula and Clay enact an "encounter" of unnerving gazes through the ambiguous medium of "darkness" and "glass," the play unfolds as a nightmarish kaleidoscope of cryptic postures, startling challenges, and cunning retorts. To all appearances, Lula and Clay are equally theatrical creatures—one extravagantly "made up" in the guise of a demonic temptress (her "red hair" and "loud lipstick" set off by concealing sunglasses), the other hidden behind layers of alienating screens (magazine; "three-button suit and striped tie"; "mirrors ... curses in code"). Their entangled projections of racial identity and sexual appetite fuel fantasies of power and fulfillment, evoking but not challenging hackneyed scenerios of American cultural interaction. As these protagonists hurtle through an estranging space that is at once fake ("paste the lights, as admitted props") and realistic ("loud scream of the actual train"), we witness a ghoulish masquerade of seduction, menace, and delusion from which, seemingly, there is no exit, not even that of death.

Read thusly, *Dutchman* evidently offers a mirror-image of the vision set forth in "The Revolutionary Theatre." Here, conflict serves rather than subverts established canons, and the "victim's" sacrifice neutralizes rather than promotes the promise of his revolt. But, of course, to read *Dutchman* this way is to elevate the play's overt narrative over its subterranean alternative. For against the ritual implication of Lula's scripting and containment of Clay's potential agency—her effort to author his genealogy and direct him within a limited and intelligible repertoire of "types"—we should recall the singular, stunning moment of Clay's eruptive speech on the "black heart" that throbs beneath the veils of all theatrical "act, lies, device." Driven by a seething and robust lyricism, Clay rises to discard his mask, and the consuming need to deflect liberating violence that it satisfies. He rises to expound a self free of pretense and illusion, a "wanton" self prepared to enter the authentic moral and historical crucible of revolutionary avowal. Expressing the very will-to-transformation that Baraka champions in "The Revolutionary Theatre" and that

Lula herself imagines with fear and loathing—"you mix it up [...] Turning pages. Change, change, change. Till shit, I don't know you"—Clay thereby discloses a dynamic *anti*theatrical presence in the very drama that testifies to the repression and defeat of his desire.

The tension between Clay's speech and the dramatic continuum which it contests suggests that underlying the protagonists' exchanges, with their evocations of minstrelsy and "drawing room" flirtation, simmers a volatile crucible of judgment and insurrection. The effects of this double dramatic structure for the characters are alternately bracing and fatal, but for the audience they are no less consequential: if we read the enframing narrative as authoritative, we remain bound to the theatre as a site of sacrificial suppression, where all rebellious energies become mere functions of an unchangeable historical "reality"; if, to the contrary, we privilege the emergence of a "pure, pumping black" voice, we may take the play as an instrument of sacrificial excess, an incitement to "run through the streets" in fidelity to the "real" of emancipatory performance. Thereby establishing for the spectator the grounds for deciding between opposed views of dramatic meaning—each governed by distinctive notions of mimesis, action, catharsis, and identification—*Dutchman* returns us neither to the prefabricated theatre of the bourgeois auditorium nor to the improvised scaffold of the worker's meeting-hall, but instead to the theatre's origins as the most vitally expressive sphere of the *polis*, a nexus of the "political" and the "performative." In this, Baraka's play, notwithstanding changing details of social history and evolving conventions of theatrical style, retains its power to shock and to move, remaining, like its doomed but visionary hero, "a ghost of the future" we shall all compose together.

CHARACTERS

CLAY, twenty-year-old negro
LULA, thirty-year-old white woman
RIDERS OF COACH, white and black
YOUNG NEGRO
CONDUCTOR

In the flying underbelly of the city. Steaming hot, and summer on top, outside. Underground. The subway heaped in modern myth.

Opening scene is a man sitting in a subway seat, holding a magazine but looking vacantly just above its wilting pages. Occasionaly he looks blankly toward the window on his right. Dim lights and darkness whistling by against the glass. [Or pass the lights, as admitted props, right on the subway windows. Have them move, even dim and flicker. But give the sense of speed. Also stations, whether the train is stopped or the glitter and activity of these stations merely flashes by the windows.]

The man is sitting alone. That is, only his seat is visible, though the rest of the car is outfitted as a complete subway car. But only his seat is shown. There might be, for a time, as the play begins, a loud scream of the actual train. And it can recur throughout the play, or continue on a lower key once the dialogue starts.

The tram slows after a time, pulling to a brief stop at one of the stations. The man looks idly up, until he sees a woman's face staring at him through the window; when it realizes that the man has noticed the face, it begins very premeditatedly to smile. The man smiles too, for a moment, without a trace of self-consciousness. Almost an instinctive though undesirable response. Then a kind of awkwardness or embarrassment sets in, and the man makes to look away, is further embarrassed, so he brings back his eyes to where the face was, but by now the train is moving again, and the face would seem to be left behind by the way the man turns his head to look back through the other windows at the slowly fading platform. He smiles then; more comfortably confident, hoping perhaps that his memory of this brief encounter will be pleasant. And then he is idle again.

Scene 1

Train roars. Lights flash outside the windows.

LULA *enters from the rear of the car in bright, skimpy summer clothes and sandals. She carries a net bag full of paper books, fruit, and other anonymous articles. She is wearing sunglasses, which she pushes up on her forehead from time to time.* LULA *is a tall, slender, beautiful woman with long red hair hanging straight down her back, wearing only loud lipstick in somebody's good taste. She is eating an apple, very daintily. Coming down the car toward* CLAY.

She stops beside CLAY'S *seat and hangs languidly from the strap, still managing to eat the apple. It is apparent that she is going to sit in the seat next to* CLAY, *and that she is only waiting for him to notice her before she sits.*

CLAY *sits as before, looking just beyond his magazine, now and again pulling the magazine slowly back and forth in front of his face in a hopeless effort to fan himself. Then he sees the woman hanging there beside him and he looks up into her face, smiling quizzically.*

LULA: Hello.

CLAY: Uh, hi're you?

LULA: I'm going to sit down ... O.K.?

CLAY: Sure.

LULA: [*Swings down onto the seat, pushing her legs straight out as if she is very weary.*] Oooof! Too much weight.

CLAY: Ha, doesn't look like much to me. [*Leaning back against the window, a little surprised and maybe stiff.*]

LULA: It's so anyway.

[*And she moves her toes in the sandals, then pulls her right leg up on the left knee, better to inspect the bottoms of the sandals and the back of her heel. She appears for a second not to notice that* CLAY *is sitting next*

139

to her or that she has spoken to him just a second before. CLAY *looks at the magazine, then out the black window. As he does this, she turns very quickly toward him.*]

Weren't you staring at me through the window?

CLAY: [*Wheeling around and very much stiffened.*] What?

LULA: Weren't you staring at me through the window? At the last stop?

CLAY: Staring at you? What do you mean?

LULA: Don't you know what staring means?

CLAY: I saw you through the window ... if that's what it means. I don't know if I was staring. Seems to me you were staring through the window at me.

LULA: I was. But only after I'd turned around and saw you staring through that window down in the vicinity of my ass and legs.

CLAY: Really?

LULA: Really. I guess you were just taking those idle potshots. Nothing else to do. Run your mind over people's flesh.

CLAY: Oh boy. Wow, now I admit I was looking in your direction. But the rest of that weight is yours.

LULA: I suppose.

CLAY: Staring through train windows is weird business. Much weirder than staring very sedately at abstract asses.

LULA: That's why I came looking through the window ... so you'd have more than that to go on. I even smiled at you.

CLAY: That's right.

LULA: I even got into this train, going some other way than mine. Walked down the aisle ... searching you out.

CLAY: Really? That's pretty funny.

LULA: That's pretty funny ... God, you're dull.

CLAY: Well, I'm sorry, lady, but I really wasn't prepared for party talk.

140

LULA: No, you're not. What are you prepared for? [*Wrapping the apple core in a Kleenex and dropping it on the floor.*]

CLAY: [*Takes her conversation as pure sex talk. He turns to confront her squarely with this idea.*] I'm prepared for anything. How about you?

LULA: [*Laughing loudly and cutting it off abruptly.*] What do you think you're doing?

CLAY: What?

LULA: You think I want to pick you up, get you to take me somewhere and screw me, huh?

CLAY: Is that the way I look?

LULA: You look like you been trying to grow a beard. That's exactly what you look like. You look like you live in New Jersey with your parents and are trying to grow a beard. That's what. You look like you've been reading Chinese poetry and drinking lukewarm sugarless tea.[*Laughs, uncrossing and recrossing her legs.*] You look like death eating a soda cracker.

CLAY: [*Cocking his head from one side to the other, embarrassed and trying to make some comeback, but also intrigued by what the woman is saying ... even the sharp city coarseness of her voice, which is still a kind of gentle sidewalk throb.*] Really? I look like all that?

LULA: Not all of it. [*She feints a seriousness to cover an actual somber tone.*] I lie a lot. [*Smiling.*] It helps me control the world.

CLAY: [*Relieved and laughing louder than the humor.*] Yeah, I bet.

LULA: But it's true, most of it, right? Jersey? Your bumpy neck?

CLAY: How'd you know all that? Huh? Really, I mean about Jersey ... and even the beard. I met you before? You know Warren Enright?

LULA: You tried to make it with your sister when you were ten.

[CLAY *leans back hard against the back of the seat, his eyes opening now, still trying to look amused.*]

But I succeeded a few weeks ago. [*She starts to laugh again.*]

CLAY: What're you talking about? Warren tell you that? You're a friend of Georgia's?

141

LULA: I told you I lie. I don't know your sister. I don't know Warren Enright.

CLAY: You mean you're just picking these things out of the air?

LULA: Is Warren Enright a tall skinny black black boy with a phony English accent?

CLAY: I figured you knew him.

LULA: But I don't. I just figured you would know somebody like that. [*Laughs.*]

CLAY: Yeah, yeah.

LULA: You're probably on your way to his house now.

CLAY: That's right.

LULA: [*Putting her hand on* CLAY's *closest knee, drawing it from the knee up to the thigh's hinge, then removing it, watching his face very closely, and continuing to laugh, perhaps more gently than before.*] Dull, dull, dull. I bet you think I'm exciting.

CLAY: You're O.K.

LULA: Am I exciting you now?

CLAY: Right. That's not what's supposed to happen?

LULA: How do I know? [*She returns her hand, without moving it, then takes it away and plunges it in her bag to draw out an apple.*] You want this?

CLAY: Sure.

LULA: [*She gets one out of the bag for herself.*] Eating apples together is always the first step. Or walking up uninhabited Seventh Avenue in the twenties on weekends. [*Bites and giggles, glancing at Clay and speaking in loose sing-song.*] Can get you involved ... boy! Get us involved. Um-huh. [*Mock seriousness.*] Would you like to get involved with me, Mister Man?

CLAY: [*Trying to be as flippant as Lula, whacking happily at the apple.*] Sure. Why not? A beautiful woman like you. Huh, I'd be a fool not to.

LULA: And I bet you're sure you know what you're talking about. [*Taking him a little roughly by the wrist, so he cannot eat the apple, then shaking the wrist.*] I bet you're sure of almost everything anybody ever asked you about ... right? [*Shakes his wrist harder.*] Right?

CLAY: Yeah, right ... Wow, you're pretty strong, you know? Whatta you, a lady

142

wrestler or something?

LULA: What's wrong with lady wrestlers? And don't answer because you never knew any. Huh. [*Cynically.*] That's for sure. They don't have any lady wrestlers in that part of Jersey. That's for sure.

CLAY: Hey, you still haven't told me how you know so much about me.

LULA: I told you I didn't know anything about *you* ... you're a well-known type.

CLAY: Really?

LULA: Or at least I know the type very well. And your skinny English friend too.

CLAY: Anonymously?

LULA: [*Settles back in seat, single-mindedly finishing her apple and humming snatches of rhythm and blues song.*] What?

CLAY: Without knowing us specifically?

LULA: Oh boy. [*Looking quickly at Clay.*] What a face. You know, you could be a handsome man.

CLAY: I can't argue with you.

LULA: [*Vague, off center response.*] What?

CLAY: [*Raising his voice, thinking the train noise has drowned part of his sentence.*] I can't argue with you.

LULA: My hair is turning gray. A gray hair for each year and type I've come through.

CLAY: Why do you want to sound so old?

LULA: But it's always gentle when it starts. [*Attention drifting.*] Hugged against tenements, day or night.

CLAY: What?

LULA: [*Refocusing.*] Hey, why don't you take me to that party you're going to?

CLAY: You must be a friend of Warren's to know about the party.

LULA: Wouldn't you like to take me to the party? [*Imitates clinging vine.*] Oh, come on, ask me to your party.

CLAY: Of course I'll ask you to come with me to the party. And I'll bet you're a friend of Warren's.

LULA: Why not be a friend of Warren's? Why not? [*Taking his arm.*] Have you asked me yet?

CLAY: How can I ask you when I don't know your name?

LULA: Are you talking to my name?

CLAY: What is it, a secret?

LULA: I'm Lena the Hyena.

CLAY: The famous woman poet?

LULA: Poetess! The same!

CLAY: Well, you know so much about me ... what's my name?

LULA: Morris the Hyena.

CLAY: The famous woman poet?

LULA: The same. [*Laughing and going into her bag.*] You want another apple?

CLAY: Can't make it, lady. I only have to keep one doctor away a day.

LULA: I bet your name is ... something like ... uh, Gerald or Walter, Huh?

CLAY: God, no.

LULA: Lloyd, Norman? One of those hopeless colored names creeping out of New Jersey. Leonard? Gag ...

CLAY: Like Warren?

LULA: Definitely. Just exactly like Warren. Or Everett.

CLAY: Gag ...

LULA: Well, for sure, it's not Willie.

CLAY: It's Clay.

LULA: Clay? Really? Clay what?

CLAY: Take your pick. Jackson, Johnson, or Williams.

LULA: Oh, really? Good for you. But it's got to be Williams. You're too pretentious to be a Jackson or Johnson.

CLAY: Thass right.

LULA: But Clay's O.K.

CLAY: So's Lena.

LULA: It's Lula.

CLAY: Oh?

LULA: Lula the Hyena.

CLAY: Very good.

LULA: [*Starts laughing again.*] Now you say to me, "Lula, Lula, why don't you go to this party with me tonight?" It's your turn, and let those be your lines.

CLAY: Lula, why don't you go to this party with me tonight, huh?

LULA: Say my name twice before you ask, and no huh's.

CLAY: Lula, Lula, why don't you go to this party with me tonight?

LULA: I'd like to go, Clay, but how can you ask me to go when you barely know me?

CLAY: That is strange, isn't it?

LULA: . What kind of reaction is that? You're supposed to say, "Aw, come on, we'll get to know each other better at the party."

CLAY: That's pretty corny.

LULA: What are you into anyway? [*Looking at him half sullenly but still amused.*] What thing are you playing at, Mister? Mister Clay Williams? [*Grabs his thigh, up near the crotch.*] What are you thinking about?

CLAY: Watch it now, you're gonna excite me for real.

LULA: [*Taking her hand away and throwing her apple core through the window.*] I bet. [*She slumps in the seat and is heavily silent.*]

CLAY: I thought you knew everything about me? What happened?

[LULA *looks at him, then looks slowly away, then over where the other aisle would be. Noise of the train. She reaches in her bag and pulls out one of the paper books. She puts it on her leg and thumbs the pages listlessly.* CLAY *cocks his head to see the title of the book. Noise of the train.* LULA *flips pages and her eyes drift. Both remain silent.*]

Are you going to the party with me, Lula?

LULA: [*Bored and not even looking.*] I don't even know you.

CLAY: You said you know my type.

LULA: [*Strangely irritated.*] Don't get smart with me, Buster. I know you like the palm of my hand.

CLAY: The one you eat the apples with?

LULA: Yeh. And the one I open doors late Saturday evening with. That's my door. Up at the top of the stairs. Five flights. Above a lot of Italians and lying Americans. And scrape carrots with. Also … [*Looks at him.*] the same hand I unbutton my dress with, or let my skirt fall down. Same hand. Lover.

CLAY: Are you angry about anything? Did I say something wrong?

LULA: Everything you say is wrong. [*Mock smile.*]That's what makes you so attractive. Ha. In that funnybook jacket with all the buttons.[*More animate, taking hold of his jacket.*] What've you got that jacket and tie on in all this heat for? And why're you wearing a jacket and tie like that? Did your people ever burn witches or start revolutions over the price of tea? Boy, those narrow-shoulder clothes come from a tradition you ought to feel oppressed by. A three-button suit. What right do you have to be wearing a three-button suit and striped tie? Your grandfather was a slave, he didn't go to Harvard.

CLAY: My grandfather was a night watchman.

LULA: And you went to a colored college where everybody thought they were Averell Harriman.

CLAY: All except me.

LULA: And who did you think you were? Who do you think you are now?

CLAY: [*Laughs as if to make light of the whole trend of the conversation.*] Well, in college I thought I was Baudelaire. But I've slowed down since.

146

LULA: I bet you never once thought you were a black nigger.

[*Mock serious, then she howls with laughter.* CLAY *is stunned but after initial reaction, he quickly tries to appreciate the humor.* LULA *almost shrieks.*] A black Baudelaire.

CLAY: That's right.

LULA: Boy, are you corny. I take back what I said before. Everything you say is not wrong. It's perfect. You should be on television.

CLAY: You act like you're on television already.

LULA: That's because I'm an actress.

CLAY: I thought so.

LULA: Well, you're wrong. I'm no actress. I told you I always lie. I'm nothing, honey, and don't you ever forget it. [*Lighter.*] Although my mother was a Communist. The only person in my family ever to amount to anything.

CLAY: My mother was a Republican.

LULA: And your father voted for the man rather than the party.

CLAY: Right!

LULA: Yea for him. Yea, yea for him.

CLAY: Yea!

LULA: And yea for America where he is free to vote for the mediocrity of his choice! Yea!

CLAY: Yea!

LULA: And yea for both your parents who even though they differ about so crucial a matter as the body politic still forged a union of love and sacrifice that was destined to flower at the birth of the noble Clay ... what's your middle name?

CLAY: Clay.

LULA: A union of love and sacrifice that was destined to flower at the birth of the noble Clay Clay Williams. Yea! And most of all yea yea for you, Clay Clay. The Black Baudelaire! Yes! [*And with knifelike cynicism.*] My Christ. My Christ.

147

CLAY: Thank you, ma'am.

LULA: May the people accept you as a ghost of the future. And love you, that you might not kill them when you can.

CLAY: What?

LULA: You're a murderer, Clay, and you know it. [*Her voice darkening with significance.*] You know goddamn well what I mean.

CLAY: I do?

LULA: So we'll pretend the air is light and full of perfume.

CLAY: [*Sniffing at her blouse.*] It is.

LULA: And we'll pretend the people cannot see you. That is, the citizens. And that you are free of your own history. And I am free of my history. We'll pretend that we are both anonymous beauties smashing along through the city's entrails. [*She yells as loud as she can.*] GROOVE!

Black

Scene 2

Scene is the same as before, though now there are other seats visible in the car. And throughout the scene other people get on the subway. There are maybe one or two seated in the car as the scene opens, though neither CLAY *nor* LULA *notices them.* CLAY'*s tie is open.* LULA *is hugging his arm.*

CLAY: The party!

LULA: I know it'll be something good. You can come in with me, looking casual and significant. I'll be strange, haughty, and silent, and walk with long slow strides.

CLAY: Right.

LULA: When you get drunk, pat me once, very lovingly on the flanks, and I'll look at you cryptically, licking my lips.

CLAY: It sounds like something we can do.

LULA: You'll go around talking to young men about your mind, and to old men about your plans. If you meet a very close friend who is also with someone like me, we can stand together, sipping our drinks and exchanging codes of lust. The atmosphere will be slithering in love and half-love and very open moral decision.

CLAY: Great. Great.

LULA: And everyone will pretend they don't know your name, and then ... [*She pauses heavily.*] later, when they have to, they'll claim a friendship that denies your sterling character.

CLAY: [*Kissing her neck and fingers.*] And then what?

LULA: Then? Well, then we'll go down the street, late night, eating apples and winding very deliberately toward my house.

CLAY: Deliberately?

LULA: I mean, we'll look in all the shopwindows, and make fun of the queers. Maybe we'll meet a Jewish Buddhist and flatten his conceits over some very pretentious coffee.

149

CLAY: In honor of whose God?

LULA: Mine.

CLAY: Who is ... ?

LULA: Me ... and you?

CLAY: A corporate Godhead.

LULA: Exactly. Exactly. [*Notices one of the other people entering.*]

CLAY: Go on with the chronicle. Then what happens to us?

LULA: [*A mild depression, but she still makes her description triumphant and increasingly direct.*] To my house, of course.

CLAY: Of course.

LULA: And up the narrow steps of the tenement.

CLAY: You live in a tenement?

LULA: Wouldn't live anywhere else. Reminds me specifically of my novel form of insanity.

CLAY: Up the tenement stairs.

LULA: And with my apple-eating hand I push open the door and lead you, my tender big-eyed prey, into my ... God, what can I call it ... into my hovel.

CLAY: Then what happens?

LULA: After the dancing and games, after the long drinks and long walks, the real fun begins.

CLAY: Ah, the real fun. [*Embarrassed, in spite of himself.*] Which is ... ?

LULA: [*Laughs at him.*] Real fun in the dark house. Hah! Real fun in the dark house, high up above the street and the ignorant cowboys. I lead you in, holding your wet hand gently in my hand ...

CLAY: Which is not wet?

LULA: Which is dry as ashes.

CLAY: And cold?

LULA: Don't think you'll get out of your responsibility that way. It's not cold at all. You Fascist! Into my dark living room. Where we'll sit and talk endlessly, endlessly.

CLAY: About what?

LULA: About what? About your manhood, what do you think? What do you think we've been talking about all this time?

CLAY: Well, I didn't know it was that. That's for sure. Every other thing in the world but that. [*Notices another person entering, looks quickly, almost involuntarily up and down the car, seeing the other people in the car.*] Hey, I didn't even notice when those people got on.

LULA: Yeah, I know.

CLAY: Man, this subway is slow.

LULA: Yeah, I know.

CLAY: Well, go on. We were talking about my manhood.

LULA: We still are. All the time.

CLAY: We were in your living room.

LULA: My dark living room. Talking endlessly.

CLAY: About my manhood.

LULA: I'll make you a map of it. Just as soon as we get to my house.

CLAY: Well, that's great.

LULA: One of the things we do while we talk. And screw.

CLAY: [*Trying to make his smile broader and less shaky.*] We finally got there.

LULA: And you'll call my rooms black as a grave. You'll say, "This place is like Juliet's tomb."

CLAY: [*Laughs.*] I might.

LULA: I know. You've probably said it before.

CLAY: And is that all? The whole grand tour?

LULA: Not all. You'll say to me very close to my face, many, many times, you'll say, even whisper, that you love me.

CLAY: Maybe I will.

LULA: And you'll be lying.

CLAY: I wouldn't lie about something like that.

LULA: Hah. It's the only kind of thing you will lie about. Especially if you think it'll keep me alive.

CLAY: Keep you alive? I don't understand.

LULA: [*Bursting out laughing, but too shrilly.*] Don't understand? Well, don't look at me. It's the path I take, that's all. Where both feet take me when I set them down. One in front of the other.

CLAY: Morbid. Morbid. You sure you're not an actress?. All that self-aggrandizement.

LULA: Well, I told you I wasn't an actress ... but I also told you I lie all the time. Draw your own conclusions.

CLAY: Morbid. Morbid. You sure you're not an actress? All scribed? There's no more?

LULA: I've told you all I know. Or almost all.

CLAY: There's no funny parts?

LULA: I thought it was all funny.

CLAY: But you mean peculiar, not ha-ha.

LULA: You don't know what I mean.

CLAY: Well, tell me the almost part then. You said almost all. What else? I want the whole story.

LULA: [*Searching aimlessly through her bag. She begins to talk breathlessly, with a light and silly tone.*] All stories are whole stories. All of 'em. Our whole story ... nothing but change. How could things go on like that forever? Huh? [*Slaps him on the shoulder, begins finding things in her bag, taking them out and throwing them over her shoulder into the aisle.*] Except I do go on as I do. Apples and long walks with deathless intelligent lovers. But you mix it up. Look out the window, all the time. Turning pages. Change change change. Till, shit, I don't know you. Wouldn't, for that matter. You're too serious. I bet you're even too serious to be psychoanalyzed. Like all those Jewish poets from Yonkers, who leave their mothers looking for other mothers, or others' mothers, on whose baggy tits they lay their fumbling heads. Their poems are always funny, and all about sex.

CLAY: They sound great. Like movies.

LULA: But you change. [*Blankly.*] And things work on you till you hate them;

[*More people come into the train. They come closer to the couple, some of them not sitting, but swinging drearily on the straps, staring at the two with uncertain interest.*]

CLAY: Wow. All these people, so suddenly. They must all come from the same place.

LULA: Right. That they do.

CLAY: Oh? You know about them too?

LULA: Oh yeah. About them more than I know about you. Do they frighten you?

CLAY: Frighten me? Why should they frighten me?

LULA: 'Cause you're an escaped nigger.

CLAY: Yeah?

LULA: 'Cause you crawled through the wire and made tracks to my side.

CLAY: Wire?

LULA: Don't they have wire around plantations?

CLAY: You must be Jewish. All you can think about is wire. Plantations didn't have any wire. Plantations were big open whitewashed places like heaven, and everybody on 'em was grooved to be there. Just strummin' and hummin' all day.

LULA: Yes, yes.

153

CLAY: And that's how the blues was born.

LULA: Yes, yes. And that's how the blues was born. [*Begins to make up a song that becomes quickly hysterical. As she sings she rises from her seat, still throwing things out of her bag into the aisle, beginning a rhythmical shudder and twistlike wiggle, which she continues up and down the aisle, bumping into many of the standing people and tripping over the feet of those sitting. Each time she runs into a person she lets out a very vicious piece of profanity, wiggling and stepping all the time.*] And that's how the blues was born. Yes. Yes. Son of a bitch, get out of the way. Yes. Quack. Yes. Yes. And that's how the blues was born. Ten little niggers sitting on a limb, but none of them ever looked like him. [*Points to* CLAY, *returns toward the seat, with her hands extended for him to rise and dance with her.*] And that's how blues was born. Yes. Come on, Clay. Let's do the nasty. Rub bellies. Rub bellies.

CLAY: [*Waves his hands to refuse. He is embarrassed, but determined to get a kick out of the proceedings.*] Hey, what was in those apples? Mirror, mirror on the wall, who's the fairest one of all? Snow White, baby, and don't you forget it.

LULA: [*Grabbing for his hands, which he draws away.*] Come on, Clay. Let's rub bellies on the train. The nasty. The nasty. Do the gritty grind, like your ol' rag-head mammy. Grind till you lose your mind. Shake it, shake it, shake it, shake it! OOOOweeee! Come on, Clay. Let's do the choo-choo train shuffle, the navel scratcher.

CLAY: Hey, you coming on like the lady who smoked up her grass skirt.

LULA: [*Becoming annoyed that he will not dance, and becoming more animated as if to embarrass him still further.*] Come on, Clay … let's do the thing. Uhh! Uhh! Clay! Clay! You middle-class black bastard. Forget your social-working mother for a few seconds and let's knock stomachs. Clay, you liver-lipped white man. You would-be Christian. You ain't no nigger, you're just a dirty white man. Get up, Clay. Dance with me, Clay.

CLAY: Lula! Sit down, now. Be cool.

LULA: [*Mocking him, in wild dance.*] Be cool. Be cool. That's all you know … shaking that wildroot cream-oil on your knotty head, jackets buttoning up to your chin, so full of white man's words. Christ. God. Get up and scream at these people. Like scream meaningless shit in these hopeless faces. [*She screams at people in train, still dancing.*] Red trains cough Jewish underwear for keeps! Expanding smells of silence. Gravy snot whistling like sea birds. Clay. Clay, you got to break out. Don't sit there dying the way they want you to die. Get up.

CLAY: Oh, sit the fuck down. [*He moves to restrain her.*] Sit down, goddamn it.

LULA: [*Twisting out of his reach.*] Screw yourself, Uncle Tom. Thomas Woolly-head. [*Begins to dance a kind of jig, mocking* CLAY *with loud forced humor.*] There is Uncle Tom ... I mean, Uncle Thomas Woolly-Head. With old white matted mane. He hobbies on his wooden cane. Old Tom. Old Tom. Let the white man hump his ol' mama, and he jes' shuffle off in the woods and hide his gentle gray head. Ol' Thomas Woolly-Head.

> [*Some of the other riders are laughing now. A drunk gets up and joins* LULA *in her dance, singing, as best he can, her "song."* CLAY *gets up out of his seat and visibly scans the faces of the other riders.*]

CLAY: Lula! Lula!

> [*She is dancing and turning, still shouting as loud as she can. The drunk too is shouting, and waving his hands wildly.*]

Lula ... you dumb bitch. Why don't you stop it? [*He rushes half stumbling from his seat, and grabs one of her flailing arms.*]

LULA: Let me go! You black son of a bitch. [*She struggles against him.*] Let me go! Help!

> [CLAY *is dragging her towards her seat, and the drunk seeks to interfere. He grabs* CLAY *around the shoulders and begins wrestling with him.* CLAY *clubs the drunk to the floor without releasing* LULA *who is still screaming.* CLAY *finally gets her to the seat and throws her into it.*]

CLAY: Now you shut the hell up. [*Grabbing her shoulders.*] Just shut up. You don't know what you're talking about. You don't know anything. So just keep your stupid mouth closed.

LULA: You're afraid of white people. And your father was. Uncle Tom Big Lip!

CLAY: [*Slaps her as hard as he can, across the mouth.* LULA's *head bangs against the back of the seat. When she raises it again,* CLAY *slaps her again.*] Now shut up and let me talk.

[*He turns toward the other riders, some of whom are sitting on the edge
of their seats. The drunk is on one knee, rubbing his head, and singing
softly the same song. He shuts up too when he sees* CLAY *watching him.
The others go back to newspapers or stare out the windows.*]

Shit, you don't have any sense, Lula, nor feelings either. I could murder you
now. Such a tiny ugly throat. I could squeeze it flat, and watch you turn blue,
on a humble. For dull kicks. And all these weak-faced ofays squatting around
here, staring over their papers at me. Murder them too. Even if they expected
it. That man there … [*Points to well-dressed man.*] I could rip that Times right
out of his hand, as skinny and middle-classed as I am, I could rip that paper
out of his hand and just as easily rip out his throat. It takes no great effort.
For what? To kill you soft idiots? You don't understand anything but luxury.

LULA: You fool!

CLAY: [*Pushing her against the seat.*] I'm not telling you again, Tallulah Bankhead!
Luxury. In your face and your fingers. You telling me what I ought to do.

   [*Sudden scream frightening the whole coach.*]

Well, don't! Don't you tell me anything! If I'm a middle-class fake white man
… let me be. And let me be in the way I want. [*Through his teeth.*] I'll rip your
lousy breasts off! Let me be who I feel like being. Uncle Tom. Thomas.
Whoever. It's none of your business. You don't know anything except what's
there for you to see. An act. Lies. Device. Not the pure heart, the pumping
black heart. You don't ever know that. And I sit here, in this buttoned-up suit,
to keep myself from cutting all your throats. I mean wantonly. You great lib-
erated whore! You fuck some black man, and right away you're an expert on
black people. What a lotta shit that is. The only thing you know is that you
come if he bangs you hard enough. And that's all. The belly rub? You wanted
to do the belly rub? Shit, you don't even know how. You don't know how.
That ol' dipty-dip shit you do, rolling your ass like an elephant. That's not
my kind of belly rub. Belly rub is not Queens. Belly rub is dark places, with
big hats and overcoats held up with one arm. Belly rub hates you. Old baldheaded four-eyed ofays popping their fingers … and don't know yet what they're
doing. They say, "I love Bessie Smith." And don't even understand that Bessie
Smith is saying, "Kiss my ass, kiss my black unruly ass." Before love, suffering, desire, anything you can explain, she's saying, and very plainly, "Kiss my

black ass." And if you don't know that, it's you that's doing the kissing.

Charlie Parker? Charlie Parker. All the hip white boys scream for Bird. And Bird saying, "Up your ass, feeble-minded ofay! Up your ass." And they sit there talking about the tortured genius of Charlie Parker. Bird would've played not a note of music if he just walked up to East Sixty-seventh Street and killed the first ten white people he saw. Not a note! And I'm the great would-be poet. Yes. That's right! Poet. Some kind of bastard literature ... all it needs is a simple knife thrust. Just let me bleed you, you loud whore, and one poem vanished. A whole people of neurotics, struggling to keep from being sane. And the only thing that would cure the neurosis would be your murder. Simple as that. I mean if I murdered you, then other white people would begin to understand me. You understand? No. I guess not. If Bessie Smith had killed some white people she wouldn't have needed that music. She could have talked very straight and plain about the world. No metaphors. No grunts. No wiggles in the dark of her soul. Just straight two and two are four. Money. Power. Luxury. Like that. All of them. Crazy niggers turning their backs on sanity. When all it needs is that simple act. Murder. Just murder! Would make us all sane. [*Suddenly weary.*] Ahhh. Shit. But who needs it? I'd rather be a fool. Insane. Safe with my words, and no deaths, and clean, hard thoughts, urging me to new conquests. My people's madness. Hah! That's a laugh. My people. They don't need me to claim them. They got legs and arms of their own. Personal insanities. Mirrors. They don't need all those words. They don't need any defense. But listen, though, one more thing. And you tell this to your father, who's probably the kind of man who needs to know at once. So he can plan ahead. Tell him not to preach so much rationalism and cold logic to these niggers. Let them alone. Let them sing curses at you in code and see your filth as simple lack of style. Don't make the mistake, through some irresponsible surge of Christian charity, of talking too much about the advantages of Western rationalism, or the great intellectual legacy of the white man, or maybe they'll begin to listen. And then, maybe one day, you'll find they actually do understand exactly what you are talking about, all these fantasy people. All these blues people. And on that day, as sure as shit, when you really believe you can "accept" them into your fold, as half-white trusties late of the subject peoples. With no more blues, except the very old ones, and not a watermelon in sight, the great missionary heart will have triumphed, and all of those ex-coons will be stand-up Western men, with eyes for clean hard useful lives, sober, pious and sane, and they'll murder you. They'll murder you, and have very rational explanations. Very much like your own. They'll cut your throats,

157

and drag you out to the edge of your cities so the flesh can fall away from your bones, in sanitary isolation.

LULA: [*Her voice takes on a different, more businesslike quality.*] I've heard enough.

CLAY: [*Reaching for his books.*] I bet you have. I guess I better collect my stuff and get off this train. Looks like we won't be acting out that little pageant you outlined before.

LULA: No. We won't. You're right about that, at least. [*She turns to look quickly around the rest of the car.*] All right!

[*The others respond.*]

CLAY: [*Bending across the girl to retrieve his belongings.*] Sorry, baby, I don't think we could make it.

[*As he is bending over her, the girl brings up a small knife and plunges it into* CLAY's *chest. Twice. He slumps across her knees, his mouth working stupidly.*]

LULA: Sorry is right. [*Turning to the others in the car who have already gotten up from their seats.*] Sorry is the rightest thing you've said. Get this man off me! Hurry, now!

[*The others come and drag* CLAY's *body down the aisle.*]

Open the door and throw his body out.

[*They throw him off.*]

And all of you get off at the next stop.

[LULA *busies herself straightening her things. Getting everything in order. She takes out a notebook and makes a quick scribbling note. Drops it in her bag. The train apparently stops and all the others get off, leaving her alone in the coach.*

Very soon a YOUNG NEGRO *of about twenty comes into the coach, with a couple of books under his arm. He sits a few seats in back of* LULA. *When he is seated she turns and gives him a long slow look. He looks up from his book and drops the book on his lap. Then an old* NEGRO CONDUCTOR *comes into the car, doing a sort of restrained soft shoe, and half mumbling the words of some song. He looks at the young man,*] *briefly, with a quick greeting.*]

CONDUCTOR: Hey, brother!

YOUNG MAN: Hey.

[*The* CONDUCTOR *continues down the aisle with his little dance and the mumbled song.* LULA *turns to stare at him and follows his movements down the aisle. The* CONDUCTOR *tips his hat when he reaches her seat, and continues out the car.*]

CURTAIN

FUNNYHOUSE OF A NEGRO

ADRIENNE KENNEDY

———⟫●⟪———

Obie award-winning original production by
Barr-Albee-Wilder, at the East End Theatre, 1964,
directed by Michael Kahn

INTRODUCTION

by Adrienne Kennedy

Funnyhouse of a Negro was completed in Rome, Italy, the week before our second son Adam was born in Salvator Mundi Hospital. I was twenty-nine. And I believed if I didn't complete this play before my child's birth and before my thirtieth birthday, I would never finish it.

My son Joe Jr. and I lived in a beautiful tranquil apartment about fifteen minutes from Piazza di Spagna. Hall steps led to a miniature living room that opened onto a terrace that overlooked Rome. I sat at the dark desk in the cool mimature room with pages I had started in Ghana on the campus of Legon (Achimoto Guest House). They seemed a disjointed raging mass of paragraphs typed on thin transparent typing paper I had bought at the campus of Legon's bookstore. The entire month of July each morning when my son Joe went to Fregene with a play group of children run by an American couple, I tried to put the pages in order.

Ten months earlier at the end of September 1960 my husband Joe and I left New York on the Queen Elizabeth. It was my first sight of Europe and Africa. We stopped in London, Paris, Madrid, Casablanca and lived in Monrovia, Liberia, before we settled in Accra, Ghana.

The imagery in *Funnyhouse of a Negro* was born by seeing those places: Queen Victoria, the statue in front of Buckingham Palace, Patrice Lumumba on posters and small cards all over Ghana, murdered just after we arrived in Ghana, fall 1960; the savannahs in Ghana, the white frankopenny trees; the birth of Ghana newly freed from England, scenes of Nkrumah on cloth murals and posters. And this was the first time in my life that it was impossible to keep my hair straightened. In Ghana and for the rest of the thirteen month trip I stopped straightening my hair.

After Ghana in February 1961 I had chosen Rome to wait for my husband to finish his work in Nigeria. Rome was the land my high school Latin teacher had sung of: the Forum, the Tiber, the Palatine, Caesar. When my son Joe was at the Parioli Day School I walked in the Forum for hours that spring of 1961. I rode the bus on the Appian Way, the rhythms of my teacher speaking out loud in my mind. Wandering through Rome while Joe was at school I was more alone than I have ever been. At noon I returned to the Penstoni Sabrina for lunch, often a pasta soup made of star shaped pasta, then went into our room while waiting for my son to return on the bus at the American Embassy and stared at the pages. There were paragraphs about Patrice Lumumba and Queen Victoria. I had always liked the Duchess of Hapsburg since I'd seen the Chapultapec Palace in Mexico. There were lines about her. But the main character talked in monologues about her hair and savannahs in Africa. At that moment *Funnyhouse of Negro* and *The Owl Answers* were all a part of one work. It wasn't until late July and the impetus of my son's impending birth that the two works split apart and my character Sarah (with her selves Queen Victoria, Patrice Lumumba, Duchess of Hapsburg and Jesus) was born.

In May, two months earlier, my mother had written me that my father had left Cleveland and returned to Georgia to live after thirty-five years. I cried when I read the letter, walking from American Express up the Piazza di Spagna steps. So Jesus (who I had always mixed with my social worker father) and the landscape and memories of Georgia and my grandparents became intertwined with the paragraphs on the Ghanian savannahs and Lumumba and his murder.

So trying (for the first time in my life) to comb my unstraightened hair, trying to out race the birth of my child, rereading the divorce news letters from my mother ... in the July Italian summer mornings, alone in the miniature room, near the Roman Forum, I finished *Funnyhouse of a Negro* the last week of July 1961. Our son Adam was born August 1.

CHARACTERS

NEGRO-SARAH

DUCHESS OF HAPSBURG, One of herselves

QUEEN VICTORIA REGINA, One of herselves

JESUS, One of herselves

PATRICE LUMUMBA, One of herselves

SARAH'S LANDLADY, Funnyhouse Lady

RAYMOND, Funnyhouse Man

THE MOTHER

Author's Note:

Funnyhouse of a Negro is perhaps clearest and most explicit when the play is placed in the girl Sarah's room. The center of the stage works well as her room, allowing the rest of the stage as the place for herselves. Her room should have a bed, a writing table and a mirror. Near her bed is a statue of Queen Victoria; other objects might be her photographs and her books. When she is placed in her room with her belongings, then the director is free to let the rest of the play happen around her.

BEGINNING: *Before the closed Curtain* A WOMAN *dressed in a white nightgown walks across the Stage carrying before her a bald head. She moves as one in a trance and is mumbling something inaudible to herself. Her hair is wild, straight and black and falls to her waist. As she moves, she gives the effect of one in a dream. She crosses the Stage from Right to Left. Before she has barely vanished, the CURTAIN opens. It is a white satin Curtain of a cheap material and a ghastly white, a material that brings to mind the interior of a cheap casket, parts of it are frayed and look as if it has been gnawed by rats.*

SCENE: *Two women are sitting in what appears to be a Queen's chamber. It is set in the middle of the Stage in a strong white LIGHT, while the rest of the Stage is in unnatural BLACKNESS. The quality of the white light is unreal and ugly. The Queen's chamber consists of a dark monumental bed resembling an ebony tomb, a low, dark chandelier with candles, and wine-colored walls. Flying about are great black RAVENS.* QUEEN VICTORIA *is standing before her bed holding a small mirror in her hand. On the white pillow of her bed is a dark, indistinguishable object.* THE DUCHESS OF HAPS-BURG *is standing at the foot of the bed. Her back is to us as is the* QUEEN's. *Throughout the entire scene, they do not move.* BOTH WOMEN *are dressed in royal gowns of white, a white similar to the white of the Curtain, the material cheap satin. Their headpieces are white and of a net that falls over their faces. From beneath both their headpieces springs a headful of wild kinky hair. Although in this scene we do not see their faces, I will describe them now. They look exactly alike and will wear masks or be made up to appear a whitish yellow. It is an alabaster face, the skin drawn tightly over the high cheekbones, great dark eyes that seem gouged out of the head, a high forehead, a full red mouth and a head of frizzy hair. If the characters do not wear a mask then the face must be highly powdered and possess a hard expressionless quality and a stillness as in the face of Death. We hear KNOCKING.*

VICTORIA: [*Listening to the knocking.*] It is my father. He is arriving again for the night. [*The* DUCHESS *makes no reply.*] He comes through the jungle to find me. He never tires of his journey.

DUCHESS: How dare he enter the castle, he who is the darkest of them all, the darkest one? My mother looked like a white woman, hair as straight as any white woman's. And at least I am yellow, but he is black, the blackest one of them all. I hoped he was dead. Yet he still comes through the jungle to find me.

[*The KNOCKING is louder.*]

VICTORIA: He never tires of the journey, does he, Duchess? [*Looking at herself in the mirror.*]

DUCHESS: How dare he enter the castle of Queen Victoria Regina, Monarch of England? It is because of him that my mother died. The wild black beast put his hands on her. She died.

VICTORIA: Why does he keep returning? He keeps returning forever, coming back ever and keeps coming back forever. He is my father.

DUCHESS: He is a black Negro.

VICTORIA: He is my father. I am tied to the black Negro. He came when I was a child in the south, before I was born he haunted my conception, diseased my birth.

DUCHESS: Killed my mother.

VICTORIA: My mother was the light. She was the lightest one. She looked like a white woman.

DUCHESS: We are tied to him unless, of course, he should die.

VICTORIA: But he is dead.

DUCHESS: And he keeps returning.

[*The KNOCKING is louder; BLACKOUT. The LIGHTS go out in the Chamber. Onto the Stage from the Left comes the FIGURE in the white nightgown carrying the bald head. This time we hear her speak.*]

MOTHER: Black man, black man, I never should have let a black man put his hands on me. The wild black beast raped me and now my skull is shining. [*She disappears to the Right.*]

[*Now the LIGHT is focused on a single white square wall that is to the Left of the Stage, that is suspended and stands alone, of about five feet in dimension and width. It stands with the narrow part facing the audience. A CHARACTER steps through. She is a faceless, dark character with a hangman's rope about her neck and red blood on the part that would be her face. She is the NEGRO. The most noticeable aspect of*] *her looks is her wild kinky hair. It is a ragged head with a patch of hair missing from the crown which the* NEGRO *carries in her hand. She is dressed in black. She steps slowly through the wall, stands still before it and begins her monologue.*]

NEGRO: Part of the time I live with Raymond, part of the time with God, Maxmillian and Albert Saxe Coburg. I live in my room. It is a small room on the top floor of a brownstone in the West Nineties in New York, a room filled with my dark old volumes, a narrow bed and on the wall old photographs of castles and monarchs of England. It is also Victoria's chamber. Queen Victoria Regina's. Partly because it is consumed by a gigantic plaster statue of Queen Victoria who is my idol and partly for other reasons; three steps that I contrived out of boards lead to the statue which I have placed opposite the door as I enter the room. It is a sitting figure, a replica of one in London, and a thing of astonishing whiteness. I found it in a dusty shop on Morningside Heights. Raymond says it is a thing of terror, possessing the quality of nightmares, suggesting large and probable deaths. And of course he is right. When I am the Duchess of Hapsburg I sit opposite Victoria in my headpiece and we talk. The other time I wear the dress of a student, dark clothes and dark stockings. Victoria always wants me to tell her of whiteness. She wants me to tell her of a royal world where everything and everyone is white and there are no unfortunate black ones. For as we of royal blood know, black is evil and has been from the beginning. Even before my mother's hair started to fall out. Before she was raped by a wild black beast. Black was evil.

As for myself I long to become even a more pallid Negro than I am now; pallid like Negroes on the covers of American Negro magazines; soulless, educated and irreligious. I want to possess no moral value, particularly value as to my being. I want not to be. I ask nothing except anonymity. I am an English major, as my mother was when she went to school in Atlanta. My father majored in social work. I am graduated from a city college and have occasional work in libraries, but mostly spend my days preoccupied with the placement and geometric position of words on paper. I write poetry filling white page after white page with imitations of Edith Sitwell. It is my dream to live in rooms with European antiques and my Queen Victoria, photographs of Roman ruins, walls of books, a piano, oriental carpets and to eat my meals on a white glass table. I will visit my friends' apartments which will contain books, photographs of Roman ruins, pianos and oriental carpets. My friends will be white.

I need them as an embankment to keep me front reflecting too much upon the fact that I am a Negro. For, like all educated Negroes—out of life and death essential—I find it necessary to maintain a stark fortress against recognition of myself. My white friends, like myself, will be shrewd, intellectual and anxious for death. Anyone's death. I will mistrust them, as I do myself, waver in their opinion of me, as I waver in the opinion of myself. But if I had not wavered in my opinion of myself, then my hair would never have fallen out. And if my hair hadn't fallen out, I wouldn't have bludgeoned my father's head with an ebony mask.

In appearance I am good-looking in a boring way; no glaring Negroid features, medium nose, medium mouth and pale yellow skin. My one defect is that I have a head of frizzy hair, unmistakably Negro kinky hair; and it is indistinguishable. I would like to lie and say I love Raymond. But I do not. He is a poet and is Jewish. He is very interested in Negroes.

> [*The* NEGRO *stands by the wall and throughout her following speech, the following characters come through the wall, disappearing off into varying directions in the darkened night of the Stage:* DUCHESS, QUEEN VICTORIA, JESUS, PATRICE LUMUMBA. JESUS *is a hunchback, yellow-skinned dwarf, dressed in white rags and sandals.* PATRICE LUMUMBA *is a black man. His head appears to be split in two with blood and tissue in eyes. He carries an ebony mask.*]

SARAH (NEGRO): The rooms are my rooms; a Hapsburg chamber, a chamber in a Victorian castle, the hotel where I killed my father, the jungle. These are the places myselves exist in. I know no places. That is, I cannot believe in places. To believe in places is to know hope and to know the emotion of hope is to know beauty. It links us across a horizon and connects us to the world. I find there are no places only my funnyhouse. Streets are rooms, cities are rooms, eternal rooms. I try to create a space for myselves in cities, New York, the midwest, a southern town, but it becomes a lie. I try to give myselves a logical relationship but that too is a lie. For relationships was one of my last religions. I clung loyally to the lie of relationships, again and again seeking to establish a connection between my characters. Jesus is Victoria's son. Mother loved my father before her hair fell out. A loving relationship exists between myself and Queen Victoria, a love between myself and Jesus but they are lies.

> [*Then to the Right front of the Stage comes the WHITE LIGHT. It goes to a suspended stairway. At the foot of it, stands the* LANDLADY. *She is a tall, thin, white woman dressed in a black and red hat and appears to be talking to someone in a suggested open doorway in a corridor of a*

rooming house. She laughs like a mad character in a funnyhouse throughout her speech.]

LANDLADY: [*Who is looking up the stairway.*] Ever since her father hung himself in a Harlem hotel when Patrice Lumumba was murdered she hides herself in her room. Each night she repeats: He keeps returning. How dare he enter the castle walls, he who is the darkest of them all, the darkest one? My mother looked like a white woman, hair as straight as any white woman's. And I am yellow but he, he is black, the blackest one of them all. I hoped he was dead. Yet he still comes through the jungle.

I tell her: Sarah, honey, the man hung himself. It's not your blame. But, no, she stares at me: No, Mrs. Conrad, he did not hang himself, that is only the way they understand it, they do, but the truth is that I bludgeoned his head with an ebony skull that he carries about with him. Wherever he goes, he carries black masks and heads.

She's suffering so till her hair has fallen out. But then she did always hide herself in that room with the walls of books and her statue. I always did know she thought she was somebody else, a Queen or something, somebody else.

Blackout

SCENE: *Funnyman's place.*

The next scene is enacted with the DUCHESS *and* RAYMOND. *Raymond's place is suggested as being above the Negro's room and is etched in with a prop of blinds and a bed. Behind the blinds are mirrors and when the blinds are opened and closed by Raymond this is revealed.* RAYMOND *turns out to be the funnyman of the funnyhouse. He is tall, white and ghostly thin and dressed in a black shirt and black trousers in attire suggesting an artist. Throughout his dialogue he laughs. The* DUCHESS *is partially disrobed and it is implied from their attitudes of physical intimacy —he is standing and she is sitting before him clinging to his leg. During the scene* RAYMOND *keeps opening and closing the blinds.*

DUCHESS: [*Carrying a red paper bag.*] My father is arriving and what am I to do?

[RAYMOND *walks about the place opening the blinds and laughing.*]

FUNNYMAN: He is arriving from Africa, is he not?

DUCHESS: Yes, yes, he is arriving from Africa.

FUNNYMAN: I always knew your father was African.

DUCHESS: He is an African who lives in the jungle. He is an African who has always lived in the jungle. Yes, he is a nigger who is an African who is a missionary teacher and is now dedicating his life to the erection of a Christian mission in the middle of the jungle. He is a black man.

FUNNYMAN: He is a black man who shot himself when they murdered Patrice Lumumba.

DUCHESS: [*Goes on wildly.*] Yes, my father is a black man who went to Africa years ago as a missionary teacher, got mixed up in politics, was revealed and is now devoting his foolish life to the erection of a Christian mission in the middle of the jungle in one of those newly freed countries. Hide me. [*Clinging to his knees.*] Hide me here so the nigger will not find me.

FUNNYMAN: [*Laughing.*] Your father is in the jungle dedicating his life to the erection of a Christian mission.

DUCHESS: Hide me here so the jungle will not find me. Hide me.

FUNNYMAN: Isn't it cruel of you?

DUCHESS: Hide me from the jungle.

FUNNYMAN: Isn't it cruel?

DUCHESS: No, no.

FUNNYMAN: Isn't it cruel of you?

DUCHESS: No. [*She screams and opens her red paper bag and draws from it her fallen hair. It is a great mass of dark wild hair. She holds it up to him. He appears not to understand. He stares at it.*] It is my hair. [*He continues to stare at her.*] When I awakened this morning it had fallen out, not all of it but a mass from the crown of my head that lay on the center of my pillow. I arose and in the greyish winter morning light of my room I stood staring at my hair, dazed by my sleeplessness, still shaken by nightmares of my mother. Was is true, yes, it was my hair. In the mirror I saw that, although my hair remained on both sides, dearly on the crown and at my temples my scalp was bare. [*She removes her black crown and shows him the top of her head.*]

FUNNYMAN: [*Staring at her.*] Why would your hair fall out? Is it because you are cruel? How could a black father haunt you so?

DUCHESS: He haunted my very conception. He was a wild black beast who raped my mother.

FUNNYMAN: He is a black Negro. [*Laughing.*]

DUCHESS: Ever since I can remember he's been in a nigger pose of agony. He is the wilderness. He speaks niggerly groveling about wanting to touch me with his black hand.

FUNNYMAN: How tormented and cruel you are.

DUCHESS: [*As if not comprehending.*] Yes, yes, the man's dark, very dark-skinned. He is the darkest, my father is the darkest, my mother is the lightest. I am in between. But my father is the darkest. My father is a nigger who drives me to misery. Any time spent with him evolves itself into suffering. He is a black man and the wilderness.

FUNNYMAN: How tormentcd and cruel you are.

DUCHESS: He is a nigger.

FUNNYMAN: And your mother, where is she?

172

DUCHESS: She is in the asylum. In the asylum bald. Her father was a white man. And she is in the asylum.

[*He takes her in his arms. She responds wildly.*]

Blackout

KNOCKING is heard it continues, then somewhere near the Center of the Stage a FIGURE appears in the darkness, a large dark faceless MAN carrying a mask in his hand.

MAN: It begins with the disaster of my hair. I awaken. My hair has fallen out, not all of it, but a mass from the crown of my head that lies on the center of my white pillow. I arise and in the greyish winter morning light of my room I stand staring at my hair, dazed by sleeplessness, still shaken by nightmares of my mother. Is it true? Yes. It is my hair. In the mirror I see that although my hair remains on both sides, clearly on the crown and at my temples my scalp is bare. And in my sleep I had been visited by my bald crazy mother who comes to me crying, calling me to her bedside. She lies on the bed watching the strands of her own hair fall out. Her hair fell out after she married and she spent her days lying on the bed watching the strands fall from her scalp, covering the bedspread until she was bald and admitted to the hospital. Black man, black man, my mother says, I never should have let a black man put his hands on me. She comes to me, her bald skull shining. Black diseases, Sarah, she says. Black diseases. I run. She follows me, her bald skull shining. That is the beginning.

Blackout

SCENE: *Queen's Chamber. Her hair is in a small pile on the bed and in a small pile on the floor, several other small piles of hair are scattered about her and her white gown is covered with fallen out hair.* QUEEN VICTORIA *acts out the following scene: She awakens [In pantomime.] and discovers her hair has fallen. It is on her pillow. She arises and stands at the side of the bed with her back toward us, staring at hair. The* DUCHESS *enters the room, comes around, standing behind* VICTORIA, *and they stare at the hair.* VICTORIA *picks up a mirror. The* DUCHESS *then picks up a mirror and looks at her own hair. She opens the red paper bag that she is carrying and takes out her hair, attempting to place it back on her head [For unlike* VICTORIA, *she does not wear her headpiece now.] The LIGHTS remain on. The unidentified MAN returns out of the darkness and streaks. He carries the mask.*

MAN: [PATRICE LUMUMBA.] I am a nigger of two generations. I am Patrice Lumumba. I am a nigger of two generations. I am the black shadow that haunted my mother's conception. I belong to the generation born at the turn of the century and the generation born before the depression. At present I reside in New York City in a brownstone in the West Nineties. I am an English major at a city college. My nigger father majored in social work, so did my mother. I am a student and have occasional work in libraries. But mostly I spend my vile days preoccupied with the placement and geometric position of words on paper. I write poetry filling white page after white page with imitations of Sitwell. It is my vile dream to live in rooms with European antiques and my statue of Queen Victoria, photographs of Roman ruins, walls of books, a piano and oriental carpets and to eat my meals on a white glass table. It is also my nigger dream for my friends to eat their meals on white glass tables and to live in rooms with European antiques, photographs of Roman ruins, pianos and oriental carpets. My friends will be white. I need them as an embankment to keep me from reflecting too much upon the fact that I am Patrice Lumumba who haunted my mother's conception. They are necessary for me to maintain recognition against myself. My white friends, like myself, will be shrewd intellectuals and anxious for death. Anyone's death. I will despise them as I do myself. For if I did not despise myself then my hair would not have fallen and if my hair had not fallen then I would not have bludgeoned my father's face with the ebony mask.

[*The LIGHT remains on him. Before him a BALD HEAD is dropped on a wire, SOMEONE screams. Another wall is dropped, larger than the first one was. This one is near the front of the Stage facing thus. Throughout the following monologue, the CHARACTERS:* DUCHESS, VICTORIA, JESUS *go back and forth. As they go in their backs are to us but the* NEGRO *faces us, speaking.*]

I always dreamed of a day when my mother would smile at me. My father ... his mother wanted him to be Christ. From the beginning in the lamp of their dark room she said—I want you to be Jesus, to walk in Genesis and save the race. You must return to Africa, find revelation in the midst of golden savannas, nim and white frankopenny trees, white stallions roaming under a blue sky, you must walk with a white dove and heal the race, heal the misery, take us off the cross. She stared at him anguished in the kerosene light ... At dawn he watched her rise, kill a hen for him to eat at breakfast, then go to work down at the big house till dusk, till she died.

His father told him the race was no damn good. He hated his father and adored his mother. His mother didn't want him to marry my mother and sent a dead chicken to the wedding. I DON'T want you marrying that child, she wrote, she's not good enough for you, I want you to go to Africa. When they first married they lived in New York. Then they went to Africa where my mother fell out of love with my father. She didn't want him to save the black race and spent her days combing her hair. She would not let him touch her in their wedding bed and called him black. He is black of skin with dark eyes and a great dark square brow. Then in Africa he started to drink and came home drunk one night and raped my mother. The child from the union is me. I clung to my mother. Long after she went to the asylum I wove long dreams of her beauty, her straight hair and fair skin and grey eyes, so identical to mine. How it anguished him. I turned from him, nailing him on the cross, he said, dragging him through grass and nailing him on a cross until he bled. He pleaded with me to help him find Genesis, search for Genesis in the midst of golden savannas, nim and white frankopenny trees and white stallions roaming under a blue sky, help him search for the white doves, he wanted the black man to make a pure statement, he wanted the black man to rise from colonialism. But I sat in the room with my mother, sat by her bedside and helped her comb her straight black hair and wove long dreams of her beauty. She had long since begun to curse the place and spoke of herself trapped in blackness. She preferred the company of night owls. Only at night did she rise, walking in the garden among the trees with the owls. When I spoke to her she saw I was a black man's child and she preferred speaking to owls. Nights my father came from his school in the village struggling to embrace me. But I fled and hid under my mother's bed while she screamed of remorse. Her hair was falling badly and after a while we had to return to this country.

He tried to hang himself once. After my mother went to the asylum he had hallucinations, his mother threw a dead chicken at him, his father laughed and said the race was no damn good, my mother appeared in her nightgown screaming she had trapped herself in blackness. No white doves flew. He had left Africa and was again in New York. He lived in Harlem and no white doves flew. Sarah, Sarah, he would say to me, the soldiers are coming and a cross they are placing high on a tree and are dragging me through the grass and nailing me upon the cross. My blood is gushing. I wanted to live in Genesis in the midst of golden savannas, nim and white frankopenny trees and white stallions roaming under a blue sky. I wanted to walk with a white dove. I wanted to be a Christian. Now I am Judas. I betrayed my mother. I sent your mother to the asylum. I created a yellow child who hates me. And he tried to hang himself in a Harlem hotel.

Blackout

[*A BALD HEAD is dropped on a string. We hear LAUGHING.*]

SCENE: DUCHESS's *place.*

The next scene is done in the Duchess of Hapsburg's place which is a chandeliered ballroom with SNOW falling, a black and white marble floor, a bench decorated with white flowers, all of this can be made of obviously fake materials as they would be in a funnyhouse. The DUCHESS is wearing a white dress and as in the previous scene a white headpiece with her kinky hair springing out from under it. In the scene are the DUCHESS and JESUS: JESUS enters the room, which is at first, dark, then suddenly BRILLIANT, he starts to cry out at the DUCHESS, who is seated on a bench under the chandelier, and pulls his hair from the red paper bag holding it up for the DUCHESS to see.

JESUS: My hair.

[*The DUCHESS does not speak, JESUS again screams.*]

My hair. [*Holding the hair up, waiting for a reaction from the duchess.*]

DUCHESS: [*As if oblivious.*] I have something I must show you. [*She goes quickly to shutters and darkens the room, returning standing before JESUS. She then slowly removes her headpiece and from under it takes a mass of her hair.*] When I awakened I found it fallen out, not all of it but a mass that lay on my white pillow. I could see, although my hair hung down at the sides, clearly on my white scalp it was missing. [*Her baldness is identical to JESUS's.*]

Blackout

The LIGHTS come back up. They are BOTH sitting on the bench examining each other's hair, running it through their fingers, then slowly the DUCHESS *disappears behind the shutters and returns with a long red comb. She sits on the bench next to* JESUS *and starts to comb her remaining hair over her baldness.* [*This is done slowly.*] JESUS *then takes the comb and proceeds to do the same to the* DUCHESS *of Hapsburg's hair. After they finish they place the* DUCHESS's *headpiece back on and we can see the strands of their hair falling to the floor.* JESUS *then lies down across the bench while the* DUCHESS *walks back and forth, the* KNOCKING *does not cease. They speak in unison, as the* DUCHESS *walks about and* JESUS *lies on the bench in the falling snow, staring at the ceiling.*

DUCHESS AND JESUS: [*Their hair is falling more now, they are both hideous.*] My father isn't going to let alone. [*KNOCKING.*] Our father isn't going to let us alone, our father is the darkest of us all, my mother was the fairest, I am in between, but my father is the darkest of them all. He is a black man. Our father is the darkest of them all. He is a black man. My father is a dead man.

[*Then they suddenly look up at each other and scream, the LIGHTS go to their heads and we see that they are totally bald. There is a KNOCK-ING. LIGHTS go to the stairs and the* LANDLADY.]

LANDLADY: He wrote to her saying he loved her and asked her forgiveness. He begged her to take him off the cross (*He had dreamed she would.*), stop them from tormenting him, the one with the chicken and his cursing father. Her mother's hair fell out, the race's hair fell out because he left Africa, he said. He had tried to save them. She must embrace him. He said his existence depended on her embrace. He wrote her from Africa where he is creating his Christian center in the jungle and that is why he came here. I know that he wanted her to return there with him and not desert the race. He came to see her once before he tried to hang himself, appearing in the corridor of my apartment. I had let him in. I found him sitting on a bench in the hallway. He put out his hand to her, tried to take her in his arms, crying out—Forgiveness, Sarah, is it that you never will forgive me for being black? Sarah, I know you were a child of torment. But forgiveness. That was before his breakdown. Then, he wrote her and repeated that his mother hoped he would be Christ but he failed. He had married her mother because he could not resist the light. Yet, his mother from the beginning in the kerosene lamp of their dark rooms in Georgia said: I want you to be Jesus, to walk in Genesis and save the race, return to Africa, find revelation in the black. He went away.

But Easter morning, she got to feeling badly and went into Harlem to see him; the streets were filled with vendors selling lilies. He had checked out of that hotel. When she arrived back at my brownstone he was here, dressed badly, rather drunk, I had let him in again. He sat on a bench in the dark hallway, put out his hand to her, trying to take her in his arms, crying out—forgiveness, Sarah, forgiveness for my being black, Sarah. I know you are a child of torment. I know on dark winter afternoons you sit alone weaving stories of your mother's beauty. But Sarah, answer me, don't turn away, Sarah. Forgive my blackness. She would not answer. He put out his hand to her. She ran past him on the stairs, left him there with his hand out to me, repeating his past, saying his mother hoped he would be Christ. From the beginning in the kerosene lamp of their dark rooms, she said, "Wally, I want you to be Jesus, to walk in Genesis and save the race. You must return to Africa, Wally, find revelation in the midst of golden savannas, nim and white frankopenny trees and white stallions roaming under a blue sky. Wally, you must find the white dove and heal the pain of the race, heal the misery of the black man, Wally, take us off the cross, Wally." In the kerosene light she stared at me anguished from her old Negro face—but she ran past him leaving him. And now he is dead, she says, now he is dead. He left Africa and now Patrice Lumumba is dead.

[*The next scene is enacted back in the* DUCHESS *of Hapsburg's place.* JESUS *is still in the Duchess's chamber, apparently he has fallen asleep and as we see him he awakens with the* DUCHESS *by his side, and sits here as in a trance. He rises terrified and speaks.*]

JESUS: Through my apocalypses and my raging sermons I have tried so to escape him, through God Almighty I have tried to escape being black. [*He then appears to rouse himself from his thoughts and calls:*] Duchess, Duchess.

[*He looks about for her there is no answer. He gets up slowly, walks back into the darkness and there we see that she is hanging on the chandelier, her bald head suddenly drops to the floor and she falls upon* JESUS. *He screams.*]

I am going to Africa and kill this black man named Patrice Lumumba. Why? Because all my life I believed my Holy Father to be God, but now I know that my father is a black man. I have no fear for whatever I do, I will do in the name of God, I will do in the name of Albert Saxe Coburg, in the name of Victoria, Queen Victoria Regina, the monarch of England, I will.

180

Blackout

SCENE: *In the jungle, RED SUN, FLYING THINGS, wild black grass. The effect of the jungle is that it, unlike the other scenes, is over the entire stage. In time this is the longest scene in the play and is played the slowest, as the slow, almost standstill stages of a dream. By lighting the desired effect would be—suddenly the jungle has overgrown the chambers and all the other places with a violence and a dark brightness, a grim yellowness.*

JESUS *is the first to appear in the center of the jungle darkness. Unlike in previous scenes, he has a nimbus above his head. As they each successively appear, they all too have nimbuses atop their heads in a manner to suggest that they are saviours.*

JESUS: I always believed my father to be God.

[*Suddenly they all appear in various parts' of the jungle.* PATRICE LUMUMBA, *the* DUCHESS, VICTORIA, *wandering about speaking at once. Their speeches are mixed and repeated by one another.*]

ALL: He never tires of the journey, he who is the darkest one, the darkest one of them all. My mother looked like a white woman, hair as straight as any white woman's. I am yellow but he is black, the darkest one of us all. How I hoped he was dead, yet he never tires of the journey. It was because of him that my mother died because she let a black man put his hands on her. Why does he keep returning? He keeps returning forever, keeps returning and returning and he is my father. He is a black Negro. They told me my Father was God but my father is black. He is my father. I am tied to a black Negro. He returned when I lived in the south back in the twenties, when I was a child, he returned. Before I was born at the turn of the century, he haunted my conception, diseased my birth … killed my mother. He killed the light. My mother was the lightest one. I am bound to him unless, of course, he should die.

But he is dead.
And he keeps returning. Then he is not dead.
Then he is not dead.
Yet, he is dead, but dead he comes knocking at my door.

[*This is repeated several times, finally reaching a loud pitch and then* ALL *rushing about the grass. They stop and stand perfectly still.* ALL *speaking tensely at various times in a chant.*]

I see him. The black ugly thing is sitting in his hallway, surrounded by his ebony masks, surrounded by the blackness of himself. My mother comes into the room. He is there with his hand out to me, groveling, saying—Forgiveness, Sarah, is it that you will never forgive me for being black.

> Forgiveness, Sarah, I know you are a nigger of torment.
> Why? Christ would not rape anyone.
> You will never forgive me for being black.
> Wild beast. Why did you rape my mother? Black beast, Christ
>   would not rape anyone.

He is in grief from that black anguished face of his. Then at once the room will grow bright and my mother will come toward me smiling while I stand before his face and bludgeon him with an ebony head.

Forgiveness, Sarah, I know you are a nigger of torment.

[*Silence. Then they suddenly begin to laugh and shout as though they are in victory. They continue for some minutes running about laughing and shouting.*]

Blackout

Another WALL drops. There is a white plaster statue of Queen Victoria which represents the Negro's room in the brownstone, the room appears near the staircase highly lit and small. The main prop is the statue but a bed could be suggested. The figure of Victoria is a sitting figure, one of astonishing repulsive whiteness, suggested by dusty volumes of books and old yellowed walls.

The Negro SARAH *is standing perfectly still, we hear the KNOCKING, the LIGHTS come on quickly, her* FATHER's *black figure with bludgeoned hands rushes upon her, the LIGHT GOES BLACK and we see her hanging in the room.*

LIGHTS come on the laughing LANDLADY. *And at the same time remain on the hanging figure of the* NEGRO.

LANDLADY: The poor bitch has hung herself.

[FUNNYMAN RAYMOND *appears from his room at the commotion.*]

The poor bitch has hung herself.

RAYMOND: [*Observing her hanging figure.*]   She was a funny little liar.

LANDLADY: [*Informing him.*]   Her father hung himself in a Harlem hotel when Patrice Lumumba died.

RAYMOND: Her father never hung himself in a Harlem hotel when Patrice Lumumba was murdered. I know the man. He is a doctor, married to a white whore. He lives in the city in rooms with European antiques, photographs of Roman ruins, walls of books and oriental carpets. Her father is a nigger who eats his meals on a white glass table.

END

SLAVS!

TONY KUSHNER

—————✦—————

On June 6, 1994, a staged reading of Slavs! *was given as a benefit for the Lesbian Avengers Civil Rights Organizing Project at the Walter Kerr Theatre in New York City. The reading was produced by David Binder, James Calleri and David G. O'Connell and directed by Michael Mayer.*

INTRODUCTION

by Michael Cadden

Tony Kushner is America's best-known contemporary political playwright. His Pulitzer Prize-winning *Angels in America: A Gay Fantasia on National Themes* (1991-2), which has been produced in regional theatres and universities around the country as well as on Broadway, announces in its subtitle its political focus ("National Themes"), its formal structure ("Fantasia"), and the subjectivity of its author ("Gay"). Rarely has an author been so willing to lay all his cards on the table, from the advertising campaign which must necessarily feature the play's controversial title to the epic's final "fabulous" monologue. Because *Angels in America* was commissioned by Oskar Eustis of San Francisco's Eureka Theatre through a Special Projects Grant from the National Endowment of the Arts, Kushner says he had a special obligation to tackle the relationship between individual lives and the society which both produces and reflects them, "Since the writing was funded by a Federal grant, I felt the play ought to have a national dimension, and as it was a considerable sum, I wanted to give the taxpayers their money's worth."

No doubt some taxpayers balked at Kushner's depiction of Reagan's America as a period of moral chaos in which the rule of self-interest was allowed a Satanic sway over the land, and at his suggestion that gay lives had become central to an examination of all things American because of the role they had come to play in the worlds of religion, law, medicine, and politics. But in many quarters *Angels in America* was hailed as the most important American drama since Miller's *Death of a Salesman*, Williams' *A Streetcar Named Desire*, and O'Neill's *Long Day's Journey Into Night*—what Kushner refers to as "the three great postwar pillars upon which the stature of serious American playwrighting rests." But as much as Kushner owes to this domestic theatrical tradition, he is equally a product of a European tradition initiated by Bertolt Brecht a tradition which for Kushner is best exemplified in the work of such British playwrights as Caryl Churchill, Edward Bond, David Hare, David Edgar, and Howard Brenton. What Kushner values most in both the American and the European traditions is a dramatist's ability to connect the personal and the political, to link individual suffering to large social issues. Indeed, Kushner has suggested that, "since it's true that everything is political (though not exclusively so) it becomes meaningless to talk about political and nonpolitical theatre, and more useful to speak of a theatre that presents the world as it is, an interwoven web of the public and the private."

Like most of his favorite European playwrights, Kushner defines himself as a socialist. For him, socialism means "beginning to struggle in a really, really powerful way with why economic justice and equality are so incredibly uncomfortable for us, and why we still define our worth by how much money we individually can make at the expense of other people, and why we find sharing and collective enterprise and motivations that are not competitive so phenomenally difficult." Given this definition, it comes as no surprise that Kushner is particularly interested in dramatizing moments when history itself seems to "crack wide open," allowing his characters to see through the ideologies which had heretofore governed their lives.

Slavs! (*Thinking About the Longstanding Problems of Virtue and Happiness*), which premiered in 1994 at the Humana Festival of New American Plays at the Actors Theatre of Louisville, began life as part of *Angels in America*. Kushner had originally intended the second half of *Angels*, entitled *Perestroika*, to draw parallels between the breakdown of moral and political consensus in both the United States and the Soviet Union during the 1980s and 90s. "Soviet" scenes were to kick off each act in order to suggest that the millennium that was fast approaching was not only "national"; but as the "American" scenes grew in length, all but one of the "Soviet" scenes—the opening moments *Perestroika*—were dropped. They later became the starting point for *Slavs!*

Like *Angels*, *Slavs!* is set in what Kushner diagnoses as a period of disintegration—in this instance the collapse of the Soviet Empire. It opens on the day in March 1985 when Mikhail Gorbachev succeeded Konstantin Chernenko as General Secretary of the Communist Party, marking the beginning of the end for the U.S.S.R.; and it ends in 1992, as the new Commonwealth of Independent States struggles to reconcile its free-market present with the ideals of a now tarnished Soviet past. For a playwright of Kushner's socialist convictions, it was clearly important to examine both the failure of the collectivist experiment and the failure of the system that was taking its place. As he said in an interview with New York Times reporter William Harris, "Free-market capitalism is the coming thing, but that doesn't mean we have to assume it's a good thing. I wanted the play to speak to the particular dilemma that we're faced with now, those of us who believe that there's still a necessity for the collective, as well as the individual."

Kushner's comment echoes the quotation from an essay by Marxist critic Raymond Williams which serves as a Prologue to *Slavs!* and which gave the playwright a portion of his title. According to Williams, "The idea of socialism … is based on the idea and the practice of a society." Consequently, "in thinking about the longstanding problems of virtue and happiness, people who began from the idea of a society did not immediately refer to the problems of a general human nature or to the inevitable conditions of existence; they looked first at the precise forms of the society in which they were living and at how these might, where necessary, be changed." As a political playwright, Kushner sees his job as the analysis of "the precise forms of the society" which his characters inhabit. As to "how these might, where necessary, be changed," *Slavs!* has nothing to say. Questions are the province of the writer; answers are for the audience to tackle. Hence, the play ends with an old Politburo member's restatement of Lenin's appropriation of "a novel, by Chernyshevsky, the title and contents of which asked the immortal question; which Lenin asked and in asking stood the world on its head; the question which challenges to both contemplation and, if we love the world, to action; the question which implies: Something is terribly wrong with the world, and avers: Human beings can change it; the question asked by the living and, apparently, by the fretful dead as well: What is to be done?" What indeed.

CHARACTERS

FIRST BABUSHKA - a snow sweep of indeterminate age.

SECOND BABUSHKA - another snow sweep of indeterminate age.

VASSILY VOROVILICH SMUKOV - a high-ranking Politburo member, a pessimistic man in his seventies.

SERGE ESMERELDOVICH UPGOBKIN - a high-ranking Politburo member, an optimistic man in his eighties.

ALEKSII ANTEDILLUVIANOVICH PRELAPSARIANOV - a Politburo member of incalcuable rank, the world's oldest living Bolshevik, considerably older than ninety.

IPPOLITE IPPOPOLITOVICH POPOLITIPOV - an appartchik of some importance, a sour man in his sixties.

YEGOR TREMENS RODENT - an appartchik of less importance, attached to Popolitipov; a nervous type in his fifties.

KATERINA SERAFIME GLEB - a security guard at the Pan-Soviet Archives for the Study of Cerebro-Cephalognomical Historico-Biological Materialism (also known as PASOVACERCEPHHIBIMAT). An inebriated young woman in her twenties.

BONFILA BEZHUKHOVA BONCH-BRUEVICH - a pediatric oncologist, a pleasant woman in her thirties.

BIG BABUSHKA - yet another snow sweep of indeterminate age, garrulous, large, with a moustache.

MRS. SHASTLIVYI DOMIK - an unhappy, angry woman in her forties.

VODYA DOMIK - a silent little girl, eight years old.

The play takes place in Moscow, March 1985; and Talmenka, Siberia, 1992.

Author's Note:

For the information on the Soviet nuclear catastrophe which is addressed in Act Three, I am indebted primarily to a series of articles by John-Thor Dahlburg which ran in the *Los Angeles Times*, September 2-4, 1992; to Grigori Medvedev's *The Truth About Chernobyl*; and to Dr. Don Pizzarello of New York University Medical Center.

PROLOGUE

The idea of socialism, as the word itself indicates, is based on the idea and the practice of a *society*. This may seem, at first sight, to do nothing to distinguish it from other political ideas, but that is only because we haven't looked closely enough. The very idea of a *society*—that is, a definite form of human relationships in certain specific conditions at a particular moment in history—is itself comparatively modern. *Society* used to mean mainly the company of other people. The idea of a *society* was to distinguish one form of social relationships from another, and to show that these forms varied historically and could change. Thus, in thinking about the longstanding problems of virtue and happiness, people who began from the idea of a society did not immediately refer the problems to a general human nature or to inevitable conditions of exsistence; they looked first at the precise forms of the society in which they were living and at how these might, where necessary, be changed.

—RAYMOND WILLIAMS
"Walking Backwards into the Future"

[Two babushkas, dressed in knee-length cheap winter coats, their legs encased in thick white support hose, their feet shod in rubber galoshes, their heads of course wrapped in floral—or geometric—print scarves tied under the chin, are sweeping snow from the entrance steps of the Hall of the Soviets, the Kremlin, March 1985. As they sweep, the snow falls; they talk.]

FIRST BABUSHKA: However reluctant one may be to grant it, history and the experience of this century presses upon us the inescapable conclusion that there is a direct continuum from Dictatorship of the Proletariat and the embrace of violence as a means of effecting change that one finds in later Marx and Engels to dictatorship plain and simple—you missed a spot—and state terror.

SECOND BABUSHKA: True enough. But Marx's defense of revolutionary violence must be set in its proper context, namely: the nineteenth-century evolutionary-socialist error-of-belief in the Inevitability of Gradualism, which sought not so much to transform society into something new …

FIRST BABUSHKA: … But rather to create merely an "improved" version of the society one sought to change.

SECOND BABUSHKA: Exactly.

FIRST BABUSHKA: But is it not a false antinomy to predicate as the only alternative to Reformism or Gradualism a vanguard-driven …

[Two Politburo members, V. V. SMUKOV and S. E. UPGOBKIN, very impressive in greatcoats and big fur hats enter.]

SECOND BABUSHKA: *[Seeing them.]* Shhhh! Shhhhhh!

[The babushkas clam up tight. They sweep.]

VASSILY VOROVILICH SMUKOV: Morning grandma.

[The babushkas suddenly become sweet, toothless old ladies, smiling, head-bobbing, forelock-tugging mumblers.]

FIRST BABUSHKA: Good morning sirs!

SECOND BABUSHKA: How-de-doo! Mind the ice, don't slip!

[UPGOBKIN and SMUKOV start up the steps.]

FIRST BABUSHKA: Big doings today, sirs …

VASSILY VOROVILICH SMUKOV: Oh, the usual mischief …

SERGE ESMERELDOVICH UPGOBKIN: [*Watching them sweep.*] Heavy snows for March. Your labor, I fear, is *Sisyphean!*

SECOND BABUSHKA: And what's more, sir, it's *completely pointless!* We sweep, it falls, we sweep some more, it falls some more …

FIRST BABUSHKA: It's hopeless, hopeless!

[*The two babushkas laugh and laugh.*]

VASSILY VOROVILICH SMUKOV: That's the spirit, grandma! Sweep! Sweep!

[*The babushkas sweep; they are all laughing.* SMUKOV *and* UPGOB-KIN *take each other's arm, climb the stairs and disappear into the Hall. The babushkas instantly stop laughing.*]

FIRST BABUSHKA: So where was I?

SECOND BABUSHKA: … a vanguard-driven …

FIRST BABUSHKA: Yes! A vanguard-driven revolution as the only alternative to Reaction. For the People make their own history.

SECOND BABUSHKA: Limits are set by the conditions of their social development.

FIRST BABUSHKA: But those conditions are themselves affected by the state of their economic relations. [*She stops sweeping.*] Sweeping snow. In Moscow. It *is* sisyphean.

SECOND BABUSHKA: [*A shrug.*] Nevertheless. *Sweep,* "grandma."

FIRST BABUSHKA: Grandma yourself. [*Sweeping again.*] Big doings today …

SECOND BABUSHKA: Big.

ACT ONE

"O tell me of the Russians, Communist, my son!
Tell me of the Russians, my honest young man!"
"They are moving for the people, mother; let me alone.
For I'm worn out with reading and want to lie down."

—JOHN BERRYMAN
"Communist"

Scene 1

[*In an anteroom outside the Politburo Chamber in the Hall of the Soviets in the Kremlin. March 1985.* SMUKOV *and* UPGOBKIN, *in suits now, are sitting and talking. A samovar stands nearby, brewing tea.*]

VASSILY VOROVILICH SMUKOV: People are not capable of change.
They used to be, maybe, but not anymore. In the old days you could ask anything of the people and they'd do it: Live without bread, without heat in the winter, take a torch to their own houses—as long as they believed they were building socialism there was no limit to how much they could adapt, transform. Moldable clay in the hands of history.

SERGE ESMERELDOVICH UPGOBKIN: And you feel it's different now?

VASSILY VOROVILICH SMUKOV: Well, you see.
We are all grown less pliable, unsure of our footing, unsure of the way, brittle bones and cataracts ... How are your cataracts, by the way, Serge Esmereldovich?

SERGE ESMERELDOVICH UPGOBKIN: [*Shrugs.*] Old eyes get tough, cloudy. This one [*Points to one eye.*] is not really an eye anymore, it's a bottle cork, it's a walnut. This one [*Points to the other eye.*] lets in milky light. I live in a world of milk-white ghosts now, luminous beings, washed clean of detail. And I hear better, Vashka: in every voice, a million voices whispering, [*Imitates whispering; it sounds like the sea.*] Sssssshhhhh. shhssshhh ... More tea?

VASSILY VOROVILICH SMUKOV: No; I'll have to get up to pee in the middle of Aleksii's speech.

SERGE ESMERELDOVICH UPGOBKIN: Whereas I intend to drink two more cups, so the pressure on my bladder will keep me awake.

VASSILY VOROVILICH SMUKOV: At least in the bad old days you could sleep through the speeches and not worry that you'd miss a thing. Now the speeches are longer and you have to stay awake to boo. It's miserable: democracy. Grishin or Gorbachev, Gorbachev or Grishin. I vote *not* to vote! I am a true apostle of the old scientific creed: Geriatrical Materialism. Our motto: Stagnation is our only hope. Our sacred text: silence. Not this interminable debate, blah blah blah, my side, your side—really, this is logorrhea, not revolution.

SERGE ESMERELDOVICH UPGOBKIN: Patience.
There are no shortcuts to the new era. The terrain is vast. Aeons to traverse, everything is implicated, everything encompassed, the world, the universe … Today this anteroom is the anteroom to History, Vashka! Beyond those doors, inside that chamber, History is aborning! Inhale its perfumes! A harsh and unnaturally protracted winter is losing its teeth. A great pressure has built up to this,. Vashka, a great public desperation. There is no choice. You'll see that people can change, and change radically. From crown to toe, every cell formed anew. We set the process in motion with our words.

VASSILY VOROVILICH SMUKOV: People, I think, would rather die than change.

SERGE ESMERELDOVICH UPGOBKIN: Do you really think so?
I believe precisely the opposite.
We would rather change than die.
We have been ordered into motion by History herself,
Vashka. When the sun comes out, the sky cracks open,
the silent flowers twist and sway …

Scene 2

[ALEKSII ANTEDILLUVIANOVICH PRELAPSARIANOV, *the world's oldest Bolshevik, speaking in the Chamber of Deputies. He is unimaginably old and totally blind; his voice is thin and high, but he speaks with great passion.*]

ALEKSII ANTEDILLUVIANOVICH PRELAPSARIANOV: And *Theory? Theory?* How are we to proceed without *Theory?* Is it enough to reject the past, is it wise to move forward in this blind fashion, without the Cold Brilliant Light of Theory to guide the way? What have these reformers to offer in the way of Theory? What beautiful system of thought have they to present to the world, to the befuddling, contrary tumult of life, to this mad swirling planetary disorganization, to the Inevident Welter of fact, event, phenomenon, calamity? Do they have, as we did, a beautiful Theory, as bold, as Grand, as comprehensive a construct … ? You can't imagine, when we first read the Classic Texts, when in the dark vexed night of our ignorance and terror the seed-words sprouted and shoved incomprehension aside, when the incredible bloody vegetable struggle up and through into Red Blooming gave us Praxis, True Praxis, True Theory married to Actual Life … You who live in this Sour Little Age cannot imagine the sheer grandeur of the prospect we gazed upon: like standing atop the highest peak in the mighty Caucasus, and viewing in one all-knowing glance the mountainous, granite order of creation. We were One with the Sidereal Pulse then, in the blood in our heads we heard the tick of the Infinite. You cannot imagine it. I weep for you.And what have you to offer now, children of this Theory? What have you to offer in its place? Market Incentives? Watered-down Bukharinite stopgap makeshift Capitalism? NEPmen! Pygmy children of a gigantic race!

Change? Yes, we must must change, only show me the Theory, and I will be at the barricades, show me the book of the next Beautiful Theory, and I promise you these blind eyes will see again, just to read it, to devour that text. Show me the words that will reorder the world, or else keep silent.

The snake sheds its skin only when a new skin is ready; if he gives up the only membrane he has before he can replace it, naked he will be in the world, prey to the forces of chaos: without his skin he will be dismantled, lose coherence and die. Have you, my little serpents, a new skin?

Then we dare not, we cannot move ahead.

Scene 3

[*Outside the Chamber of Deputies again, the Kremlin.* IPPOLITE IPPOPOLI-
TOVICH POPOLITIPOV *and* YEGOR TREMENS RODENT, *two middle-aged
deputies, are talking.* POPOLITIPOV *is in a rage over the debate in the adjoining chamber.* RODENT *is freaked out.* RODENT *is* POPOLITIPOV's *protégé, and
is profoundly deferential.*]

IPPOLITE IPPOPOLITOVICH POPOLITIPOV: The heart is not progressive. The
heart is conservative, no matter what the mind may be. Why don't they get
that? The mind may make its leaps ahead; the heart will refuse to budge, shatter at the prospect. Yearn to go back to what it loves. That's the function of
the organ, that's what it's there for: to fall in love. And love is profoundly reactionary, you fall in love and that instant is fixed, love is always fixed on the past.

YEGOR TREMENS RODENT: Oh true. Oh I am all terror these days. Sleep with
the light on. No idea of what: just terror. Popolitipov, look! I'm shaking!

IPPOLITE IPPOPOLITOVICH POPOLITIPOV: Now debate that, reformers! The
conservative, fractable human heart!

> [SERGE ESMERELDOVICH UPGOBKIN *enters, leading* ALEKSII ANTE-
> DILLUVIANOVICH PRELAPSARIANOV *to a comfy chair.*]

YEGOR TREMENS RODENT: [*To* POPOLITIPOV.] Sssshhhh.

> [POPOLITIPOV *and* RODENT *move a discreet distance away from the
> two old Bolsheviks.*]

ALEKSII ANTEDILLUVIANOVICH PRELAPSARIANOV: [*As* UPGOBKIN *helps him
to his chair.*] Stop hovering, Serge Esmereldovich, you're practically bugger-
ing me!

SERGE ESMERELDOVICH UPGOBKIN: I have to stand this close, otherwise I don't
see ...

ALEKSII ANTEDILLUVIANOVICH PRELAPSARIANOV: Nothing to see! I'm fine!
And your breath is terrible. Please, you give me the fidgets. It's just a vein, just
a weak vein in my head.

SERGE ESMERELDOVICH UPGOBKIN: I'll get some tea for you ... [*Looking about.*]

197

If I can find the samovar.

YEGOR TREMENS RODENT: There, comrade Upgobkin, it's over there …

ALEKSII ANTEDILLUVIANOVICH PRELAPSARIANOV: *I'm* the blind one! You just have cataracts! I'm *blind*!

IPPOLITE IPPOPOLITOVICH POPOLITIPOV: Is Comrade Minister Prelapsarianov not feeling well?

ALEKSII ANTEDILLUVIANOVICH PRELAPSARIANOV: HOURS! HOURS OF TALK! What do they think they have to say! Such pretentiousness, they fart and they whinny and I HAVE AN ANEURISM! [*He has gotten overexcited.*] Oh, oh, oh …

SERGE ESMERELDOVICH UPGOBKIN: Some hot tea … [*He pours in a stiff shot of vodka from a hip flask.*]

IPPOLITE IPPOPOLITOVICH POPOLITIPOV: [*Quietly, to* RODENT.] For decades a mostly respectable torpor. Now: Expect madness.

YEGOR TREMENS RODENT: [*Also quiet.*] In Omsk thousands saw a radiant orb in the sky, larger than the moon. Sea monsters were seen swimming in some Kazakhstan lake. Strange space creatures reported landed in Gorki …

IPPOLITE IPPOPOLITOVICH POPOLITIPOV: With three eyes. And they marched about the square.

YEGOR TREMENS RODENT: Six eyes. Tiny tiny head, big big body, six eyes.

IPPOLITE IPPOPOLITOVICH POPOLITIPOV: I really think it was only three.

YEGOR TREMENS RODENT: Two rows of three each, which makes six.

IPPOLITE IPPOPOLITOVICH POPOLITIPOV: Aha.

SERGE ESMERELDOVICH UPGOBKIN: [*Offering the teacup to* PRELAPSARIANOV.] Can you swallow it?

ALEKSII ANTEDILLUVIANOVICH PRELAPSARIANOV: My head, my head, inside my brain, there's an itch, a little worm … Sssshhhh. Sssshhhh … [*He cradles his head.*]

YEGOR TREMENS RODENT: The theory is that radioactivity escaped from the explosion at the plutonium plant at Mayak is calling to them, the creatures, from across space, and they come perhaps with food and magic farm equipment, or personal computers, or with death rays to kill us all, and in Novy Sibirsk, people whose grandparents were merely babies when the Czar was killed are rumored to have used black arts to resurrect ... Rasputin. *Rasputin.*

IPPOLITE IPPOPOLITOVICH POPOLITIPOV: This cannot be what Lenin intended.

YEGOR TREMENS RODENT: Fantasy is the spiritual genius of Slavic peoples. And icons weep blood again. As if seventy years of socialism had never happened at all.

ALEKSII ANTEDILLUVIANOVICH PRELAPSARIANOV: [*Sitting suddenly bolt upright.*] Wait. Wait. OH! OH!

SERGE ESMERELDOVICH UPGOBKIN: Aleksii? Aleksii!

YEGOR TREMENS RODENT: Is Comrade Minister all right, is ...

> [ALEKSII ANTEDILLUVIANOVICH *stands, staring ahead, dropping the teacup.*]

IPPOLITE IPPOPOLITOVICH POPOLITIPOV: Serge Esmereldovich, is he ... ?

ALEKSII ANTEDILLUVIANOVICH PRELAPSARIANOV: I see it now! Now I see! For ninety years I have wondered and wondered and wondered WHY is the Good Cause always defeated by the Bad, WHY Injustice and never Justice anywhere, WHY does Evil always always triumph and Good cast down in the gutter to be shat upon, WHY THIS HORROR AND WHY THIS HEARTACHE and NOW I GET IT! Because God ... is a Menshevik! Because God ... is a Petty-Bourgeois! Because God is a Reactionary, and Progressive People are THE POLITICAL ENEMIES OF GOD! He HATES US! Now! Now AT LAST I *SEE* —[*He collapses and dies.*]

SERGE ESMERELDOVICH UPGOBKIN: Aleksii? Aleksii!?

YEGOR TREMENS RODENT: Oh my God ...

SERGE ESMERELDOVICH UPGOBKIN: Oh help, oh help, oh somebody somebody, Aleksii Antedilluvianovich Prelapsarianov is dead!

Scene 4

[SMUKOV *enters.*]

VASSILY VOROVILICH SMUKOV: Did I hear … ?
Oh my. A dead body.

SERGE ESMERELDOVICH UPGOBKIN: Aleksii Antedilluvianovich Prelapsarianov
is dead.

VASSILY VOROVILICH SMUKOV: Oh dear, he spoke too long. So many words,
we were afraid this might happen.

IPPOLITE IPPOPOLITOVICH POPOLITIPOV: The strain on the heart.

YEGOR TREMENS RODENT: No, it was his brain. A vessel popped upstairs. His
face is royal purple.

IPPOLITE IPPOPOLITOVICH POPOLITIPOV: But popped because: The griev-
ing heart avenged itself on the forward-moving mind. The heart drowned the
brain in blood. So that the whole animal could rest, safe from the future, secure
in the past. As I was saying, the mind may …

YEGOR TREMENS RODENT: Someone ought to call security, we can't leave him
lying …

SERGE ESMERELDOVICH UPGOBKIN: His heart had little reason to murder his
mind, Ippolite Ippopolotovich, Aleksii's mind was hardly moving in a forward
direction.

VASSILY VOROVILICH SMUKOV: I thought in the main his arguments were sound.
As I understood it …

IPPOLITE IPPOPOLITOVICH POPOLITIPOV: The brain inhabits the body like
a virus inhabits a cell. It takes control of the nucleus and selfishly mismanages
the entirety till disaster results. It does not do to think too much! You reformers, you vanguard, you taskmaster brain …

YEGOR TREMENS RODENT: Oh you are making too much of this, Poppy. Comrade
Minister Prelapsarianov was ninety-five years old. No wonder, it was past his
time.

IPPOLITE IPPOPOLITOVICH POPOLITIPOV: Illness is a metaphor, Yegor; the human body, the body politic, the human soul, the soul of the state. Dynamic and immobile all at once, lava and granite, the head and the heart. It's all tension and tearing, and which will win? An infarction [*Clutches his heart.*] or a stroke? [*Clutches his head.*]

VASSILY VOROVILICH SMUKOV: I don't know what you're talking about, Popolitipov, but one thing is clear: We should not move until we know where we're going. They should chisel that on poor Aleksii's tombstone, that was his best bit. Wait patiently till the way is clear.

SERGE ESMERELDOVICH UPGOBKIN: And imagination? That faculty? Which Angels are said to lack, but people possess? Dialectics can only lead us so far, to the edge of what is known. But after that … ? We see so poorly, almost blind. We who …

YEGOR TREMENS RODENT: Careful, Serge Esmereldovich, if you're going to make a speech, look at what happened to poor Comrade Minister, and you're almost as old as he is … was.

SERGE ESMERELDOVICH UPGOBKIN: Then let me follow him into oblivion. Let me make that leap. Because you can only creep so far, and then you must leap, Rodent, you must use your own legs and your own will, or life itself will simply toss you in the air, but willing or resisting, I promise you all, you will leap! Does the heart plot to kill the mind, does it shatter that not sprouted seed, the brain, before the New Blooms blossom? Then let the heart beware, for my brain will dream the New, I will make that leap, and let the strain be too much, let the strain explode my recalcitrant heart, let my heart burst like a bomb while my sparks leap their synapses! We must dream the New! And by Caution we never can! By Leaping! [*He begins to leap in the air, over and over, going higher and higher.*]

IPPOLITE IPPOPOLITOVICH POPOLITIPOV: Stop it, Serge Esmereldovich Upgobkin, you'll …

SERGE ESMERELDOVICH UPGOBKIN: [*As he leaps, to* POPOLITIPOV.] Leap, you unregenerate Stalinist! Leap, you bursitic Brezhnevite! Leap, leap, Procrustean, legless Legachevite, leap!
So what if they dissolve the entire Union, so what if the Balkans are all re-Balkanized, so what if the Ukraine won't sell us their wheat, and Georgia secedes, and Germany reunites, and all our reforms go only to squelch real revolution!

201

VASSILY VOROVILICH SMUKOV: Oh, well, now that would really be terrible, we…

SERGE ESMERELDOVICH UPGOBKIN: [*Still leaping, continuing over the above, to* SMUKOV.] LEAP! HIGH! See if you can see it! The NEW! The UNIMAG-INED! The THAT-FOR-WHICH-OUR-DREAMS-ARE-ACHING! For what is hope but desiring forwards!? [*To Rodent.*] Are you a man, or are you a mollusc? Will you never dare? Will you be dead forever?

YEGOR TREMENS RODENT: NO!

SERGE ESMERELDOVICH UPGOBKIN: Then LEAP!

[UPGOBKIN *and* RODENT *leap and leap.*]

VASSILY VOROVILICH SMUKOV: Serge, Serge, please don't overexert yourself, what has gotten into you?

SERGE ESMERELDOVICH UPGOBKIN: The NEW! The NEW! The NEW!

IPPOLITE IPPOPOLITOVICH POPOLITIPOV: [*Over the above.*] Yegor Tremens Rodent, stop that at once!

[POPOLITIPOV *stops* RODENT, *pulls him down to earth.*]

IPPOLITE IPPOPOLITOVICH POPOLITIPOV: Control yourself, dammit.

VASSILY VOROVILICH SMUKOV: Look at him! Serge …

[UPGOBKIN *is leaping higher and higher. His face is upturned, he is no longer with his comrades, he is beatific, he is smiling enormously. From above there is a violently brief burst of radiance, and the instant it falls on* UPGOBKIN *he collapses and dies. And the light is gone.*]

YEGOR TREMENS RODENT: *Now* I am calling security. And no more metaphors, anyone, please.
Two bodies, two bodies, what a scandal this will make.

IPPOLITE IPPOPOLITOVICH POPOLITIPOV: Was it his heart, or was it his head?

YEGOR TREMENS RODENT: Heart.

VASSILY VOROVILICH SMUKOV: Still smiling. That smile. What on earth do you suppose he saw?

[*They look up, wondering.*]

ACT TWO

"That's why I loved you, for your magnanimous
heart! And you do not need my forgiveness, nor
I yours: it's all the same whether you forgive or not,
all my life you will remain a wound in my soul,
and I in yours—that's how it should be."

—FYODOR DOSTOEVSKY
The Brothers Karamazov

[*Translated by Richard Pevear and Larrissa Volokhonsky.*]

And, oh, how blue the cornflowers,
how black the earth, how red the kerchief
of the female comrade!

—JOHN ASH
"A History of Soviet Organ Music"

Scene 1

[*In the small, dank, dark, dismal room that serves as the guards' chamber of the Pan-Soviet Archives for the Study of Cerebro-Cephalognomical Historico-Biological Materialism [Also known as PASOVACERCEPHHIBIMAT —pronounced "passovah-sayr-seff-HIB-i-mat".] The night following the afternoon of Act One. A table for a desk, an old swivel chair missing a wheel, and a security-system, video monitor surveilling an adjoining room in which big glass jars sit in neat rows on shelves. In the jars float human brains. [We see this room only on the video screen.] In the guardroom, KATHERINA SERAFIMA GLEB, a young woman in her twenties who is wearing the uniform of a security guard, is sitting, staring into space. An old samovar, much, less impressive than the samovar in Act One, stands on the table, brewing tea. POPOLITIPOV, wearing a voluminous greatcoat and a big fur hat, covered in snow, bursts in, carrying an ancient*] *battered guitar case.*]

IPPOLITE IPPOPOLITOVICH POPOLITIPOV: You.

KATHERINA SERAFIMA GLEB: What?

IPPOLITE IPPOPOLITOVICH POPOLITIPOV: Have replaced myself in me.

KATHERINA SERAFIMA GLEB: What?

IPPOLITE IPPOPOLITOVICH POPOLITIPOV: The soul in me that on Judgment Day looked to ascend to bright Heaven has been smitten, obliterated, replaced in me by you.

KATHERINA SERAFIMA GLEB: Too creepy.

IPPOLITE IPPOPOLITOVICH POPOLITIPOV: I am not merely yours, Katherina, I *am* you, I have *become* you.

KATHERINA SERAFIMA GLEB: I said, too creepy.

IPPOLITE IPPOPOLITOVICH POPOLITIPOV: I would like to run my tongue against the salty soft shag covering your upper lip.

KATHERINA SERAFIMA GLEB: Too personal.

IPPOLITE IPPOPOLITOVICH POPOLITIPOV: I want to fuck you.

KATHERINA SERAFIMA GLEB: Don't try anything, Poppy, I'm warning you.

IPPOLITE IPPOPOLITOVICH POPOLITIPOV: Can I sing you a song?

KATHERINA SERAFIMA GLEB: Your voice is repulsive. No. Do you have a cigarette?

IPPOLITE IPPOPOLITOVICH POPOLITIPOV: No. In me there is a yearning, and it complains to me of wanting you, it strains against my skin towards you, it is like the wet lapping of the tide, the pull of the moon on the ocean, like the rise of sap through frozen wood when winter is shattered by the burnt thrust of spring.

KATHERINA SERAFIMA GLEB: Too romantic.

IPPOLITE IPPOPOLITOVICH POPOLITIPOV: Like the hydraulic rush of the river through the dam, the whine of turbines, voltage crossing across a continent

204

of wire.

KATHERINA SERAFIMA GLEB: Too technological.

IPPOLITE IPPOPOLITOVICH POPOLITIPOV: Like the inchoate voluptuous seething of the masses as they surge towards revolutionary consciousness.

KATHERINA SERAFIMA GLEB: [*Overlapping on "surge".*] Too political. Too corny.

IPPOLITE IPPOPOLITOVICH POPOLITIPOV: When I was a child ...

KATHERINA SERAFIMA GLEB: Too psychological.

IPPOLITE IPPOPOLITOVICH POPOLITIPOV: [*Screams, then:*] Give yourself to me, I beg you, Katherina Serafima, or I will blow my brains out. I will lie down in a snowbank or under a train or ...

KATHERINA SERAFIMA GLEB: You were supposed to bring cigarettes, Poppy.

IPPOLITE IPPOPOLITOVICH POPOLITIPOV: I burn my flesh with cigarettes, dreaming of you, I scrape my knuckles along roughcast walls, look, bloody scabs, I deliberately lace my shoes too tight, and cinch my belt till my intestines squirm under pressure, in pain, I refuse myself sleep, dreaming of you, I've slept maybe six, maybe seven hours this whole month. sleep-deprived, trussed and hobbled and why? I mean, are you clever? No. Are you kind? Most certainly not. And yet there is in all your attributes considered and parts taken together a summational. additive kind of perfection: I love you.

KATHERINA SERAFIMA GLEB: You're old.

IPPOLITE IPPOPOLITOVICH POPOLITIPOV: I love you.

KATHERINA SERAFIMA GLEB: I hate you.

IPPOLITE IPPOPOLITOVICH POPOLITIPOV: [*Shouting.*] I LOVE YOU!

KATHERINA SERAFIMA GLEB: I'm a lesbian.

IPPOLITE IPPOPOLITOVICH POPOLITIPOV: Pervert.

KATHERINA SERAFIMA GLEB: Asshole.

IPPOLITE IPPOPOLITOVICH POPOLITIPOV: Abomination!

KATHERINA SERAFIMA GLEB: Exploiter!

IPPOLITE IPPOPOLITOVICH POPOLITIPOV: Wanton! Abuser!

KATHERINA SERAFIMA GLEB: Harasser! Torturer! *Apparatchik!*

> [*He lunges for her. She dodges easily. He falls heavily. She steps on his neck.*]

KATHERINA SERAFIMA GLEB: I warned you.

IPPOLITE IPPOPOLITOVICH POPOLITIPOV: Get off.

KATHERINA SERAFIMA GLEB: Cigarettes.

> [*He hands them to her. She releases him.*]

KATHERINA SERAFIMA GLEB: I'm tired of this, Poppy, I'm going to find an easier way to get a decent smoke. I really am a lesbian, you know. I have a new girlfriend. I'll never have sex with you. I don't want to touch you, and frankly, Poppy, it's not fair you should make me go through this mortifying business over and over and over again, night after night after night; know what? You're a pig.

IPPOLITE IPPOPOLITOVICH POPOLITIPOV: I cannot help myself. [*He begins to remove an ancient guitar from the guitar case.*]

KATHERINA SERAFIMA GLEB: Just because you got me a soft job. A soft, *boring* job. Which I hate. This place is creepy. Know what? At night I hear them slithering.

IPPOLITE IPPOPOLITOVICH POPOLITIPOV: Who?

KATHERINA SERAFIMA GLEB: The brains. They rub their spongy rivules and volutes against the smooth glass sides of their jars. Sometimes they bubble. As if breathing.

IPPOLITE IPPOPOLITOVICH POPOLITIPOV: The brains are dead brains, Katherina.

KATHERINA SERAFIMA GLEB: Then why don't they throw them out?

IPPOLITE IPPOPOLITOVICH POPOLITIPOV: They study them. The great minds of the Party. Political minds. Scientific minds. Even an artist or two.

KATHERINA SERAFIMA GLEB: In my opinion they should throw them out. Most of the older ones are falling apart. No one could make a proper study of them.

Sometimes when I get bored, I grab the jars and shake them up. The brain cells of Vyshinsky. The brain cells of Iron Feliks Dzerzhinsky. Whirl like snowflakes in a crystal snowball.

IPPOLITE IPPOPOLITOVICH POPOLITIPOV: Become my mistress or I will report you.

KATHERINA SERAFIMA GLEB: When you die, Poppy, will they put your brain in a jar?

[POPOLITIPOV *begins to play softly, serenading her.*]

KATHERINA SERAFIMA GLEB: [*Listens to the music a beat, then:*] Some nights I pretend that I am not simply night watchman but I lead midnight tours through here for insomniac Muscovites whose anxieties or guilty consciences keep them awake. This is my speech:
[*To the audience.*] Welcome to The Pan-Soviet Archives for the Study of Cerebro-Cephalognomical Historico-Biological Materialism, also known as PASOVACERCEPHHIBIMAT. Here the Party has stored the brains of its bygone leaders, an unbroken line of brains stretching back to Red October. Beginning of course with Lenin, most people think his brain is still in his body in the crypt, but it's not, it's here, it is MASSIVE, 1,340 grams of solid brain-flesh, the heaviest brain ever extracted, it's a wonder the poor man could hold his head up his brain was so grotesquely HUGE. Ranked beside it are many other famous brains, all floating in some sort of sudsy limegreen mummifying juice, all the famous Bolshevik brains except for those which got flushed in the notorious dead-brain Purges of 1937. Stalin's brain is here; Brezhnev's, which is dingy-yellow like an old tooth; Andropov's, and now I suppose Chernenko's; he died last week but his brain's not here yet: Maybe they couldn't find it. [*She goes to* POPPY *and tousle-pulls his hair.*] [*Teasingly, torturing him.*] Let's talk politics.

IPPOLITE IPPOPOLITOVICH POPOLITIPOV: [*Strumming.*] I don't want to talk politics with you, my Katushka, I want to pluck my guitar for you, pick pick pick I pick my heart to pieces.

KATHERINA SERAFIMA GLEB: Gorbachev will replace Chernenko.
Right?
Come on, Poppy. Tell me! Gorbachev will be our honored leader next?
His wife is a Jewess.

IPPOLITE IPPOPOLITOVICH POPOLITIPOV: [*Continuing to strum.*] No she ...

KATHERINA SERAFIMA GLEB: That's what they say: Jewess.

[POPOLITIPOV *continues to play under this.*]

KATHERINA SERAFIMA GLEB: I'm not an anti-Semite, I have nothing to do with Jews, but that's what they say.
Tea?

> [POPOLITIPOV *nods his head "yes," still playing.* KATHERINA *goes to the samovar, lifts the lid, reaches within and withdraws an alarmingly large bottle of vodka. She takes a huge swallow and hands it to* POPOLITIPOV, *who does the same; while he drinks, she hums his tune; and then he starts playing again; throughout all this the music never stops.*]

IPPOLITE IPPOPOLITOVICH POPOLITIPOV: Gorbachev isn't a Jew. Nor is Raisa Maxsimovna. She just likes to dress fancy. A strange lust for the sort of pleasures one associates with adolescence seems to have overtaken everyone: panic, mania, nausea, rage. The pleasures of adulthood are forsaken.

KATHERINA SERAFIMA GLEB: What are the pleasures of adulthood?

IPPOLITE IPPOPOLITOVICH POPOLITIPOV: Heartbreak. Agony deep as bone marrow. Quiet, nuanced despair.

> [*He looks at her. She drinks vodka. He drinks vodka. He plays again.*]

KATHERINA SERAFIMA GLEB: Gorbachev will come, trailing free-market anarchy in his wake! Burger King! Pizza Hut! The International Monetary Fund! Billions in aid will flow! Solzhenitsyn will come back from Vermont to thrash and purify us! Kentucky Fried Chicken franchises! Toxic waste! Everything will change then, because Gorbachev is crafty and sly in the manner of Jews. He'll defeat the deadbeat nomenklatura, every last one, including you, Poppy, and then there will be no more politics, we will become like Americans, I will be in a heavy-metal band! There will be *surprises*: most of them unpleasant, but at least unanticipated, and the Great Grey Age of Boredom will finally lift.

> [*She takes a swig of vodka, he takes a swig of vodka.*]

IPPOLITE IPPOPOLITOVICH POPOLITIPOV: To the Great Age of Boredom.

KATHERINA SERAFIMA GLEB: I am inexpressibly, immeasurably sad. Sad sad.

IPPOLITE IPPOPOLITOVICH POPOLITIPOV: Because you are a Slav. Sorrow is the spiritual genius of Slavic peoples.

KATHERINA SERAFIMA GLEB: Bullshit. I don't believe in national identities. Reactionary! I am an anarchist.

IPPOLITE IPPOPOLITOVICH POPOLITIPOV: You are a nihilist.

KATHERINA SERAFIMA GLEB: I am an internationalist. [*Swig of vodka.*] Like Trotsky! [*Swig of vodka.*] The Jew!

> [*Pause. He looks at her.*]

IPPOLITE IPPOPOLITOVICH POPOLITIPOV: When I was a child, I was an ugly child, a graceless child, and did not believe I would be loved and was in fact not loved by anyone.

KATHERINA SERAFIMA GLEB: Poor Poppy. Poor Poppy the Slav.

IPPOLITE IPPOPOLITOVICH POPOLITIPOV: My mother dead in the Great Patriotic War, in the snow, German bullet through her spine, her belly, but I was already a young man by then so it can't have been then that I lost her love, but earlier, earlier, a point towards which my memories refuse to travel— I cannot blame them. My father was a bastard, the Germans got him too.

KATHERINA SERAFIMA GLEB: [*Swigging vodka.*] Poppy the orphan.

IPPOLITE IPPOPOLITOVICH POPOLITIPOV: The Party adopted me. The Party was not Love, but Necessity; it rebuilt the ruined world. Through the Party I came to love.

KATHERINA SERAFIMA GLEB: Love.

> [*Vodka. Sorrow.*]

IPPOLITE IPPOPOLITOVICH POPOLITIPOV: The Party dispenses miracles. The Party drove away the Czar, immortalized Lenin, withstood France and Britain and the United States, made Communism in one country, electrified Russia, milled steel, built railways, abolished distance, defeated Germany, suspended time, became Eternal, dispersed the body of each and every member, molecule by molecule, across an inconceivably vast starry matrix encompassing the infinite: so that, within the Party, everything is; so that everything human, even Marx—was shown as limited and the Party, Illimitable; and through the illimitable Party the human is exalted, becomes Divine, occupant of a great chiming spaciousness that is not distance but time, time which never moves nor passes, light which does not travel and yet is light: And love, pure love, even in a degraded, corrupt and loveless world, love can finally be born.

[*Little pause, more vodka.*]

IPPOLITE IPPOPOLITOVICH POPOLITIPOV: Do you understand what I am saying to you, Katushka?

KATHERINA SERAFIMA GLEB: [*Softly; deeply moved.*] Not a word.

IPPOLITE IPPOPOLITOVICH POPOLITIPOV: [*Very tenderly.*] That night, that night, when I saw you that night, I was walking in the Arbat, you had fallen in the snow, sleeping in the gutter, dirty, drunk, rude, radiant: I was overwhelmed with lust, and then followed—love. Love. Love. Love. Love.

[*They are very close; he has almost won.*]

Even in a corrupt and loveless world, love can be born.

[KATHERINA *leaps to her feet and screams, a long, loud, howl of joy; she rushes across the room at* DR. BONFILA BEZHUKHOVNA BONCH-BRUEVICH, *who is just entering the room, carrying a wrapped parcel, wearing hat and coat, covered in snow.* KATHERINA *kisses* BONFILA *passionately.*]

IPPOLITE IPPOPOLITOVICH POPOLITIPOV: [*Aghast.*] Good *GOD*!

BONFILA BEZHUKHOVNA BONCH-BRUEVICH: [*Seeing* POPOLITIPOV.] Oh my *GOD*.

KATHERINA SERAFIMA GLEB: *GOD* I'm happy! [*To* POPOLITIPOV.] Hello, Poppy!

BONFILA BEZHUKHOVNA BONCH-BRUEVICH: [*Horror-stricken, bowing her head slightly.*] Comrade Commissar, I …

KATHERINA SERAFIMA GLEB: See? Lesbians! This is my girlfriend, Doctor Bonf …

BONFILA BEZHUKHOVNA BONCH-BRUEVICH: [*Cutting her off.*] I'm interrupting.

[BONFILA *turns to leave,* KATHERINA *grabs her arm.*]

KATHERINA SERAFIMA GLEB: No, Poppy was interrupting, Poppy is always interrupting, but now he's going. Aren't you, Poppy? [*Screaming with rage.*] GO,

POPPY!!!

BONFILA BEZHUKHOVNA BONCH-BRUEVICH: [*To* KATHERINA.] You're drunk.

KATHERINA SERAFIMA GLEB: No I'm not.

BONFILA BEZHUKHOVNA BONCH-BRUEVICH: Yes you are!

KATHERINA SERAFIMA GLEB: You're mad at me.
[*To* POPOLITIPOV.] See what you've done.
I need a drink.
[*To* POPOLITIPOV.] See, my sadness is gone, I must not be a true Slav after all. I'm happy you can see her, now maybe you will know that I cannot love you: ever, ever. And she is a physician, she cures people, not an ineffectual aged paperpushing-timeserver-apparatchik-with-a-dacha like you who only bleeds the people dry.

   [*Awkward pause.*]

BONFILA BEZHUKHOVNA BONCH-BRUEVICH: Did I interrupt ...
[*Pointing to the guitar that* POPPY *clutches.*] Comrade Commissar was playing the ...

IPPOLITE IPPOPOLITOVICH POPOLITIPOV: [*Putting the guitar away; very, very darkly.*] Not anymore. Doctor ... ?

KATHERINA SERAFIMA GLEB: Bonch-Bruevich!

BONFILA BEZHUKHOVNA BONCH-BRUEVICH: [*Simultaneously.*] Comrade Commissar, I ...
[*To* KATHERINA, *hearing that she has said her name.*] Shut up.
I'll go.
I'll go.
Somebody should go.
This is mortifying.

IPPOLITE IPPOPOLITOVICH POPOLITIPOV: Is it?
[*Pleasant.*] Things change. Some things. We are all liberals.
[*Homicidally angry to* KATHERINA.] Horseleech! Viper's spawn!
[*Pleasant again.*] You are a doctor. Of ... ?
[*Military command.*] Do you have a specialty.

BONFILA BEZHUKHOVNA BONCH-BRUEVICH: Pediatric oncology.

KATHERINA SERAFIMA GLEB: [*Sad.*] Kids with cancer.

IPPOLITE IPPOPOLITOVICH POPOLITIPOV: Moscow?

BONFILA BEZHUKHOVNA BONCH-BRUEVICH: I ... Yes.

IPPOLITE IPPOPOLITOVICH POPOLITIPOV: [*Trying to keep it together but coming unglued.*] That's convenient for both of you. You are lucky. Moscow is an agreeable posting, for cosmopolitans such as you and I. Many doctors have to report to places more remote, arctic outposts ...

 [*Little pause; becoming suddenly profoundly sad and weary.*]

Doctor, may I ask you a health-related question?

BONFILA BEZHUKHOVNA BONCH-BRUEVICH: Certainly.

IPPOLITE IPPOPOLITOVICH POPOLITIPOV: [*In confidence, in earnest.*] If a man were to shoot himself, against which of the various customary vulnerable points of the body would you advise he position the barrel of his gun?

BONFILA BEZHUKHOVNA BONCH-BRUEVICH: I ...

IPPOLITE IPPOPOLITOVICH POPOLITIPOV: Temple? Soft palate? Heart?

KATHERINA SERAFIMA GLEB: I have a friend who died by shooting himself in the armpit. The bullet went through his shoulder and into his nose.

 [KATHERINA *bursts into gales of drunken laughter. A beat;* BONFILA *and* POPOLITIPOV *stare at* KATHERINA.]

BONFILA BEZHUKHOVNA BONCH-BRUEVICH: [*Softly, deferentially.*] I would advise him not to shoot himself, Comrade Commissar. I would advise him to live.

IPPOLITE IPPOPOLITOVICH POPOLITIPOV: Say his life had become unbearable.

BONFILA BEZHUKHOVNA BONCH-BRUEVICH: Life is almost never literally unbearable. We choose whether or not we bear up. We choose.

IPPOLITE IPPOPOLITOVICH POPOLITIPOV: Circumstances may dictate otherwise. History.

BONFILA BEZHUKHOVNA BONCH-BRUEVICH: People make their own history.

IPPOLITE IPPOPOLITOVICH POPOLITIPOV: Limits are set by the conditions of their social development.

KATHERINA SERAFIMA GLEB: [*By rote, a thing she learned in school.*] Those conditions are themselves affected by the state of their economic relations.

[*Pause. The others look at* KATHERINA.]

KATHERINA SERAFIMA GLEB: Which in turn are related to a particular stage of the mode of production.

[*She sits heavily slumps over, falls asleep.*]

IPPOLITE IPPOPOLITOVICH POPOLITIPOV: [*Crossing to the sleeping Kat; he looks at her, then:*] Her head is stuffed full of pottery shards, rags, ash and wind. She is the Revolution's Great-Granddaughter. She is ... a barbarian.

BONFILA BEZHUKHOVNA BONCH-BRUEVICH: She's immature. And can't drink.
And I think she doesn't like you very much.

IPPOLITE IPPOPOLITOVICH POPOLITIPOV: I must be going.

KATHERINA SERAFIMA GLEB: [*Still slumped over, drowsy.*] Try the armpit, Poppy.

IPPOLITE IPPOPOLITOVICH POPOLITIPOV: [*A beat; then, bracing himself for the mortal blow.*] If I shoot myself, Katherina, will you miss me?.

KATHERINA SERAFIMA GLEB: [*Looking up.*] Maybe. For a day or two. Maybe.
The cigarettes, definitely.
Not really. No.
Oh Poppy, I'm sorry, but you're a pig, you know, and I would like to be kind, but I can't. [*She sleeps.*]

IPPOLITE IPPOPOLITOVICH POPOLITIPOV: We have not made kind people. [*To* BONFILA, *not without menace.*] We have not made a world that makes people kind.

[*He leaves.*]

BONFILA BEZHUKHOVNA BONCH-BRUEVICH: Is he really going to shoot himself?

[KATHERINA *snores, loudly.*]

Scene 2

[*The guardroom. Several hours later.* KATHERINA *and* BONFILA *sit at the table, both drunk,* KATHERINA *more drunk; the parcel, still wrapped, is on the table between them. Also on the table is a now nearly empty bottle of vodka.*]

BONFILA BEZHUKHOVNA BONCH-BRUEVICH: My great-grandfather was Vladimir Dimitrievich Bonch-Bruevich. Do you know who that is?

[KATHERINA *shakes her head "no".*]

BONFILA BEZHUKHOVNA BONCH-BRUEVICH: First Secretary of the Sovnarkom.
The Council of People's Commissars. 1918. A founder of the Party.

KATHERINA SERAFIMA GLEB: Never heard of him.

BONFILA BEZHUKHOVNA BONCH-BRUEVICH: It's your history.

KATHERINA SERAFIMA GLEB: I have no history. What's in the package?

BONFILA BEZHUKHOVNA BONCH-BRUEVICH: My great-grandfather is the man who embalmed Lenin. He selected the design for the tomb.

KATHERINA SERAFIMA GLEB: You're angry with me because I'm drunk.

BONFILA BEZHUKHOVNA BONCH-BRUEVICH: Not as angry as I was when I was sober.

KATHERINA SERAFIMA GLEB: Promise we'll be lovers forever.

BONFILA BEZHUKHOVNA BONCH-BRUEVICH: No.

KATHERINA SERAFIMA GLEB: Promise we'll be lovers till I'm sober.

BONFILA BEZHUKHOVNA BONCH-BRUEVICH: Yes.

KATHERINA SERAFIMA GLEB: If you leave me I'll kill you.

BONFILA BEZHUKHOVNA BONCH-BRUEVICH: Oh bullshit.

KATHERINA SERAFIMA GLEB: Is Poppy dead yet, do you think?
You've been my lover for more than a month, and look, you still visit me

214

late at night, you bring me mysterious packages …

BONFILA BEZHUKHOVNA BONCH-BRUEVICH: Three weeks, it's only been …
It's still new to me, all this …

KATHERINA SERAFIMA GLEB: You won't leave me, will you?

BONFILA BEZHUKHOVNA BONCH-BRUEVICH: I love you.

KATHERINA SERAFIMA GLEB: That's not what I asked. Everyone loves me,
but I'm unbearable.
I need someone who will … stay, or …
I'm sad again.

BONFILA BEZHUKHOVNA BONCH-BRUEVICH: My great-grandfather was also
a great Slavophile, a folklorist.

KATHERINA SERAFIMA GLEB: Sadness is the spiritual genius of the Slavic peoples.

BONFILA BEZHUKHOVNA BONCH-BRUEVICH: Uh-huh.
He wrote that the revolts of the Old Believers against Peter the Great were
early stirrings of the Revolution among the peoples.

KATHERINA SERAFIMA GLEB: Peter the Great, 1672-1725.

BONFILA BEZHUKHOVNA BONCH-BRUEVICH: My great-grandfather also collected icons. And he planned the Lenin Cult.

KATHERINA SERAFIMA GLEB: Lenin: 1870-1923.

BONFILA BEZHUKHOVNA BONCH-BRUEVICH: 1924. When Lenin died, peas-
ants from Tsarskoe Selo sent this to my great-grandpa, to put in the tomb.

[*She unwraps the package. It's an old icon, with a metal candleholder
attached, in which is a red glass, inside of which is a candle.*]

BONFILA BEZHUKHOVNA BONCH-BRUEVICH: See? It's Lenin. They painted
his face over an icon of St. Sergius of Radonezh, who lived six hundred years
ago …

[*Little pause.* KATHERINA *drinks most of the rest of the vodka, passes
the last swallow to* BONFILA, *who drinks it.*]

BONFILA BEZHUKHOVNA BONCH-BRUEVICH: … and who is said to have been a great worker of miracles.

KATHERINA SERAFIMA GLEB: We need more vodka.

BONFILA BEZHUKHOVNA BONCH-BRUEVICH: There is no more vodka.

KATHERINA SERAFIMA GLEB: We must go out and get some more vodka.

BONFILA BEZHUKHOVNA BONCH-BRUEVICH: It's too late. It must be four A.M. There won't be a store open.

KATHERINA SERAFIMA GLEB: Why won't you make love to me?

BONFILA BEZHUKHOVNA BONCH-BRUEVICH: *Here?*

KATHERINA SERAFIMA GLEB: Oh who gives a fuck where? Sure, here. If you love me what would it matter.

BONFILA BEZHUKHOVNA BONCH-BRUEVICH: Too creepy.

KATHERINA SERAFIMA GLEB: Do it, here. Put your hand down my coveralls, slip it deep inside me, blow hot fog-breath in my ears till my brains cook, let me lick your cunt till my whole face is wet, put my hair in your mouth, nip my buttocks, let me scream joyfully as if a hungry animal I want to feed is eating me up!

BONFILA BEZHUKHOVNA BONCH-BRUEVICH: You embarrass me.

KATHERINA SERAFIMA GLEB: You're afraid of sex with me.

BONFILA BEZHUKHOVNA BONCH-BRUEVICH: *Nonsense.*

     [*Little pause.*]

I'm afraid of sex with you in front of a Deputy Secretary Of …

KATHERINA SERAFIMA GLEB: He's off shooting himself.
     We're alone. I still have all my clothes on. Something's wrong.

BONFILA BEZHUKHOVNA BONCH-BRUEVICH: He won't shoot himself, and tomorrow he'll have us both arrested. Ten years in an institution!

KATHERINA SERAFIMA GLEB: Under Gorbachev people will not be …

BONFILA BEZHUKHOVNA BONCH-BRUEVICH: [*Overlap.*] Or maybe he'll have me transferred, just me, alone, to some godforsaken town in Uzbekistan; it was very, very, very stupid of you to kiss me like that in the open like that, to …

KATHERINA SERAFIMA GLEB: He's probably dead by now—Poppy—and anyway he wouldn't …

BONFILA BEZHUKHOVNA BONCH-BRUEVICH: [*Overlap, continuous from above.*] … to draw down attention like that, to deliberately …
HOW THE HELL DO—YOU KNOW WHAT HE'D … You're ignorant. You don't know anything.

[*Pause.*]

KATHERINA SERAFIMA GLEB: St. Sergius of Radonezh. 1314-1392. You're yelling because you're afraid of me.

BONFILA BEZHUKHOVNA BONCH-BRUEVICH: Yes.

[*They kiss. It gets hot, then hotter, then cold.*]

BONFILA BEZHUKHOVNA BONCH-BRUEVICH: Sexual deviance is symptomatic of cultures of luxury, in which monied classes cultivate morbid fascinations with biological functions, especially sex, tending towards narcissistic, antisocial, unproductive behavior such as … Anyway I don't believe in lesbians, I believe in the working class as the only repository for real historical agency. You're right I am afraid of you.

KATHERINA SERAFIMA GLEB: Why did you come?

BONFILA BEZHUKHOVNA BONCH-BRUEVICH: To show you this. [*The icon.*] My great-grandmother is dying. She's one hundred and five years old. Endurance is the spiritual genius of Slavic peoples. She gave me this. She says it still works miracles.

KATHERINA SERAFIMA GLEB: Who do you pray to when you light the candle, Lenin or St. Sergius?

BONFILA BEZHUKHOVNA BONCH-BRUEVICH: She didn't say.

KATHERINA SERAFIMA GLEB: What miracles has it worked?

BONFILA BEZHUKHOVNA BONCH-BRUEVICH: She didn't say that either.

KATHERINA SERAFIMA GLEB: Let's pray for vodka.

BONFILA BEZHUKHOVNA BONCH-BRUEVICH: Shouldn't it be for something less frivolous?

KATHERINA SERAFIMA GLEB: I pray for you to love me enough to be true to your promise.

BONFILA BEZHUKHOVNA BONCH-BRUEVICH: What promise.

KATHERINA SERAFIMA GLEB: That you'll never leave me.

BONFILA BEZHUKHOVNA BONCH-BRUEVICH: Till you're sober.

KATHERINA SERAFIMA GLEB: [*Very serious.*] Then I must never be sober again. Let's pray for vodka.

BONFILA BEZHUKHOVNA BONCH-BRUEVICH: Match.

[KATHERINA *gives her one.* BONFILA *lights the candle. The room darkens.* KATHERINA *kneels, bows her head.*]

KATHERINA SERAFIMA GLEB: St. Lenin or St. Sergius, whoever you are. Please hear the prayer of your little daughter. Look down on her from heaven, she's in the room of dead brains; send vodka. So that I may stay pathetically drunk so that she will never leave me, because I'm full of violence and self-pity and lies, but I do have decent feelings too, and dreams that are beautiful, that I'm not ashamed of having, and there was no earthly thing I could attach them to until I made her love me. Please help me little father. Please hear my prayer.

[*Pause. A big babushka enters, covered in snow.*]

BIG BABUSHKA: [*No pauses.*] Kat, I'll tell you what, I was sweeping the snow off the steps up front and along comes this huge truckload of soldiers plowing down the street, sliding on the ice and bang it smacks into a telephone pole and goes over on its side and all the soldiers come tumbling out, and I rush over to see was anyone hurt, and someone was because a soldier's running up and down the street spattering blood in the snow and we can't get him to stop because naturally they're all drunken idiots from the sticks and he's screaming "I'm dying, I'm dying, mother, mother," and all the yelling frightens a dog who bites a cop who swings a club which smashes a big store window; dog, glass, blood, soldiers, and finally we got the boy calmed down and sent him off wrapped up in a bandage and the dog's run off and the cop sees it's a liquor store window he's smashed so he gives me a big bottle of this vodka to shut me up about it (because everyone knows my mouth) which I can't drink because my liver's already the size of my head and so here, I've brought it to you, you drunken slut, because I'm fond of you as if you were my own granddaughter, now I got to go finish sweeping the snow before more falls. [*The big babushka slams a big bottle of vodka down on the table. She squints at the icon.*] St. Sergius of Radonezh with the face of Great Lenin.

[*She crosses herself and exits.* KATHERINA *and* BONFILA *look at the vodka and each other, agape.*]

Scene 3

[*Even later.* KATHERINA *is asleep with her head in* BONFILA's *lap.* BONFILA *strokes* KATHERINA's *hair and looks at the icon, before which the candle is still burning. The second bottle of vodka stands, almost empty, beside the first empty bottle.*]

BONFILA BEZHUKHOVNA BONCH-BRUEVICH: [*Very softly.*] Little father: You left us alone and see the state we've fallen into? Shouldn't you come back to us now? We have suffered and suffered and Paradise has not arrived. Shouldn't you come back and tell us what went wrong?
She says your brain is in a jar next door: Your body is across town. Pull yourself together, leave your tomb, come claim your brain, remember speech, and action, and once more, having surveyed the wreckage we have made, tell your children: What is to be done?

Shouldn't you come back now?

[*Little red candle lights blink on everywhere.*]

BONFILA BEZHUKHOVNA BONCH-BRUEVICH: [*Like on Christmas morning.*] Kat. Wake up. Kat. Wake up. Katherina.

KATHERINA SERAFIMA GLEB: What?

BONFILA BEZHUKHOVNA BONCH-BRUEVICH: [*Looking about at the lights, wonderingly.*] Do you ...

KATHERINA SERAFIMA GLEB: [*Asleep.*] What is it?

BONFILA BEZHUKHOVNA BONCH-BRUEVICH: [*Standing.*] Do you see? Do you see? It's ...

[*A little girl, dressed in a shirt and pullover sweater, enters, and silently looks at* BONFILA. BONFILA *screams.* KATHERINA *stands up abruptly.*]

KATHERINA SERAFIMA GLEB: [*Terrified, blind.*] I drank too much. Much too much. I've blinded myself. [*She gropes about for* BONFILA.] B! B! Don't leave me! Don't leave me!
The lights are going out.

[*The lights go out.*]

ACT THREE

I'm hanging on to the tram strap
of these terrible times,
and I don't know why I'm alive.

—OSIP MANDELSTAM
The Moscow Notebooks
(*Translated by Richard and Elizabeth McKane*)

Scene I

[*Talmenka, Siberia; 1992. A white room in a medical facility. The little girl who appeared at the end of Act Two,* VODYA DOMIK, *is now sitting in a wooden chair. She is expressionless, and mostly very still, although she blinks and occasionally, though infrequently, scratches her arm or shifts in the chair. She sits alone for a few beats.* YEGOR TREMENS RODENT *enters, wearing hat, coat, mittens, muffler, umbrella, galoshes; he's carrying a cheap overstuffed briefcase. He is, as always, timorous and deferential, but in the intervening years he's gotten nasty. He tries to hide this; as the scene progresses it emerges.*
An old samovar stands in the corner, dead cold. Near it a kettle on a hotplate.
RODENT *looks at* VODYA, *who stares ahead. Several beats pass.*]

YEGOR TREMENS RODENT: Hello little girl.

[VODYA *has no reaction whatsoever, and has none throughout what follows.* RODENT's *tone is maddeningly unvaried: mild, cheerful, each attempt exactly the same as the one preceding, rather like a parrot.*]

YEGOR TREMENS RODENT: Hello little girl.
    Hello little girl.
    Hello.
    Hello.
    Hello little girl.
    Hello little girl.
    Hello little girl.
    Hello. Hello. Hello. Little girl.

[*Pause. He thinks, then:*]

Hello little girl.
Hello little girl.
Hello little girl. [*Getting a little ratty-panic.*]
Hello. Hello. Hello little girl. Little girl.
    Little girl.
    Little ...

[*He pauses again to look around and to think.* BONFILA *comes in, looking different—older, more tired—than in the previous act.* RODENT *doesn't hear her come in.*]

YEGOR TREMENS RODENT: Hello little girl.
Hello little girl.
Hello little girl.

BONFILA BEZHUKHOVNA BONCH-BRUEVICH: She doesn't ...

YEGOR TREMENS RODENT: [*Badly frightened.*] *OH*!!

BONFILA BEZHUKHOVNA BONCH-BRUEVICH: She doesn't speak. Deputy Councilor Rodent?

YEGOR TREMENS RODENT: [*Shaken, nervous.*] Assistant Deputy Councilor. Rodent, um, yes.
[*Inclining his head towards* VODYA.] She ... is ... Mute?
Deaf-mute, or ... ?

[BONFILA *shrugs.*]

BONFILA BEZHUKHOVNA BONCH-BRUEVICH: Welcome to Talmenka.

[*She exits.* RODENT *looks at the door through which she has exited, then turns back to* VODYA, *looks at her for a minute and then, exactly as before.*]

YEGOR TREMENS RODENT: Hello little girl.
Hello little girl.
Hello little girl.
Hello little girl.
Want a boiled sweet?
[*Mildly malicious.*] No, I don't have any boiled sweets.

222

Hello little girl.
Hello little girl.
Hello little ...

[MRS. SHASTLIVYI DOMIK, VODYA's *mother, enters abruptly; she is dressed pretty much like a young babushka. She isn't loud but every word she speaks is a bullet aimed at the person she's addressing.* RODENT *spins to face her.*]

MRS. SHASTLIVYI DOMIK: Her name is Vodya. Domik.

YEGOR TREMENS RODENT: Why doesn't she ...

MRS. SHASTLIVYI DOMIK: She doesn't.

[MRS. DOMIK *exits abruptly.* RODENT *looks at* VODYA. *A beat, then:*]

YEGOR TREMENS RODENT: Hello little girl.
Hello little ...

[BONFILA *and* MRS. DOMIK *enter together.*]

BONFILA BEZHUKHOVNA BONCH-BRUEVICH: Assistant Deputy Councilor Y. T. Rodent, this is Mrs. Shastlivyi Domik, the child's mother.

MRS. SHASTLIVYI DOMIK: Her name is Vodya.

BONFILA BEZHUKHOVNA BONCH-BRUEVICH: Assistant Deputy Councilor Rodent has come from Moscow. He's come to make a report to President Yeltsin.

YEGOR TREMENS RODENT: [*Nervous little laugh, then:*] Well, not *directly* to ...

BONFILA BEZHUKHOVNA BONCH-BRUEVICH: [*Overlap.*] He's come to see what's going on here. About the children.

[*They all look at* VODYA.]

YEGOR TREMENS RODENT: [*Official, but still nervous.*] Can she hear what we say?

BONFILA BEZHUKHOVNA BONCH-BRUEVICH: Probably.

YEGOR TREMENS RODENT: But she doesn't speak.

BONFILA BEZHUKHOVNA BONCH-BRUEVICH: No.

YEGOR TREMENS RODENT: *Can* she, I mean is she …

BONFILA BEZHUKHOVNA BONCH-BRUEVICH: Theoretically, yes, I mean she's *able*, she has a larynx, a tongue, she … So theoretically, yes but …

MRS. SHASTLIVYI DOMIK: [*Overlapping on second "theoretically".*] She doesn't speak. She never speaks.

YEGOR TREMENS RODENT: How old is she.

BONCH-BRUEVICH and DOMIK: [*Together.*] Eight.

[*Pause.*]

YEGOR TREMENS RODENT: I …

[*Nervous laugh.*]

Well how horrible.

[*Pause.*]

BONFILA BEZHUKHOVNA BONCH-BRUEVICH: Several of the children have died before their sixth birthday. She's the oldest. She's our survivor.

YEGOR TREMENS RODENT: I thought … um, I was told she'd be, um, um, um, yellow.

BONFILA BEZHUKHOVNA BONCH-BRUEVICH: They're all yellow at birth, we have no idea why, really but. That's why they're called Yellow Children. The jaundice fades by their first birthday.
The older they get the more we see it. Nervous-system damage, renal malformation, liver, cataracts at three, bone-marrow problems.

YEGOR TREMENS RODENT: See what?

BONFILA BEZHUKHOVNA BONCH-BRUEVICH: What?

YEGOR TREMENS RODENT: You said, "the more we see it." What is "*it*"?

BONFILA BEZHUKHOVNA BONCH-BRUEVICH: [*A beat, then a bit more assertive, confrontational.*] They mostly don't walk until … How old was Vodya?

MRS. SHASTLIVYI DOMIK: Four.

BONFILA BEZHUKHOVNA BONCH-BRUEVICH: And they don't speak. A few have words, minimal speech, she doesn't.

224

We've ruled out pretty much everything you'd normally look for: pesticides, industrial pollutants, something the parents are eating. They eat badly here but ...

MRS. SHASTLIVYI DOMIK: We've always eaten badly.

[*Little pause.*]

YEGOR TREMENS RODENT: So it isn't the diet.

MRS. SHASTLIVYI DOMIK: We've always eaten badly.

BONFILA BEZHUKHOVNA BONCH-BRUEVICH: It's genetic. Inherited. Probably chromosome alteration due to her parents' exposure to ionizing radiation. Or her parents' parents. In significantly high doses, wave, not particulate, not on the ground or on food, but from a ...
In 1949, two hundred and fifty miles from here, in Kazakhstan, in the Semipalatinsk area, the army detonated a nuclear warhead. They detonated the warhead to put out a minor oil fire. An experiment. No one of course was evacuated.

YEGOR TREMENS RODENT: [*Shrugs sadly.*] Stalin.

BONFILA BEZHUKHOVNA BONCH-BRUEVICH: [*Even more aggressive.*] The place I worked in last year, Chelyabinsk, there's a cave, full of something in leaky barrels. Unmarked railway cars used to pass through the town late at night, smoking, on their way to the cave, you could smell the fumes everywhere. Not Stalin. Last year.

YEGOR TREMENS RODENT: It's a storage facility.

BONFILA BEZHUKHOVNA BONCH-BRUEVICH: So, basically, you ask what's wrong with her. Well, in my opinion and in the opinion of my colleagues, she's a mutation. A nuclear mutant. Third generation. She has a sister who's "healthy"; I wonder what her children will be like?

YEGOR TREMENS RODENT: [*To* MRS. DOMIK.] I'm sorry.

[MRS. DOMIK *walks out.*]

BONFILA BEZHUKHOVNA BONCH-BRUEVICH: In Altograd, which is where I was before I was in Chelyabinsk, there's twenty times the normal rate for thyroid cancer. There's a lake full of blind fish. Everyone has nosebleeds. Everyone's chronically fatigued. Leukemia is epidemic. The reactor plant

225

near there has cracks in the casing, steam comes through several times a month, it's the same kind as at Chernobyl, it was supposed to be closed, it isn't, and the caves in Chelyabinsk? The stuff you have in there, probably cesium, strontium, certainly bomb-grade plutonium, piled up since when? 1950? It's seeping into the aquifer; sixty feet per year. Do you know what that means? There's a river nearby. Millions drink from it. This is documented. The Dnieper's already shot from Chernobyl, and people still drink from that. Millions. The plutonium in that cave. Three hundred pounds of it could kill every person on the planet. You have thirty *tons* down there, in rusting drums. The people of Altograd voted for you to move it, a referendum, last year: Why? Why hasn't it been moved?

YEGOR TREMENS RODENT: To where?

BONFILA BEZHUKHOVNA BONCH-BRUEVICH: The whole country's a radioactive swamp, waste dumps, warheads, malfunctioning reactors, there are six hundred nuclear waste sites in *Moscow*, for God's sake. Hundreds upon hundreds of thousands of people have been exposed.

[*Little pause.*]

YEGOR TREMENS RODENT: The world has changed with an unimaginable rapidity. People grow impatient. Everything is new now, and everything is terrible. In the old days I would not have been forced to do this sort of work. [*With a little menace.*] In the old days you would not speak to me like this.

[*Little pause.*]

BONFILA BEZHUKHOVNA BONCH-BRUEVICH: All I ever see are the regional authorities, and they're just the same old Party bosses who just ...

YEGOR TREMENS RODENT: [*Official.*] But you see, doctor, there's nothing to be done. We have no place to put it. We used to dump it into the sea, the ... That's frowned on by the International Community, it's understandable, they'll take away our loans if we ... We have no money. Trillions. It would cost trillions. And some of these places will simply never be inhabitable again. Regardless of the money. Twenty thousand years.

[MRS.DOMIK *slams back into the room, stands glowering.*]

YEGOR TREMENS RODENT: And anyway, we're broke.

BONFILA BEZHUKHOVNA BONCH-BRUEVICH: And now you're offering to process and store radioactive and toxic waste from the West.

YEGOR TREMENS RODENT: [*Overlap.*] They'll pay us.

BONFILA BEZHUKHOVNA BONCH-BRUEVICH: [*Overlap.*] But store it where?

YEGOR TREMENS RODENT: [*Overlap.*] We need the money. The Russian People need the ...

BONFILA BEZHUKHOVNA BONCH-BRUEVICH: [*Overlap.*] You've conducted tests. On uninformed citizens. Whole populations, the Russian People ...

YEGOR TREMENS RODENT: [*Overlap, snide.*] I, personally, never did that.

BONFILA BEZHUKHOVNA BONCH-BRUEVICH: [*Overlap.*] The West doesn't do that. Expose its citizens unknowingly to radiation, to ... Even the United States would never do that.

YEGOR TREMENS RODENT: Oh don't be so certain ...

BONFILA BEZHUKHOVNA BONCH-BRUEVICH: I am ... certain, the Western democracies, even capitalist countries don't ...

YEGOR TREMENS RODENT: [*Overlap.*] Then move to the West. Anyone can, now. If they'll let you in. Which of course they won't. What do you want from me?

BONFILA BEZHUKHOVNA BONCH-BRUEVICH: I want to know.

YEGOR TREMENS RODENT: What?

BONFILA BEZHUKHOVNA BONCH-BRUEVICH: BECAUSE I AM ... *STILL*, A SOCIALIST! Isn't that absurd! After all I've seen I still believe ... And, and I want to know! And you, SOMEONE MUST TELL ME! How this ... How this came to pass. How any of this came to pass. In a socialist country. In the world's first socialist country.

   [*Little pause.*]

YEGOR TREMENS RODENT: Naïveté.

BONFILA BEZHUKHOVNA BONCH-BRUEVICH: It's the spiritual genius of Slavic peoples.

YEGOR TREMENS RODENT: [*A brief pause; trying to figure her out, now he's got the*

227

upper hand.] What are you doing in Siberia.

BONFILA BEZHUKHOVNA BONCH-BRUEVICH: I was transferred by the Ministry of Health Services in 1985.

YEGOR TREMENS RODENT: You must have made someone angry.

BONFILA BEZHUKHOVNA BONCH-BRUEVICH: As a matter of fact I did. Not angry, jealous. He had me transferred.

YEGOR TREMENS RODENT: But things are different now. You could go back.

BONFILA BEZHUKHOVNA BONCH-BRUEVICH: Yes.

YEGOR TREMENS RODENT: In fact, you could have gone back there five years ago, in 1987 you could have gone back. [*With mock enthusiasm.*]   Perestroika!

BONFILA BEZHUKHOVNA BONCH-BRUEVICH: I suppose so. I was afraid.

YEGOR TREMENS RODENT: Of the man who had you transferred?

BONFILA BEZHUKHOVNA BONCH-BRUEVICH: No.
Someone I disappointed. I disappointed a friend, I hurt her, badly, and I was afraid to face her again. So I stayed here. Why are you asking me … ?

YEGOR TREMENS RODENT: [*Shrug, nasty smile.*] The Steppes, the Taiga, it's an unhealthy place. Siberia, doctor, is making you shrill.

MRS. SHASTLIVYI DOMIK: [*Suddenly, to* RODENT, *very upset.*] Compensation. Money. You're from Moscow, do you understand me?

YEGOR TREMENS RODENT: Yes, I understand what comp …

MRS. SHASTLIVYI DOMIK: [*Continuous from above, and throughout this section she runs right over what* RODENT *says, taking only little breaths when he begins to speak.*] I want to be compensated. Look at her. Look. She'll never be anything.

YEGOR TREMENS RODENT: I'm truly sorry about your …

MRS. SHASTLIVYI DOMIK: [*Overlap.*] I will need to be compensated. Look. Look. What am I supposed to do with …

YEGOR TREMENS RODENT: I have forms for you to fill out and …

MRS. SHASTLIVYI DOMIK: [*Overlap.*] How am I supposed to feed her? You cut back on my assistance …

YEGOR TREMENS RODENT: It's very hard all over Russia, Mrs ...

MRS. SHASTLIVYI DOMIK: [*Overlap.*] I can't live without my assistance and you took most of it, it's a pittance, how am I supposed to feed her, she eats, and watch her, she has to be watched every second and you closed down the day hospital, you cut assistance so compensate me. And medicine, now I have to pay for medicine, more than half the money we have goes for ...

YEGOR TREMENS RODENT: Austerity measures are necessary to ... Doctor, can you get her to ...

MRS. SHASTLIVYI DOMIK: [*Overlap.*] ... for medicine, and how do I pay for that medicine is expensive when I can't work because what work is there that *pays*, that really *pays*, and with *inflation* ...

YEGOR TREMENS RODENT: The transition to a free-market economy requires sacrifice.

MRS. SHASTLIVYI DOMIK: [*Overlap.*] ... my God, inflation, money's worthless and who has what you need for the black market, it's impossible, I should be compensated and ...

YEGOR TREMENS RODENT: The World Bank is promising ...

BONFILA BEZHUKHOVNA BONCH-BRUEVICH: [*Simultaneous with* RODENT.] Mrs. Domik, I think you should maybe sit and I'll get some tea ...

MRS. SHASTLIVYI DOMIK: [*Overlap.*] ... and anyway who'll mind her if I work. [*To* BONFILA.] I DONT WANT TEA, and what have you ever done for her, huh, except tests and tests and tests, you haven't helped any of the children, and she's not dying she's *growing*, and who's supposed to mind her if I have to work all day, she doesn't just sit now, she wanders, across roads, and ... Well? WHAT ABOUT MY DAUGHTER? WHAT ABOUT MY DAUGHTER? WHAT ARE YOU GOING TO DO ABOUT MY DAUGHTER? WHO'LL PAY FOR THAT?.

BONFILA BEZHUKHOVNA BONCH-BRUEVICH: Please, Mrs. Domik, there are other patients in the ...

MRS. SHASTLIVYI DOMIK: Take her!

> [MRS.DOMIK *yanks* VODYA *out of the chair and drags her over to* RODENT, *who recoils with fear.* MRS. DOMIK *shoves the child against*

RODENT.]

MRS. SHASTLIVYI DOMIK: She's not a, a, a person! NO! Take her to Yeltsin! Take her to Gorbachev! Take her to Gaidar! Take her to Clinton! *YOU* care for her! YOU did this! YOU did this! She's *YOURS.*

[MRS.DOMIK *exits.* BONFILA *takes* VODYA *and leads her back to her chair.*]

YEGOR TREMENS RODENT: Um, um um …

[BONFILA *goes out of the room.* RODENT *goes over to* VODYA *and pats her on the head.* MRS. DOMIK *comes back in, alone, wearing a coat and scarf, and carrying the same for* VODYA.]

MRS. SHASTLIVYI DOMIK: Get your filthy fucking hands off my child.

[RODENT *moves away from* VODYA, *sits.* MRS. DOMIK *bundles* VODYA *up, preparing to leave.*]

YEGOR TREMENS RODENT: [*Quietly, carefully, furtively.*] Mrs. Domik, may I speak to you, not as a representative of the government but in confidence, as one Russian to another?

[*Little pause.*]

This nation is failing apart. It is in the hands of miscreants and fools. The government does not serve the people, but betrays the people to foreign interests. The tragedy of your daughter is but one instance, a tragic instance of the continuance of the crimes of the Communist era through to the present day. Chaos threatens. The land is poisoned. The United States is becoming our landlord. Dark-skinned people from the Caucasus regions, Muslims, Asiatics, swarthy inferior races have flooded Moscow, and white Christian Russians such as you and I are expected to support them. There is no order and no strength; the army is bound hand and foot by foreign agents pretending to be our leaders, but they are not our leaders. They stand idly by as the United Nations imposes sanctions and threatens war against our brother Slavs in Serbia who are fighting to liberate Bosnia; the great Pan-Slavic Empire has been stolen from us again by the International Jew. Not because we are weak: We have enormous bombs, chemicals, secret weapons. Because we lack a leader, a man of iron and will; but the leader is coming, Mrs. Domik, already he is here, already I and millions like us who have joined the Liberal Democratic Party of Russia support him. We need more women. Motherland Mrs. Domik is the spiritual genius of Slavic peoples.

[*Reaching in his briefcase.*] Would you like some literature?

> [*He proffers a pamphlet;* MRS.DOMIK *takes it, looks it over as if examining a rotten piece of fruit; she fixes* RODENT *with a look, smiling in an ugly way; then crumples his pamphlet and drops it on the floor.*]

MRS. SHASTLIVYI DOMIK: [*Smiling.*] Listen, you fucking ferret, I'm not a fucking "Russian like you," I'm a Lithuanian, and I fucking hate Russians; and why am I here in Siberia, because fucking Stalin sent my grandma here fifty years ago. My grandpa and my great-uncles and great-aunts died tunneling through the Urals on chain gangs. Their father and his brother were shot in Vilnius, their children were shot fighting Germans, my sister starved to death and my brother killed himself under fucking Brezhnev after fifteen years in a psychiatric hospital, I've tried twice to do the same—and my *daughter* ...
Fuck this century. Fuck your leader. Fuck the state. Fuck all governments, fuck the motherland, fuck your mother, your father and you.

> [MRS.DOMIK *takes* VODYA's *hand and exits.* RODENT, *ashen with terror, puts his literature back in his briefcase, stands, begins to put his coat and gear on.* BONFILA *enters.*]

BONFILA BEZHUKHOVNA BONCH-BRUEVICH: Leaving?

YEGOR TREMENS RODENT: Mm-hmm.

BONFILA BEZHUKHOVNA BONCH-BRUEVICH: Would you like to meet more of the children?

YEGOR TREMENS RODENT: Er, um, no, no, not necessary.

BONFILA BEZHUKHOVNA BONCH-BRUEVICH: We could go through files ...

YEGOR TREMENS RODENT: Send them to my office, send them to Moscow.

> [*Little pause.*]

BONFILA BEZHUKHOVNA BONCH-BRUEVICH: I also didn't go back to Moscow... You know when you asked me earlier? Why didn't I go back? Because I thought I could do some good here. In the face of all this impossibility, twenty thousand years, that little girl who won't live five more years, I still believe that good can be done, that there's work to be done. Good hard work.

YEGOR TREMENS RODENT: [*A little smile.*] To the Motherland. To the work ahead. Goodbye.

[*He exits.* BONFILA *is alone for a beat. She kicks the little chair in which* VODYA *had been sitting, sending it clattering across the room. Another brief beat, and then* KATHERINA *enters, dressed in a medical assistant's coat.*]

KATHERINA SERAFIMA GLEB: I'm dying for a smoke. Did you remember the cigarettes?

[BONFILA *takes a pack of cigarettes out of her labcoat pocket, and gives them to* KATHERINA.]

BONFILA BEZHUKHOVNA BONCH-BRUEVICH: They're bad for your health.

KATHERINA SERAFIMA GLEB: Yeah, yeah. To Moscow. I want to go to Moscow.

BONFILA BEZHUKHOVNA BONCH-BRUEVICH: You say that every single day.

KATHERINA SERAFIMA GLEB: Some day you'll say yes.

BONFILA BEZHUKHOVNA BONCH-BRUEVICH: Are you sorry you followed me here?

KATHERINA SERAFIMA GLEB: I didn't follow you, you *begged* me to come. Siberia sucks.
I'm done for the day. Are you ready for home?

BONFILA BEZHUKHOVNA BONCH-BRUEVICH: I'm ready.

EPILOGUE

Are the democracies that govern the world's richest countries capable of solving the problems that communism has failed to solve? That is the question. Historical communism has failed, I don't deny it. But the problems remain—those same problems which the communist utopia pointed out and held to be solvable, and which now exist, or very soon will, on a world scale. That is why one would be foolish to rejoice at the defeat and to rub one's hands saying: "We always said so!" Do people really think that the end of historical communism (I stress the word "historical") has put an end to poverty and the thirst for justice? In our world the two-thirds society rules and prospers without having anything to fear from the third of poor devils. But it would be good to bear in mind that in the rest of the world, the two-thirds (or four-fifths or nine-tenths) society is on the other side.

—NORBERTO BOBBIO
"The Upturned Utopia"
(*Translated by Patrick Camiller*)

[S. E. UPGOBKIN *and* A. A. PRELAPSARIANOV *are in Heaven, a gloomy, derelict place like a city after an earthquake. They are dressed in high fur hats and greatcoats. Snow falls on them. They are seated on wooden crates. Between them is another crate they are using as a table. They are playing cards. A samovar stands on a fourth crate, brewing tea.*]

SERGE ESMERELDOVICH UPGOBKIN: I spent my many years on earth loud in proclaiming the faith that there is no God.

ALEKSII ANTEDILLUVIANOVICH PRELAPSARIANOV: Now you have been dead almost ten years. What do you think now?

SERGE ESMERELDOVICH UPGOBKIN: I am bewildered. I expected more from the Afterlife, in the way of conclusive proof, in some form or another ...

ALEKSII ANTEDILLUVIANOVICH PRELAPSARIANOV: But the Ancient of Days remains evasive, ineffable, in Heaven as on earth.
Heaven, I had been led to believe in my childhood, was not such a dark and gloomy place, which forces upon me the suspicion that my mother *lied* to me each night as I knelt by my bed, praying; a suspicion I cannot entertain. Your deal.

SERGE ESMERELDOVICH UPGOBKIN: And I must admit I am tired of playing cards with you, Aleksii Antedilluvianovich.

ALEKSII ANTEDILLUVIANOVICH PRELAPSARIANOV: I believe I have improved my card game considerably, Serge Esmereldovich.

SERGE ESMERELDOVICH UPGOBKIN: After ten years of playing, Aleksii, it would actually be more interesting to me if your game had *not* improved. Can we think of nothing else to do?

ALEKSII ANTEDILLUVIANOVICH PRELAPSARIANOV: We could look down on the earth, see how things are going for Russia.

[*Little pause.*]

SERGE ESMERELDOVICH UPGOBKIN: Let's not.

ALEKSII ANTEDILLUVIANOVICH PRELAPSARIANOV: Your deal.

SERGE ESMERELDOVICH UPGOBKIN: Tea?

[*Aleksii nods "yes";* SERGE *gets the tea.*]

ALEKSII ANTEDILLUVIANOVICH PRELAPSARIANOV: We could look down on
the earth and see how things are going elsewhere. Cuba. Rwanda. Bosnia.
Pakistan. [*Beat.*] Afghanistan?

SERGE ESMERELDOVICH UPGOBKIN: God forbid.

ALEKSII ANTEDILLUVIANOVICH PRELAPSARIANOV: Yes, perhaps not. It is *depressing*.

SERGE ESMERELDOVICH UPGOBKIN: It is *very* depressing.

ALEKSII ANTEDILLUVIANOVICH PRELAPSARIANOV: It is.

SERGE ESMERELDOVICH UPGOBKIN: [*Getting very frustrated.*] I had at least
expected to see, if not the face of God or the face of Absolute Nothingness,
then the Future, at least the Future: But ahead there is only a great cloud of
turbulent midnight, and not even the dead can see what is to come.

   [VODYA DOMIK *enters.*]

ALEKSII ANTEDILLUVIANOVICH PRELAPSARIANOV: [*Moved, sad, wondering.*]
Look, Serge, a child has come.

SERGE ESMERELDOVICH UPGOBKIN: Hello little girl.

VODYA DOMIK: Hello.

ALEKSII ANTEDILLUVIANOVICH PRELAPSARIANOV: How sad to see a little one
wandering Night's Plutonian Shore.

VODYA DOMIK: Plutonium? Is there plutonium even here?

ALEKSII ANTEDILLUVIANOVICH PRELAPSARIANOV: No, no, *Plutonian-n-n-n*,
not plutonium-m-m-m. I was quoting the great American poet, Edgar Allan
Poe.

SERGE ESMERELDOVICH UPGOBKIN: I prefer Emerson. So dialectical! But moral
and spiritual too, like Dostoevsky. If Dostoevsky had lived in America, and had
had a sunnier disposition, he might have been Emerson. They were contemporaries. The world is fantastical! I miss it so.

ALEKSII ANTEDILLUVIANOVICH PRELAPSARIANOV: [*To* VODYA.] Welcome to
Nevermore.

SERGE ESMERELDOVICH UPGOBKIN: How did you die, child?

VODYA DOMIK: Cancer, a wild profusion of cells; dark flowerings in my lungs, my brain, my blood, my bones; dandelion and morning glory vine seized and overwhelmed the field; life in my body ran riot. And here I am.

ALEKSII ANTEDILLUVIANOVICH PRELAPSARIANOV: I died from speaking too much.

SERGE ESMERELDOVICH UPGOBKIN: I died from leaping.

ALEKSII ANTEDILLUVIANOVICH PRELAPSARIANOV: He leapt, he died, and still he cannot see the New.

SERGE ESMERELDOVICH UPGOBKIN: It is bitter.

VODYA DOMIK: The socialist experiment in the Soviet Union has failed, grand-fathers.

ALEKSII ANTEDILLUVIANOVICH PRELAPSARIANOV: It has.

VODYA DOMIK: And what sense are we to make of the wreckage?
Perhaps the principles were always wrong. Perhaps it is true that social justice, economic justice, equality, community, an end to master and slave, the withering away of the state: These are desirable but not realizable on the earth.

> [*Little pause.*]

Perhaps the failure of socialism in the East speaks only of the inadequacy and criminal folly of any attempt to organize more equitably and rationally the production and distribution of the wealth of nations. And chaos, market fluctuations, rich and poor, colonialism and war are all that we shall ever see.

> [*Little pause.*]

Perhaps, even, the wreckage that became the Union of Soviet Socialist Republics is so dreadful to contemplate that the histories and legends of Red October, indeed of hundreds of years of communitarian, millenarian and socialist struggle, will come to seem mere prelude to Stalin, the gulags, the death of free thought, dignity and human decency; and "socialist" become a foul epithet; and to the ravages of Capital there will be no conceivable alternative.

ALEKSII ANTEDILLUVIANOVICH PRELAPSARIANOV: It is bitter.

SERGE ESMERELDOVICH UPGOBKIN: It is very bitter.

236

VODYA DOMIK: I am inexpressibly sad, grandfathers. Tell me a story.

[*Little pause.*]

SERGE ESMERELDOVICH UPGOBKIN: I have this one story, a Russian story ...

ALEKSII ANTEDILLUVIANOVICH PRELAPSARIANOV: Whatever they do, whatever the glory or ignominy, as we move through history, Russians make great stories.

SERGE ESMERELDOVICH UPGOBKIN: I have this one story, but I can say only that it happened, and not what it means:

[VODYA *climbs up on his lap.*]

SERGE ESMERELDOVICH UPGOBKIN: Vladimir Ilyich Ulyanov was very sad. He was seventeen years old, and the secret police had just hanged his brother Sasha, for having plotted to kill the Czar. All this was long ago. Because he already missed his brother very much, Vladimir, who was to become Great Lenin, decided to read his brother's favorite book: a novel, by Chernyshevsky, the title and contents of which asked the immortal question; which Lenin asked and in asking stood the world on its head; the question which challenges us to both contemplation and, if we love the world, to action; the question which implies: Something is terribly wrong with the world, and avers: Human beings can change it; the question asked by the living and, apparently, by the fretful dead as well: What is to be done?

[*Little pause.*]

VODYA DOMIK: What *is* to be done?

ALEKSII ANTEDILLUVIANOVICH PRELAPSARIANOV: Yes. What is to be done?

END

OPEN ADMISSIONS

SHIRLEY LAURO

⟹⊙⟸

*Originally produced at The Double Image Theatre
under the aegis of Ensemble Studio Theatre.
Director, Richard Southern. Stage Manager, John Clinton.*

INTRODUCTION

by Romulus Linney

"Why do you do what you do?" Calvin asks Alice that question in Shirley Lauro's *Open Admissions*. It is a simple question. On the surface it is asked by an African American male college student baffled by the grading behavior of a white female college professor. But it explodes before us, in a one act play that in thirty minutes gives us centuries of weary, well meant oppression, and the fury that it provokes.

The immediate political reality of open admissions in a university, admirably specific and dramatic, quickly becomes a huge tapestry of human dilemmas not only of one nation, but of many. The professor cannot understand that she is racist. The student cannot understand why he is not given what is his, which he was promised. Underlying the struggle of one person trying to comprehend another turn and twist other, more threatening disasters. The woman believes she may be raped or murdered or both by the man. The man believes that his honesty and intelligence is mocked and betrayed by a deceitful woman who will destroy his life. Both are right and both are wrong. The rising conflict in this concise and theatrically marvelous situation is tightened and compressed into a coiled spring of tremendous force, which must be released. It is a measure of the depth and truth of Shirley Lauro's *Open Admissions* that when the spring flies open, nothing is solved, everything understood.

THE CHARACTERS

PROFESSOR ALICE MILLER- Professor of Speech Communications, started out to be a Shakespearean scholar. Has been teaching Speech at a city college in New York for 12 years. She is overloaded with work and exhausted.
Late thirties. Wears skirt, blouse, sweater, coat, gloves. Carries briefcase.

CALVIN JEFFERSON- 18, a freshman in Open Admissions Program at the College. Black, powerfully built, handsome, big. At first glance a street person but this is belied by his intensity. Wears jacket, jeans, cap, sneakers. Has been at the College 3 months, hoping it will work out.

TIME: *The present. Late fall. 6 o'clock in the evening.*

PLACE: *A cubicle Speech Office at a city college in New York.*

The play begins on a very high level of tension and intensity and builds from there. The level of intensity is set by CALVIN *who enters the play with a desperate urgency, as though he had arrived at the Emergency Room of a Hospital, needing immediate help for a serious problem. He also enters in a state of rage and frustration but is containing these feelings at first. The high level of tension is set by both* ALICE *and* CALVIN *and occurs from the moment* CALVIN *enters.* ALICE *wants to leave. She does not want the scene to take place. The audience's experience from the start should be as if they had suddenly tuned in on the critical round of a boxing match.*

CALVIN*'s speech is "Street Speech" jargon. Run-on sentences and misspellings in the text are for the purpose of helping the actor with the pronunciations and rhythms of the language.*

The Speech office of PROFESSOR ALICE MILLER *in a city college in New York. A small cubicle with partitions going 3/4 of the way up. Windowless, airless, with a cold antiseptic quality and a strong sense of impersonalness and transience. The cubicle has the contradictory feelings of claustrophobia and alienation at the same time. It is a space used by many teachers during every day of the week.*

On the glass-windowed door it says:

> SPEECH COMMUNICATIONS DEPT.
> Prof. Alice Miller, B.A., M.A., Ph.D.

There are other names beneath that.

In the cubicle there is a desk with nothing on it except a phone, a chair with a rain coat on it, a swivel chair and a portable black board on which has been tacked a diagram of the "Speech Mechanism." Room is bare except for these things.

AT RISE: *Cubicle is in darkness. Muted light filters through glass window on door from hallway. Eerie feeling. A shadow appears outside door. Someone enters, snapping on light. It is* ALICE. *She carries a loose stack of essays, a book sack loaded with books and a grade book, one Shakespeare book, two speech books, and a portable cassette recorder. She closes the door, crosses to the desk, puts the keys in her purse, puts purse and booksack down and dials "0."*

243

ALICE: Outside please. [*Waits for this, then dials a number.*] Debbie? Mommy, honey ... A "93?" Terrific! Listen, I just got through. I had to keep the class late to finish ... So, I can't stop home for dinner. I'm going right to the meeting ... no, I'll be safe ... don't worry. But you go put the double lock on, ok? And eat the cold meatloaf. [*She puts essays in book sack.*] See you later. Love you too. [*She kisses the receiver.*] Bye. [*She hangs tip, puts on coat, packs up purse and book sack, crosses to door and snaps off light. Then opens door to go.*]

   [CALVIN *looms in doorway.*]

ALICE: OOHH! You scared me!

CALVIN: Yes ma'am, I can see I scared you okay. I'm sorry.

ALICE: Calvin Washington? 10:30 section?

CALVIN: Calvin Jefferson. 9:30 section.

ALICE: Oh, right. Of course. Well, I was just leaving. Something you wanted?

CALVIN: Yes, Professor Miller. I came to talk to you about my grades. My grade on that Shakespeare project especially.

ALICE: Oh. Yes. Well. What did you get, Calvin? A "B" wasn't it? Something like that?

CALVIN: Umhmm. Thass right. Somethin like that ...

ALICE: Yes. Well, look, I don't have office hours today at all. It's very dark already. I just stopped to make a call. But if you'd like to make an appointment for a conference, I'm not booked yet next month. Up 'till then, I'm just jammed.

CALVIN: Thass two weeks! I need to talk to you right now!

ALICE: Well what exactly is it about? I mean the grade is self-explanatory— "Good" — "B" work. And I gave you criticism in class the day of the project, didn't I? So what's the problem?

CALVIN: I wanna sit down and talk about why I got that grade! And all my grades in point of fact.

ALICE: But I don't have office hours today. It's very late and I have another commitment. Maybe tomor—[*She tries to leave.*]

CALVIN: [*Voice rising.*] I have to talk to you *now*!

244

ALICE: Look, tomorrow there's a Faculty Meeting. l can meet you here afterwards ... around 12:30. Providing Professor Roth's not scheduled to use the desk.

CALVIN: I got a job tomorrow! Can't you talk to me right now?

ALICE: But what's it about? I don't see the emergen—-

CALVIN: [*Voice rising loudly.*] I jiss *tole* you what it's about! My project and my *grades* is what it's about!

ALICE: [*Glancing down the hall, not wanting a commotion overheard.*] All right! Just stop shouting out here, will you? [*She snaps on light and crosses to desk.*] Come on in. I'll give you a few minutes now.

[*He comes in.*]

ALICE: [*She puts purse and book sack down and sits at desk.*] Okay. Now then. What?

CALVIN: [*Closes door and crosses UC. Silent for a moment, looking at her.*] How come all I ever git from you is "B"?

ALICE: [*Stunned.*] What?

CALVIN: This is the third project I did for you. An all I ever git is "B".

ALICE: Are you joking? This is what you wanted to talk about? "B" is an excellent grade!

CALVIN: No it's not! "A" is "excellent." "B" is "good."

ALICE: You don't think you deserved an "A" on those projects, do you?

CALVIN: No. But I got to know how to improve myself somehow, so maybe sometime I can try for a "A". I wouldn't even mind on one of those projects if I got a "C". Thass average — if you know what l mean? Or a "D". But all I ever git from you is "B". It don't matter what I do in that Speech Communications Class, seems like. I come in the beginnin a it three months ago? On the Open Admissions? Shoot, I didn't know which end was up. I stood up there and give this speech you assigned on "My Hobby." You remember that?

ALICE: [*Reads note on desk.*] About basketball?

CALVIN: Huh-uh. That was Franklin Perkins give that speech. Sits in the back row?

245

ALICE: [*Tosses note in wastebasket.*] Oh. Yes. Right. Franklin.

CALVIN: Umhmm. I give some dumb speech about "The Hobby a Makin Wooden Trays."

ALICE: Oh, yes. Right. I remember that.

CALVIN: Except I didn't have no hobby makin wooden trays, man. I made one in high school one time, thass all.

ALICE: [*Leafs through pages of speech books.*] Oh, well, that didn't matter. It was the speech that counted.

CALVIN: Umhmm? Well, that was the sorriest speech anybody ever heard in their lives! I was scared to death and couldn't put one word in front a the other any way I tried. Supposed to be 5 minutes. Lasted 2! And you gave me a "B"!

ALICE: [*Rises, crosses to DR table and puts speech book down.*] Well, it was your first time up in class, and you showed a lot of enthusiasm and effort. I remember that speech.

CALVIN: Everybody's firss time up in class, ain't it?

ALICE: Yes. Of course.

CALVIN: [*Crosses DR to* ALICE.] That girl sits next to me, that Judy Horowitz — firss time she was up in class too. She give that speech about "How to Play the Guitar?" And man, she brought in charts and taught us to read chords and played a piece herself an had memorized the whole speech by heart. An you give *her* a "B".

ALICE: [*Crosses to desk, picks up book sack and puts it on desk.*] Well, Judy's organization on her outline was a little shaky as I recall.

CALVIN: [*Crosses end of desk.*] I didn' even turn no outline in.

ALICE: [*Picks up purse and puts it on desk.*] You didn't?

CALVIN: [*Leans in.*] Huh-uh. Didn' you notice?

ALICE: Of course! It's —just — well, it's been sometime—[*She quickly takes the grade book from the book sack and looks up his name.*] Let me see, oh, yes. Right. Here, I see. You didn't hand it in...

CALVIN: Thass right, I didn'.

ALICE: You better do that before the end of the term.

CALVIN: I can't. Because I don' know which way to do no outline!

ALICE: [*Looks up name in grade book and marks it with red pencil.*] Oh. Well...that's all right. Don't worry about it, okay? [*She puts grade book away.*] Just work on improving yourself in other ways.

CALVIN: What other ways? Only thing you ever say about anything I ever done in there is how I have got to get rid of my "Substandard Urban Speech!"

ALICE: [*Picks up 2 files from desk and crosses to UCR file cabinet.*] Well, yes, you do! You see, that's your real problem, Calvin! "Substandard Speech." It under-cuts your "Positive Communicator's Image!" Remember how I gave a lecture about that? About how all of you here have Substandard Urban Speech because this is a Sub — an *Urban* College. [*She puts on gloves.*] Remember? But that's perfectly okay! It's okay! Just like I used to have Substandard Midwestern Speech when I was a student. Remember my explaining about that? How I used to say "crik" for "creek," and "kin" for "can" and "tin" for "ten?" [*She crosses in back of desk and chuckles at herself.*] Oh, and my breathiness! [*She picks up purse.*] That was just my biggest problem of all: Breathiness. I just about worked myself to death up at Northwestern U. getting it right straight out of my speech. Now, that's what you have to do too, Calvin. [*She picks up book sack and keys.*] Nothing to be ashamed of—but get it right straight out! [*She is ready to leave. She pats* CALVIN *on the shoulder and crosses UC.*]

CALVIN: [*Pause. Looks at her.*] Thass how come I keep on gittin "B"?

ALICE: "That's."

CALVIN: [*Steps in to* ALICE.] Huh?

ALICE: "That's." Not "Thass." Can't you hear the difference? "That's" one of the words in the Substandard Black Urban Pattern. No final "T's". Undermining your Positive Image...labeling you. It's "Street Speech." Harlemese. Don't you remember? I called everyone's attention to your particular syndrome in class the minute you started talking?

    [*He looks at her, not speaking.*]

ALICE: It's "last," not "lass;" "first," not "firss." That's your friend, that good old "Final T!" Hear *it* when I talk?

CALVIN: Sometimes. When you say *it*, h*it*tin *it* like tha*t*!

ALICE: Well, you should be going over the exercises on it in the speech book all the time, and recording yourself on your tape recorder.

[*She pats book sack.*]

CALVIN: I don't got no tape recorder.

ALICE: Well, borrow one! [*She turns away.*]

CALVIN: [*Crosses in back of* ALICE *to her right.*] On that Shakespeare scene I jiss did? Thass why I got a "B"? Because of the "Final T's?"

ALICE: [*Backs DS a step.*] Well, you haven't improved your syndrome, have you?

CALVIN: How come you keep on answerin me by axin me somethin else?

ALICE: And that's the other one.

CALVIN: What "other one?"

ALICE: Other most prevalent deviation. You said: "axing" me something else.

CALVIN: Thass right. How come you keep axin me somethin else?

ALICE: "Asking me," Calvin, "asking me!"

CALVIN: I jiss did!

ALICE: No, no, Look. That's classic Substandard Black! Text book case. [*She puts purse and booksack down and crosses to diagam on blackboard.*] See, the jaw and teeth are in two different positions for the two sounds, and they make two completely different words! [*She writes "ass-king, "and "axing" on the blackboard, pronouncing them in an exaggerated way for him to see.*] "ass-king" and "ax-ing". I am "ass-king" you the question. But, the woodcutter is "ax-ing" down the tree. Can't you hear the difference? [*She picks up his speech book from desk.*] Here.

[CALVIN *follows her to desk.*]

ALICE: Go over to page 105. It's called a "Sharp S" problem with a medial position "sk" substitution. See? "skin, screw, scream" —those are "sk" sounds in the Primary Position. "Asking, risking, frisking,"—that's medial position. And "flask, task, mask"—that's final position. Now you should be working on those, Calvin. Reading those exercises over and over again. I mean the way you did the Othello scene was just ludicrous: "Good gentlemen, I ax thee —" [*She crosses to the board and points to "ax-ing". She chuckles.*] That meant Othello was chopping the gentlemen down!

CALVIN: How come I had to do the Othello scene anyhow? Didn git any choice. An Franklin Perkins an Sam Brown an Lester Washington they had to too.

ALICE: What do you mean?

CALVIN: An Claudette Jackson an Doreen Simpson an Melba Jones got themselves assigned to Cleopatra on the Nile?

ALICE: Everyone was assigned!

CALVIN: Uh-huh. But everybody else had a choice, you know what I mean? That Judy Horowitz, she said you told her she could pick outa five, six different characters. And that boy did his yesterday? That Nick Rizoli? Did the Gravedigger? He said he got three, four to choose off of too.

ALICE: [*Crosses to* CALVIN.] Well some of the students were "right" for several characters. And you know, Calvin, how we talked in class about Stanislavsky and the importance of "identifying" and "feeling" the part?

CALVIN: Well how Doreen Simpson "identify" herself some Queen sittin on a barge? How I supposed to "identify" some Othello? I don't!

ALICE: [*Crosses to blackboard, picks up fallen chalk.*] Oh, Calvin, don't be silly.

CALVIN: [*Crosses center.*] Well, I don'! I'm not no kind a jealous husband. I haven' got no wife. I don' even got no girlfriend, hardly! And thass what it's all about ain't it? So what's it I'm supposed to "identify" with anyhow?

ALICE: [*Turns to* CALVIN.] Oh, Calvin, what are you arguing about? You did a good job!

CALVIN: "B" job, right?

ALICE: Yes.

CALVIN: [*Crosses to* ALICE.] Well, what's that "B" standin for? Cause I'll tell you somethin you wanna know the truth: I stood up there didn' hardly know the sense a anythin I read, couldn't hardly even read it at all. Only you didn't notice. Wasn't even listenin, sittin there back a the room jiss thumbin through your book.

[ALICE *crosses to desk.*]

CALVIN: So you know what I done? Skip one whole paragraph, tess you out— you jiss kep thumbin through your book! An then you give me a "B"! [*He has followed* ALICE *to desk.*]

ALICE: [*Puts papers in box and throws out old coffee cup.*] Well that just shows how well you did the part!

CALVIN: You wanna give me somethin I could "identify" with, how come you ain' let me do that other dude in the play...

ALICE: Iago?

CALVIN: Yeah. What is it they calls him? Othello's ...

ALICE: Subordinate.

CALVIN: Go right along there with my speech syndrome, wouldn' it now? See, Iago has to work for the Man. I identifies with him! He gits jealous man. Know what I mean? Or that Gravedigger? Shovelin dirt for his day's work! How come you wouldn't let me do him? Thass the question I wanna ax you!

ALICE: [*Turns to* CALVIN.] "Ask me," Calvin, "Ask me!"

CALVIN: [*Steps SR.*] "Ax you?" Okay, man. [*Turns to* ALICE.] Miss Shakespeare, Speech Communications 1! [*Crosses US of* ALICE.] Know what I'll "ax" you right here in this room, this day, at this here desk right now? I'll "ax" you how come I have been in this here college 3 months on this here Open Admissions an I don't know nothin more than when I came in here? You know what I mean? This supposed to be some big break for me. This here is where all them smart Jewish boys has gone from the Bronx Science and went an become some Big Time Doctors at Bellvue. An some Big Time Judges in the Family Court an like that there. And now it's supposed to be my turn.

[ALICE *looks away and* CALVIN *crosses R of* ALICE.]

CALVIN: You know what I mean? [*He crosses UR.*] An my sister Jonelle took me out of foster care where I been in 6 homes and 5 schools to give me my chance. [*He crosses DR.*] Livin with her an she workin 3 shifts in some "Ladies Restroom" give me my opportunity. An she say she gonna buss her ass git me this education I don't end up on the streets! [*Crosses on a diagonal to* ALICE.] Cause I have got *brains*!

[ALICE *sits in student chair.* CALVIN *crosses in back, to her left.*]

CALVIN: You understand what I am Communicatin to you? My high school has tole me I got brains an can make somethin outta my life if I gits me the chance! And now this here's supposed to be my chance! High school says you folks gonna bring me up to date on my education and git me even. Only nothin is happenin to me in my head except I am gettin more and more confused about what I knows and what I don't know! [*He sits in swivel chair.*] So what I wanna "ax" you is: How come you don't sit down with me and teach me which way to git my ideas down instead of givin me a "B."

[ALICE *rises and crosses UR.*]

CALVIN: I don't even turn no outline in? Jiss give me a "B." [*He rises and crosses R of* ALICE.] An Lester a "B!" An Melba a "B!" An Sam a "B!" What's that "B" standin for anyhow? Cause it surely ain't standin for no piece of work!

ALICE: Calvin don't blame me!

[CALVIN *crosses DR.*]

ALICE: I'm trying! God knows I'm trying! The times are rough for everyone. I'm a Shakespearean scholar, and they have me teaching beginning Speech. I was supposed to have 12 graduate students a class, 9 classes a week, and they gave me 35 Freshmen a class, 20 classes a week. I hear 157 speeches a week! You know what that's like? And I go home late on the subway scared to death! In Graduate School they told me I'd have a first rate career. Then I started here and they said: "Hang on! Things will improve!" But they only got worse...and worse! Now I've been here for 12 years and I haven't written one word in my field! I haven't read 5 research books! I'm exhausted ...and I'm finished! We all have to bend. I'm just hanging on now...supporting my little girl...earning a living...and that's all... [*She crosses to desk.*]

CALVIN: [*Faces* ALICE.] What I'm supposed to do, feel sorry for you? Least you can *earn* a livin! Clean office, private phone, name on the door with all them B.A.'s, M.A.'s, Ph.D.'s.

ALICE: You can have those too. [*She crosses DR to* CALVIN.] Look, last year we got 10 black students into Ivy League Graduate Programs. And they were no better than you. They were just perceived [*Points to blackboard.*] as better. Now that's the whole key for you...to be perceived as better! So you can get good recommendations and do well on interviews. You are good looking and ambitious and you have a fine native intelligence. You can make it, Calvin. All we have to do is work on improving your Positive Communicator's Image...by getting rid of that Street Speech. Don't you see?

CALVIN: See what? What you axin *me* to see?

ALICE: "*Asking*" me to see, Calvin. "*Asking*" me to see!

CALVIN: [*Starts out of control at this, enraged, crosses UC and bangs on file cabinet.*] Ooooeee! Ooooeee! You wanna *see*? You wanna *see*? Ooooeee!

ALICE: Calvin stop it! STOP IT!

CALVIN: "Calvin stop it? .... Stop it?" [*Picks up school books from desk.*] There any black professors here?

ALICE: [*Crosses UR.*] No! They got cut... the budget's low ...they got ...

CALVIN: [*Interrupting.*] Cut? They got CUT? [*Crosses to* ALICE *and backs her to the DS edge of desk.*] Gonna cut you, lady! Gonna cut you, throw you out the fuckin window, throw the fuckin books out the fuckin window, burn it all mother fuckin down. FUCKIN DOWN!!!

ALICE: Calvin! Stop it! STOP IT! YOU HEAR ME?

CALVIN: [*Turns away center stage.*] I CAN'T!! *YOU* HEAR *ME*? I CAN'T! *YOU* HEAR *ME*! I CAN'T! YOU GOTTA GIVE ME MY EDUCATION! GOTTA TEACH ME! GIVE ME SOMETHING NOW! GIVE ME NOW! NOW! NOW! NOW! NOW! NOW!

[CALVIN *tears up text book. He starts to pick up torn pages and drops them. He bursts into wailing, bellowing cry in his anguish and despair, doubled over in pain and grief. It is a while before his sobs subside. Finally,* ALICE *speaks.*]

ALICE: Calvin...from the bottom of my heart...I want to help you...

CALVIN: [*Barely able to speak.*] By changin my words? Thass nothin.. nothin! I got to know them big ideas ... and which way to git em down...

ALICE: But how can I teach you that? You can't write a paragraph, Calvin...or a sentence...you can't spell past 4th grade...the essay you wrote showed that...

CALVIN: [*Rises.*] What essay?

ALICE: [*Crosses to UL files, gets essay and hands it to* CALVIN.] The autobiograph-
           ical one...you did it the first day...

CALVIN: You said that was for your reference...didn't count...

ALICE: Here...

CALVIN: [*Opens it up. Stunned.*] "F?" Why didn't you tell me I failed?

ALICE: [*Crosses to desk, puts essay down.*] For what?

CALVIN: [*Still stunned.*] So you could teach me how to write.

ALICE: [*Crosses DL.*] In 16 weeks?

CALVIN: [*Still can't believe this.*] You my teacher!

ALICE: That would take years! And speech is my job. You need a tutor.

CALVIN: I'm your job. They outa tutors!

ALICE: [*Turns to him.*] I can't do it, Calvin. And that's the real truth. I'm one per-
           son, in one job. And I can't. Do you understand? And even if I could, it would-
           n't matter. All that matters is the budget...and the curriculum...and the
           grades...and how you look...and how you talk!

CALVIN: [*Pause. Absorbing this.*] Then I'm finished, man.

           [*There is a long pause. Finally:*]

ALICE: [*Gets essay from desk, refiles it and returns to desk.*] No, you're not. If you'll
           bend and take what I can give you, things will work out for you … Trust me
           … Let me help you Calvin … Please … I can teach you speech …

CALVIN: [*Crosses to UC file cabinet. Long Pause.*] Okay … all right, man … [*Crosses
           to student chair and sits.*]

ALICE: [*Crosses to desk, takes off rain coat and sits in swivel chair.*] Now, then, we'll
           go through the exercise once then you do it at home … please, repeat after me,
           slowly … "asking" … "asking" … "asking" …

CALVIN: [*Long pause.*] Ax-ing …

ALICE: Ass-king …

CALVIN: [*During the following, he now turns from* ALICE, *faces front, and gazes out beyond the audience; on his fourth word, lights begin to fade to black.*] Ax-ing … Aks-ing … ass-king … asking … asking … asking …

Blackout

END OF PLAY

EXECUTION OF JUSTICE

EMILY MANN

———⟫•⟪———

Originally commissioned by the
Eureka Theatre Company, San Francisco.

Produced on Broadway by Lester and Marjorie Osterman and
Mortimer Caplin in Association with Norton & Stark, Inc.

Professional Premiere at the Actors Theatre of Louisville.

INTRODUCTION

by Oskar Eustis

When *Execution of Justice* first burst on the American theater in 1984, the effect was galvanic: produced across the country in dozens of theaters, it announced with breathtaking audacity that the theater could speak in the largest terms and the most immediate, speak from today's headlines about issues that go back millennia, and create powerful, emotional theatricality from utterly factual materials. Created during Reagan's first term, *Execution* was a powerful refutation of a theater that seemed to have become increasingly domestic, commercial and despair-ridden. The hungry response from theaters of all sizes across the nation suggested that not even its immense cast was enough to deter their desire to produce theater that mattered. *Execution* is a milestone in the history of documentary drama, managing to capture a crucial historical moment in the development of the gay movement in this country even as it tackles fundamental issues of justice, politics and violence.

Execution of Justice is built on the achievement of *Still Life*, Emily Mann's Obie-Award winning play about the impact of the Vietnam War on America. Like *Execution*, *Still Life* is built on documentary materials, interviews with a Vietnam vet, his wife and his lover. Like *Execution*, *Still Life* tackles great public events by looking at their impact on individuals, and reports objective events only through the eyes of participants. *Still Life* and *Execution* both depend on the interweaving and juxtaposition of documentary materials, through collage and collision opening up a world of meanings that would remain hidden if the plays respected a more straightforward, organic narrative strategy. *Execution of Justice* differs from *Still Life* in the size of its canvas and the daring of its dramatic conceit.

Still Life, perhaps the greatest depiction of the Vietnam War we have in American drama, is an intensely focused miniature, a laser-like penetration past the middle-class domestication of America's self-image into the roiling and unresolved mass of contradictions that Vietnam exposed and created for our country. The brilliance of *Still Life* is in its unwavering commitment to the quotidian and domestic: who would imagine that a monologue about the preparation of a family spaghetti dinner would become a Rosetta stone unlocking the ravages of a war in Southeast Asia on an American housewife?

What begins as a play whose form we think we recognize—the adultery play, the triangle of Minnesota artist, wife and lover—devolves into a horror of war crimes, atrocity and guilt. Emily Mann succeeds at something the Weathermen failed to accomplish: she brings the war home.

Execution of Justice, on the other hand, has an absolutely enormous range of characters, and takes place almost exclusively in public space, literal and imaginative. By focusing on a single, shocking incident—the murders of Mayor George Moscone and Supervisor Harvey Milk by ex-supervisor Dan White—*Execution* exposes the contradictory passions and conflicts of an entire city. Just as in *Still Life* one small family grouping becomes the lens through which America is viewed, in *Execution of Justice* San Francisco becomes the symbol and archetype for an America caught in what Patrick Buchanan would later call a "cultural war". Dramatically, this means that Mann sets out to do something much more difficult and dangerous than what she had tackled in her earlier work: she creates a collective protagonist. The city of San Francisco is the fractured, challenged central actor of *Execution*, and the *agon* of the city the dramatic focus of this extraordinary play.

While working on *Still Life*, Emily Mann first explored the idea of traumatic memory, how certain events can be so damaging to a sense of self that the mind continually returns to them, running them over and over, unable to forget, or forgive, or move further because the memory so violates a sense of self that it cannot be processed. In *Still Life*, an atrocity in Vietnam is the traumatic memory that Mark must relive again and again, unable to resolve the contradictions in his personal life because of the paralyzing guilt he carries with him. Mark also carries the weight of metaphor; he unwittingly embodies the American trauma in Vietnam, the wound to a nation's democratic self-image created by its participation in an imperialist war, the unresolved contradiction that still rages today in our political debates.

Execution of Justice is a traumatic memory as well, but the trauma is not that of an individual but of an entire city. Early on in the process of developing the play, Mann made the crucial choice to focus on the trial rather than on the murders as the central event of the play. In so doing, she found her title and focused her theme: rather than exploring the characters of the victims (both of whom were extraordinary men and deserve full biographies), or even the motivations and psychology of the killer (and Dan White's character was as fascinating as it was twisted), Emily chose to focus on what could have led a group of jurors to decide that the cold-blooded executions of their mayor and a city supervisor, at City Hall, were crimes worthy of a maximum jail sentence of seven years. Mann's insight that the verdict, even more than the initial crime, was the real trauma opened up a much richer world to explore than the mere fact of the crimes themselves. One route would have led to psychobiography; the road she took required her to solve the problem of how to create a collective protagonist, a problem that political playwrights have been struggling with for centuries.

Once she had determined that San Francisco was to be her protagonist and the trial her frame, Mann had to struggle with the nature of her dramatic form. The central problem with the trial was all that was *not* put into evidence: how do you dramatize an absence? Her solution was ingenious and opened doors we did not even know were closed: she created the "Chorus of Uncalled Witnesses," voices that had been silenced at the trial but demanded to speak in the theater, and slowly the structure of the play began to come into focus. The play was to become the *trial that should have happened*, and the actual playing of the script every night became the traumatic reliving of the trial, structured the way we remember traumatic events: memory interrupted by bitter commentary, obsessive hoping for a different result, analysis and emotion stirred into an unbearable mix because the simple fact of what happened cannot be remembered in tranquility.

The aspiration is unmistakably Greek. The Theater of Dionysus, at least the one that we of the political theater imagine, was where all the people of the City gathered on the side of the hill to hear the great issues of their age debated. These people knew that their collective identity was more important than any individual identity, and that their community was strengthened by the debate of intense, contradictory experiences. The very earliest surviving dramatic text we have, *The Persians* by Aeschylus, asks those Athenians to look at their most bitter enemy, defeated a mere eight years previously at the cost of the lives and limbs of family members of every audience member present, to feel empathy for their enemy's losses, and to remember that not long ago the Persians felt that they were God's chosen people, just as the Athenians did today. Contradiction and civic identity were at the core of the Athenian theater, and for two and a half millennia the theater has sought to recapture that sense of civic centrality that we imagine our Greek colleagues felt.

When the Cop and Sister Boom Boom descend onto the stage, when The Chorus of Uncalled Witnesses interrupt the action to explain what should have happened, when the audience for *Execution of Justice* at Berkeley Rep interrupted the actor playing Schmidt and refused to allow him to finish his final summation, the theater was asking to be restored to its central civic function.

INTRODUCTION

Justice may not always be possible in the courts, the play seems to argue, but at least the Theater is here, to remind us of what Justice is and could be.

CHARACTERS

DAN WHITE
MARY ANN WHITE
COP
SISTER BOOM

CHORUS OF UNCALLED WITNESSES:
  JIM DENMAN, White's Jailer
  YOUNG MOTHER
  MILK'S FRIEND
  GWENN CRAIG, Vice President of
    the Harvey Milk Democratic Club
  City Supervisor HARRY BRITT, Milk's
    Successor
  JOSEPH FREITAS, District Attorney
  MOURNER

TRIAL CHARACTERS:
  THE COURT
  COURT CLERK
  DOUGLAS SCHMIDT, Defense Attorney
  THOMAS F. NORMAN, Prosecuting
    Attorney
  JOANNA LU, TV Reporter
  PROSPETIVE JURORS
  JUROR #3
  FOREMAN
  BAILIFF
Inspector FRANK FALZON, Homicide
Inspector EDWARD ERDELATZ

WITNESSES FOR THE PEOPLE:
  CORONER STEPHENS
  RUDY NOTHENBERG, Deputy Mayor,
    Moscone's Friend
  BARBARA TAYLOR, Reporter
  OFFICER BYRNE, Department of Records
  WILLIAM MELIA, Civil Engineer
  CYR COPERTINI, Secretary to the Mayor
  CARL HENRY CARLSON, Aide to Harvey
    Milk
  RICHARD PABICH, Assistant to Harvey
    Milk

WITNESSES FOR THE DEFENSE
  DENISE APCAR, Aide to WHITE
  Fire Chief SHERRATT
  Fireman FREDIANI
  Police Officer SULLIVAN
  City Supervisor LEE DOLSON
  Psychiatrists:
  DR. JONES
  DR. SOLOMON
  DR. BLINDER
  DR. LUNDE
  DR. DELMAN

IN REBUTTAL FOR THE PEOPLE
  City Supervisor CAROL RUTH SILVER
  DR. LEVY, psychiatrist

RIOT POLICE

THE TIME: *1978 to the present*
THE PLACE: *San Francisco*
THE WORDS COME FROM: *Trial Transcripts, Reportage and
  Interviews*

ACT I

MURDER

A BARE STAGE.
A WHITE SCREEN OVERHEAD.
ON SCREEN: IMAGES OF SAN FRANCISCO.
HOT, FAST MUSIC. IMAGES OF MILK AND MOSCONE
PUNCTUATE THE VISUALS.

PEOPLE ENTER. A DAY IN SAN FRANCISCO. A MAELSTROM OF
URBAN ACTIVITY.

WITHOUT WARNING: ON SCREEN. [video, if possible.]

DIANNE FEINSTEIN: *[Almost unable to stand.]* As President of the Board of
Supervisors, It is my duty to make this announcement: Mayor George Moscone
… and Supervisor Harvey Milk … have been shot … and killed.

   [GASPS AND CRIES. A LONG MOMENT.]

   The suspect is Supervisor DAN WHITE.

THE CROWD IN SHOCK. THEY CANNOT MOVE. THEN
THEY RUN. OUT OF THE CHAOS, DAN WHITE APPEARS
ON SCREEN: A CHURCH WINDOW FADES UP.
A SHAFT OF LIGHT.
DAN WHITE PRAYS.

ON AUDIO: HYPERREAL SOUNDS OF MUMBLED
HAIL MARYS.
SOUNDS OF A WOMAN'S HIGH HEELS ECHOING,
MOVING FAST.
SOUND OF BREATHING HARD, RUNNING.

MARY ANN WHITE ENTERS, BREATHLESS.
WHITE LOOKS UP. SHE APPROACHES HIM.

WHITE: I shot the Mayor and Harvey.

[*She crumples. Lights change.*]

CLERK: This is the matter of the People versus Daniel James White.

[*Amplified gavel. Lights change.*]

COP: [*Quiet.*] Yeah, I'm wearing a "Free Dan White" t-shirt. [*indicating on shirt "NO MAN IS AN ISLAND."*] You haven't seen what
I've seen
—my nose shoved into what I think stinks.
Against everything I believe in.
There was a time in San Francisco when you knew a guy
by his parish.

[SISTER BOOM BOOM *enters.*]

Sometimes I sit in Church and I think of those
disgusting drag queens dressed up as nuns
and I'm a cop,
and I'm thinkin',
there's gotta be a law, you know,
because they're makin' me think things I don't want to think
and I gotta keep my mouth shut.

[BOOM BOOM *puts out cigarette.*]

COP: Take a guy out of his sling—fist fucked to death—
they say it's mutual consent, it ain't murder,
and I pull this disgusting mess down, take him to the morgue,
I mean, my wife asks me, "Hey, how was your day?"
I can't even tell her.
I wash my hands before I can even look at my kids.

[*They are very aware of each other, but possibly never make eye contact.*]

BOOM BOOM: God bless you one.
God bless you all.

COP: See, Danny knew—he believes in the rights of minorities. Ya know, he just knew—we are a minority, too.

BOOM BOOM: I would like to open with a reading from the Book of Dan. [*Opens book.*]

COP: We been workin' this job three generations—my father was a cop—and then they put—Moscone, Jesus, the mayor—Jesus—Moscone put this N-negro loving, faggot loving Chief telling us what to do he doesn't even come from the neighborhood, he doesn't even come from this city! He's tellin' us what to do in a force that knows what to do. He makes us paint our cop cars faggot blue— he called it "lavender gloves" for the queers, handle 'em, treat 'em with "lavender gloves," he called it. He's cuttin' off our balls. The City is stinkin' with degenerates— I mean, I'm worried about my kids, I worry about my wife, I worry about me and how I'm feelin' mad all the time. You gotta understand that I'm not alone— it's real confusion—

BOOM BOOM: "As Dan came to his day of reckoning, he feared not for he went unto the lawyers and the doctors and the jurors, and they said, 'Take heart, for in this you will receive not life but three to seven with time off for good behavior—'" [*Closes book reverently.*]

COP: Take a walk with me sometime. See what I see every day … Like I'm supposed to smile when I see two baldheaded, shaved-head men with those tight pants and muscles, chains everywhere, French-kissin' on the street, putting their hands all over each other's asses, I'm supposed to smile, walk by, act as if this is RIGHT??!!

BOOM BOOM: As gay people and as people of color and as women we all know the cycle of brutality and ignorance which pervades our culture.

COP: I got nothin' against people doin' what they want, if I don't see it.

BOOM BOOM: And we all know that brutality only begets more brutality.

COP: I mean, I'm not makin' some woman on the streets for everyone to see.

BOOM BOOM: Violence only sows the seed for more violence.

COP: I'm not ...

BOOM BOOM: And I hope Dan White knows that.

COP: I can't explain it any better.

BOOM BOOM: Because the greatest, most efficient information gathering and dispersal network is the Great Gay Grapevine.

COP: Just take my word for it—

BOOM BOOM: And when Dan White gets out of jail, no matter where Dan White goes, someone will recognize him.

COP: Walk into a leather bar with me some night—They—they're—there are queers who'd agree with me—it's disgusting.

BOOM BOOM: All over the world, the word will go out,
And we will know where Dan White is.

COP: The point is: Dan White showed you could fight City Hall.

BOOM BOOM: [Pause.] Now we are all aware, as I said,
Of this cycle of brutality and murder.
And the only way we can break that horrible cycle is with
love, understanding and forgiveness.
And there are those who were before me here today—
gay brothers and sisters
who said that we must somehow learn to
love, understand and forgive
the sins that have been committed against us
and the sins of violence
And it sort of grieves me that some of us are not
Understanding and loving and forgiving of Dan White.
And after he gets out,
after we find out where he is ...
[Long, wry look.]

I mean, not, y'know,
with any malice or planning....
[*Long look.*]
You know, you get so depressed and your blood sugar
goes up
and you'd be capable of just about *ANYTHING!*
[*Long pause. Smiles.*]
And some angry faggot or dyke who is not
understanding, loving and forgiving—
is going to perform a horrible act of violence and brutality
against Dan White.
And if we can't break the cycle before somebody gets Dan White
somebody will get Dan White.
and when they do,
I beg you all to
love, understand and forgive. [*He throws a kiss, laughs.*]

    [*Lights fade to black.*]

CLERK: This is the matter of the People vs. Daniel James White and the record will show that the Defendant is present with his counsel and the District Attorney is present and this is out of presence of the jury.

    [*Court setting up. TV lights.*]

JOANNA LU: [*On camera.*] The list of prospective witnesses that the defense has presented for the trial of the man accused of killing the liberal Mayor of San Francisco, George Moscone, and the first avowedly homosexual elected official, City Supervisor Harvey Milk, reads like a Who's Who of City Government [*Looks at list.*] … Judges, Congressmen, current and former Supervisors, and even a State Senator. The D.A. has charged White with two counts of first degree murder, invoking for the first time the clause in the new California capital punishment law that calls for the gas chamber for any person who has assassinated a public official in an attempt to prevent him from fulfilling his official duties. Ironically, Harvey Milk and George Moscone vigorously lobbied against the death penalty while Dan White vigorously supported it. This is Joanna Lu at the Hall of Justice.

    [*Gavel. Spotlight on clerk.*]

CLERK: Ladies and gentlemen, this is the information in the case now pending before you: the People of the State of California, Plaintiff, versus Daniel James White, Defendant. Action Number: 98663, Count One.

> [*Gavel.*]
> [*Lights.*]
> [*On screen: JURY SELECTION.*]

COURT: Mr. Schmidt, you may continue with your jury selection—

SCHMIDT: Thank you, Your Honor.

CLERK: It is alleged that Daniel James White did willfully unlawfully and with malice aforethought murder George R. Moscone, the duly elected Mayor of the City and County of San Francisco, California.

SCHMIDT: Have you ever supported controversial causes, like homosexual rights, for instance?

JUROR #1:   [WOMAN.] I have gay friends ... I, uh ... once walked with them in a Gay Freedom Day Parade.

SCHMIDT: Your Honor, I would like to strike the juror,

JUROR #1:   [WOMAN.] I am str ... l am heterosexual.

COURT: Agreed.

> [*Gavel.*]

CLERK: The defendant Daniel James White is further accused of a crime of felony to wit: that said defendant Daniel James White did willfully, unlawfully and with malice aforethought, murder Harvey Milk, a duly elected Supervisor of the City and County of San Francisco, California.

SCHMIDT: With whom do you live, sir?

JUROR #2:   [MAN.] My roommate.

SCHMIDT: What does he or she do?

JUROR #2:   [MAN.] He works at the Holiday Inn.

SCHMIDT: Your Honor, I ask the court to strike the juror for cause.

COURT: Agreed.

   [*Gavel.*]

CLERK: Special circumstances: it is alleged that Daniel James White in this proceeding has been accused of more than one offense of murder.

JUROR #3.   I worked briefly as a San Francisco policeman, but I've spent most of my life since then as a private security guard.

SCHMIDT: As you know, serving as a juror is a high honor and responsibility.

JUROR #3:   Yes, sir.

SCHMIDT: The jury serves as the conscience of the community.

JUROR #3:   Yes, sir. I know that, sir.

SCHMIDT: Now, sir, as a juror you take an oath that you will apply the laws of the State of California as the Judge will instruct you. You'll uphold that oath, won't you?

JUROR #3:   Yes, sir.

SCHMIDT: Do you hold any views against the death penalty no matter how heinous the crime?

JUROR #3:   No, sir. I support the death penalty.

SCHMIDT: Why do you think Danny White killed Milk and Moscone?

JUROR #3:   I have certain opinions. I'd say it was social and political pressures...

SCHMIDT: I have my jury.

COURT: Mr. Norman?

   [*No response. Fine with him.*]

   [*Gavel.*]

JOANNA LU: [*On camera.*] The jury has been selected quickly for the Dan White trial. It appears the prosecution and the defense want the same jury. The prosecuting attorney, Assistant D.A. Tom Norman, exercised only 3 out of 27 possible peremptory challenges. By all accounts, there are no Blacks, no gays, and no Asians. One juror is an ex-policeman, another the wife of the county jailer, four of the seven women are old enough to be Dan White's mother. Most of the jurors are working and middle-class Catholics. Speculation in the press box is that the prosecution feels that it has a law-and-order jury. In any case, Dan White will certainly be judged by a jury of his peers. [*Turns.*] I have with me this morning District Attorney Joseph Freitas, Jr.

[*TV lights on* FREITAS.]

May we ask, sir, the prosecution's strategy in the trial of Dan White?

FREITAS: I think it's a clear case—We'll let the facts speak for themselves—

CLERK: And the Defendant, Daniel James White, has entered a plea of not guilty to each of the charges and allegations contained in this information.

[WHITE *enters.* MRS. WHITE *enters.*]

COURT: Mr. Norman, do you desire to make an opening statement at this time?

NORMAN: I do, Judge.

COURT: All right. You may proceed.

[*Lights change.*]
[*On screen. ACT ONE MURDER.*][*Gavel.*]
[*All screens go to white.*]

NORMAN: [*Opening statement. The prosecution.*] Your Honor, members of the jury, and you must be the judges now, [*Actor takes in audience.*] counsel for the defense: [*To audience.*] Ladies and gentlemen—I am Thomas F. Norman and I am the Assistant District Attorney, and I appear here as trial representative to Joseph Freitas Jr., District Attorney. Seated with me is Frank Falzon, Chief Inspector of Homicide for San Francisco.

George R. Moscone was the duly-elected Mayor of San Francisco.

[*On screen: portrait of* MOSCONE.]

Harvey Milk was the duly-elected Supervisor or City Councilman of District 5 of San Francisco.

[*On screen: portrait of* HARVEY MILK.]

The defendant in this case, Mr. Daniel James White, had been the duly-

269

elected Supervisor of District 8 of San Francisco, until for personal reasons of his own he tendered his resignation in writing to the Mayor on or about November the 10th, 1978, which was approximately 17 days before this tragedy occurred.

Subsequent to tendering his resignation he had the feeling that he wanted to withdraw that resignation, and that he wanted his job back. George Moscone, it appears, had told the accused that he would give him his job back or, in other words, appoint him back to the Board if it appeared that there was substantial support in District Number 8 for that appointment—

Material was received by the Mayor in that regard, and in the meantime, Mr. Daniel James White had resorted to the courts in an effort to withdraw his written resignation.

It appears that those efforts were not met with much success.

[*On screen: The defense,* DOUGLAS SCHMIDT.]

SCHMIDT: Ladies and Gentlemen, the prosecutor has quite skillfully outlined certain of the facts that he believes will be supportive of his theory of first-degree murder.

I intend to present ALL the facts, including some of the background material that will show, not so much what happened on November 27th, but WHY those tragedies occurred on November 27th.

The evidence will show, and it's not disputed, that Dan White did, indeed, shoot and kill George Moscone and I think the evidence is equally clear that Dan White did shoot and kill Harvey Milk.

Why then should there be a trial?
The issue in this trial is properly to understand WHY that happened.

[*On screen: Chief Medical Examiner and* CORONER *for the City and County of San Francisco.*]
[*Lights.*]
[CORONER *sits.*]

STEPHENS: [*Holding photo.*] In my opinion and experience, Counsel, the larger tattoo pattern at the side of the Mayor's head is compatible with a firing distance of about one foot, and the smaller tattoo pattern within the larger tattoo pattern is consistent with a firing distance of a little less than one foot.

That is: The wounds to the head were received within a distance of one foot when the Mayor was already on the floor incapacitated.

[NORMAN *looks to jury.*]
[*On screen: Image of figure shooting man in head from a distance of one foot, leaning down "Coup De Grace."*]

SCHMIDT: Why? ... Good people, fine people, with fine backgrounds, simply don't kill people in cold blood, it just doesn't happen, and obviously some part of them has not been presented thus far. Dan White was a native of San Francisco. He went to school here, went through high school here. He was a noted athlete in high school. He was an army veteran who served in Vietnam, and was honorably discharged from the army. He became a policeman thereafter, and after a brief hiatus developed, again returned to the police force in San Francisco, and later transferred to the fire department. He was married in December of 1976, [*HE indicates* MARY ANN WHITE.] and he fathered his son in July 1978.

Dan White was a good policeman and Dan White was a good fireman. In fact, he was decorated for having saved a woman and her child in a very dangerous fire, but the complete picture of Dan White perhaps was not known until some time after these tragedies on November 27th. The part that went unrecognized was since his early manhood, Daniel White was suffering from a mental disease. The disease that Daniel White was suffering from is called depression, sometimes called manic depression or uni-polar depression.

NORMAN: Doctor, what kind of a wound was that in your opinion?

STEPHENS: These are gunshot wounds of entrance, Counsel. The cause of death was multiple gunshot wounds ... particularly the bullet that passed through the base of the Supervisor's brain. This wound would cause instant or almost instant death. I am now holding People's 30 and 29 for identification. In order for this wound to be received, Counsel ... the Supervisor's left arm has to be relatively close to the body with the palm turned away from the body and the thumb towards the body.

NORMAN: Can you illustrate that for us?

STEPHENS: Yes, Counsel. The left arm has to be in close to the body and slightly forward with the palm up. The right hand has to be palm away with the thumb pointed towards the body and the elbow in slightly to the body with the arm raised. In this position, all of these wounds that I have just described in People's 30 and 29 line up.

NORMAN: Thank you.

[*Freeze on position. Lights.*]

SCHMIDT: [*To jury.*] Dan White came from a vastly different lifestyle than Harvey Milk, who was a homosexual leader and politician. Dan White was an idealistic young man, a working class young man. He was deeply endowed with and believed very strongly in the traditional American values, family and home; like the District he represented. [*Indicates jury.*] Dan White believed people when they said something. He believed that a man's word, essentially, was his bond. I don't think Dan White was particularly insightful as to what his underlying problem was, but he was an honest man, and he was fair, perhaps too fair for politics in San Francisco.

[DAN WHITE *campaign speech:*]
[*Hear sounds of* ROCKY *on audio, crowd response throughout.*]

DAN: Do you like my new campaign song?

[*Crowd cheers.*]

Yeah!

[*On screen: Live video or slides of* WHITE *giving speech, cameras.*]

[*To camera.*] For years, we have witnessed an exodus from San Francisco by many of our family members, friends and neighbors. Alarmed by the enormous increase in crime, poor educational facilities and a deteriorating social structure, they have fled to temporary havens … In a few short years these malignancies of society will erupt from our city and engulf the tree-lined, sun-bathed communities which chide us for daring to live in San Francisco. That is, unless we who have remained—can transcend the apathy which has caused us to lock our doors while the tumult rages unchecked through our streets—Individually we are helpless. Yet you must realize there are thousands and thousands of angry frustrated people such as yourselves waiting to unleash a fury that can and will eradicate the malignancies which blight our beautiful city. I am not going to be forced out of San Francisco by splinter groups of radicals, social deviates, and incorrigibles. UNITE AND FIGHT WITH DAN WHITE.

[*Crowd cheers.*]
[*Lights change.*]
[*Screens go to white.*]

SCHMIDT: I think Dan White saw the city deteriorating as a place for the average and decent people to live.

COURT: Mr. Nothenberg, please be sworn.

SCHMIDT: The irony is ... that the young man with so much promise in seeking the job on the Board of Supervisors actually was destined to construct his own downfall. After Dan White was elected he discovered there was a conflict of interest if he was a fireman and an elected official. His wife, Mary Ann, was a school teacher and made a good salary. But after their marriage, it was discovered that the wife of Dan White had become ... pregnant and had to give up her teaching job. So the family income plummeted from an excess of $30,000 to $9,600, which is what a San Francisco supervisor—city councilman— is paid. I believe all the stress and the underlying mental illness culminated in his resignation that he turned in to the Mayor on November 10th, 1978.

[*On screen.* MR. NOTHENBERG, *Deputy Mayor.*]
[*Lights.*]

NORMAN: Would you read that for us?

NOTHENBERG: Dear Mayor Moscone: I have been proud to represent the people of San Francisco from District 8 for the past ten months, but due to personal responsibilities which I feel must take precedent over my legislative duties, I am resigning my position effective today. I am sure that the next representative to the Board of Supervisors will receive as much support from the people of San Francisco as I have. Sincerely, Dan White. It is so signed.

SCHMIDT: [*To jury.*] Some days after November the 10th, pressure was brought to bear on Dan White to go back to the job that he had worked so hard for, and there was a one-way course that those persons could appeal to Dan White, and that was to appeal to his sense of honor: Basically—Dan you are letting the fire department down, letting the police department down. It worked. That type of pressure worked, because of the kind of man Dan White is. He asked the Mayor for his job back.

NORMAN: Mr. Nothenberg, on or about Monday the 27th of November last year, do you know whether Mayor Moscone was going to make an appointment to the Board of Supervisors, particularly for District No. 8?

NOTHENBERG: Yes, he was.

SCHMIDT: The Mayor said: We have political differences, but you are basically a good man, and you worked for the job and I'm not going to take you to fault. That letter was returned to Dan White.

NORMAN: Do you know whom his appointee to District 8 was going to be?

NOTHENBERG: Yes, I do.

NORMAN: Who was that, please.

NOTHENBERG: It was going to be a gentleman named Don Horanzey.

NORMAN: Thank you.

SCHMIDT: As I said, Dan White believed a man's word was his bond. Mayor Moscone had said: If there was any legal problem he would simply reappoint Dan White. Thereafter it became: Dan White there is no support in District 8 and unless you can show some broad base support, the job will not be given to you, and finally, the public statement coming from the Mayor's office: it's undecided. But you will be notified, prior to the time that any decision is made. They didn't tell Dan White. But they told Barbara Taylor.

> [*Blackout-Audio on phone.*]
> [*Spotlight* WHITE *and* TAYLOR.]

TAYLOR: I'm Barbara Taylor from KCBS. I'd like to speak to Dan White.

WHITE: Yuh.

TAYLOR: I have received information from a source within the Mayor's office that you are not getting that job. I am interested in doing an interview to find out your reaction to that. Mr. White?

> [*Long pause.*]
> [*Spotlight* DAN WHITE.]

WHITE: I don't know anything about it.

> [*Click.*]
> [*Dial tone.*]
> [*Lights change.*]

TAYLOR: [*Live.*] Well, the Mayor's office told me: "The only one in favor of the appointment of Dan White is Dan White himself."

NORMAN: Thank you, Miss Taylor.

SCHMIDT: After that phone call, Denise Apcar, Dan's aide, told Dan White that there were going to be supporters down at City Hall the next morning to show support to the Mayor's office. In one day they had collected 1100 signatures in District 8 in support of Dan White.

But the next morning,—Denise called Dan and told him the Mayor was unwilling to accept the petitioners.

[*On screen:* DENISE APCAR, *aide to* DAN WHITE.]

APCAR: Yes. I told Danny—I don't remember my exact words—that the Mayor had "circumvented the people."

NORMAN: Did you believe at that time that the Mayor was going to appoint someone other than Dan White?

APCAR: Oh, yes.

NORMAN: At that time, were your feelings such that you were angry?

APCAR: Definitely. Well the Mayor had told him … and Dan always felt that a person was going to be honest when they said something. He believed that up until the end—

NORMAN: You felt and believed that Mr. Milk had been acting to prevent the appointment of Mr. Dan White to his vacated seat on the Board of Supervisors?

APCAR: Yes. I was very much aware of that.

NORMAN: Had you expressed that opinion to Mr. White?

APCAR: Yes.

NORMAN: Did Mr. White ever express that opinion also to you?

APCAR: He wasn't down at City Hall very much that week so I was basically the person that told him these things.

NORMAN: Did you call Mr. White and tell him that you had seen Harvey Milk come out of the Mayor's office after you had been informed the Mayor was not in?

APCAR: Yes, I did. Then he called me back and said, "Denise, come pick me up. I want to see the Mayor."

NORMAN: When you picked him up, did he do anything unusual?

APCAR: Well ... he didn't look at me and normally he would turn his body a little bit towards the driver and we would talk, you know, in a free-form way, but this time he didn't look at me at all. He was squinting hard. He was very nervous, he was agitated. He was rubbing his hands, blowing into his hands and rubbing them like he was cold, like his hands were cold. He acted very hurt. Yes. He was, he looked like he was going to cry. He was doing everything he could to restrain his emotion.

NORMAN: [*Looks to the jury.*] Did you ever describe him as acting quote "all fired up?" unquote.

APCAR: Yes, yes I—I believe I said that.

NORMAN: Did he mention at that time that he also was going to talk to Harvey Milk?

APCAR: Yes, he did.

NORMAN: Did he ever say he was going to quote "really lay it on the Mayor?" unquote.

APCAR: It's been brought to my attention I said that, yes.

NORMAN: When you were driving Mr. White downtown, was there some discussion relative to a statement you made. Quote "Anger had run pretty high all week towards the Mayor playing pool on us, dirty, you know?" unquote.

APCAR: I believe I was describing my anger. At the time I made those statements I was in shock and I spoke freely and I'm sure I've never used those terms before.

NORMAN: When you made those statements it was 2 hours and 5 minutes after the killings occurred, was it not?

APCAR: Yes.

NORMAN: Miss Apcar—When you were driving Mr. White to City Hall did you know he was carrying a loaded gun?

APCAR: No. I did not.

NORMAN: Thank you.

SCHMIDT: Yes, Dan White went to City Hall and he took a .38 caliber revolver
with him, and that was not particularly unusual for Dan White. Dan White
was an ex-policeman, and as a policeman one is required to carry, off-duty, a
gun, and as an ex-policeman—well I think it's common practice. And as it's
been mentioned Dan White's life was being threatened continuously by the
White Panther party and other radical groups. And additionally, remember,
there was the atmosphere of terror created by the Jonestown People's Temple
Tragedy.

> [*Screens flood with Jonestown image.*]

Only a week before the City Hall tragedy, 900 people, mostly San Franciscans—
men, women, and children—died in the jungle. Rumors surfaced that hit lists
had been placed on public officials in San Francisco. Assassination squads. And
in hindsight, of course, we can all realize that this did not occur, but at the time
there were 900 bodies laying in Guyana to indicate that indeed people were
bent on murder.

> [*Screen.* OFFICER BYRNE, *Department of Records.*]
> [*Lights.*]

NORMAN: Officer Byrne, do persons who were once on the police force who
have resigned their position, do they have the right to carry a concealed
firearm on their person?

SCHMIDT: And I think it will be shown that Jim Jones himself was directly allied
with the liberal elements of San Francisco politics and was hostile to the conservative elements.

BYRNE: No, a resigned person would not have that right.

SCHMIDT: And so, it would be important to understand that there were threats
directed towards conservative persons like Dan White.

NORMAN: Officer, have you at my instance and request examined those particular records to determine whether there is an official permit issued by the Chief
of Police to a Mr. Daniel James White to carry a concealed firearm?

BYRNE: Yes, I have.

NORMAN: What have you found?

BYRNE: I find no permit.

NORMAN: Thank you.

[*Lights.*]

SCHMIDT: Yes, it's a violation of the law to carry a firearm without a permit, but that firearm was registered to Dan White. And indeed, many officials at City Hall carried guns because of this violent atmosphere including ex-police Chief, Supervisor Al Nelder and the current Mayor of San Francisco, Dianne Feinstein.

COURT: Mr. Melia, please be sworn.

SCHMIDT: Upon approaching the door on Polk Street, Mr. White observed a metal detection machine. Knowing that he did not know the man that was on the metal detection machine, he simply went around to the McAllister Street well door, where he expected to meet his aide. He did not find Denise Apcar there. She'd gone to put gas in her car. He waited for several moments, but knowing that it was imminent, the talk to the Mayor, he stepped through a window at the Department of Public Works.

[*Screen: Slide of windows with man in front demonstrating procedure.*]

Which doesn't require any physical prowess, and you can step through those windows, and the evidence will show that though now they are barred, previously it was not uncommon for people to enter and exit there. They are very large windows, and are large, wide sills,

[*Screen shows windows which are the windows he stepped through. They are actually small, high off the ground: Now they are barred.*]

and it's quite easy to step into the building through these windows.

[*On screen. Slide of man in three piece suit trying to get leg up.*] [*Screen.* WILLIAM MELIA, JR., *Civil Engineer.*]

MELIA: At approximately 10:35 I heard the window open. I heard someone jump to the floor and then running through the adjoining room. I looked up and caught a glance of a man in a suit running past the doorway of my office into the City Hall hallway.

NORMAN: What did you do?

MELIA: I got up from my desk and called after him: "Hey, wait a second."

NORMAN: Did that person wait or stop?

MELIA: Yes, they did.

NORMAN: Do you see that person here in this courtroom today?

MELIA: Yes, I do.

NORMAN: Where is that person?

MELIA: It's Dan White. [*Pause.*] He said to me: "I had to get in. My aide was supposed to come down and let me in the side door, but never showed up." I had taken exception to the way he had entered our office, and I replied: "AND YOU ARE?" And he replied: "I'm Dan White, the City Supervisor." He said, "Say, I've got to go," and with that, he turned and ran out of the office.

NORMAN: Did you say that he ran?

MELIA: Right.

NORMAN: Uh huh Mr. Melia—had you ever seen anyone else enter or exit through that window or those windows along that side?

MELIA: Yes, I had. It was common for individuals that worked in our office to do that.

NORMAN: Individuals who worked in your office … Were you alarmed when you learned that a Supervisor crawled or walked through that window, or stepped through that window?

MELIA: Was I alarmed?

NORMAN: Yes.

MELIA: Yes. I was … alarmed.

NORMAN: Thank you.

    [NORMAN *looks to jury*.]

SCHMIDT: [*Annoyed.*] I think it's significant at this point also because the fact that he crawled through the window appears to be important—it's significant to reiterate that as Mr. Melia just testified people often climb through that window, and indeed, on the morning of the 27th, Denise had the key to the McAllister Street well door. So, Dan White stepped through the window, identified himself, traveled up to the second floor.

[*Screen:* MRS. CYR COPERTINI *appointment secretary to the* MAYOR.]

And then approached the desk of Cyr Copertini and properly identified himself, and asked to see the Mayor.

[*Lights.*]

CYR: I am the appointment secretary to Mayor Feinstein.

NORMAN: In November of last year and particularly on November 27th what was your then occupation?

CYR: I was appointment secretary to the Elected Mayor of San Francisco, George Moscone.

[WITNESS *deeply moved.*]

NORMAN: Mrs. Copertini—Were you aware that there was anything that was going to happen that day of November 27th of interest to the citizens of San Francisco, uh … I mean, such as some public announcement?

CYR: … There was to be a news conference to announce the new supervisor for the Eighth District, at 11:30.

NORMAN: Mrs. Copertini, at approximately 10:30 a.m. you saw Mr. Daniel White, he appeared in front of your desk … do you recall what he said?

CYR: He said: "Hello, Cyr. May I see the Mayor?" I said: "He has someone with him, but let me go check with him." I went into the Mayor and told him that Supervisor White was there to see him. He was a little dismayed. He was a little uncomfortable by it and said: "Oh, all right. Tell him I'll see him, but he will have to wait a coupla minutes—"

I asked the Mayor, "Shouldn't I have someone in there with him," and he said: "No, no, I'll see him alone." And I asked him again. And he said,

"No, no, I'll see him alone." And then I went back. I said to Dan White, "it will be a few minutes."

He asked me how I was and how things were going. Was I having a nice day.

NORMAN: Was there anything unusual about his tone of voice?

CYR: No. I don't think so. He seemed nervous. I asked him would he like to see the newspaper while he was waiting? He said: "No, he wouldn't," and I said:

"Well, that's alright. There's nothing in it anyway unless you want to read about Caroline Kennedy having turned 21." And he said: "21? Is that right." He said: "Yeah, that's all so long ago. It's even more amazing when you think that John John is now 18."

> [*Lights change. Music "Deus Irae."*]
> [*Boys Choir.*]

DENMAN: The only comparable situation I ever remember was when JFK was killed.

CYR: It was about that time he was admitted to the Mayor's office.

NORMAN: Did you tell Mr. Daniel White that he could go in?

CYR: Yes.

DENMAN: I remember that in my bones, in my body.

NORMAN: Did he respond in any way to that?

DENMAN: Just like this one.

CYR: He said: "Good girl, Cyr."

NORMAN: Good girl, Cyr?

CYR: Right.

DENMAN: When Camelot all of a sudden turned to hell.

NORMAN: Then what did he do?

CYR: Went in.

NORMAN: After he went in there did you hear anything of an unusual nature that was coming from the Mayor's office?

CYR: After a time I heard a … commotion.

[Lights change.]

YOUNG MOTHER: I heard it on the car radio, I literally gasped.

NORMAN: Explain that to us, please.

YOUNG MOTHER: I wanted to pull over to the side of the road and scream.

CYR: Well, I heard—a series of noises—first a group and then one—

YOUNG MOTHER: Just scream.

CYR: I went to the window to see if anything was happening out in the street.

YOUNG MOTHER: Then I thought of my kids.

CYR: And the street was rather extraordinarily calm.

DENMAN: I noticed when I looked outside that there was an unusual quiet.

CYR: For that hour of the day there is usually more—there wasn't really anything out there.

DENMAN: I went to the second floor and started walking toward the Mayor's office.

YOUNG MOTHER: I wanted to get them out of school and take them home,

NORMAN: Could you describe these noises for us?

YOUNG MOTHER: I wanted to take them home and [*She makes a hugging gesture with her arms.*] lock the door.

CYR: Well, they were dull thuds rather like—

DENMAN: And there was this strange combination of panic and silence that you rarely see.

CYR: I thought maybe it was an automobile door that somebody had tried to shut, by, you know, pushing, and then finally succeeding.

DENMAN: It was like a silent slow-motion movie of a disaster.

NORMAN: Do you have any recollection that you can report with any certainty to us as to how many sounds there were?

CYR: No. As I stood there I—I thought I ought to remember—

[WITNESS *breaks down.*]

DENMAN: There was this hush and aura, people were moving with strange faces, as if the world had just come to an end.

NOTHENBERG: [MOSCONE'*s friend.*] George loved this city, and felt what was wrong could be fixed.

NORMAN: Do you want a glass of water?

[CYR *sobs.*]

DENMAN: And I asked someone what had happened and he said: "the Mayor has been shot."

CYR: I ought to remember that pattern in case it is something, but I—

NOTHENBERG: [MOSCONE'*s friend.*] He knew—it was a white racist town. A Catholic town. But he believed in people's basic good will.

[CYR *sobs.*]

COURT: Just a minute. Do you want a recess?

NOTHENBERG: [MOSCONE'*s friend.*] He never suspected, I bet, Dan White's psychotic behavior.

NORMAN: Do you want a recess?

NOTHENBERG: [MOSCONE'*s friend.*] That son of a bitch killed someone I loved. I mean, I loved the guy.

CYR: No. I'm all right.

COURT: Are you sure you are all right?

CYR: Yes.

YOUNG MOTHER: I just thought of my kids.

[*Pause.*]

NOTHENBERG: [MOSCONE'*s friend.*] I loved his idealism. I loved his hope.

CYR: Then what happened was Rudy Nothenberg left to tell the press that the conference would start a few minutes late.

NOTHENBERG: [MOSCONE's *friend*.] I loved the guy.

CYR: And then he came back to me right away and said: "Oh, I guess we can go ahead. I just saw Dan White leave."

NOTHENBERG: [MOSCONE's *friend*.] I loved his almost naive faith in people.

CYR: So then he went into the Mayor's office and said: "Well, he's not here." And I said: "Well, maybe he went into the back room."

NOTHENBERG: [MOSCONE's *friend*.] I loved his ability to go on.

CYR: Then he just gave a shout saying: "Gary, get in here. Call an ambulance. Get the police."

NOTHENBERG: See, I got too tired to stay in politics and do it. George and I were together from the beginning. Me, Phil Burton, Willie Brown. Beatin' all the old Irishmen.

DENMAN: I heard right away that Dan White had done it.

NOTHENBERG: But George believed, as corny as this sounds, that you do good for the people. I haven't met many of those and George was one of those. Maybe those are the guys that get killed. I don't know.

  [CYR *crying*.]

NORMAN: All right. All this you told us about occurred in San Francisco, didn't it?

CYR: [*Deeply moved*.] Yes.

SCHMIDT: Dan White, as it was quite apparent at that point had CRACKED because of his underlying mental illness …

  [*Screen:* CARL HENRY CARLSON, *Aide to* HARVEY MILK.]

CARLSON: I heard Peter Nardoza, Diane Feinstein's aide, say: Diane wants to see you and Dan White said: "That'll have to wait a couple of minutes, I have something to do first."

NORMAN: I have something to do first?

CARLSON: Yes.

NORMAN: Do you recall in what manner Mr. White announced himself?

SCHMIDT: There were stress factors due to the fact that he hadn't been notified,

CARLSON: He appeared at the door which was normally left open. Stuck his head
in and asked: "Say, Harv, can I see you for a minute?"

SCHMIDT: and the sudden emotional surge that he had in the Mayor's office
was simply too much for him

NORMAN: What did Harvey Milk do at that time if anything?

CARLSON: He turned around.

SCHMIDT: and he cracked.

CARLSON: He turned around

SCHMIDT: The man cracked.

CARLSON: and said "Sure." and got up and went across the hall …

SCHMIDT: He shot the Mayor.

CARLSON: to the office designated as Dan White's office on the chart.

SCHMIDT: reloaded his gun, basically on instinct, because of his police training, and was about to leave the building at that point

NORMAN: After they went across the hall to Mr. White's office …

SCHMIDT: and he looked down the hall,

NORMAN: Would you tell us what next you heard or saw?

SCHMIDT: he saw somebody that he believed to be an aide to Harvey Milk.

CARLSON: A few seconds, probably 10, 15 seconds later, I heard a shot, or the
sound of gunfire.

SCHMIDT: He went down to the Supervisor's area to talk to Harvey Milk.

COURT: Excuse me. Would you speak out. Your voice is fading a bit.

SCHMIDT: At that point, in the same state of rage, emotional upheaval with the
stress of 10 years of mental illness having cracked this man—

CORONER: [*Demonstrates as he speaks.*] The left arm has to be close to the body and slightly forward with the palm up.

SCHMIDT: ninety seconds from the time he shot the Mayor, Dan White shot and killed Harvey Milk.

CARLSON: After the shot, I heard Harvey Milk scream."oh, no." And then the first—the first part of the second "no" which was then cut short by the second shot.

CORONER: The right hand has to be palm away with the thumb pointed towards the body and the elbow in slightly to the body with the arm raised.

NORMAN: How many sounds of shots did you hear altogether, Mr. Carlson?

CARLSON: Five or six. I really didn't consciously count them.

CORONER: In this position all of these wounds that I have just described in People's 30 and 29 line up.

> [*Blackout on* CORONER *in position.*]
> [*Pause.*]

CARLSON: A few moments later the door opened, the door opened, and Daniel White walked out, rushed out, and proceeded down the hall.

NORMAN: Now, Mr. Carlson, when Daniel White first appeared at the office of Harvey Milk and said, "Say, Harv, can I see you for a minute?", could you describe his tone of voice in any way?

CARLSON: He appeared to be very normal, usual friendly self. I didn't, I didn't feel anything out of the ordinary. It was just very typical Dan White.

> [*Music out, lights change.*]

GWENN: I'd like to talk about when people are pushed to the wall.

SCHMIDT: Harvey Milk was against the re-appointment of Dan White.

GWENN: In order to understand the riots, I think you have to understand that the Dan White verdict did not occur in a vacuum.

SCHMIDT: Basically, it was a political decision. It was evident there was a liberal wing of the Board of Supervisors, and there was a smaller conservative wing, and Dan White was a conservative politician for San Francisco.

[*Screen:* RICHARD PABICH, *Legislative Assistant to* HARVEY MILK.]
[*Lights.*]

PABICH   My address is 542-A Castro Street.

GWENN: I don't think I have to say what their presence meant to us, and what their loss meant to us—

NORMAN: What did you do after you saw Dan White run down the hall and put the key in the door of his old office, Room 237?

GWENN: The assassinations of our friends Harvey Milk and George Moscone were a crime against us all.

PABICH   Well, I was struck in my head, sort of curious as to why he'd been running.

GWENN: And right here, when I say "us," I don't mean only gay people.

PABICH   And he was—it looked like he was in a hurry. I was aware of the political situation.

GWENN: I mean all people who are getting less than they deserve.

PABICH   I was aware that Harvey was taking the position to the Mayor that Mr. White shouldn't be reappointed. Harvey and I had talked earlier that day … that it would be a significant day.

[*Lights.*]
[*Subliminal music.*]

MILK'S FRIEND: After Harvey died, I went into a depression that lasted about a year, I guess. They called it depression, anyway. I thought about suicide, well, I more than thought about it.

SCHMIDT: Mr. Pabich, Mr. Milk had suggested a replacement for Dan White, hadn't he?

PABICH   He had, to my understanding, recommended several people, and basically took the position that Dan White should not be reappointed.

MILK'S FRIEND: I lost my job. I stayed in the hospital for, I would guess, two months or so. They put me on some kind of drug that … well, it helped, I guess.

I mean, I loved him and it was …

SCHMIDT: Was he requesting that a homosexual be appointed?

PABICH   No, he was not.

MILK'S FRIEND: Well, he was gone and that couldn't change.

SCHMIDT: I have nothing further. Thank you.

MILK'S FRIEND: He'd never be here again, I knew that.

COURT: All right. Any redirect, Mr. Norman?

NORMAN: No. Thank you for coming, Mr. Pabich.

> [PABICH *exits.*]

GWENN: It was as if Dan White had been given the go-ahead. It was a free-for-all, a license to kill.

> [PABICH *with* JOANNA LU.]
> [*TV lights.*]

PABICH   [*On camera.*] It's over. Already I can tell it's over. He asked me a question, a clear queer-baiting question, and the jury didn't bat an eye. [*Starts to exit, then.*] Dan White's going to get away with murder.

JOANNA LU: Mr. Pabich.

MILK'S FRIEND: I had this recurring dream. We were at the Opera, Harvey and I. I was laughing. Harvey was laughing. Then Harvey leaned over and said to me: When you're watching Tosca, you know you're alive. That's when I'd wake up.

GWENN: I remember the moment I heard Harvey had been shot—[*She breaks down.*]

MILK'S FRIEND: And I'd realize—like for the first time all over again—he's dead.

> [*Hyperreal sounds of high heels on marble, echoing, moving fast.*
> *Mumbled Hail Marys.*]
> [*Fade lights up slowly on* SCHMIDT, NORMAN.]

SCHMIDT: From here I think the evidence will demonstrate that Dan White ran down to Denise's office, screamed at his aide to give him the key to her car. And he left, went to a church, called his wife, went into St. Mary's Cathedral, prayed, and his wife got there, and he told her, the best he could, what he remembered he had done, and then they walked together to the Northern Police Station where he turned himself in; asked the officer to look after his wife, asked the officer to take possession of an Irish poster he was carrying …

[*Screen: Slide. Stain glass window, cover of Uris book.*]
[*IRELAND: A Terrible Beauty.*]

and then made a statement, what best he could recall had occurred.

[FALZON *hands on shoulders.*]

FALZON: Why … I feel like hitting you in the fuckin' mouth … How could you be so stupid? How?

WHITE: I … I want to tell you about it … I want to, to explain.

FALZON: Do you want a lawyer, Danny?

WHITE: No, Frank I want to talk to you.

FALZON: Okay, if you want to talk to me, I'm gonna get my tape recorder and read you your rights and do it right.

NORMAN: The people at this time move the tape recorded statement into evidence.

FALZON: Today's date is Monday, November 27th, 1978. The time is presently 12:05. We're inside the Homicide Detail, Room 454, at the Hall of Justice. Present is Inspector Edward Erdelatz, Inspector Frank Falzon and for the record, sir, your full name?

WHITE: Daniel James White.

FALZON: Would you, normally in a situation like this, ah … we ask questions, I'm aware of your past history as a police officer and also as a San Francisco fireman. I would prefer, I'll let you do it in a narrative form as to what happened this morning if you can lead up to the events of the shooting and then backtrack as to why these events took place. [*Looks at* ERDELATZ.]

WHITE: Well, it's just that I've been under an awful lot of pressure lately, financial pressure, because of my job situation, family pressure because of ah … not being able to have the time with my family. [*Sob.*]

FALZON: Can you relate these pressures you've been under, Dan, at this time? Can you explain it to Inspector Erdelatz and myself?

WHITE: It's just that I wanted to serve

[FALZON *nods.*]

the people of San Francisco well and I did that. Then when the pressures got too great, I decided to leave. After I left, my family and friends offered their support and said, whatever it would take to allow me to go back into office,— well they would be willing to make that effort. And then it came out that Supervisor Milk and some others were working against me to get my seat back on the Board. He didn't speak to me, he spoke to the City Attorney but I was in the office and I heard the conversation.

I could see the game that was being played, they were going to use me as a *scapegoat*, whether I was a good supervisor or not, was not the point. This was a political opportunity and they were going to degrade me and my family and the job that I had tried to do an, an more or less HANG ME OUT TO DRY. And I saw more and more evidence of this during the week when the papers reported that ah … someone else was going to be reappointed. The Mayor told me he was going to call me before he made any decision, he never did that. I was troubled, the pressure, my family again, my, my son's out to a babysitter.

FALZON: Dan, can you tell Inspector Erdelatz and myself, what was your plan this morning? What did you have in mind?

WHITE: I didn't have any devised plan or anything, it's, I was leaving the house to talk, to see the Mayor and I went downstairs, to, to make a phone call and I had my gun down there.

FALZON: Is this your police service revolver, Dan?

WHITE: This is the gun I had when I was a policeman. It's in my room an ah … I don't know, I just put it on. I, I don't know why I put it on, it's just …

FALZON: You went directly from your residence to the Mayor's office this morning?

WHITE: Yes, my, my aide picked me up but she didn't have any idea ah … you know that I had a gun on me or, you know, and I went in to see him an, an he told me he wasn't going to reappoint me and he wasn't intending to tell me about it. Then ah … I got kind of fuzzy and then just my head didn't feel right and I,

FALZON: Was this before any threats on your part, Dan?

WHITE: I, I never made any threats.

FALZON: There were no threats at all?

WHITE: I, I … oh no.

FALZON: When were you, how, what was the conversation, can you explain to Inspector Erdelatz and myself the conversation that existed between the two of you at this time?

WHITE: It was pretty much just, you know, I asked, was I going to be reappointed. He said, no I am not, no you're not. And I said, why, and he told me, it's a political decision and that's the end of it, and that's it and then he could obviously see, see I was obviously distraught an then he said, let's have a drink and I, I'm not even a drinker, you know I don't, once in awhile, but I'm not even a drinker. But I just kinda stumbled in the back and he was all, he was all smiles—he was talking an nothing was getting through to me. It was just like a roaring in my ears an, an then … it just came to me, you know, he …

FALZON: You couldn't hear what he was saying, Dan?

WHITE: Just small talk that, you know, it just wasn't registering. What I was going to do now, you know, and how this would affect my family, you know, an, an just, just all the time knowing he's going to go out an, an lie to the press and, an tell 'em, you know, that I, I wasn't a good supervisor and that people didn't want me an then that was it. Then I, I just shot him, that was it, it was over.

FALZON: What happened after you left there, Dan?

WHITE: Well, I, I left his office by one of the back doors an, I was going to go down the stairs and then I saw Harvey Milk's aide across the hall at the Supervisor's an then it struck me about what Harvey had tried to do an I said, well I'll go talk to him. He didn't know I had, I had heard his conversation and he was all smiles and stuff and I went in and, you know, I, I didn't agree with him on a lot of things but I was always honest you know, and here they were devious. And then he started kinda smirking, 'cause he knew, he knew I wasn't going to be reappointed—And ah … I started to say you know how hard I worked for it and what it meant to me and my family and then my reputation as, as a hard worker, good honest person and he just kind of smirked at me as if to say, too bad an then, and then, I just got all flushed an, an hot, and I shot him.

FALZON: This occurred inside your room, Dan?

WHITE: Yeah, in my office, yeah.

FALZON: And when you left there did you go back home?

WHITE: No, no, no I drove to the, the Doggie Diner on, on Van Ness and I called my wife and she, she didn't know, she …

FALZON: Did you tell her, Dan?

[*Sobbing.*]

WHITE: I called up, I didn't tell her on the phone. I just said … she was working. I just told her to meet me at the cathedral.

FALZON: St. Mary's?

[*Sobbing.*]

WHITE: She took a cab, yeah. She didn't know. She knew I'd been upset and I wasn't even talking to her at home because I just couldn't explain how I felt and she had no, nothing to blame about it, she was, she always has been great to me but it was, just the pressure hitting me an just my head's all flushed and expected that my skull's going to crack. Then when she came to the church, I, I told her and she kind of slumped an she, she couldn't say anything.

FALZON: How is she now do you, do you know is she, do you know where she is?

WHITE: I don't know now. She, she came to Northern Station with me. She asked me not to do anything about myself, you know that she, she loved me and she'd stick by me and not to hurt myself.

ERDELATZ: Dan, right now are you under a doctor's care?

WHITE: No.

ERDELATZ: Are you under any medication at all?

WHITE: No.

ERDELATZ: When is the last time you had your gun with you prior to today?

WHITE: I guess it was a few months ago. I, I was afraid of some of the threats that were made an, I, I, just wanted to make sure to protect myself you know this, this city isn't safe you know and there's a lot of people running around an well I don't have to tell you fellows, you guys know that.

ERDELATZ: When you left home this morning, Dan, was it your intention to confront the Mayor, Supervisor Milk or anyone else with that gun?

WHITE: No, I, I, what I wanted to do was just, talk to him you know, I, I ah, I didn't even know if I was going to be reappointed or not be reappointed. *Why do we do things, you know, why did I, I don't know.* No, I, I just wanted to talk to him that's all an at least have him be honest with me and tell me why he was doing it, not because I was a bad supervisor or anything but, you know, I never killed anybody before, I never shot anybody …

ERDELATZ: Why did …

WHITE: ……I didn't even, I didn't even know if I wanted to kill him. I just shot him, I don't know.

ERDELATZ: What type of gun is that you were carrying, Dan?

WHITE: It's a .38, a two-inch .38.

ERDELATZ: And do you know how many shots you fired?

WHITE: Uh … no I don't, I don't. I, I out of instinct when I, I reloaded the gun ah … you know, it's just the training I guess I had, you know.

ERDELATZ: Where did you reload?

WHITE: I reloaded in my office, when I was I couldn't out in the hall.

   [*Pause.*]

ERDELATZ: When you say you reloaded, are you speaking of following the shooting in the Mayor's office?

WHITE: Yeah.

ERDELATZ: Inspector Falzon?

FALZON: No questions. Is there anything you'd like to add, Dan, before we close this statement?

WHITE: Yes. Just that I've been honest and worked hard, never cheated anybody and I wanted to do a good job, I'm trying to do a good job and I saw this city as it's going, kind of downhill and I was always just a lonely vote on the board. I was trying to do a good job for the city.

FALZON: Inspector Erdelatz and I ah … appreciate your cooperation and the truthfulness of your statement.

> [*Lights change.*]
> [DAN WHITE *sobbing.* MARY ANN WHITE *sobbing.*
> JURORS *sobbing.*]
> [FALZON *moved.*]

NORMAN: I think that is all. You may examine.

COURT: Do you want to take a recess at this time?

SCHMIDT: Why don't we take a brief recess?

COURT: Let me admonish you, ladies and gentlemen of the jury, not to discuss this case among yourselves nor with anyone else, not allow anyone to speak to you about the matter, no are you to form or express an opinion until the matter has been submitted to you.

> [*Gavel.*]
> [*House light up.*]
> [*On screen: Recess.*]

INTERMISSION

ACT II

IN DEFENSE OF MURDER

AS AUDIENCE ENTERS, ON SCREEN
DOCUMENTARY IMAGES OF MILK *AND* MOSCONE
COMPANY/AUDIENCE WATCH

MOSCONE: * My late father was a guard at San Quentin, and who I was visiting one day, and who showed to me, and then explained the function of, the uh, the uh death chamber. And it just seemed inconceivable to me, though I was pretty young at the time, that in this society that I had been trained to believe was the most effective and efficient of all societies, that the only way we could deal with violent crime would be to do the ultimate ourselves, and that's to governmentally sanction the taking of another person's life.

MILK: * [FALZON *enters*.] Two days after I was elected I got a phone call—the voice was quite young. It was from Altoona, Pennsylvania. And the person said, "Thanks." And you've got to elect gay people so that that young child, and the thousands upon thousands like that child, know that there's hope for a better world. There's hope for a better tomorrow. Without hope, they'll only gaze at those blacks, the Asians, the disabled, the seniors, the us'es, the us'es. Without hope, the us'es give up. I know that you cannot live on hope alone. But without it, life is not worth living. And you, and you, and you, gotta give 'em hope. Thank you very much.

> [*Lights up. Courtroom.*]
> [FALZON *on witness stand.*]
> [DAN WHITE *at defense table sobbing.*]
> [MARY ANN WHITE *behind him sobbing.*]
> [*On tape.*]

---

* Dialogue: from *The Times of Harvey Milk*, a film by Robert Epstein and Richard Schmeichen.

WHITE: [*Voice.*] Just that I've been honest and worked hard, never cheated anybody and I wanted to do a good job, I'm trying to do a good job and I saw this city as it's going, kind of downhill and I was always just a lonely vote on the board. I was trying to do a good job for the city.

FALZON: Inspector Erdelatz and I ah … appreciate your cooperation and the truthfulness of your statement.

> [FALZON *switches tape off.*]

NORMAN: I think that is all. You may examine.

> [*Lights change, company exits.*]
> [*On screen:* INSPECTOR FRANK FALZON, *witness for the prosecution.*] [*Dissolve on screen: ACT TWO—IN DEFENSE OF MURDER.*]

SCHMIDT: Inspector Falzon, you mentioned that you had known Dan White in the past, prior to November 27, 1978?

FALZON: Yes, sir, quite well.

SCHMIDT: About how long have you known him?

FALZON: According to Dan,
it goes way back to the days
we attended St. Elizabeth's Grammar School together,
but we went to different high schools.
I attended St. Ignatius, and he attended Riordan.
He walked up to me one day at the Jackson Playground,
with spikes over his shoulders, glove in his hand,
and asked if he could play on the team.
I told him it was the police team,
and he stated that he was a new recruit at Northern Station,
wanted to play on the police softball team,
and since that day Dan White and I have been very good friends.

SCHMIDT: You knew him fairly well then, that is fair?

FALZON: As well as I know anybody, I believed.

SCHMIDT: Can you tell me, when you saw him first on November 27th, 1978, how did he appear physically to you?

296

FALZON: Destroyed. This was not the Dan White I had
known, not at all.
That day I saw a shattered individual,
both mentally and physically in appearance,
who appeared to me to be shattered.
Dan White, the man I knew
prior to Monday, the 27th of November, 1978,
was a man among men.

SCHMIDT: Knowing, with regard to the shootings of Mayor Moscone and Harvey
Milk, knowing Dan White as you did, is he the type of man that could have
pre-meditatedly and deliberately shot those people?

NORMAN: Objection as calling for an opinion and conclusion.

COURT: Sustained.

SCHMIDT: Knowing him as you do, have you ever seen anything in his past that
would lead you to believe he was capable of cold-bloodedly shooting somebody?

NORMAN: Same objection.

COURT: Sustained.

SCHMIDT: Your Honor, at this point I have anticipated that maybe there would
be some argument with regard to opinions not only as to Inspector Falzon,
but with a number of other witnesses that I intend to call, and accordingly I
have prepared a memorandum of what I believe to be the appropriate law. [*Shows
memo.*]

COURT: I have no quarrel with your authorities, but I think the form of the questions that you asked was objectionable.

SCHMIDT: The questions were calculated to bring out an opinion on the state
of mind and—I believe that a lay person, if he is an intimate acquaintance, surely
can hazard such an opinion. I believe that Inspector Falzon, as a police officer, has an opinion.

COURT: Get the facts from this witness. I will let you get those facts whatever
they are.

SCHMIDT: All right, we will try that. Inspector Falzon, again, you mentioned that you were quite familiar with Dan White; can you tell me something about the man's character, as to the man that you knew prior to the—prior to November 27th, 1978?

NORMAN: Objection as being irrelevant and vague.

COURT: Overruled. [*To* FALZON.] Do you understand the question?

FALZON: I do, basically, your Honor.

COURT: All right, you may answer it.

NORMAN: Well, your Honor, character for what?

COURT: Overruled. [*To* FALZON.] You may answer it.

FALZON: The Dan White that I knew prior to Monday, November 27, 1978,
was a man who seemed to excel in pressure situations,
and it seemed that the greater the pressure, the more enjoyment
that Dan had,
exceeding at what he was trying to do.

Examples would be in his sports life,
that I can relate to,
and for the first time in the history of the State of California,
there was a law enforcement softball tournament held in 1971.

The San Francisco Police Department entered
that softball tournament along with other major departments,
Los Angeles included,
and Dan White was not only named on the All Star Team
at the end of the tournament,
but named the most valuable player.

He was just outstanding under pressure situations,
when men would be on base
and that clutch hit was needed.

Another example of Dan White's
attitude toward pressure
was that when he decided to run
for the District 8 Supervisor's seat,
and I can still vividly remember the morning

he walked into the Homicide Detail and sat down to—
announce that he was going to run for City Supervisor,

I said: "How are you going to do it, Dan?
Nobody heard of Dan White.
How are you going to go out there,
win this election?
He said: "I'm going to do it the way the people
want it to be done,
knock on their doors, go inside, shake their hands,
let them know what Dan White stands for."

And he said: "Dan White is going to represent them.
There will be a voice in City Hall, you watch, I'll make it."

He did what he said he was going to do,
he ran, won the election.

SCHMIDT: Given these things that you mentioned about Dan White, outstanding under pressure, is there anything in his character that you saw of him, prior to those tragedies of the 27th of November, that would have led you to believe that he would ever kill somebody cold-bloodedly?

NORMAN: Objection, irrelevant.

COURT: Overruled.

NORMAN: Let me state my grounds for the record.

COURT: Overruled.

NORMAN: Thank you, Judge. It's irrelevant and called for his opinion and speculation.

COURT: Overruled. [Gavel. To FALZON.] You may answer that.

FALZON: Yes, your Honor.
     I'm aware—I'm hesitating only because
     there was something I saw in Dan's personality
     that didn't become relevant to me
     until I was assigned this case.
     He had a tendency to run, occasionally,
     from situations.

I saw this flaw, and I asked him about it,
and his response was that his ultimate goal
was to purchase a boat, just travel around the world,
get away from everybody,
He wanted to be helpful to people,
and yet he wanted to run away from them.
That did not make sense to me.

Otherwise, to me,
Dan White was an exemplary individual,
a man that I was proud to know
and be associated with.

SCHMIDT: Do you think he cracked? Do you think there was something wrong with him on November 27th?

NORMAN: Objection as calling for an opinion and speculation.

COURT: Sustained.

SCHMIDT: I have nothing further. [*Turns back.*] Inspector, I have one last question. Did you ever see him act out of revenge as to the whole time you have known him?

NORMAN: Objection. That calls for speculation.

COURT: No, overruled, and this is as to his observations and contacts. Overruled.

FALZON: The only time Dan White
could have acted out in revenge
is when he took the opposite procedure
in hurting himself,
by quitting the San Francisco Police Department.

SCHMIDT: Nothing further. Thank you, sir.

NORMAN: Inspector Falzon, you regard yourself as a close friend to Mr. Daniel White, don't you?

FALZON: Yes, sir.

NORMAN: Do you regard yourself as a very close friend of Mr. Daniel White?

FALZON: I would consider myself a close friend of yours, if that can relate to you my closeness with Dan White.

NORMAN: Of course, you haven't known me as long as you have known Mr. Daniel White, have you, Inspector?

FALZON: Just about the same length of time, Counsel.

NORMAN: Inspector Falzon, while you've expressed some shock at these tragedies, would you subscribe to the proposition that there's a first for everything?

FALZON: It's obvious in this case; yes, sir.

NORMAN: Thank you.

> [NORMAN *sits.*]
> [FALZON *gets up and takes his seat.*]
> [*Beside* NORMAN.]

NORMAN: The Prosecution rests.

> [*Blackout.*]

> [*On screen: The Prosecution rests.*]
> [*Commotion in court.*]

COURT: Order.

> [*Gavel.*]
> [*Lights up.*]
> [FREITAS *alone.*]

FREITAS: I was the D.A.
Obviously in some respects, the trial ruined me. This trial ...

> [*On screen: Dissolve into picture of* DAN WHITE *as fire hero.*]
> [*Screen:* THE DEFENSE. *Subliminal music.*]
> [*Lights up.*]

SHERRATT [*Fire Chief.*] Dan White was an excellent fire fighter. In fact, he was commended for a rescue at Geneva Towers. The award hasn't been given to him as yet, uh ...

FREDIANI. [*Fireman.*] Dan White was the valedictorian of the Fire Department class. He was voted so by members of the class.

[*On screen:* DAN WHITE *as Valedictorian.*]

MILK'S FRIEND: When I was in the hospital, what galled me most was the picture of Dan White as the All American Boy.

SHERRATT: but a meritorious advisory board and fire commission were going to present Mr. White with a class C medal.

[*On screen:* DAN WHITE *as fire hero.*]

FREDIANI. Everybody liked Dan.

SCHMIDT: Did you work with Dan as a policeman?

SULLIVAN   [*Policeman.*] Yes, I did.

MILK'S FRIEND: Maybe as a gay man, I understand the tyranny of the All American Boy.

[*On screen:* DAN WHITE *as police officer.*]

FREDIANI. He loved sports and I loved sports.

[*On screen:* DAN WHITE *as Golden Gloves boxer.*]

SULLIVAN   Dan White as a police officer,
was a very fair police officer on the street.

MILK'S FRIEND: Maybe because I am so often his victim.

GWENN: I followed the trial in the papers.

SCHMIDT: Having had the experience of being a police officer, is it unusual for persons that have been police officers to carry guns?

SULLIVAN   Uh, pardon me, Mr. Schmidt?

GWENN: I thought then something was wrong with this picture.

SCHMIDT: I say, is it uncommon that ex-police officers would carry guns?

GWENN: Something was wrong, we thought, when the Chief Inspector of Homicide became the chief character witness for the defense.

SULLIVAN   No, it is a common thing that former police officers will carry guns.

GWENN: Why didn't the Chief Inspector of Homicide ask Dan White how he got into City Hall with a loaded gun?

SCHMIDT: Without a permit?

SULLIVAN: Yes.

GWENN: Dan White reloaded after shooting the Mayor. If it was "reflex," police training, why didn't he reload again after shooting Harvey Milk?

SCHMIDT: Is there anything in his character that would have led you to believe he was capable of shooting two persons?

NORMAN: Objection.

COURT: Overruled.

SULLIVAN: No, nothing whatever.

GWENN: And what can explain the coup de grace shots
White fired into the backs of their heads as they lay there helpless on the floor?

DOLSON: [*City Supervisor.*] Dan in my opinion was a person who saved lives.

GWENN: Where is the prosecution?

FREITAS: I mean, I would have remained in politics. Except for this. I was voted out of office.

SCHMIDT: [*To* DOLSON.] Supervisor Dolson, you saw him on November 27th, 1978, did you not?

DOLSON: I did.

FREITAS: In hindsight, you know.
I would have changed a lot of things.

SCHMIDT: What did you see?

FREITAS: But hindsight is always perfect vision.

[*Slide:* DAN WHITE *as City Supervisor outside City Hall.*]

DOLSON: What I saw made me want to cry ...
Dan was always so neat.
Looked like a Marine on Parade ...

GWENN: What pressures were you under *indeed*?

DOLSON: And here he was, this kid, who was badly disheveled
and he had his hands cuffed behind him,
which was something I never expected to see.
He looked [*sobs.*] absolutely *devastated*.

GWENN: As the "VICTIM" sat in the courtroom
we heard of policemen and firemen sporting
FREE DAN WHITE t-shirts
as they raised 100,000 dollars for Dan White's defense fund,
and the same message began appearing
in spray paint on walls around the city.
FREE DAN WHITE.

DOLSON: I put my arm around him, told him that everything
was going to be all right,
but how everything was going to be all right,
I don't know.

[WITNESS *deeply moved.*]
[MARY ANN WHITE *sobs.*]

GWENN: And the trial was still happening.

SCHMIDT: [*Deeply moved.*] Thank you. I have nothing further.

[DOLSON *sobs.*]

GWENN: But the tears at the Hall of Justice
are all for Dan White.

[*Gavel.*]
[*They exit.*]
[*Lights change.*]

[*The ex-D.A. alone in an empty courtroom.*]
[*Nervous, fidgeting.*]

FREITAS: I was voted out of office.

[*On screen:* JOSEPH FREITAS, JR., *former D.A.*]

Well, I'm out of politics and I don't know whether
I'll get back into politics
because it certainly did set back my personal ah …
aspirations as a public figure dramatically.
I don't know.

You know, there was an attempt to not allow our office to
prosecute the case
because I was close to Moscone myself.
And we fought against that.

I was confident—
[*Laughs.*]
I chose Tom Norman because he was the senior homicide prosecutor
for fifteen years and he was quite successful at it.
I don't know …

The was a great division in the city then, you know.
The city was divided all during that period.
George was a liberal Democrat and Dick Hongisto.
I was considered a liberal Democrat
and George as you'll remember was elected
Mayor over John Barbagelata who was the leader
of what was considered the Right in town.
And it was a narrow victory.
So, after his election, Barbagelata persisted in attacking them
and keeping
I thought—
keeping the city divided.

It divided on emerging constituencies like
the gay constituency.
That's the one that was used to cause
the most divisive emotions more than any other.
So the divisiveness in the city was there.

I mean that was the whole point of this political fight
between Dan White
and Moscone and Milk:
The fight was over who controlled the city.

The Right couldn't afford to lose Dan.
He was their saving vote on the Board of Supervisors.
He blocked the Milk/Moscone agenda.
Obviously Harvey Milk didn't want Dan White on the Board.

So, it was political, the murders.

Maybe I should have,
again in hindsight, possibly Tom,
even though his attempts to do that may have been
ruled inadmissible,
possibly Tom should have been a little stronger in that area.
But again, at the time … I mean,
even the press was shocked at the outcome …

But—
Well, I think that what the jury had already bought was
White's background—
Now that's what was really on trial.
Dan White sat there and waved his little American flag
and they acquitted him.
They convicted George and Harvey.
Now if this had been a poor Black or a poor Chicano
or a poor white janitor who'd been fired,
or the husband of an alleged girlfriend of Moscone's,
I don't think they would have bought the diminished capacity
defense.
But whereas they have a guy who was a member of a
County Board of Supervisors who left the police department,
who had served in the army, who was a fireman,
who played baseball—
I think that's what they were caught up in—
that kind of person *must* have been crazy to do this.
I would have interpreted it differently.
Not to be held to a higher standard, but uh …
that he had all the tools to be responsible.

One of the things people said was:
"Why didn't you talk more about
George's background, his family life, etc.?"

Well ...
One of the reasons is that Tom Norman did know,
that had he opened up that area,
they were prepared,
yeah—
they were prepared to smear George—to bring up the incident in
Sacramento. With the woman—
[And other things.]
It would be at best a wash,
so why get into it?

If you know they're going to bring out things that aren't positive.
We wanted to let the city heal.
We—And after Jonestown ...
Well it would have been the city on trial.
If the jury had stuck to the facts alone,
I mean, the confession alone was enough to convict him ...
I mean, look at this kid that shot Reagan,
it was the same thing. All the way through that,
they said, my friends—
"Well, Christ, look at what the prosecutors went through on that one, Joe."
It's tragic that that has to be the kind of experience
that will make you feel better.

And then about White being anti-gay
well ...
White inside himself may have been anti-gay,
but that Milk was his target ...
As I say—*Malice was there.*
Milk led the fight to keep White off the Board,
which makes the murder all the more rational.
I know the gay community thinks the murder was anti-gay:
political in that sense. But
I think, they're wrong. Y' know, some people—
 in the gay community
—ah—even said I threw the trial.
Before this, I was considered a great friend to the gay community.
Why would I want to throw the trial
—this trial
in an election year?

Oh, there were accusations you wouldn't believe ...
At the trial, a woman ...
it may have been one of the jurors—
I can't remember ...
Actually said—
"But what would Mary Ann White do without her husband?"
And I remember my outrage.
She never thought,
"What will Gina Moscone do without George?"

I must tell you that it's hard for me to talk about a lot
of these things,
all of this is just the—just
the tip of the iceberg.

We thought—Tommy and I—Tom Norman and I—
We thought it was an open and shut case of first degree murder.

    [*Lights.*]

    [*On screen: THE PSYCHIATRIC DEFENSE.*]
    [*Lights up on four psychiatrists in conservative dress, in either
    separate witness stands or a multiple stand unit.*]

NORMAN: It wasn't just an automatic reaction when he fired those last two shots
into George Moscone's *brains* was it, Doctor?

COURT: Let's move on Mr. Norman.
You are just arguing with the witnesses now.

NORMAN: Your Honor—

COURT: Let's move on.

SOLOMON: I think he was out of control and in an unreasonable state. And I think
if the gun had held, you know, maybe more bullets, maybe he would have shot
more bullets. I don't know.

LUNDE: This wasn't just some mild case of the blues.

SOLOMON: I think that, you know, maybe Mr. Moscone would have been just
as dead with one bullet. I don't know.

JONES: I think he was out of control.

DELMAN: Yes.

NORMAN: George Moscone was shot four times, Doctor. The gun had five cartridges in it. Does that change your opinion in any way?

SOLOMON: No. I think he just kept shooting for awhile.

[NORMAN *throws his notes down.*]

SCHMIDT: Now, there is another legal term we deal with in the courtroom, and that is variously called "malice" or "malice aforethought" … ? And this must be present in order to convict for murder in the first degree.

JONES: Okay, let me preface this by saying I am not sure how malice is defined. I'll give you what my understanding is. In order to have malice, you would have to be able to do certain things: to be able to be intent to kill somebody unlawfully. You would have to be able to do something for a base and anti-social purpose. You would have to be aware of the duty imposed on you not to do that, not to unlawfully kill somebody or do something for a base, anti-social purpose, that involved a risk of death, and you would have to be able to act, despite having that awareness of that, that you are not supposed to do that, and so you would have to know that you were not supposed to do it, and then also act despite—keeping in mind that you are not supposed to do it. Is that your answer—your question?

SCHMIDT: I think so.

JONES: [*Laughs.*] I felt that he had the capacity
   to do the first three:
   that he had the capacity to intend to kill,
   but that doesn't take much, you know,
   to try to kill somebody,
   it's not a high-falutin' mental state.
   I think he had the capacity to do something
   for a base and anti-social purpose.
   I think he had the capacity to know that there was a duty
   imposed on him not to do that,
   but *I don't think he had the capacity to hold that notion*
   in his mind while he was acting;
   so that I think that the depression,

plus the moment, the tremendous emotions of the
moment, with the depression,
reduced his capacity for conforming conduct.
In fact, I asked him:
"Why didn't you hit them?"
And he was flabbergasted that I asked such a thing,
because it was contrary to his code of behavior,
you know, he was taken aback, kind of—
to hit them seemed ridiculous to him—
because it would have been so unfair,
since he could have defeated them so easily
in a fist fight.

SCHMIDT: Thank you. [*He sits. To* NORMAN.] You may examine.

* [NORMAN: Doctor Jones, when let off at City Hall the accused was let off at the Polk Street entrance and then walked a block and a half to Van Ness Avenue—Why wouldn't he just enter City Hall through the main entrance?

JONES: He got towards the top of the stairs, then looked up, saw the metal detector and thought: "Oh, my goodness, I got that gun."

NORMAN: Doctor, why would he care whether there was a metal detector there, and that a gun would have been discovered upon his person?

JONES: Well, I would presume that would mean some degree of hassle. I mean, I presume that the metal detector would see if somebody is trying to bring a weapon in.

NORMAN: That is usually why they have it. Did he realize at that time that he was unlawfully carrying a concealable firearm?

JONES: I presume so.]

NORMAN: Dr. Jones, if it's a fact that Dan White shot George Moscone twice in the body, and that when George Moscone fell to the floor disabled, he shot twice more into the right side of George Moscone's head at a distance of between 12 and 18 inches, he made a decision at that time, didn't he, to either discharge the gun into the head of George Moscone, or not discharge the gun into the head of George Moscone?

---

*Note: The bracketed section was cut in the Broadway production.

JONES: If decision means he behaved in that way, then, yes.

NORMAN: Well, didn't he have to make some kind of choice based upon some reasoning process?

JONES: Oh, no, not based on reasoning necessarily. I think—I don't think that I—you know, great emotional turmoil in context of major mood disorder—he was enraged and anxious and frustrated in addition to the underlying depression. I think that after Moscone says "How's your family?" or, "What's your wife going to do?" at that point, I think that it's—it's over.

NORMAN: It's over for George Moscone.

SOLOMON: I think that if you look at the gun as a transitional object, you can see that transitional objects are clung to in—in situations of great—of anxiety and insecurity, as one sees with children.

[COURT—*raises eyes, gives up.*]

NORMAN: Doctor, are you telling us that a person who has lived an otherwise law-abiding life and an otherwise moral life could not premeditate and deliberate as is contemplated by the definition of first degree murder?!

SOLOMON: I'm not saying that absolutely. Obviously, it's more difficult for a person who lives a highly moral life. And this individual, Dan White, had, if you want—a hypertrophy complex. Hypertrophy meaning over developed, morally; rigidly, overdeveloped, In fact, if Mr. White were to receive a light sentence I think there is a distinct possibility he could take his own life.
But I would say in general, yes.
I don't think you'd kill Mr. Schmidt if you lost this case.

NORMAN: It's unlikely.

SOLOMON: You may be very angry, but I don't think you will do it because I think you are probably a very moral and law abiding citizen, and I think if you did it, I would certainly recommend a psychiatric examination, because I think there would be a serious possibility that you had flipped.

[*Pause.*]

It's most interesting to me how split off his feelings were at this time.

LUNDE: Dan White had classical symptoms that are described in diagnostic manuals for depression and, of course, he had characteristics of compulsive personality, which happens to be kind of a bad combination in those sorts of people.

NORMAN: [*Frustrated.*] Dr. Solomon you are aware that he took a gun with him when he determined to see George Moscone, a loaded gun?

SOLOMON: Yes.

NORMAN: Why did he take that gun, in your opinion, Dr. Solomon?

SOLOMON: I might say that I think there are symbolic aspects to this.

NORMAN: Symbolic aspects, now Doctor …

COURT: Let's move on to another question.

NORMAN: Well, Your Honor …

COURT: Let's move on.

NORMAN: [*Frustrated.*] All right. Dr. Delman, after he went in the building armed with a gun through a window and went up to see George Moscone, at the time he came in to see George Moscone, do you feel that he was angry with George Moscone?

DELMAN: Yes.

NORMAN: When George Moscone told him that he wasn't going to appoint him, do you think that that brought about and increased any more anger?

DELMAN: Yes.

NORMAN: All right. Now there was some point in there when he shot George Moscone, isn't that true?

DELMAN: Yes.

NORMAN: Do you know how many times he shot him?

DELMAN: I believe it's four.

NORMAN: Well, Doctor, do you put any significance upon the circumstances that he shot George Moscone twice in the head?

DELMAN: The question is, "Do I put any significance in it?"

NORMAN: Yes.

DELMAN: I really have no idea why that happened.

NORMAN: Well, Doctor, do you think he knew that if you shot a man twice in the head that it was likely to surely kill him?!

DELMAN: I'm sure that he knew that shooting a man in the head would kill him, Mr. Norman.

NORMAN: Thank you! [*He sits.*]

SCHMIDT: But, it is your conclusion, Doctor, that Dan White could not premeditate or deliberate, within the meaning we have discussed here, on November 27th, 1978?

DELMAN: That is correct.

>   [NORMAN *slaps hands to head.*]
>   [BLINDER *enters.*]

SCHMIDT: Thank you.

BLINDER: I teach forensic psychiatry.
I teach about the uses and abuses
of psychiatry in the judicial system.
The courts tend to place psychiatry in a position
where it doesn't belong. Where it becomes the sole arbiter
between guilt and innocence.
There is also a tendency in the stresses of the adversary system
to polarize psychiatric testimony so that a psychiatrist
finds himself trying to put labels on normal
stressful behavior,
and *everything* becomes a mental illness.
And I think that is an abuse.

>   [*He refers to his notes.*]

Dan White found City Hall rife of corruption.
With the possible exceptions of Dianne Feinstein and Harvey Milk,
the supervisors seemed to make their judgments, their votes,
on the basis of what was good for them,
rather than what was good for the City.

And this was a very frustrating thing for Mr. White:
to want to do a good job for his constituents
and find he was continually defeated.

In addition to these stresses, there were
attacks by the press
and there were threats of literal attacks on Supervisors.
He told me a number of Supervisors like himself
carried a gun to scheduled meetings.
Never any relief from these tensions.

Whenever he felt things were not going right,
He would abandon his usual program of exercise and good nutrition
and start gorging himself on junk foods:
Twinkies, Coca-Cola.

Soon Mr. White was just sitting in front of the TV.
Ordinarily, he reads. (Mr. White has always been an
identifiable Jack London adventurer.)

But now, getting very depressed about the fact he would
not be reappointed,
he just sat there before the TV
binging on Twinkies.

   [*On screen: The Twinkie Defense.*]

He couldn't sleep.
He was tossing and turning on the couch in the living room
so he wouldn't disturb his wife on the bed.

Virtually no sexual contact at this time.
He was dazed, confused, had crying spells,
became increasingly ill,
and wanted to be left alone.

He told his wife:
"Don't bother cooking any food for me.
I will just munch on these potato chips,"

Mr. White stopped shaving and refused to go
out of the house to help Denise rally support.

314

He started to receive information that he would not be reappointed
from unlikely sources.
This was very stressing to him.

Again, it got to be cupcakes, candy bars.
He watched the sun come up on Monday morning.

Finally, at 9:00 Denise called.
He decides to go down to City Hall.
He shaves and puts on his suit.
He sees his gun—lying on the table.
Ammunition.
He simultaneously puts these in his pocket.
Denise picks him up.
He's feeling anxious about a variety of things.
He's sitting in the car hyperventilating,
blowing on his hands, repeating:
"Let him tell me to my face why he won't reappoint me.
Did he think I can't take it?
I am a man.
I can take it."

He goes down to City Hall, and I sense that time is short
so let me bridge this by saying that as I believe
it has been testified to,
he circumvents the mental (*sic*) detector,
goes to the side window,
gets an appointment with the Mayor.
The Mayor almost directly tells him,
"I am not going to reappoint you."

The Mayor puts his arm around him saying;
"Let's have a drink.
What are you going to do now, Dan?
Can you get back into the Fire Department?
What about your family?
Can your wife get her job back?
What's going to happen to them now?"

Somehow this inquiry directed to his family struck a nerve.
The Mayor's voice started to fade out and Mr. White felt

"As if I were in a dream."
He started to leave and then inexplicably turned around
and like a reflex
drew his revolver.
He had no idea how many shots he fired.

The similar event occurred
in Supervisor Milk's office.

He remembers being shocked by the sound of the gun
going off—for the second time like a cannon.

He tells me that he was aware he engaged
in a lethal act,
but tells me he gave no thought to his wrongfulness.
As he put it to me:
"I had no chance to even think about it."

He remembers running out of the building
driving, I think, to church,
making arrangements to meet his wife,
and then going from the church
to the Police Department.

> [*Pause.*]
> [*Exhausted.*]

SCHMIDT: Doctor, you have mentioned the ingestion of sugar and sweets and that sort of thing. There are certain theories with regard to sugar and sweets and the ingestion thereof, and I'd like to just touch on that briefly with the jury. Does that have any significance, or could it possibly have any significance?

BLINDER: [*Turns to jury.*] First, there is a substantial body of evidence that in susceptible individuals, large quantities of what we call junk food, high sugar content food with lots of preservatives, can precipitate anti-social and even violent behavior.

There have been studies, for example, where they have taken so-called career criminals and taken them off all their junk food and put them on meat and potatoes and their criminal records immediately evaporate. [*Pause.*] It's contradictory and ironic, but the way it works is that for such a person, the American Dream is a Nightmare. For somebody like Dan White.

SCHMIDT: Thank you, Doctor.

[*Lights fade on psychiatrists.*]
[*Pause.*]
[*Lights up on* MARY ANN WHITE, *blazing white.
She is almost blinded.*] [*She comes
forward.*]

SCHMIDT: You are married to that man, is that correct?

MARY ANN: Yes.

SCHMIDT: When did you first meet him?

MARY ANN: I met him [WITNESS *sobbing.*]

SCHMIDT: If you want to take any time// just let us know

MARY ANN: [*Pulling herself together.*] I met him in April, 1976 ...

SCHMIDT: And you were married// and you took a trip?

MARY ANN: Yes. Yes, we went to Ireland on our honeymoon because Danny
just had this feeling that Ireland could be this place that could be really peace-
ful for him. He just really likes—loves—everything about Ireland and so we —
[*Sobbing.*]

SCHMIDT: Excuse me.

MARY ANN: —so we went there// for about five wee—

SCHMIDT: During that period did you notice anything// unusual about his behavior?

MARY ANN: Yes, I mean, you know, when we went I thought—went thinking
it was going to be kind of romantic, and when we got there, the thing that
attracted me most to Danny was his vitality, energy and the fact that he always
had the ability to inspire in you something that made you want to do your best
like he did, and when we got there, when we got to Ireland ... it was all of a
sudden, he went into like a two-week long mood, like I had seen before, but

I had never seen one, I guess, all the way through, because when we were going
out, I might see him for a day, and being a fireman, he would work a day, and
then I wouldn't see him, and when we got to Ireland ... I mean, I was just newly

Note: //=Overlap ... Next speaker starts, first speaker continues.

married and I thought: "What did I do?"

SCHMIDT: After he was on the Board, did you notice these moods// become more frequent?

MARY ANN: Yes, he had talked to me about how hard the job was on him. You know, from June he started to talk about how it was. Obviously you can sense when you are not sleeping together, and you are not really growing together and he would say, "Well, I can't—I can't really think of anyone else when I don't even like myself." And I said, "It's just him. He's not satisfied with what I'm doing and I don't like myself//and so I can't … "

SCHMIDT: Did you see him on the morning of … November 27th?

MARY ANN: Yes//I did.

SCHMIDT: And at that time did he indicate what he was going to do//that day?

MARY ANN: It was just, he was going to stay *home*. He wasn't leaving the house.

SCHMIDT: Later that morning, did you receive a call//to meet him somewhere?

MARY ANN: Yes. I did. Yes, I went to St. Mary's Cathedral.
I went and saw him.
I could see that he had been crying, and I, I
just kind of looked at him
and he just looked at me
and he said,
he said,
"I shot the Mayor and Harvey."

SCHMIDT: [*Looks to* NORMAN *as if to say,* "*Any questions?*" NORMAN *nods no.*] Thank you.

> [DAN WHITE *sobs.*]
> [SCHMIDT *puts hand on* WHITE's *shoulder.*]
> [MARY ANN WHITE *stumbles off the stand*
> *to her husband.*]
> [WHITE *shields his eyes.*]
> [*She looks as if she will embrace him.*]

SCHMIDT: The defense is prepared to rest at this time.

> [MARY ANN WHITE *sobs.*]

[*Hyperreal sound of a woman's high heels
on marble echoing.*]
[*Mumbled "Hail Marys."*]

COURT: Let me admonish you, ladies gentlemen of the jury, not to discuss this
case among yourselves nor with anyone else, not to allow anyone to speak to
you about the case, nor are you to form or express an opinion until the matter has been submitted to you.

[*Gavel.*]
[*On screen. The Defense rests.*]
[ALL *exit.*]

MILK'S FRIEND: [*Enters alone.*] *We got back from the airport the night of the
27th
And my roommate said;
There's going to be a candle-light march.
By now, we thought it had to have reached City Hall.
So we went directly there. From the airport to City Hall.
And there were maybe 75 people there.
And I remember thinking;
My God is this all anybody ... cared?
Somebody said: No, the march hasn't gotten here yet.
So we then walked over to Market Street
which was 2 or 3 blocks away.
And looked down it.
And Market Street runs in a straight line
out to the Castro area.
And as we turned the corner,

[*On screen. The screens flooded with
candles and the candle-light march
music. Barber's "Adagio."*]

there were people as wide as this wide street
As far as you could see.

[*The entire company enters holding*

---

*Dialogue from *The Times of Harvey Milk*, a film by Robert Epstein and Richard Schmeichen.

candles.]
[*After awhile.*]

YOUNG MOTHER: *Thousands and thousands of people,
And that feeling of such loss.

[*Music continues.*]

GWENN: *It was one of the most eloquent expressions of a
community's response to violence
that I have ever seen …

A MOURNER: [*Wearing a black arm band.*] I'd like to read from the transcript of
Harvey Milk's political will. [*Reads.*]
This is Harvey Milk speaking on Friday, November 18.
This tape is to be played only in the event of my death
by assassination.

[*On screen: Pictures of* MILK.]

I've given long and considerable thought to this,
and not just since the election.
I've been thinking about this for some time
prior to the election and certainly over the years.
I fully realize that a person who stands for what I stand for—
a gay activist—
becomes the target for a person who is insecure, terrified,
afraid or very disturbed themselves.

[DAN WHITE *enters. Stops.*]

Knowing that I could be assassinated at any moment
or any time,
I feel it's important that some people should understand
my thoughts.
So the following are my thoughts, my wishes, my desires,
I'd like to pass them on and have them played for the appropriate people.
The first and most obvious concern is that
if I was to be shot and killed,

---

*Dialogue from *The Times of Harvey Milk*, a film by Robert Epstein and Richard Schmeichen.

the mayor has the power,
George Moscone.

> [*On screen: Pictures of* MOSCONE,
> *the funeral, the mourners, the widow.*]

of appointing my successor …
to the Board of Supervisors.
I cannot prevent some people
from feeling angry and frustrated and mad,
but I hope
that they would not demonstrate violently.
If a bullet should enter my brain,
let that bullet destroy every closet door.

> [*Gavel.*]
> [*All* MOURNERS *blow out candles.*]
> [DAN WHITE *sits.*]
> [*Blackout.*]

> [*On screen: The People's rebuttal/*DR. LEVY *Psychiatrist*]
> [*Lights up.*]

LEVY: I interviewed the defendant several hours after the shootings of
     November 27th.
     In my opinion, one can get a more accurate diagnosis
     the closer one examines the suspect
     after a crime has been committed.
     At that time, it appeared to me that Dan White had
     no remorse for the death of George Moscone.
     It appeared to me, he had no remorse
     for the death of Harvey Milk.
     There was nothing in my interview which would suggest to me
     there was any mental disorder.
     I had the feeling that there was some depression but it was not
     depression that I would consider as a diagnosis.

     In fact, I found him to be less depressed
     than I would have expected him to be.
     At that time I saw him, it seemed that he felt himself to be quite justified.
     [*Looks to notes.*]

I felt he had the capacity to form malice.
I felt he had the capacity to premeditate. And ...
I felt he had the capacity to deliberate, to arrive at a
course of conduct weighing considerations.

NORMAN: Did you review the transcript of the proceeding wherein the testimonies of Drs. Jones, Blinder, Solomon, Delman and Lunde were given?

LEVY: Yes. I found nothing in them that would cause me to revise my opinion.

NORMAN: Thank you, Dr. Levy. [*Sits.*]

[SCHMIDT *stands.*]

SCHMIDT: Dr. Levy, are you a full professor at the University of California?

LEVY: No. I am an associate clinical professor.

[SCHMIDT *smiles, looks to jury.*]

SCHMIDT: May I inquire of your age, sir?

LEVY: I'm 55.

SCHMIDT: Huh. [*Picking up papers.*] Doctor, your report is dated November 27, 1978, is it not?

LEVY: Yes.

SCHMIDT: And yet the report was not written on November 27, 1978?

LEVY: No. It would have been within several days//of that time.

SCHMIDT: And then it was dated November 27, 1978?

LEVY: Yes.

SCHMIDT: Well, regardless of the backdating, or whatever, when did you come to your forensic conclusions?

LEVY: I'd say the conclusion would have been on November 27th.

SCHMIDT: And that was after a two-hour talk with Dan White?

LEVY: Yes.

SCHMIDT: Doctor, would it be fair to say that you made some snap decisions?

LEVY: I don't believe// I did.

SCHMIDT: Did you consult with any other doctors?

LEVY: No.

SCHMIDT: Did you review any of the witnesses' statements?

LEVY: No.

SCHMIDT: Did you consult any of the material that was available to you, save and except for the tape of Dan White on the same date?

LEVY: No. That was all that was made available to me// at that time.

SCHMIDT: Now I don't mean to be facetious, but this is a fairly important case, is that fair?

LEVY: I would certainly think so,// yes.

SCHMIDT: But you didn't talk further with Mr. White?

LEVY: No. I was not requested to.

SCHMIDT: And you didn't request to talk to him further?

LEVY: No, I was not going to do a complete assessment.

SCHMIDT: Well, in fact, you didn't do a complete assessment, is that fair?

LEVY: *I was not asked to do a complete assessment.*

COURT: Doctor, you are fading away.

LEVY: I was not asked to do a complete assessment.

SCHMIDT: Thank you.

> [*Blackout.*]
> [*Commotion in court,* JOANNA *tries to
> get interview from* LEVY.]

SCHMIDT: [*In black.*] She wants to tell the story so it's not responsive to the questions.

> [*Lights up.*]
> [*On screen:* SUPERVISOR CAROL RUTH SILVER,

for the prosecution.]

SILVER: [*Very agitated, speaking fast, heated.*] The prosecution asked in what other case did a dispute between Dan White and Harvey Milk arise! And it was the Polk Street closing was another occasion when Harvey requested that Polk Street, which is a heavily gay area in San Francisco, I am sure everybody knows, and on Halloween had traditionally had a huge number of people in costumes and so forth down there and has// traditionally been recommended for closure by the Police Department and—

SCHMIDT: I am going to object to this, Your Honor.

SILVER: It was recommended—

COURT: Just ask the next question. Just ask the next question.

SILVER: I am sorry.

NORMAN: Did Mr. Milk and Mr. White take positions that were opposite to each other?

SILVER: Yes.

NORMAN: Was there anything that became, well, rather loud and perhaps hostile in connection or consisting between the two?

SILVER: Not loud but very hostile.
You have to first understand that this street closure
was recommended by the Police Chief and had been done customarily in
the years past// and is, was—came up as an uncontested issue practically.

SCHMIDT: Your Honor, I again—

COURT: Please, just make your objection.

SCHMIDT: I'd like to.

COURT: Without going through contortions.

SCHMIDT: There is an objection.

COURT: All right. Sustained.

NORMAN: Miss Silver, did you know, or did you ever see Mr. White to appear to be depressed or to be withdrawn?

SILVER: No.

NORMAN: Thank you. [*Sits.*]

[SILVER *flabbergasted, upset.*]

COURT: All right. Any questions, Mr. Schmidt?

SCHMIDT: Is it Miss Silver?

SILVER: Yes.

SCHMIDT: Miss Silver, you never had lunch with Dan White, did you?

SILVER: Did I ever have lunch?

[*Subliminal music.*]

NOTHENBERG: George Moscone was socially brilliant in that he could find the injustice.

SCHMIDT: I mean the two of you?

SILVER: I don't recall having done so// but I—

NOTHENBERG: His mind went immediately to what can we do?

SCHMIDT: Did you socialize frequently?

NOTHENBERG: What can we practically do?

SILVER: No, when his son was born// I went to a party at his house and that kind of thing.

SCHMIDT: Did Mr. Norman contact you last week, or did you// contact him?

NOTHENBERG: I was with George registering voters in Mississippi in 1964.

SILVER: On Friday morning I called his office.

NOTHENBERG: Y'know, he'd never seen that kind of despair before, but when he saw it he said right out: "This is intolerable."

SILVER: Because I was reading the newspaper—

SCHMIDT: Yes.

SILVER: And it appeared// to me that—

COURT: Don't tell us.

NOTHENBERG: And whenever he said: "this is *intolerable*,"

SILVER: I'm sorry.

NOTHENBERG: in all the years I knew him, he always *did* something about it.

COURT: The jurors are told not to read the newspaper, and I am hoping that they haven't// read the newspapers.

SILVER: I apologize.

COURT: Okay.

SCHMIDT: Miss Silver—

COURT: I am sorry, I didn't want to cut her off—

SILVER: No, I understand.

COURT: from any other answer.

SCHMIDT: I think she did complete the answer, Judge.
In any event, you contacted Mr. Norman, did you not?

SILVER: Yes, I did.

SCHMIDT: And at that time, you offered to Mr. Norman to round up people who could say that Dan White never looked depressed at City Hall, is that fair?

SILVER: That's right. Well, I offered to testify to that effect and I suggested that there were other people// who could similarly testify to that fact.

SCHMIDT: In fact, you expressed it though you haven't sat here and listened to the testimony in this courtroom?

SILVER: No, I have never been here before Friday when I was subpoenaed// and spent some time in the jury room.

SCHMIDT: But to use your words, after having read what was in the paper, you said that the defense sounded like "bullshit" to you? That's correct.

DENMAN: I thought I would be a chief witness for the prosecution.

SCHMIDT: Would that suggest then that perhaps you have a bias in this case?

DENMAN: What was left unsaid was what the trial should have been about.

SILVER: I certainly have a bias.

SCHMIDT: You are a political enemy of Dan White's is that fair?

SILVER: No, that's not true.

DENMAN: Before, y'know, there was a lot of talk about assassinating the Mayor among thuggish elements of the Police Officers Association.

SCHMIDT: Did you have any training in psychology or psychiatry?

DENMAN: And those were the cops Dan White was closest to.

SILVER: No more than some of the kind of C.E.B. courses// lawyer's psychology for lawyers kind of training.

DENMAN: I think he knew a lot of guys would think he did the right thing and yeah they would make him a hero.

SCHMIDT: I mean, would you be able to diagnosis, say, *manic depression depressed type*, or could you distinguish that from *uni-polar depression*?

SILVER: No.

DENMAN: I was Dan White's jailer for 72 hours after the assassinations.

SCHMIDT: Did you ever talk to him about his dietary habits or anything like that.

DENMAN: There were no tears.

SILVER: I remember a conversation about nutrition or something like that but I can't remember// the substance of it.

SCHMIDT: I don't have anything further.

DENMAN: There was no shame.

COURT: Any redirect, Mr. Norman?

NORMAN: Yes.

DENMAN: You got the feeling that he knew exactly what he was doing and there was no remorse.

NORMAN: Miss Silver, you were asked if you had a bias in this case. You knew Harvey Milk very well and you liked him, didn't you?

SILVER: I did; and also George Moscone.

NORMAN: Miss Silver, speaking of a bias, had you ever heard the Defendant say anything about getting people of whom Harvey Milk numbered himself?

[*Lights up on* MILK'*s friend.*]

SILVER: In the Polk Street debate—

MILK'S FRIEND: The night Harvey was elected, I went to bed early because it was more happiness than I had been taught to deal with.

SILVER: Dan White got up and gave—
a long diatribe—

MILK'S FRIEND: Next morning we put up signs saying "thank you."

SILVER: Just a—a very unexpected and very uncharacteristic of Dan, long hostile speech about how gays and their lifestyles had to be contained and we can't// *encourage* this kind of thing and—

SCHMIDT: I am going to object to this, your Honor.

COURT: Sustained, okay.

MILK'S FRIEND: During that, Harvey came over and told me
that he had made a political will
because he expected he'd be killed.
And then in the same breath, he said (I'll never forget it):
"It works, it works … "

NORMAN: All right … that's all.

MILK'S FRIEND: The system works// …

NORMAN: Thank you.

DENMAN: When White was being booked, it all seemed fraternal. One officer gave Dan a pat on the behind when he was booked, sort of a "Hey, catch you later, Dan," pat.

COURT: Any recross?

DENMAN: Some of the officers and deputies were standing around with half-smirks on their faces. Some were actually laughing.

SCHMIDT: Just a couple.

DENMAN: The joke they kept telling was,
   "Dan White's mother says to him when he comes home,
   'No, dummy, I said milk and baloney, not Moscone!'" [*Pause.*]

SCHMIDT: Miss Silver, you are a part of the gay community also, are you?

SILVER: Myself?

SCHMIDT: Yes.

SILVER: You mean, am I gay?

SCHMIDT: Yes.

SILVER: No, I'm not.

SCHMIDT: I have nothing further.

MOSCONE'S FRIEND: George would have said, "This is intolerable," and he'd have done something about it.

COURT: All right, Miss Silver you may leave. Next witness, please.

   [*Lights*]
   [SILVER *exits towards door.*]
   [JOANNA *with TV lights.*]

JOANNA LU: Miss Silver, Supervisor Silver, would you like to elaborate on Mr. White's anti-gay feelings or hostility to Harvey Milk or George Moscone?

SILVER: No comment, right now.

   [SILVER *distraught, rushes past.*]

JOANNA LU: Did you feel you were baited, did you have your say?

SILVER: [*Blows up.*] I said I have no comment at this time!!!

   [*She exits.*]

COURT: Mr. Norman? Next witness?

NORMAN: Nothing further.
Those are all the witnesses we have to present.

COURT: The People rest?

NORMAN: Yes.

COURT: Does the defense have any witnesses?

SCHMIDT: [*Surprised.*] Well, we can discuss it, Your Honor. I am not sure there is anything to rebut.

> [*Light change.*]
> [*Commotion in court.*]
> [*On screen: The People Rest.*]
> [*Lights up on* SCHMIDT:]
> [*He is at a podium, a parish priest*
> *at a pulpit.*]
> [*Dissolve to on screen: Summations.*]

SCHMIDT: I'm nervous. I'm very nervous. I sure hope I say all the right things. I can't marshal words the way Mr. Norman can—but—I believe strongly in things.

Lord God! I don't say to you to forgive Dan White. I don't say to you to just let Dan White walk out of here a free man. He is guilty. But, the degree of responsibility is the issue here. The state of mind is the issue here. It's not who was killed; it's why. It's not who killed them; but why. The state of mind is the issue here.

Lord God! The pressures.
Nobody can say that the things that happened to him days
or weeks preceeding wouldn't make a reasonable and ordinary man
at least mad,
angry in some way.

Surely—surely, that had to have arisen, not to kill,
not to kill, just to be mad, to act irrationally,
because if you kill, when you are angry,
or under the heat of passion,
if you kill, then the law will punish you,
and you will be punished by God—
God will punish you,

but the law will also punish you.

Heat of passion fogs judgement, makes one act irrationally,
in the very least,
and my God,
that is what happened at the very least.

Forget about the mental illness,
forget about all the rest of the factors
that came into play at the same time;
Surely he acted irrationally, impulsively—out of some passion.

Now ... you will recall at the close of the prosecution's case,
it was suggested to you this was a calm, cool, deliberating,
terrible terrible person
that had committed two crimes like these,
and these are terrible crimes,
and that he was emotionally stable at that time
and there wasn't anything wrong with him.

He didn't have any diminished capacity.
Then we played these tapes he made directly after
he turned himself in at Northern Station.

My God,
that was not a person that was calm and collected and cool
and able to weigh things out.
It just wasn't.

The tape just totally fogged me up the first time I heard it.
It was a man that was, as Frank Falzon said, broken.
Shattered.

This was not the Dan White that everybody had known.

Something happened to him and he snapped.
That's the word I used in my opening statement.
Something snapped here.

The pot had boiled over here,
and people that boil over in that fashion,
they tell the truth.

Have the tape played again, if you can't remember what was said.
He said in no uncertain terms,

"My God,
why did I do these things?
What made me do this?
How on earth could I have done this?
I didn't intend to hurt anybody.
My God,
what happened to me?
Why?"

Play the tape.
If everybody says the tape is truthful, play the tape.
I'd agree it's truthful.

With regard to the reloading and some of these little
discrepancies that appeared to come up.
I am not even sure of the discrepancies,
but if there were discrepancies,
listen to it in context.
"Where did you reload?"
"I reloaded in my office, I think."
"And then did you leave the Mayor's office?"
"Yes, then I left the Mayor's office."

That doesn't mean anything to me at all.
It doesn't mean anything to me at all.
And I don't care where the reloading took place!

But listen to the tape.
It says in no uncertain terms,
"I didn't intend to hurt anybody.
I didn't intend to do this."
Why do we do things?

I don't know.
It was a man desperately trying to grab at something …

"What happened to me?
How could I have done this?"

If the District Attorney concedes that what is
on the tape is truthful,
and I believe that's the insinuation we have here,
then, by golly,
there is voluntary manslaughter,
nothing more and nothing less. I say this to you in all honesty.

And if you have any doubts our law tells you,
you have to judge in favor of Dan White.

Now, I don't know what more I can say.
He's got to be punished
and he will be punished.
He's going to have to live with this for the rest of his life.
His child will live with it
and his family will live with it
and God will punish him
and the law will punish him,
and they will punish him severely.
And this is the type of case where, I suppose
I don't think Mr. Norman will do it
but you can make up a picture of a dead man
or two of them for that matter
and you can wave them around and say
somebody is going to pay for this
and somebody *is* going to pay for this.
But it's not an emotional type thing.
I get emotional about it
but *you* can't
because you have to be objective about the facts.

But please, please
Just justice.
That's all.
Just justice here.

[SCHMIDT *appears to break for a moment.*]

Now I get one argument.
I have made it.

And I just hope that—
I just hope that you'll come to the same conclusion
that I have come to,
and thank you for listening to me.

NORMAN: Ladies and gentlemen,
I listened very carefully to the summation just given you.
It appears to me, members of the jury,
to be a very facile explanation and rationalization
as to premeditation and deliberation.
The evidence that has been laid before you
screams for murder in the first degree.

What counsel for the defense has done is suggest to you
to *excuse* this kind of conduct and call it something that
it isn't,
to call it voluntary manslaughter.

Members of the jury, you are the triers of fact here.
You have been asked to hear this tape recording again.
The tape recording has been aptly described
as something very moving. We all feel a sense of sympathy,
a sense of empathy for our fellow man, but you are not to let
sympathy influence you in your judgment.

To reduce the charge of murder to something less—
to reduce it to voluntary manslaughter—
means you are saying that this was not murder.
That this was an intentional killing of a human being
upon a quarrel, or heat of passion.
But ladies and gentlemen,
that quarrel must have been so extreme
at the time
that the defendant could not—
was incapable of forming
those qualities of thought which are
malice, premeditation and deliberation.
But the evidence in this case doesn't suggest that at all.
Not at all.
If the defendant had picked up a vase or something

that happened to be in the mayor's office
and hit the mayor over the head and killed him
you know, you know that argument for voluntary manslaughter
might be one which you could say the evidence admits
a reasonable doubt. But—

Ladies and gentlemen:
THE FACTS ARE:
It was *he*—Dan White – who brought the gun to the City Hall;
the gun was not there.
It was *he* who brought the extra cartridges for the gun;
they were not found there.

He went to City Hall and when he got there he went
to the Polk Street door.

There was a metal detector there.
He knew he was carrying a gun.
He knew that he had extra cartridges for it.

Instead of going through the metal detector,
he *decided* to go around the corner.
He was capable at that time of expressing anger.
He was capable of, according to the doctor—
well, parenthetically, members of the jury,
I don't know how they can look in your head and tell you
what you are able to do. But—
they even said that he was capable of knowing at that time
that if you pointed a gun at somebody and you fired that gun
that you would surely kill a person.

He went around the corner, and climbed
through a window into City Hall.

He went up to the Mayor's office.
He appeared, according to witnesses,
to act calmly in his approach, in his speech.

He chatted with Cyr Copertini; he was capable of
carrying on a conversation to the extent that he was
able to ask her how she was, after having asked to see

the Mayor.

[*Looks to audience.*]

He stepped into the Mayor's office.
After some conversation,
he shot the Mayor twice in the body.
Then he shot the Mayor in the head twice
while the Mayor was disabled on the floor.
The evidence suggests that in order to shoot the Mayor
twice in the head
he had to *lean down* to do it.

[*And* NORMAN *does.*]
[*Looks to jury.*]

Deliberation is premeditation.
It has malice.
I feel stultified to even bring this up.
This is the definition of murder.

He reloaded the gun.
Wherever he reloaded the gun, it was *he* who
reloaded it!

He did see Supervisor Milk
whom he knew was acting against his appointment
and he was capable of expressing anger in that regard.

He entered the Supervisor's area (a block from the Mayor's
office across City Hall)
and was told, "Dianne wants to see you."
He said, "That is going to have to wait a moment.
I have something to do first."

Then he walked to Harvey Milk's office, put his head
in the door and said
"Can I see you a moment, Harv?"
The reply was. "Yes."

He went across the hall and put three bullets
into Harvey Milk's body,

one of which hit Harvey directly in the back.
When he fell to the floor disabled,
two more were delivered to the back of his head.

Now what do you call that but premeditation and deliberation?
What do you call that realistically
but a cold-blooded killing?
Two *cold-blooded executions.*
It occurs to me that if you don't call them that,
then you are ignoring the objective evidence
and the objective facts here.

Members of the jury, there are circumstances here
which no doubt bring about anger,
maybe even rage, I don't know,
but the manner in which that anger was felt
and was handled
is *socially something that cannot be approved.*

Ladies and gentlemen,
the quality of your service is reflected in your verdict.

> [*He sits.*]
> [JOANNA LU *at door*
> *stops* SCHMIDT: *TV lights.*]

JOANNA LU: Mr. Schmidt, do you

SCHMIDT: Yes.

JOANNA LU: Do you feel society would feel justice is served if the jury returns two manslaughter verdicts?

SCHMIDT: Society doesn't have anything to do with it. Only those 12 people in the jury box.

> [*Gavel.*]

COURT: Ladies and gentlemen of the jury,
Now that you have heard the evidence,
we come to that part of the trial where you are instructed
on the applicable law.

In the crime of murder of the first degree
the necessary concurrent mental states are:
Malice aforethought, premeditation and deliberation.
In the crime of murder of the second degree,
the necessary concurrent mental state is:
Malice aforethought.
In the crime of voluntary manslaughter,
the necessary mental state is:
an intent to kill.
Involuntary manslaughter is an unlawful killing
without malice aforethought
and without intent to kill.

The law does not undertake to limit or define
the kinds of passion
which may cause a person to act rashly.
Such passions as desperation,
humiliation, resentment,
anger, fear, or rage
or any other high wrought emotion …
can be sufficient to reduce the killings to manslaughter
so long as they are sufficient
to obscure the reason
and render the average man likely to act rashly.

There is no malice aforethought
if the killing occurred upon a sudden quarrel
or heat of passion.

There is no malice aforethought
if the evidence shows that due to diminished capacity
caused by illness, mental defect, or intoxication,
the defendant did not have the capacity
to form the mental state constituting malice aforethought,
even though the killing was intentional,
voluntary, premeditated and unprovoked.

> [*A siren begins to cover the court.*]
> [*On screen: Images of the riot at City
> Hall begin to appear. Broken glass,*

images of cop cars burning, riot police, angry faces.]
[On audio: Explosions.
It is the riot.]

GWENN: *[On video.]* In order to understand the riots, I think you have to understand that the Dan White verdict did not occur in a vacuum—

COURT: Mr. Foreman, has the jury reached verdicts// in this case?

GWENN: that there were and are other factors which contribute to a legitimate
rage that was demonstrated dramatically at our symbol of Who's Responsible,
City Hall.

> *[On screen. Images of City Hall being*
> *stormed.*
> *Line of police in front in riot gear.]*

FOREMAN: Yes, it has, Your Honor.

GWENN: The verdict came down and the people rioted.

COURT: Please read the verdicts.

GWENN: The people stormed City Hall, burned police cars;

> *[On: screen: Image of City Hall.*
> *Line of police cars in flames.]*

FOREMAN: *[Reading.]* The jury finds the defendant Daniel James White guilty
of violating Section 192.1 of the penal code,

GWENN: Then the police came into our neighborhood. And the police rioted.

FOREMAN: Voluntary manslaughter, for the slaying of Mayor George Moscone.

> *[MARY ANN WHITE gasps.]*
> *[DAN WHITE puts head in hands.]*
> *[Explosion.]*
> *[Riot police enter.]*

GWENN: The police came into the Castro and assaulted gays.
They stormed the Elephant Walk Bar.
One kid had an epileptic seizure and was almost killed for it.
A cop drove a motorcycle up against a phone booth

where a lesbian woman was on the phone,
blocked her exit
and began beating her up.

COURT: Is this a unanimous verdict of the jury?

FOREMAN: Yes, it is, Judge.

GWENN: I want to talk about when people are pushed to the wall. [*Off video.*]

COURT: Will each juror say "yea"// or"nay?"

YOUNG MOTHER: What about the children?

MOSCONE'S FRIEND: I know who George offended. I know who Harvey offended.

JURORS: Yea, yea, yea// yea, yea, yea.

MOSCONE'S FRIEND: I understand the offense.

YOUNG MOTHER: What do I tell my kids?

GWENN: Were the ones who are responsible seeing these things?

YOUNG MOTHER: That in this country you serve more time for robbing a bank than for killing two people?

JURORS: Yea, yea, yea// yea, yea, yea.

GWENN: Hearing these things?

MILK'S FRIEND: I understand the offense.

GWENN: Do they understand about people being pushed to the wall?

YOUNG MOTHER: Accountability?

[*Yeas end.*]

MILK'S FRIEND: Assassination.
I've grown up with it
I forget it hasn't always been this way.

YOUNG MOTHER: What do I say?
That two lives are worth seven years and eight months// in jail

MILK'S FRIEND: I remember coming home from school in second grade—
JFK was killed—
Five years later, Martin Luther King.
It's a frame of reference.

[*Explosion.*]

COURT: Will the Foreman please read the verdict for the second count?

DENMAN: It's a divided city.

FOREMAN: The jury finds the defendant Daniel James White guilty of violating Section 192.1 of the penal code, voluntary manslaughter,
in the slaying of Supervisor Harvey Milk.

> [DAN WHITE *gasps.*]
> [MARY ANN WHITE *sobs.*] [NORMAN, *flushed, head in hands.*]
> [*Explosion.*]
> [*Violence ends.*]
> [*Riot police do terror control.*]
> [*TV lights.*]

BRITT: [*On camera.*] No—I'm optimistic about San Francisco.

COURT: Is this a unanimous decision by the jury?

FOREMAN: Yes, Your Honor.

BRITT: I'm Harry Britt. I was Harvey Milk's successor.

MOSCONE'S FRIEND: If he'd just killed George, he'd be in jail for life.

BRITT: Now this is an example I don't use often because people will misunderstand it, but when a prophet is killed, it's up to those who are left to build
the community or the church.

MOSCONE'S FRIEND: Dan White believed in the death// penalty ...

YOUNG MOTHER: To this jury Dan White// was their son.

NOTHENBERG: He should have gotten the death penalty.

YOUNG MOTHER: What are we teaching our sons?

BRITT: But I have hope.

MILK'S FRIEND: It was an effective assassination.

BRITT: I have hope. And as Harvey said, "you can't live// without hope."

MILK'S FRIEND: They always are.

BRITT: "And you, and you, and you—we gotta give 'em hope."

[*Riot ends.*]

JOANNA LU: [*On camera.*] Dan White was examined by the psychiatrist at the state prison. They decided against therapy. Dan White had no apparent signs of mental disorder ... Dan White's parole date was January 6, 1984. When Dan White left Soledad prison on January 6, 1984, it was five years, one month, and eight days since he turned himself in at Northern Station after the assassinations of Mayor George Moscone and Supervisor Harvey Milk. Mayor Dianne Feinstein, the current Mayor of San Francisco, has tried to keep Dan White out of San Francisco during his parole for fear he will be killed.

BOOM BOOM. [*Enters.*] Dan White! It's 1984 and Big Sister is watching you.

JOANNA LU: Dan White reportedly plans to move to Ireland after his release.

NOTHENBERG: What do you do with your feelings of revenge? With your need for retribution?

BRITT: We will never forget.

[*Riot images freeze.*]

BOOM BOOM. [*Enters.*] I would like to close with a reading from the Book of Dan. [*Opens book.*] Take of this and eat, for this is my defense. [*Raises the Twinkie. Eats it. Exits.*]

JOANNA LU: Dan White was found dead of carbon monoxide poisoning on October 21, 1985, at his wife's home in San Francisco, California.

[*Lights change.*]
[DAN WHITE *faces the court.*]

COURT: Mr. White, you are sentenced to seven years and eight months, the maximum sentence for these two counts of voluntary manslaughter. The Court feels that these sentences for the taking of life is completely inappropriate but that was the decision of the legislature. Again, let me repeat for the record:

Seven years and eight months is the maximum sentence for voluntary manslaughter, and this is the law.

> [*Gavel.*]
> [*Long pause.*]
> [WHITE *turns to the audience/jury.*]

DAN WHITE: I was always just a lonely vote on the board.
I was just trying to do a good job for the city.

> [*Long pause.*]

> [*Audio: Hyperreal sounds of a woman's
> high heels on marble.*]
> [*Mumbled Hail Marys. Rustle of an
> embrace.*]
> [SISTER BOOM BOOM *enters. Taunts police.*]
> [*Police raise riot shields.*]
> [*Blackout.*]
> [*On Screen: Execution of Justice.*]
> [*Gavel echoes.*]

> [*END OF PLAY.*]

WAITING FOR LEFTY

CLIFFORD ODETS

———<>———

*This play was first presented by the Group Theatre at the
Longacre Theatre on the evening of March 26th, 1935.*

INTRODUCTION

By Alan Wald

Waiting for Lefty and the Radical
Theater Tradition

Ever since its first production in 1934, critics have pondered the qualities, aesthetic and political, of *Waiting for Lefty*. The play has been excoriated as a simplistic exercise in "agit-prop" techniques (referring to the Soviet promotion of political propaganda through art), and defended as "transcendent" of those very conventions.[1] Less in debate are the recollections of those who viewed the first performance; their unrestrained acclamation, such as that of Harold Clurman's description of it as "the birth cry of the thirties," are regularly quoted in scholarship about Odets.[2]

Even more remarkable is the extraordinary international impact of the play. Margaret Brenman-Gibson observes that *"Waiting for Lefty* would be more frequently produced and more frequently banned all over the world—from Union Square to Moscow, from Tokyo to Johannesburg—than any other play in all of theater history."[3] One explanation for this appeal is *Waiting For Lefty*'s intimate connection with the workers theater tradition. While the tradition unfolded with certain unique features in the United States in the 1920s and 1930s, it was part of a worldwide left-wing cultural effort, with the aim of creating entertainment to which members of the non-elite classes might respond—to provide pleasure with a content that might open their eyes to the possibilities of a future and better world. Subsequently, the tradition lived on through various enterprises, usually with names such as "People's Theater," as well as specific projects such as the American Negro Theater Company, followed by various kinds of political theater in the 1960s in tandem with the New Left, Feminism, and Black Power and Chicano Power movements.

Odets's *Waiting for Lefty* appeared at the moment of orthodox "Third Period" Communism, when President Roosevelt was viewed as a fascist, the leadership of the labor movement as working at the behest of the bosses, and an

---

[1] Gabriel Miller, *Clifford Odets* (New York: Continuum, 1989). Pp. 166-167.
[2] See Harold Clurman, *The Fervent Years* (New York: Hill and Wang, 1961).
[3] Margaret Brenman-Gibson, *Clifford Odets: American Playwright. The Years from 1906-1940.*

all-out struggle for power was believed to be the order of the day. Odets was fully caught up in this dream of "a better world" modeled on some egregiously idealized vision of the Soviet Union; without that dream his play—and, indeed, his whole career—might have been still-born.

Waiting for Lefty, although borrowing episodes from a recent taxi cab strike in New York City, was also intended to dramatize a call to arms in just one of the many coordinated battles necessary to produce the "final conflict" that will lead to a truly human society. Nevertheless, the play achieved a unique rapport with its audience due to Odets's capacity to reinvigorate familiar tropes from radical culture that were in the air in 1934, along with a narrative that brought briefly to life a range of people in paradigmatic situations.

CHARACTERS

FATT	AGATE KELLER
JOE	HENCHMAN
EDNA	SECRETARY
MILLER	ACTOR
FAYETTE	REILLY
IRV	DR. BARNES
FLORRIE	DR. BENJAMIN
SID	A MAN
CLAYTON	VOICES

As the curtain goes up we see a bare stage. On it are sitting six or seven men in a semi-circle. Lolling against the proscenium down left is a young man chewing a toothpick: a gunman. A fat man of porcine appearance is talking directly to the audience. In other words he is the head of a union and the men ranged behind him are a committee of workers. They are now seated in interesting different attitudes and present a wide diversity of type, as we shall soon see. The fat man is hot and heavy under the collar, near the end of a long talk, but not too hot: he is well fed and confident. His name is HARRY FATT.

FATT: You're so wrong I ain't laughing. Any guy with eyes to read knows it. Look at the textile strike—out like lions and in like lambs. Take the San Francisco tie-up—starvation and broken heads. The steel boys wanted to walk out too, but they changed their minds. It's the trend of the times, that's what it is. All we workers got a good man behind us now. He's top man of the country— looking out for our interests—the man in the White House is the one I'm referrin' to. That's why the times ain't ripe for a strike. He's working day and night—

VOICE FROM THE AUDIENCE: For who?

The GUNMAN *stirs himself.*

FATT: For you! The records prove it. If this was the Hoover regime, would I say don't go out, boys? Not on your tintype! But things is different now. You read the papers as well as me. You know it. And that's why I'm against the strike. Because we gotta stand behind the man who's standin' behind us! The whole country—

ANOTHER VOICE: Is on the blink!

The GUNMAN *looks grave.*

FATT: Stand up and show yourself, you damn red! Be a man, let's see what you look like! [*Waits in vain.*] Yellow from the word go! Red and yellow makes a dirty color, boys. I got my eyes on four or five of them in the union here. What the hell'll they do for you? Pull you out and run away when trouble starts. Give those birds a chance and they'll have your sisters and wives in the whore houses, like they done in Russia. They'll tear Christ off his bleeding cross. They'll wreck your homes and throw your babies in the river. You think that's bunk? Read the papers! Now listen, we can't stay here all night. I gave you the facts in the case. You boys got hot suppers to go to and—

ANOTHER VOICE: Says you!

GUNMAN: Sit down, Punk!

ANOTHER VOICE: Where's Lefty?

[*Now this question is taken up by the others in unison.* FATT *pounds with gavel.*]

FATT: That's what I wanna know. Where's your pal, Lefty? You elected him chairman—where the hell did he disappear?

VOICES: We want Lefty! Lefty! Lefty!

FATT: [*Pounding.*] What the hell is this—a circus? You got the committee here. This bunch of cowboys you elected. [*Pointing to man on extreme right end.*]

MAN: Benjamin.

FATT: Yeah, Doc Benjamin. [*Pointing to other men in circle in seated order.*] Benjamin, Miller, Stein, Mitchell, Phillips, Keller. It ain't my fault Lefty took a run-out powder. If you guys—

A GOOD VOICE: What's the committee say?

OTHERS: The committee! Let's hear from the committee!

[FATT *tries to quiet the crowd, but one of the seated men suddenly comes to the front. The* GUNMAN *moves over to center stage, but* FATT *says:*]

FATT: Sure, let him talk. Let's hear what the red boys gotta say!

[*Various shouts are coming from the audience.* FATT *insolently goes back to his seat in the middle of the circle. He sits on his raised platform and relights his cigar. The* GUNMAN *goes back to his post.* JOE, *the new speaker, raises his hand for quiet. Gets it quickly. He is sore.*]

JOE: You boys know me. I ain't a red boy one bit! Here I'm carryin' a shrapnel that big I picked up in the war. And maybe I don't know it when it rains! Don't tell me red! You know what we are? The black and blue boys! We been kicked around so long we're black and blue from head to toes. But I guess anyone who says straight out he don't like it, he's a red boy to the leaders of the union. What's this crap about goin' home to hot suppers? I'm asking to your faces how many's got hot suppers to go home to? Anyone who's sure of his next meal, raise your hand! A certain gent sitting behind me can raise them both. But not in front here! And that's why we're talking strike—to get a living wage!

VOICE: Where's Lefty?

JOE: I honest to God don't know, but he didn't take no run-out powder. That Wop's got more guts than a slaughter house. Maybe a traffic jam got him, but he'll be here. But don't let this red stuff scare you. Unless fighting for a living scares you. We gotta make up our minds. My wife made up my mind last week, if you want the truth. It's plain as the nose on Sol Feinberg's face we need a strike. There's us comin' home every night—eight, ten hours on the cab. "God," the wife says, "eighty cents ain't money—don't buy beans almost. You're workin' for the company," she says to me, "Joe! you ain't workin' for me or the family no more!" She says to me, "If you don't start … "

I • JOE AND EDNA

The lights fade out and a white spot picks out the playing space within the space of seated men. The seated men are very dimly visible in the outer dark, but more prominent is FATT *smoking his cigar and often blowing the smoke in the lighted circle.*

A tired but attractive woman of thirty comes into the room, drying her hands on an apron. She stands there sullenly as JOE *comes in from the other side, home from work. For a moment they stand and look at each other in silence.*

JOE: Where's all the furniture, honey?

EDNA: They took it away. No installments paid.

JOE: When?

EDNA: Three o'clock.

JOE: They can't do that.

EDNA: Can't? They did it.

JOE: Why, the palookas, we paid three-quarters.

EDNA: The man said read the contract.

JOE: We must have signed a phoney …

EDNA: It's a regular contract and you signed it.

JOE: Don't be so sour, Edna [*Tries to embrace her.*]

EDNA: Do it in the movies, Joe—they pay Clark Gable big money for it.

JOE: This is a helluva house to come home to. Take my word!

EDNA: Take MY word! Whose fault is it?

JOE: Must you start that stuff again?

EDNA: Maybe you'd like to talk about books?

JOE: I'd like to slap you in the mouth!

EDNA: No you won't.

JOE: [*Sheepish.*] Jeez, Edna, you get me sore some time …

EDNA: But just look at me—I'm laughing all over!

JOE: Don't insult me. Can I help it if times are bad? What the hell do you want me to do, jump off a bridge or something?

EDNA: Don't yell. I just put the kids to bed so they won't know they missed a meal. If I don't have Emmy's shoes soled tomorrow, she can't go to school. In the meantime let her sleep.

JOE: Honey, I rode the wheels off the chariot today. I cruised around five hours without a call. It's conditions.

EDNA: Tell it to the A & P!

JOE: I booked two-twenty on the clock. A lady with a dog was lit … she gave me a quarter tip by mistake. If you'd only listen to me—we're rolling in wealth.

EDNA: Yeah? How much?

JOE: I had "coffee and—" in a beanery. [*Hands her silver coins.*] A buck four.

EDNA: The second month's rent is due tomorrow.

JOE: Don't look at me that way, Edna.

EDNA: I'm looking through you, not at you … Everything was gonna be so ducky! A cottage by the waterfall, roses in Picardy. You're a four-star-bust! If you think I'm standing for it much longer, you're crazy as a bedbug.

JOE: I'd get another job if I could. There's no work—you know it.

EDNA: I only know we're at the bottom of the ocean.

JOE: What can I do?

EDNA: Who's the man in the family, you or me?

JOE: That's no answer. Get down to brass tacks. Christ, gimme a break, too! A coffee cake and java all day. I'm hungry, too, Babe. I'd work my fingers to the bone if—

EDNA: I'll open a can of salmon.

354

JOE: Not now. Tell me what to do!

EDNA: I'm not God!

JOE: Jeez, I wish I was a kid again and didn't have to think about the next minute.

EDNA: But you're not a kid and you do have to think about the next minute. You got two blondie kids sleeping in the next room. They need food and clothes. I'm not mentioning anything else—But we're stalled like a flivver in the snow. For five years I laid awake at night listening to my heart pound. For God's sake, do something, Joe, get wise. Maybe get your buddies together, maybe go on strike for better money. Poppa did it during the war and they won out. I'm turning into a sour old nag.

JOE: [*Defending himself.*] Strikes don't work!

EDNA: Who told you?

JOE: Besides that means not a nickel a week while we're out. Then when it's over they don't take you back.

EDNA: Suppose they don't! What's to lose?

JOE: Well, we're averaging six-seven dollars a week now.

EDNA: That just pays for the rent.

JOE: That is something, Edna.

EDNA: It isn't. They'll push you down to three and four a week before you know it. Then you'll say, "That's somethin'," too!

JOE: There's too many cabs on the street, that's the whole damn trouble.

EDNA: Let the company worry about that, you big fool! If their cabs didn't make a profit, they'd take them off the streets. Or maybe you think they're in business just to pay Joe Mitchell's rent!

JOE: You don't know a-b-c Edna.

EDNA: I know this—your boss is making suckers outa you boys every minute. Yes, and suckers out of all the wives and the poor innocent kids who'll grow up with crooked spines and sick bones. Sure, I see it in the papers, how good orange juice is for kids. But dammit our kids get colds one on top of the other. They look like little ghosts. Betty never saw a grapefruit. I took her to the store last week and she pointed to a stack of grapefruits. "What's that!" she said. My God, Joe—the world is supposed to be for all of us.

JOE: You'll wake them up.

EDNA: I don't care, as long as I can maybe wake you up.

JOE: Don't insult me. One man can't make a strike.

EDNA: Who says one? You got hundreds in your rotten union!

JOE: The Union ain't rotten.

EDNA: No? Then what are they doing? Collecting dues and patting your back?

JOE: They're making plans.

EDNA: What kind?

JOE: They don't tell us.

EDNA: Its too damn bad about you. They don't tell little Joey what's happening in his bitsie witsie union. What do you think it is—a ping pong game?

JOE: You know they're racketeers. The guys at the top would shoot you for a nickel.

EDNA: Why do you stand for that stuff?

JOE: Don't you wanna see me alive?

EDNA: [*After a deep pause.*] No … I don't think I do, Joe. Not if you can lift a finger to do something about it, and don't. No, I don't care.

JOE: Honey, you don't understand what—

EDNA: And any other hackie that won't fight … let them all be ground to hamburger!

JOE: It's one thing to—

EDNA: Take your hand away! Only they don't grind me to little pieces! I got different plans. [*Starts to take off her apron.*]

JOE: Where are you going?

EDNA: None of your business.

356

JOE: What's up your sleeve?

EDNA: My arm'd be up my sleeve, darling, if I had a sleeve to wear. [*Puts neatly folded apron on back of chair.*]

JOE: Tell me!

EDNA: Tell you what?

JOE: Where are you going?

EDNA: Don't you remember my old boy friend?

JOE: Who?

EDNA: Bud Haas. He still has my picture in his watch. He earns a living.

JOE: What the hell are you talking about?

EDNA: I heard worse than I'm talking about.

JOE: Have you seen Bud since we got married?

EDNA: Maybe.

JOE: If I thought ... [*He stands looking at her.*]

EDNA: See much? Listen, boy friend, if you think I won't do this it just means you can't see straight.

JOE: Stop talking bull!

EDNA: This isn't five years ago, Joe.

JOE: You mean you'd leave me and the kids?

EDNA: I'd leave you like a shot!

JOE: No ...

EDNA: Yes!

[JOE *turns away, sitting in a chair with his back to her. Outside the lighted circle of the playing stage we hear the other seated members of the strike committee. "She will... she will... it happens that way," etc. This group should be used throughout for various comments, political, emotional and as general chorus. Whispering .... The fat boss now blows a heavy cloud of smoke into the scene.*]

JOE: [*Finally.*] Well, I guess I ain't got a leg to stand on.

EDNA: No?

JOE: [*Suddenly mad.*] No, you lousy tart, no! Get the hell out of here. Go pick up that bull-thrower on the comer and stop at some cushy hotel downtown. He's probably been coming here every morning and laying you while I hacked my guts out!

EDNA: You're crawling like a worm!

JOE: You'll be crawling in a minute.

EDNA: You don't scare me that much! [*Indicates a half inch on her finger.*]

JOE: This is what I slaved for!

EDNA: Tell it to your boss!

JOE: He don't give a damn for you or me!

EDNA: That's what I say.

JOE: Don't change the subject!

EDNA: This is the subject, the EXACT SUBJECT! Your boss makes this subject. I never saw him in my life, but he's putting ideas in my head a mile a minute. He's giving your kids that fancy disease called the rickets. He's making a jellyfish outa you and putting wrinkles in my face. This is the subject every inch of the way! He's throwing me into Bud Haas's lap. When in hell will you get wise—

JOE: I'm not so dumb as you think! But you are talking like a Red.

EDNA: I don't know what that means. But when a man knocks you down you get up and kiss his fist! You gutless piece of boloney.

JOE: One man can't—

EDNA: [*With great joy.*] I don't say one man! I say a hundred, a thousand, a whole million, I say. But start in your own union. Get those hack boys together! Sweep out those racketeers like a pile of dirt! Stand up like men and fight for the crying kids and wives. Goddammit! I'm tired of slavery and sleepless nights.

JOE: [*With her.*] Sure, sure! ...

EDNA: Yes. Get brass toes on your shoes and know where to kick!

JOE: [*Suddenly jumping up and kissing his wife full on the mouth.*] Listen, Edna. I'm goin' down to 174th Street to look up Lefty Costello. Lefty was saying the other day ... [*He suddenly stops.*]   How about this Haas guy?

EDNA: Get out of here!

JOE: I'll be back! [*Runs out.*]

> [*For a moment* EDNA *stands triumphant. There is a blackout and when the regular lights come up,* JOE MITCHELL *is concluding what he has been saying:*]

JOE: You guys know this stuff better than me. We gotta walk out! [*Abruptly he turns and goes back to his seat and blackout.*]

Blackout

II • LAB ASSISTANT EPISODE

Discovered: MILLER *a lab assistant, looking around; and* FAYETTE, *an industrialist.*

FAY: Like it?

MILLER: Very much. I've never seen an office like this outside the movies.

FAY: Yes, I often wonder if interior decorators and bathroom fixture people don't get all their ideas from Hollywood. Our country's extraordinary that way. Soap, cosmetics, electric refrigerators—just let Mrs. Consumer know they're used by the Crawfords and Garbos—more volume of sale than one plant can handle!

MILL: I'm afraid it isn't that easy, Mr. Fayette.

FAY: No, you're right—gross exaggeration on my part. Competition is cut-throat today. Markets up flush against a stone wall. The astronomers had better hurry—open Mars to trade expansion.

MILL: Or it will be just too bad!

FAY: Cigar?

MILL: Thank you, don't smoke.

FAY: Drink?

MILL: Ditto, Mr. Fayette.

FAY: I like sobriety in my workers ... the trained ones, I mean. The Pollacks and niggers, they're better drunk—keeps them out of mischief. Wondering why I had you come over?

MILL: If you don't mind my saying—very much.

FAY: [*Patting him on the knee.*] I like your work.

MILL: Thanks.

FAY: No reason why a talented young man like yourself shouldn't string along with us—a growing concern. Loyalty is well repaid in our organization. Did you see Siegfried this morning?

MILL: He hasn't been in the laboratory all day.

FAY: I told him yesterday to raise you twenty dollars a month. Starts this week.

MILL: You don't know how happy my wife'll be.

FAY: Oh, I can appreciate it. [*He laughs.*]

MILL: Was that all, Mr. Fayette?

FAY: Yes, except that we're switching you to laboratory A tomorrow. Siegfried knows about it. That's why I had you in. The new work is very important. Siegfried recommended you very highly as a man to trust. You'll work directly under Dr. Brenner. Make you happy?

MILL: Very. He's an important chemist!

FAY: [*Leaning over seriously.*] We think so, Miller. We think so to the extent of asking you to stay within the building throughout the time you work with him.

MILL: You mean sleep and eat in?

FAY: Yes …

MILL: It can be arranged

FAY: Fine. You'll go far, Miller.

MILL: May I ask the nature of the new work?

FAY: [*Looking around first.*] Poison gas …

MILL: Poison!

FAY: Orders from above. I don't have to tell you from where. New type poison gas for modern warfare.

MILL: I see.

FAY: You didn't know a new war was that close, did you?

MILL: I guess I didn't.

FAY: I don't have to stress the importance of absolute secrecy.

MILL: I understand!

FAY: The world is an armed camp today. One match sets the whole world blazing in forty-eight hours. Uncle Sam won't be caught napping!

MILL: [*Addressing his pencil.*] They say 12 million men were killed in that last one and 20 million more wounded or missing.

FAY: That's not our worry. If big business went sentimental over human life there wouldn't be big business of any sort!

MILL: My brother and two cousins went in the last one.

FAY: They died in a good cause.

MILL: My mother says "no!"

FAY: She won't worry about you this time. You' re too valuable behind the front.

MILL: That's right.

FAY: All right, Miller. See Siegfried for further orders.

MILL: You should have seen my brother—he could ride a bike without hands …

FAY: You'd better move some clothes and shaving tools in tomorrow. Remember what I said—you're with a growing organization.

MILL: He could run the hundred yards in 9:8 flat …

FAY: Who?

MILL: My brother. He's in the Meuse-Argonne Cemetery. Momma went there in 1926 …

FAY: Yes, those things stick. How's your handwriting, Miller, fairly legible?

MILL: Fairly so.

FAY: Once a week I'd like a little report from you.

MILL: What sort of report?

FAY: Just a few hundred words once a week on Dr. Brenner's progress.

MILL: Don't you think it might be better coming from the Doctor?

FAY: I didn't ask you that.

MILL: Sorry.

FAY: I want to know what progress he's making, the reports to be purely confidential—between you and me.

MILL: You mean I'm to watch him?

FAY: Yes!

MILL: I guess I can't do that ...

FAY: Thirty a month raise ...

MILL: You said twenty ...

FAY: Thirty!

MILL: Guess I'm not built that way.

FAY: Forty ...

MILL: Spying's not in my line, Mr. Fayette!

FAY: You use ugly words, Mr. Miller!

MILL: For ugly activity? Yes!

FAY: Think about it, Miller. Your chances are excellent ...

MILL: No.

FAY: You're doing something for your country. Assuring the United States that when those goddam Japs start a ruckus we'll have offensive weapons to back us up! Don't you read your newspapers, Miller?

MILL: Nothing but Andy Gump.

FAY: If you were on the inside you'd know I'm talking cold sober truth! Now, I'm not asking you to make up your mind on the spot. Think about it over your lunch period.

MILL: No ...

FAY: Made up your mind already?

MILL: Afraid so.

FAY: You understand the consequences?

MILL: I lose my raise

MILL: And my job!

FAY: And your job! $\left.\right\}$ *Simultaneously*

MILL: You misunderstand—

MILL: Rather dig ditches first!

FAY: That's a big job for foreigners.

MILL: But sneaking—and making poison gas—that's for Americans?

FAY: It's up to you.

MILL: My mind's made up.

FAY: No hard feelings?

MILL: Sure hard feelings! I'm not the civilized type, Mr. Fayette. Nothing suave or sophisticated about me. Plenty of hard feelings! Enough to want to bust you and all your kind square in the mouth!

[*Does exactly that.*]

Blackout

III • THE YOUNG HACK AND HIS GIRL

Opens with girl and brother. FLORENCE *waiting for* SID *to take her to a dance.*

FLOR: I gotta right to have something out of life. I don't smoke, I don't drink. So if Sid wants to take me to a dance, I'll go. Maybe if you was in love you wouldn't talk so hard.

IRV: I'm saying it for your good.

FLOR: Don't be so good to me.

IRV: Mom's sick in bed and you'll be worryin' her to the grave. She don't want that boy hanging around the house and she don't want you meeting him in Crotona Park.

FLOR: I'll meet him anytime I like!

IRV: If you do, yours truly'll take care of it in his own way. With just one hand, too!

FLOR: Why are you all so set against him?

IRV: Mom told you ten times—it ain't him. It's that he ain't got nothing. Sure, we know he's serious, that he's stuck on you. But that don't cut no ice.

FLOR: Taxi drivers used to make good money.

IRV: Today they're makin' five and six dollars a week. Maybe you wanta raise a family on that. Then you'll be back here living with us again and I'll be supporting two families in one. Well … over my dead body.

FLOR: Irv, I don't care—I love him!

IRV: You're a little kid with half-baked ideas!

FLOR: I stand there behind the counter the whole day. I think about him—

IRV: If you thought more about Mom it would be better.

FLOR: Don't I take care of her every night when I come home? Don't I cook supper and iron your shirts and … you give me a pain in the neck, too. Don't try to shut me up! I bring a few dollars in the house, too. Don't you see I want something else out of life. Sure, I want romance, love, babies. I want everything in life I can get.

IRV: You take care of Mom and watch your step!

FLOR: And if I don't?

IRV: Yours truly'll watch it for you!

FLOR: You can talk that way to a girl …

IRV: I'll talk that way to your boy friend, too, and it won't be with words! Florrie, if you had a pair of eyes you'd see it's for your own good we're talking. This ain't no time to get married. Maybe later—

FLOR: "Maybe Later" never comes for me, though. Why don't we send Mom to a hospital? She can die in peace there instead of looking at the clock on the mantelpiece all day.

IRV: That needs money. Which we don't have!

FLOR: Money, Money, Money!

IRV: Don't change the subject.

FLOR: This is the subject!

IRV: You gonna stop seeing him? [*She turns away.*] Jesus, kiddie, I remember when you were a baby with curls down your back. Now I gotta stand here yellin' at you like this.

FLOR: I'll talk to him, Irv.

IRV: When?

FLOR: I asked him to come here tonight. We'll talk it over.

IRV: Don't get soft with him. Nowadays is no time to be soft. You gotta be hard as a rock or go under.

FLOR: I found that out. There's the bell. Take the egg off the stove I boiled for Mom. Leave us alone, Irv.

[SID *comes in—the two men look at each other for a second.* IRV *exits.*]

SID: [*Enters.*]   Hello, Florrie.

FLOR: Hello, Honey. You're looking tired.

SID: Naw, I just need a shave.

FLOR: Well, draw your chair up to the fire and I'll ring for brandy and soda …
         like in the movies.

SID: If this was the movies I'd bring a big bunch of roses.

FLOR: How big ?

SID: Fifty or sixty dozen—the kind with long, long stems—big as that …

FLOR: You dope …

SID: Your Paris gown is beautiful.

FLOR: [*Acting grandly.*] Yes, Percy, velvet panels are coming back again. Madame
         La Farge told me today that Queen Marie herself designed it.

SID: Gee … !

FLOR: Every princess in the Balkans is wearing one like this. [*Poses grandly.*]

SID: Hold it. [*Does a nose camera—thumbing nose and imitating grinding of camera
         with other hand. Suddenly she falls out of the posture and swiftly goes to him, to embrace
         him, to kiss him with love. Finally:*]

SID: You look tired, Florrie.

FLOR: Naw, I just need a shave. [*She laughs tremorously.*]

SID: You worried about your mother?

FLOR: No.

SID: What's on your mind?

FLOR: The French and Indian War.

SID: What's on your mind?

FLOR: I got us on my mind, Sid. Night and day, Sid!

SID: I smacked a beer truck today. Did I get hell! I was driving along thinking of US, too. You don't have to say it—I know what's on your mind. I'm rat poison around here.

FLOR: Not to me …

SID: I know to who … and I know why. I don't blame them. We're engaged now for three years …

FLOR: That's a long time …

SID: My brother Sam joined the navy this morning—get a break that way. They'll send him down to Cuba with the hootchy-kootchy girls. He don't know from nothing, that dumb basketball player!

FLOR: Don't you do that.

SID: Don't you worry, I'm not the kind who runs away. But I'm so tired of being a dog, Baby, I could choke. I don't even have to ask what's going on in your mind. I know from the word go, 'cause I'm thinking the same things, too.

FLOR: It's yes or no—nothing in between.

SID: The answer is no—a big electric sign looking down on Broadway!

FLOR: We wanted to have kids …

SID: But that sort of life ain't for the dogs which is us. Christ, Baby! I get like thunder in my chest when we're together. If we went off together I could maybe look the world straight in the face, spit in its eye like a man should do. Goddamit, it's trying to be a man on the earth. Two in life together.

FLOR: But something wants us to be lonely like that—crawling alone in the dark. Or they want us trapped.

SID: Sure, the big shot money men want us like that.

FLOR: Highly insulting us—

SID: Keeping us in the dark about what is wrong with us in the money sense. They got the power and mean to be damn sure they keep it. They know if they give in just an inch, all the dogs like us will be down on them together—an ocean knocking them to hell and back and each singing cuckoo with stars coming from their nose and ears. I'm not raving, Florrie—

FLOR: I know you're not, I know.

SID: I don't have the words to tell you what I feel. I never finished school …

FLOR: I know …

SID: But it's relative, like the professors say. We worked like hell to send him to college—my kid brother Sam, I mean—and look what he done—joined the navy! The damn fool don't see the cards is stacked for all of us. The money man dealing himself a hot royal flush. Then giving you and me a phoney hand like a pair of tens or something. Then keep on losing the pots 'cause the cards is stacked against you. Then he says, what's the matter you can't win—no stuff on the ball, he says to you. And kids like my brother believe it 'cause they don't know better. For all their education, they don't know from nothing.

But wait a minute! Don't he come around and say to you—this millionaire with a jazz band—listen Sam or Sid or what's-your-name, you're no good, but here's a chance. The whole world'll know who you are. Yes sir, he says, get up on that ship and fight those bastards who's making the world a lousy place to live in. The Japs, the Turks, the Greeks. Take this gun—kill the slobs like a real hero, he says, a real American. Be a hero!

And the guy you're poking at? A real louse, just like you 'cause they don't let him catch more than a pair of tens, too. On that foreign soil he's a guy like me and Sam, a guy who wants his baby like you and hot sun on his face! They'll teach Sam to point the guns the wrong way, that dumb basketball player!

FLOR: I got a lump in my throat, Honey.

SID: You and me—we never even had a room to sit in somewhere.

FLOR: The park was nice …

SID: In Winter? The hallways … I'm glad we never got together. This way we don't know what we missed.

FLOR: [In a burst.] Sid, I'll go with you—we'll get a room somewhere.

SID: Naw … they're right. If we can't climb higher than this together—we better stay apart.

FLOR: I swear to God I wouldn't care.

SID: You would, you would—in a year, two years, you'd curse the day. I seen it

369

happen.

FLOR: Oh, Sid …

SID: Sure, I know. We got the blues, Babe—the 1935 blues. I'm talkin' this way
'cause I love you. If I didn't, I wouldn't care …

FLOR: We'll work together, we'll—

SID: How about the backwash? Your family needs your nine bucks. My family—

FLOR: I don't care for them!

SID: You're making it up, Florrie. Little Florrie Canary in a cage.

FLOR: Don't make fun of me.

SID: I'm not, Baby.

FLOR: Yes, you're laughing at me.

SID: I'm not.

> [*They stand looking at each other, unable to speak Finally, he turns to
> a small portable phonograph and plays a cheap, sad, dance tune. He makes
> a motion with his hand; she comes to him. They begin to dance slowly.
> They hold each other tightly, almost as though they would merge into
> each other. The music stops, but the scratching record continues to the
> end of the scene. They stop dancing. He finally unlooses her clutch and
> seats her on the couch, where she sits, tense and expectant.*]

SID: Hello, Babe.

FLOR: Hello.

> [*For a brief time they stand as though in a dream.*]

SID: [*Finally.*]   Good-by, Babe.

> [*He waits for an answer, but she is silent. They look at each other.*]

SID: Did you ever see my Pat Rooney imitation? [*He whistles Rosy O'Grady and
soft shoes to it. Stops. He asks.*]

SID: Don't you like it?

FLOR: [*Finally.*]   No. [*Buries her face in her hands.*]

370

[*Suddenly he falls on his knees and buries his face in her lap.*]

Blackout

IV • LABOR SPY EPISODE

FATT: You don't know how we work for you. Shooting off your mouth won't help. Hell, don't you guys ever look at the records like me? Look in your own industry. See what happened when the hacks walked out in Philly three months ago! Where's Philly? A thousand miles away? An hour's ride on the train.

VOICE: Two hours!!

FATT: Two hours … what the hell's the difference. Let's hear from someone who's got the practical experience to back him up. Fellers, there's a man here who's seen the whole parade in Philly, walked out with his pals, got knocked down like the rest—and blacklisted after they went back. That's why he's here. He's got a mighty interestin' word to say. [*Announces.*] TOM CLAYTON!

[*As* CLAYTON *starts up from the audience,* FATT *gives him a hand which is sparsely followed in the audience.* CLAYTON *comes forward.*]

Fellers, this is a man with practical strike experience—Tom Clayton from little ole Philly.

FATT: [*A thin, modest individual.*] Fellers, I don't mind your booing. If I thought it would help us hacks get better living conditions I'd let you walk all over me, cut me up to little pieces. I'm one of you myself. But what I wanna say is that Harry Fatt's right. I only been working here in the big town five weeks, but I know conditions just like the rest of you. You know how it is—don't take long to feel the sore spots, no matter where you park.

CLEAR VOICE: [*From audience.*] Sit down!

CLAYTON: But Fatt's right. Our officers is right. The time ain't ripe. Like a fruit don't fall off the tree until it's ripe.

CLEAR VOICE: Sit down, you fruit!

FATT: [*On his feet.*] Take care of him, boys.

VOICE: [*in audience, struggling*.] No one takes care of me.

[*Struggle in house and finally the owner of the voice runs up on stage, says to speaker:*]

SAME VOICE: Where the hell did you pick up that name! Clayton! This rat's name is Clancy, from the old Clancys, way back! Fruit! I almost wet myself listening to that one!

FATT: [*Gunman with him.*] This ain't a barn! What the hell do you think you're doing here!

SAME VOICE: Exposing a rat!

FATT: You can't get away with this. Throw him the hell outa here.

VOICE: [*Preparing to stand his ground.*] Try it yourself ... When this bozo throws that slop around. You know who he is? That's a company spy.

FATT: Who the hell are you to make—

VOICE: I paid dues in this union for four years, that's who's me! I gotta right and this pussy-footed rat ain't coming in here with ideals like that. You know his record. Lemme say it out—

FATT: You'll prove all this or I'll bust you in every hack outfit in town!

VOICE: I gotta right. I gotta right. Looka *him*, he don't say boo!

CLAYTON: You're a liar and I never seen you before in my life!

VOICE: Boys, he spent two years in the coal fields breaking up any organization he touched. Fifty guys he put in jail. He's ranged up and down the east coast—shipping, textiles, steel—he's been in everything you can name. Right now—

CLAYTON: That's a lie!

VOICE: Right now he's working for that Bergman outfit on Columbus Circle who furnishes rats for any outfit in the country before, during, and after strikes.

[*The man who is the hero of the next episode goes down to his side with other committee men.*]

CLAYTON: He's trying to break up the meeting, fellers!

VOICE: We won't search you for credentials ...

CLAYTON: I got nothing to hide. Your own secretary knows I'm straight.

VOICE: Sure. Boys, you know who this sonovabitch is?

CLAYTON: I never seen you before in my life!!

VOICE: Boys, I slept with him in the same bed sixteen years. MY OWN LOUSY BROTHER !!

FATT: [*After pause.*] Is this true?

> *No answer from* CLAYTON.

VOICE to CLAYTON: Scram, before I break your neck!

> [CLAYTON *scrams down center aisle.* VOICE *says, watching him:*]

Remember his map—he can't change that—Clancy!

> [*Standing in his place says:*]

Too bad you didn't know about this, Fatt! [*After a pause.*] The Clancy family tree is bearing nuts!

> [*Standing isolated clear on the stage is the hero of the next episode.*]

Blackout

V • THE YOUNG ACTOR

A New York theatrical producer's office. Present are a stenographer and a young actor. She is busy typing; he, waiting with card in hand.

STEN: He's taking a hot bath … says you should wait.

PHILIPS: [*The actor.*] A bath did you say? Where?

STEN: See that door? Right through there—leads to his apartment.

PHIL: Through there?

STEN: Mister, he's laying there in a hot perfumed bath. Don't say I said it.

PHIL: You don't say!

STEN: An oriental den he's got. Can you just see this big Irishman burning Chinese punk in the bedroom? And a big old rose canopy over his casting couch …

PHIL: What's that—casting couch?

STEN: What's that? You from the sticks?

PHIL: I beg your pardon?

STEN: [*Rolls up her sleeves, makes elaborate deaf and dumb signs.*] No from side walkies of New Yorkie … savvy?

PHIL: Oh, you're right. Two years of dramatic stock out of town. One in Chicago.

STEN: Don't tell him, Baby Face. He wouldn't know a good actor if he fell over him in the dark. Say you had two years with the Group, two with the Guild.

PHIL: I'd like to get with the Guild. They say—

STEN: He won't know the difference. Don't say I said it!

PHIL: I really did play with Watson Findlay in "Early Birds."

STEN: [*Withering him.*] Don't tell him!

PHIL: He's a big producer, Mr. Grady. I wish I had his money. Don't you?

STEN: Say, I got a clean heart, Mister. I love my fellow man! [*About to exit with typed letters.*] Stick around—Mr. Philips. You might be the type. If you were a woman—

PHIL: Please. Just a minute … please … I need the job.

STEN: Look at him!

PHIL: I mean … I don't know what buttons to push, and you do. What my father used to say—we had a gas station in Cleveland before the crash—"Know what buttons to push," Dad used to say, "and you'll go far."

STEN: You can't push me, Mister! I don't ring right these last few years!

PHIL: We don't know where the next meal's coming from. We—

STEN: Maybe … I'll lend you a dollar?

PHIL: Thanks very much: it won't help.

STEN: One of the old families of Virginia? Proud?

PHIL: Oh, not that. You see, I have a wife. We'll have our first baby next month … so … a dollar isn't much help.

STEN: Roped in?

PHIL: I love my wife!

STEN: Okay, you love her! Excuse me! You married her. Can't support her. No … not blaming you. But you're fools, all you actors. Old and young! Watch you parade in and out all day. You still got apples in your cheeks and pins for buttons. But in six months you'll be like them—putting on an act: Phoney strutting "pishers"—that's French for dead codfish! It's not their fault. Here you get like that or go under. What kind of job is this for an adult man!

PHIL: When you have to make a living—

STEN: I know, but—

PHIL: Nothing else to do. If I could get something else—

376

STEN: You'd take it!

PHIL: Anything!

STEN: Telling me! With two brothers in my hair!

[MR. GRADY *now enters; played by* FATT.]

Mr. Brown sent this young man over.

GRADY: Call the hospital: see how Boris is. [*She assents and exits.*]

PHIL: Good morning, Mr. Grady …

GRADY: The morning is lousy!

PHIL: Mr. Brown sent me. [*Hands over card.*]

GRADY: I heard that once already.

PHIL: Excuse me …

GRADY: What experience?

PHIL: Oh, yes …

GRADY: Where?

PHIL: Two years in stock, sir. A year with the Goodman Theatre in Chicago …

GRADY: That all?

PHIL: [*Abashed.*] Why no … with the Theatre Guild … I was there …

GRADY: Never saw you in a Guild show!

PHIL: On the road, I mean … understudying Mr. Lunt …

GRADY: What part?

[PHILIPS *can not answer.*]

You're a lousy liar, son.

PHIL: I did …

GRADY: You don't look like what I want. Can't understand that Brown. Need a big man to play a soldier. Not a lousy soldier left on

Broadway! All in pictures, and we get the nances! [*Turns to on desk.*]

PHIL: [*Immediately playing the soldier.*] I was in the ROTC in college ... Reserve Officers' Training Corps. We trained twice a week ...

GRADY: Won't help.

PHIL: With real rifles. [*Waits.*] Mr. Grady, I weigh a hundred and fifty-five!

GRADY: How many years back? Been eating regular since you left college?

PHIL: [*Very earnestly.*] Mr. Grady, I could act this soldier part. I could build it up and act it. Make it up—

GRADY: Think I run a lousy acting school around here?

PHIL: Honest to God I could! I need the job—that's why I could do it! I'm strong. I know my business! YOU'LL get an A-1 performance! 'cause I need this job! My wife's having a baby in a few weeks. We need the money. Give me a chance!

GRADY: What do I care if you can act it! I'm sorry about your baby. Use your head, son. Tank Town stock is different. Here we got investments to be protected. When I sink fifteen thousand in a show I don't take chances on some youngster. We cast to type!

PHIL: I'm an artist! I can—

GRADY: That's your headache. Nobody interested in artists here. Get a big bunch for a nickel on any corner. Two flops in a row on this lousy street nobody loves you—only God, and He don't count. We protect investments: we cast to type. Your face and height we want, not your soul, son. And Jesus Christ himself couldn't play a soldier in this show ... with all his talent. [*Crosses himself in quick repentance for this remark.*]

PHIL: Anything ... a bit, a walk-on?

GRADY: Sorry: small cast. [*Looking at papers on his desk.*] You try Russia, son. I hear it's hot stuff over there.

PHIL: Stage manager? Assistant?

GRADY: All filled, sonny. [*Stands up; crumples several papers from the desk.*] Better luck next time.

PHIL: Thanks ...

GRADY: Drop in from time to time. [*Crosses and about to exit.*] You never know when something—

[*The* STENOGRAPHER *enters with papers to put on desk.*]

What did the hospital say?

STEN: He's much better, Mr. Grady.

GRADY: Resting easy?

STEN: Dr. Martel said Boris is doing even better than he expected.

GRADY: A damn lousy operation!

STEN: Yes ...

GRADY: [*Belching.*]   Tell the nigger boy to send up a bromo seltzer.

STEN: Yes, Mr. Grady. [*He exits.*] Boris wanted lady friends.

PHIL: What?

STEN: So they operated ... poor dog!

PHIL: A dog?

STEN: His Russian Wolf Hound! They do the same to you, but you don't know it! [*Suddenly.*] Want advice? In the next office, don't let them see you down in the mouth. They don't like it—makes them shiver.

PHIL: You treat me like a human being. Thanks ...

STEN: You're human!

PHIL: I used to think so.

STEN: He wants a bromo for his hangover. [*Goes to door.*] Want that dollar?

PHIL: It won't help much.

STEN: One dollar buys ten loaves of bread, Mister. Or one dollar buys nine loaves of bread and one copy of The Communist Manifesto. Learn while you eat. Read while you run ...

PHIL: Manifesto? What's that? [*Takes dollar.*] What is that, what you said …
Manifesto?

STEN: Stop off on your way out—I'll give you a copy. From Genesis to Revelation,
Comrade Philips! "And I saw a new earth and a new heaven; for the first earth
and the first heaven were passed away; and there was no more sea."

PHIL: I don't understand that …

STEN: I'm saying the meek shall not inherit the earth!

PHIL: No?

STEN: The MILITANT! Come out in the light, Comrade.

Blackout

VI • INTERNE EPISODE

Dr. Barnes, an elderly distinguished man, is speaking on the telephone. He wears a while coat.

DR. BARNES: No, I gave you my opinion twice. You outvoted me. You did this to Dr. Benjamin yourself. That is why you can tell him yourself.

> [*Hangs up phone, angrily. As he is about to pour himself a drink from a bottle on the table, a knock is heard.*]

BARNES: Who is it?

BENJAMIN: [*Without.*]   Can I see you a minute, please?

BARNES: [*Hiding the bottle.*] Come in, Dr. Benjamin, come in.

BENJ: It's important—excuse me—they've got Leeds up there in my place—He's operating on Mrs. Lewis—the historectomy—it's my job. I washed up, prepared … they told me at the last minute. I don't mind being replaced, Doctor, but Leeds is a damn fool! He shouldn't be permitted

BARNES: [*Dryly.*] Leeds is the nephew of Senator Leeds.

BENJ: He's incompetent as hell.

BARNES: [*Obviously changing subject, picks up lab jar.*] They're doing splendid work in brain surgery these days. This is a very fine specimen …

BENJ: I'm sorry, I thought you might be interested.

BARNES: [*Still examining jar.*] Well, I am, young man, I am! Only remember it's a charity case!

BENJ: Of course. They wouldn't allow it for a second, otherwise.

BARNES: Her life is in danger?

BENJ: Of course! You know how serious the case is!

BARNES: Turn your gimlet eyes elsewhere, Doctor. Jigging around like a cricket on a hot grill won't help. Doctors don't run these hospitals. He's the Senator's nephew and there he stays.

BENJ: It's too bad.

BARNES: I'm not calling you down either. [*Plopping down jar suddenly.*] Goddammit, do you think it's my fault?

BENJ: [*About to leave.*]   I know ... I'm sorry.

BARNES: Just a minute. Sit down.

BENJ: Sorry, I can't sit.

BARNES: Stand then!

BENJ: [*Sits.*] Understand, Dr. Barnes, I don't mind being replaced at the last minute this way, but ... well, this flagrant bit of class distinction—because she's poor—

BARNES: Be careful of words like that—"class distinction." Don't belong here. Lots of energy, you brilliant young men, but idiots. Discretion! Ever hear that word?

BENJ: Too radical?

BARNES: Precisely. And some day like in Germany, it might cost you your head.

BENJ: Not to mention my job.

BARNES: So they told you?

BENJ: Told me what?

BARNES: They're closing Ward C next month. I don't have to tell you the hospital isn't self supporting. Until last year that board of trustees met deficits ... You can guess the rest. At a board meeting Tuesday, our fine feathered friends discovered they couldn't meet the last quarter's deficit—a neat little sum well over $100,000. If the hospital is to continue at all, its damn—

BENJ: Necessary to close another charity ward!

BARNES: So they say ... [*A wait.*]

BENJ: But that's not all?

BARNES: [*Ashamed.*]   Have to cut down on staff too ...

BENJ: That's too bad. Does it touch me?

BARNES: Afraid it does.

BENJ: But after all I'm top man here. I don't mean I'm better than others, but I've worked harder.

BARNES: And shown more promise …

BENJ: I always supposed they'd cut from the bottom first.

BARNES: Usually.

BENJ: But in this case?

BARNES: Complications.

BENJ: For instance?

[BARNES *hesitant*.]

BARNES: I like you, Benjamin. It's one ripping shame.

BENJ: I'm no sensitive plant—what's the answer?

BARNES: An old disease, malignant tumescent. We need an anti-toxin for it.

BENJ: I see.

BARNES: What?

BENJ: I met that disease before—at Harvard first.

BARNES: You have seniority here, Benjamin.

BENJ: But I'm a Jew!

[BARNES *nods his head in agreement.* BENJ *stands there a moment and blows his nose.*]

BARNES: [*Blows his nose.*] Microbes!

BENJ: Pressure from above?

BARNES: Don't think Kennedy and I didn't fight for you!

BENJ: Such discrimination, with all those wealthy brother Jews on the board?

BARNES: I've remarked before—doesn't seem to be much difference between wealthy Jews and rich Gentiles. Cut from the same piece!

BENJ: For myself I don't feel sorry. My parents gave up an awful lot to get me this far. They ran a little dry goods shop in the Bronx until their pitiful savings went in the crash last year. Poppa's peddling neckties ... Saul Ezra Benjamin—a man who's read Spinoza all his life.

BARNES: Doctors don't run medicine in this country. The men who know their jobs don't run anything here, except the motormen on trolley cars. I've seen medicine change—plenty—anesthesia, sterilization—but not because of rich men—in *spite* of them! In a rich man's country your true self's buried deep. Microbes! Less ... Vermin! See this ankle, this delicate sensitive hand? Four hundred years to breed that. Out of a revolutionary background! Spirit of '76! Ancestors froze at Valley Forge! What's it all mean! Slops! The honest workers were sold out then, in '76. The Constitution's for rich men then and now. Slops!

[*The phone rings.*]

BARNES: [*Angrily.*] Dr. Barnes. [*Listens a moment, looks at Benjamin.*] I see. [*Hangs up, turns slowly to the younger Doctor.*] They lost your patient.

[BENJ *stands solid with the shock of this news but finally hurls his operation gloves to the floor.*]

BARNES: That's right ... that's right. Young, hot, go and do it! I'm very ancient, fossil, but life's ahead of you, Dr. Benjamin, and when you fire the first shot say, "This one's for old Doc Barnes!" Too much dignity—bullets. Don't shoot vermin! Step on them! If I didn't have an invalid daughter—[*Goes back to his seat, blows his nose in silence.*] I have said my piece, Benjamin.

BENJ: Lots of things I wasn't certain of. Many things these radicals say ... you don't believe theories until they happen to you.

BARNES: You lost a lot today, but you won a great point.

BENJ: Yes, to know I'm right? To really begin believing in something? Not to say, "What a world!", but to say, "Change the world!" I wanted to go to Russia. Last week I was thinking about it—the wonderful opportunity to do good work in their socialized medicine—

BARNES: Beautiful, beautiful!

BENJ: To be able to work—

BARNES: Why don't you go? I might be able—

BENJ: Nothing's nearer what I'd like to do!

BARNES: Do it!

BENJ: No! Our work's here—America! I'm scared … What future's ahead, I don't know. Get some job to keep alive—maybe drive a cab—and study and work and learn my place—

BARNES: And step down hard!

BENJ: Fight! Maybe get killed, but goddam! We'll go ahead! [BENJAMIN *stands with clenched fist raised high.*]

Blackout

AGATE: LADIES AND GENTLEMEN, and don't let anyone tell you we ain't got some ladies in this sea of upturned faces! Only they're wearin' pants. Well, maybe I don't know a thing; maybe I fell outa the cradle when I was a kid and ain't been right since—you can't tell!

VOICE: Sit down, cockeye!

AGATE: Who's paying you for those remarks, Buddy?—Moscow Gold? Maybe I got a *glass eye*, but it come from working in a factory at the age of eleven. They hooked it out because they didn't have a shield on the works. But I wear it like a medal 'cause it tells the world where I belong—deep down in the working class! We had delegates in the union there—all kinds of secretaries and treasurers ... walkin' delegates, but not with blisters on their feet! Oh no! On their fat little ass from sitting on cushions and raking in mazuma.

[SECRETARY *and* GUNMAN *remonstrate in words and actions here.*]

Sit down, boys. I'm just sayin' that about unions in general. I know it ain't true here! Why no, our officers is all aces. Why, I seen our own secretary Fatt walk outa his way not to step on a cockroach. No boys, don't think—

FATT: [*Breaking in.*] You're out of order!

AGATE: [*To audience.*] Am I outa order?

ALL: No, no. Speak. Go on, etc.

AGATE: Yes, our officers is all aces. But I'm a member here—and no experience in Philly either! Today I couldn't wear my union button. The damnest thing happened. When I take the old coat off the wall, I see she's smoking. I'm a sonovagun if the old union button isn't on fire! Yep, the old celluloid was makin' the most god-awful stink: the landlady come up and give me hell! You know what happened?—that old union button just blushed itself to death! Ashamed! Can you beat it?

FATT: Sit down, Keller! Nobody's interested!

AGATE: Yes they are!

GUNMAN: Sit down like he tells you!

AGATE: [*Continuing to audience.*] And when I finish—

[*His speech is broken by* FATT *and* GUNMAN *who physically handle him. He breaks away and gets to other side of stage. The two are about to make for him when some of the committee men come forward and get in between the struggling parties.* ADATE'*s shirt has been torn.*]

AGATE: [*To audience.*] What's the answer, boys? The answer is, if we're reds because we wanna strike, then we take over their salute too! Know how they do it? [*Makes Communist salute.*] What is it? An uppercut! The good old uppercut to the chin! Hell, some of us boys ain't even got a shirt to our backs. What's the boss class tryin' to do—make a nudist colony outa us?

[*The audience laughs and suddenly* AGATE *comes to the middle of the stage so that the other cabmen back him up in a strong clump.*]

AGATE: Don't laugh! Nothing's funny! This is your life and mine! It's skull and bones every incha the road! Christ, we're dyin' by inches! For what? For the debutant-ees to have their sweet comin' out parties in the Ritz! Poppa's got a daughter she's gotta get her picture in the papers. Christ, they make 'em with our blood. Joe said it. Slow death or fight. It's war!

[*Throughout this whole speech* AGATE *is backed up by the other six workers, so that from their activity it is plain that the whole group of them are saying these things. Several of them may take alternate lines out of this long last speech.*]

You Edna, God love your mouth! Sid and Florrie, the other boys, old Doc Barnes—fight with us for right! It's war! Working class, unite and fight! Tear down the slaughter house of our old lives! Let freedom really ring.

These slick slobs stand here telling us about bogeymen. That's a new one for the kids—the reds is bogeymen! But the man who got me food in 1932, he called me Comrade! The one who picked me up where I bled—he called me Comrade too! What are we waiting for … Don't wait for Lefty! He might never come. Every minute—

[*This is broken into by a man who has dashed up the center aisle from the back of the house. He runs up on stage, says:*]

MAN: Boys, they just found Lefty!

OTHERS: What? What? What?

SOME: Shhh … Shhh …

MAN: They found Lefty …

AGATE: Where?

MAN: Behind the car barns with a bullet in his head!

AGATE: [*Crying*.] Hear it, boys, hear it? Hell, listen to me! Coast to coast! HELLO AMERICA! HELLO. WE'RE STORMBIRDS OF THE WORKING - CLASS. WORKERS OF THE WORLD … OUR BONES AND BLOOD! And when we die they'll know what we did to make a new world! Christ, cut us up to little pieces. We'll die for what is right! Put fruit trees where our ashes are! [*To audience*.] Well, what's the answer?

ALL: STRIKE!

AGATE: LOUDER!

ALL: STRIKE!

AGATE and OTHERS on STAGE: AGAIN!

ALL: STRIKE, STRIKE, STRIKE!!!

CURTAIN

AND TELL SAD STORIES OF THE DEATHS OF QUEENS ...

TENNESSEE WILLIAMS

Edited by Nicholas Moschovakis and David Roessel
[from composite typescript draft in UCLA Special Collections,
Williams Box 1 folder 2.]

First staged reading arranged by Michael Kahn at
the Shakespeare Theatre in Washington, D.C.,
as part of its Rediscovery Series play readings.
Directed by P. J. Paparelli.

INTRODUCTION

by Michael Kahn

Michael Kahn spoke about the "political Williams" with Nicholas Moschovakis and David Roessel on May 24, 2001. His remarks have been transcribed here.

A writer who strongly bases his writing on a critique of society is committing a political act. I think, also, that a writer who forces audiences to see something, hear something, that they in many ways do not want to see or hear, is committing a radical act.

Tennessee did both of those things. And that's political theatre. And he often did it better than someone who actually says, "I'm going to do a play about a strike," or "I'm going to do a play about a factory." It's less topical. I was very struck, when I did some short plays by Thornton Wilder, with how those plays were not sentimental evocations of small-town American life. They were deeply felt criticisms of small-town American life. And when I put on those plays, and Thornton came the first night to see them, he wrote me a letter saying, "You must be European, because you understand my plays." I said, "No, I'm an American, born in Brooklyn!"—but added that I saw that the plays were, in many ways, attacking complacency. Tennessee, too, is attacking those forces in our country that either repress us or are intolerant.

When I did *Cat on a Hot Tin Roof*, it hit me that it was not a play about sex, but it was really a play about America—that the family was a real microcosm of America, and the play was about his vision of American society based on greed and mendacity. So I was able to understand *Cat* in a larger sense than I had when I was young. *Sweet Bird of Youth* is a real indictment of a repressive society that does not permit anybody who is different to exist. And as I look at Tennessee's plays now, I see that they are all not only a sort of critique of American society, but in many ways they are kind of revolutionary plays, in that he puts subjects on stage that have not been there before—which is of course a pretty political, and somewhat anarchistic, act.

It's very hard to imagine now how controversial Tennessee Williams was—how shocked people were by *Cat*, and his other plays—because now they don't seem shocking at all. But the very fact that a writer of fame and success like Tennessee would continually push the envelope of the American theatre is, in itself, very radical and political. When I started doing the early one-acts, like *The Long Goodbye* and *The Strangest Kind of Love*, I began to see that obviously—early in his life—he had been influenced by some political writers, by Clifford Odets and the agitprop drama of the depression. And I was thrilled with *The Long Goodbye*, with its its echoes of Odets's style of writing, that certain toughness. So when I saw *Not About Nightingales*, it wasn't a surprise, because clearly he had gone through a political phase of writing—before he chose to be a real power through incorporating those ideas in another framework. He became a covertly political writer, as opposed to becoming an overtly political writer in the way that Arthur Miller did. I always thought that if *Camino Real*—which I think is really a work of genius—had not been so vilified, then Tennessee's desire to be abstract would have flourished. But after the incredibly hostile reception of *Camino Real* he moved away from it. I don't think Tennessee would consider himself a political writer; but he would probably be quite pleased that you are actually including him as a political writer.

Tennessee was more of a poet, you see; his concerns had to do with the vagaries of the human heart. In *And Tell Sad Stories of the Death of Queens*, the radical thing was thinking of putting these people on stage at a time when they were not put on stage. And what's even more radical is putting them on stage in a not particularly favorable light. This is not a sentimental apology for homosexuality, which, at the time when he was writing this, probably would have been the way that he would have written the play, if he had been a "gay writer." In this case the drag queens are actually a mess, often cruel to each other, very self-deluded, and lonely—and yet each has, as Candy does, his own stature. It's ahead of its time.

It is interesting to find Tennessee expressing his homosexuality in an overt way, rather than in the covert way he often did. I think we're lucky, perhaps, that many of his central characters were these great women, because much of his brilliance is in how he manipulates the kind of code that repression forced him to use. The plays are full of gay code; it was actually a problem to have Tennessee in the theatre during performances, because he would screech with laughter at some of those lines—like near the opening of *Streetcar*, when Stanley comes home bringing a piece of "meat." And I think Tennessee put them there on purpose, because he was not able to write overtly about gays in those days, and so found a way to do it by subtle and intelligent means. But here we no longer have the gender transferred. And we can see what might have been lost if he had been able to write overtly about homosexuality.

CHARACTERS

CANDY DELANEY
ALVIN KRENNING
KARL
JERRY JOHNSON

PLACE AND DATE: *New Orleans, possibly sometime between 1939-41 (or alternatively 1945-47), at the beginning of the weekend before Mardi Gras.*

Scene One

The curtain rises upon a living-room lighted by the soft blue dusk of a southern Spring, coming through French doors open upon a patio which is a tiny replica of a Japanese garden: fish-pool, fountain, weeping willow and even a short arched bridge with paper lanterns. The interior is also Japanese, or pseudo [-Japanese], with bamboo furniture, very low tables, grass-mats, polished white or pale blue porcelain bowls and vases containing artificial dogwood or cherry blossoms and log silver stems of pussy-willow, everything very delicate and pastel. A curtain of beads or bamboo separate a small bedroom, upstage.

A mechanical piano plays R. Hubbell's 1916 song "Poor Butterfly," off-key, till the entrance of CANDY, *a New Orleans "queen" uncomfortably close to his thirty-fifth birthday with the sort of face that can never look adult, a grace and slimness that will always suggest a girlish young boy. The effeminacy of* CANDY *is too natural, too innate, to require expression in mannerisms or voice: the part should be played without caricature.*

Before CANDY *enters, as the piano expires, we hear a key's nervous scratch: then* CANDY'*s breathless voice, suffering from audible shortness of breath:*

CANDY: I can never work a doorkey! No matter how long I occupy an apartment I still have trouble with doorkeys.

[*Door opens;* CANDY *enters followed by a big young merchant seaman,* KARL.]

Come in, Come on in!

KARL: [*With suspicion.*] What's this?

CANDY: My apartment.

KARL: It looks like a chop suey joint.

CANDY: I did it all over this Spring in a sort of Japanese style. I want you to take a look at the patio first so I can close the doors and discourage a call from my tenants. I have tenants upstairs, a very nice pair of boys from Alabama. But whenever I entertain they have a way of dropping down uninvited, if you know what I mean. They make themselves a little too much at home here.

KARL: You own this place?

CANDY: [*Fast, excited.*] Yes, I own three pieces of property in the Quarter, this one and two others, all in good locations, rental property. The one on Chartres has six rental units including the slave-quarters and the one on Dumaine, four units: entire slave-quarters occupied by one tenant: a real show-place, I'll show it to you right after Mass tomorrow. Mr. Frazier, the tenant's, in Biloxi, spends every week-end there: [*Winks.*] Has a friend at the air-base. And then, of course, I have my shop on Saint Charles just a block from Lee Circle, on this side of Lee Circle, a half hour's walk each way but very good for my figure. [*Laughs.*] Take a look at my lovely patio, Karl.

KARL: I can see it from here.

CANDY: Well, we'll slip out later: the air's such a lovely soft blue, like a—Luna moth's wing. Just step outside for one moment.

[KARL *ambles out.*]

Don't talk out loud, just whisper: —or my tenants will come flying downstairs, especially if they see you ...

KARL: You mentioned a shop? You said you got a shop?

CANDY: Oh, yes.

KARL: What shop?

CANDY: Interior decorating. I told you. You don't remember?

KARL: No. I forgot.

CANDY: I had a business partner till just lately, a very nice older man who used to be my sponsor. We had a beautiful relationship for seventeen years. I've had a very protected life till lately.

[*Darts back in.*]

Here he is, this is him.

[*Snatches up a framed photo.*]

Left his wife for me, sold out his business in Atlanta and we moved here in the war-years when I was eighteen, and he set me up in this shop and made me his partner in it. Well, nothing lasts forever. You dream that it will but it don't —I'll shut these doors so my tenants don't come flying down, now ...

[*Shuts patio doors.*]

No, nothing goes on forever. I worshipped Sidney Korngold. I never even noticed that he got heavy ... But Sidney had the aging man's weakness for youth ... I understood: I didn't even resent it: —oh, I had a nervous collapse when he left but I didn't reproach him for it, I put no financial obstacles in his way, I made no demands, I said, I said to him: "Sid? Whatever makes you happy is what I want for you, daddy ... "

[*Sets framed photo down with a lost look.*]

—If my tenants come down to the door, don't make a sound till they go.

KARL: Girls?

CANDY: Women? Oh, no, I'd never rent to women again in my life, they're not only very slow payers, they're messy and destructive. No. These tenants are a pair of sweet boys from Alabama: young queens, of course. I'd never consider renting to anyone else. Queens make wonderful tenants, take excellent care of the place, sometimes improve it for you. They are great home-lovers and have creative ideas. They set the styles and create the taste for the country. Don't you know that?

KARL: No.

CANDY: Just imagine this country without queens in it. It would be absolutely barbaric. Look at the homes of normal married couples. No originality: modern mixed with period, everything bunched around a big TV set in the parlor. Mediocrity is the passion among them. Conformity. Convention. Now I know the faults of queens, nobody knows the faults of queens better than I do.

KARL: Queens?

CANDY: What?

KARL: Are you queer?

CANDY: —*Baby*, are you *kidding*?!!

KARL: How about answering the question?

396

CANDY: Oh, now, really!

KARL: Huh?

CANDY: I thought that was understood in the first five minutes' talk we had in the bar.

KARL: You think I would be here if I'd thought you was a queer?

CANDY: Karl, I like you. I like you and I admire you. But really …

KARL: Really what?

CANDY: You can't expect me to seriously believe that a man who has been shipping in and out of New Orleans for five years is still not able to recognize a queen in a gay bar.

KARL: I don't go with queers.

CANDY: I know you don't. I'll tell you something. This is not the first time I have seen you. I mean this night. I have been noticing you off and on, here and there, ever since you started shipping out of this city. But up till lately I led a different life. I told you about my husband. When he broke with the normal world and took up with me as my sponsor, eighteen years ago, he changed his name. You wouldn't think it possible for any man to undergo such a complete transformation, new name, new life, new tastes and habits, even a new appearance.

   [*Turns attention to photo again.*]

I mean he —ha ha! —that's not an old picture, either. Taken two years ago, slightly less. When he turned fifty. Remarkable? Would you guess it? Doesn't he look a fast thirty? I gave that man a new lease on life. I swear that when he started going with me in Atlanta, Georgia, he was a nondescript person, already a middle-aged one! Well … I never cheated on him. I'm the monogamous type. He did the cheating. And I was so trustful I didn't suspect it till after it had been going on for years … Well, change is the heart of existence. I hold no grudge against him. We broke things off in a very dignified way. We had a joint bank account. I bought out his share of the business with my half of the money and he is now in Houston with his new chick, starting all over again, and I wish him luck with it. However he's picked a wrong one. But infatuation is even blinder than love. Specially when the victim is at the dangerous age like he is …

[Returns photograph to bureau.]

—Well, he'll wake up soon and realize that he let a good thing go for one that's basically rotten. Just younger …

[Notices KARL distracted.]

Are you lookin' fo' somethin'?

KARL: Ain't you got something to drink?

CANDY: I've got just about the best-stocked liquor cabinet in the French Quarter, baby.

KARL: Now you're talkin.

CANDY: I don't entertain very often but when I do, it's done well. You can depend on that. Let's see, you were drinkin' blended whiskey.

KARL: Never mind what I was drinkin'. I can switch without effort.

CANDY: Want something exotic?

KARL: Such as what, huh?

CANDY: Well, now, I could make you a Pimm's Cup number one, with a dash of pernod, and cucumber slices and all. I could make you a golden dawn which is a pineapple rum drink. I could make you a—

KARL: How 'bout just pouring me a healthy shot of old Grandad.

CANDY: Now you're talkin, that's the way to talk. In a little while now, when I hear my tenants go out for their nightly cruise, we'll adjourn to the patio. It will be magical then, blue dusk. I have a Hi-Fi with a speaker in the garden and in the middle of my fishpool is an island with a willow that makes a complete curtain, an absolutely private retreat from the world except for a few little glimpses of sky now and then …

KARL: You sure do go in for fancy talk, Bud.

CANDY: *[Laughing.]* Yes, I do, but y'know it's natural to me. I ornament the language so to speak. I used to write poetry once. Still do sometimes when I'm feeling sentimental.

KARL: Ain't you drinkin'?

CANDY: No. I never drink.

KARL: Why's that?

CANDY: Would you guess I have a weight problem?

KARL: You look thin to me.

CANDY: Thank you. I am.

KARL: Then why have you got a weight problem?

CANDY: Because I must starve myself to keep my figure. No calorie goes uncounted.

KARL: Jesus! —You're a card.

CANDY: The joker in the deck?

KARL: —Naw. —The queen ...

CANDY: I like you very much. I feel safe with you.

KARL: That's a mistake. Nobody's safe around me when I'm liquored up.

CANDY: I think I would be. I think you like me, too.

KARL: You're going to be disappointed.

CANDY: I don't think so.

KARL: You're not going to get what you're after.

CANDY: How do you know what I'm after?

KARL: You're different, but not that different. You want to be laid, and you won't be, not by me.

CANDY: You see? You've misunderstood me, it's happened already, just as it always does. I'd love to have anything at all between us but I would be just as happy with your true friendship, true and lasting, as with a mutual thing between us in bed. That's true. I would. I swear it.

KARL: Then you're different all right.

CANDY: Yes, I told you I was. I'm going to tell you something which you may think is a lie. You are only the second man in my life. The first was

Mr. Korngold.

[*Turning attention to photo once more.*]

He brought me out in Atlanta. When I was a chicken. Just as dumb as they come, knew there was something wrong with me but not I was queer. This man stopped me on Peachtree Street in Atlanta and asked me if I was a girl or a boy. He thought that I was a girl in boy's clothes. I told him that I was a boy, indignantly. He said, Come home with me. However he didn't take me to his home. Mr. Korngold was a respectable married man with two kiddies. However he had this double life downtown. He took me to a suite in a hotel. Which he kept under a different name. Opened a closet containing girl's clothes and wigs. Told me to get into something. I did, including the wig. And he seduced me …

KARL: Yeah?

CANDY: What he didn't know: his wife had put a tail on him, a private dick. She sued him for a divorce, naming me as the correspondent. It was not a public trial, to keep it private he had to sell his business and give this woman everything that he owned. We left Atlanta together. He was my sponsor. He put me up in business, I already had a talent for decorating. I felt obliged to make good, and I did, I made good. This was eighteen years ago.

We remained together for seventeen years. Only last year we broke up. I discovered that he'd been cheating on me in spite of the fact that I'd been completely faithful. It broke my heart. I have pride. I bought out his share in the business with my half of our joint bank-account and started from scratch on my own. He went to Texas with his new chick. People follow set patterns. Over and over. Haven't you noticed they do?

KARL: —What're you doing in there?

[*While talking,* CANDY *rises and goes through the bamboo curtain into the bed area.*]

CANDY: Changing clothes. And sex.

[*Emerges in drag.*]

I am a transvestite. Here I am.

KARL: —Are you crazy?

CANDY: No. Just very abnormal I guess.

KARL: Well, I got to admit—

CANDY: —What?

KARL: You're as much like a woman as any real one I seen.

CANDY: Thank you. That's the object.

KARL: Sure you're not one?

CANDY: Want me to show you?

KARL: No.

CANDY: How is your drink, does it need freshening, yet?

KARL: Yeah. I'm a very heavy drinker.

CANDY: You'll notice I'm being very feminine now in my talk and my mannerisms as well as appearance. Isn't that what you want?

KARL: You do this often?

CANDY: Often when I'm alone. In fact usually when I'm alone, when I come in at night, I put on my hair and slip in a fresh negligée. I have ten of them in all the rainbow colors, some of them worth a small fortune. Ha ha, not a small fortune, I mean a hundred or two ...

KARL: You must be loaded.

CANDY: Rich? No, just well off. My life expectancy isn't a long one and I see no reason to put aside much for the so-called rainy day.

KARL: You're sick?

CANDY: Haven't you noticed how short-winded I am? I have a congenital heart. I mean a congenital defect of the heart. A leakage that gradually leaks more. It's just as well. I won't look pretty much longer, even in 'drag' ... One of my upstairs tenants, the younger one, is a poet. Let me read you a poem he wrote about queers which I think is lovely, not great, no, but lovely.

[*Produces and reads lyric.*]

"I think the strange, the crazed, the queer
Will have their holiday this year,
I think, for just a little while,
There will be pity for the wild.

I think in places known as gay,
In special little clubs and bars,
Pierrot will serenade pierrot
with frantic drums and sad guitars.

I think for some uncertain reason
Mercy will be shown this season
To the lovely and misfit,
To the brilliant and deformed.

I think they will be housed and warmed
And fed and comforted a while,
Before, with such a tender smile,
The earth destroys her crooked child.

—That's it. It's dedicated to me, just to my initials, it's going to come out in a little mag soon. He's the nicer of my upstairs tenants. They occupy the slave quarters. When they go out I will show you their place because it's one of my best interiors, and very ingenious in the use of small space, only two rooms and a—

[*Noticing* KARL's *increasing restlessness.*]

—You look unhappy! Why?

KARL: Do you know any women?

CANDY: Won't I do?

KARL: No, I don't go this route.

CANDY: I told you, I just want friendship. I'm terribly lonely. Just to have the company of someone I find so attractive, to entertain him, amuse him, is all that I ask for! Really!

KARL: You're a new one, but the pitch is familiar.

CANDY: I don't deny for a moment that if you suddenly sprang up and seized me in your arms! —I wouldn't resist ...

KARL: You're barking up the wrong tree, in the wrong woods, in the wrong country.

CANDY: I only said if you did. I didn't imply it was probable that you would. I didn't even imply that it was—likely ... You like some music?

KARL: Yeah, turn on some music.

CANDY: What's your preference in music, popular or classic or—what do you like?

KARL: —I don't care, anything ...

CANDY: [*Reading an album title.*] "Waltzing with Wayne King."

KARL: Good.

CANDY: [*After the music begins.*] —I'm told I follow divinely. Shall we dance?

KARL: No.

CANDY: Why? Why not? Come on!

KARL: You look like a girl but I can't forget you're not one.

CANDY: You will when you start dancing with me. Are you afraid to?

KARL: Oh, well ...

[*Rises and dances with her.*]

CANDY: Oh, oh, oh ...

KARL: You sure can follow okay.

CANDY: Doin' what comes naturally!

KARL: [*Quitting.*] I can't, I just can't. Ha ha! —It seems too—

CANDY: Too what, honey?

KARL: —unnatural—not right. —I'd better go.

CANDY: *OH, NO!—NO!!*

KARL: Yeah, I think so.

CANDY: Don't be so conventional and inhibited, why, what for!? [(*After an awkward pause.*)] You force me to bring up a matter which is always embarrassing. Are you hard up for money?

KARL: I got a few dollars on me.

CANDY: That's not enough for a Mardi Gras weekend, baby.

KARL: Oh, I'll make out. I'll probably meet some dame over forty or fifty at Pat's or somewhere. Maybe even a B-girl who'll take my tab, and—

CANDY: She wouldn't be pretty as I am.

KARL: She'd be female.

CANDY: But would she offer you all?

KARL: What's all?

CANDY: All that I've got to offer. This lovely place at your disposal now and always. Unlimited credit at every bar in the quarter. Cash, too. A pocketful of it. And more where that pocketful came from. And no strings, Karl. Your freedom.

KARL: I want a woman tonight, having been at sea for six weeks.

CANDY: I can fix that too.

KARL: How?

CANDY: Most of my close friends are women, and all are attractive.

KARL: You mean you can fix me up with a good-looking girl?

CANDY: Easy as pie.

KARL: What would you get out of it? [*Silence.*] What would you want for all this?

CANDY: Just your companionship, later. When you come home.

KARL: My home in this town is a bed at the Salvation Army dormitory on Rampart.

CANDY: This is your home, if you'll take it.

KARL: I like to pay my own way unless I am giving something. I'm not giving nothing to you.

CANDY: You'd come home drunk. Fall in bed. I would take your shoes off, just your shoes, and blissfully fall asleep with your hand in mine.

KARL: For Christ's sake.

CANDY: No, for mine!

KARL: You're crazy. I'm going now.

CANDY: You don't believe I could fix you up with a girl who would be everything that you dream of?

KARL: It's all part of a plot. I just want some money from you. You can have what you want, now, for ten dollars. Let's get it over with, huh?

CANDY: But what I told you I wanted is what I want.

KARL: It's all you'd get.

CANDY: I know it.

KARL: And it would cost you twenty.

CANDY: Twenty's nothing. Give me your empty wallet.

[*He does. She removes bills from a teapot, which* KARL *does not see—perhaps behind the bead curtain—and puts them in his wallet. She puts the wallet in his pocket. He takes it out and carefully counts the bills. She has given him fifty dollars. He grunts. She has picked up the phone and dialed a number. She gets a response.*]

I want to speak to Helene.

KARL: Who's Helene?

CANDY: Stripper at the Dragon.

KARL: You mean really one of those strip-teasing dolls?

CANDY: Wait and see, I deliver! Helene? Candy! How are you? How about coming over between shows, honey? There's someone here you'll adore. Six foot two, eyes of blue, magnificent, young, and loaded! — Sure. —How much? —It's a deal.

405

KARL: How much!

CANDY: [*Covering phone.*] On me! [*Uncovers phone.*] How soon?

[*Turns to* KARL, *again covering phone.*]

Nine-thirty. Okay?

KARL: That's three hours from now.

CANDY: You need to shave and shower and catch forty winks, while I prepare a shrimp curry such as you've never tasted. What have you got to lose?

KARL: All right. But just don't—

CANDY: [*To phone.*] Fine, honey. I'll expect you.

[*Hangs up. Crosses to shutter doors, throws them open on the transparent blue dusk of the Japanese patio-garden.*]

Now is the hour, just now, to go in my garden!

KARL: This is the queerest deal I ever got into. What I want is another shot of that bourbon.

CANDY: Go in the garden. Cross the fishpool on the Japanese bridge. Sit down on the little Eighteenth-Century bench beneath the willow. Spring has come, this is the first evening of it! I'm going to put on my chiffon! Before you've counted to fifty, I'll bring you a drink.

KARL: Remember that you'll get nothing.

CANDY: Getting nothing is something I never forget.

[*He nods and goes out.*]

KARL: —Is this thing safe to walk on?

CANDY: Strong as steel! Guaranteed!

KARL: —Well, if it breaks, it won't be the only thing that breaks around here.

CANDY: Ha ha ha!

KARL: [*On bridge.*] It's creaking. [*Completes crossing.*] Well, I made it. Hurry up with the drink.

406

CANDY: Start counting. [*She has started changing into a long pale yellow chiffon.*] Before you get to fifty I'll –

[*Knock at door.*]

—Who's there?

ALVIN'S VOICE AT DOOR: Krenning.

CANDY: Go away, Krenning. [*Catches her breath.*] I'm not alone tonight!

ALVIN: Are you safe?

CANDY: Perfectly.

ALVIN: Sure?

CANDY: Certain!

ALVIN: Jerry saw him come in. He says he's dirt.

CANDY: Tell that jealous bitch to mind her own little business for a change!

ALVIN: He says he's the one that broke Tiny Henderson's jaw which is still wired together.

CANDY: Tell her I appreciate her concern but I am not Henderson and I am not with dirt. You all cruise every night and bring home trick after trick which I put up with despite the chance I'm taking of making a terrible scandal. This is the first person I've brought into my house since I broke up with my husband! Go away! Go away!—I'm with someone I love!

ALVIN: —Good luck.

CANDY: —Go away!

[*She pours bourbon, hurries out to the garden.*]

[*Dim to indicate passage of maybe half an hour, during which time* KARL *has become definitely drunk; their voices fade, perhaps to music, and resume as lights go back up.*]

Scene Two

Offstage voices of CANDY *and* KARL, *followed by creaking sounds of* KARL *beginning to recross the bridge over the fishpool; a sudden splash.*

Continual cursing and a soft, continual murmur of solicitude. KARL *returns dripping to interior. There are loud, enquiring cries from a gallery above.*

CANDY: [*Calling back.*] Will you all mind your own business fo' a change?

     [*Returns inside, shutting and locking the French doors. Then he rushes up to* KARL. *The enquiring cries have turned to shrill giggles and cackles.*]

     Bitches! Didn't I tell you?

KARL: You goddam faggots.

CANDY: Oh, now—

KARL: Oh, now what? This is going to cost you, Sister.

CANDY: Don't be mad at Candy! How did I know it wasn't built for a man? You take those wet things off and slip into the loveliest Chinese robe you've ever laid your blue eyes on!

KARL: Chinese shit.

CANDY: Isn't it lucky you had on dungarees?

KARL: You ain't gonna think it's so lucky before I go. I want you to know I'm takin' over this place.

CANDY: —That's just what I want you t'do.

KARL: I bet you'd dance with pleasure if I knocked you around. I'd gladly do it, too. Except you'd enjoy it too much. Where is this robe?

     [*They have retired behind the bamboo curtain and the wet dungarees, wadded, are hurled through it.*]

     And you stay away, *way* away! —Blondie.

CANDY: My name is not Blondie, it's Candy.

KARL: —Some candy ...

CANDY: Now you just dry you'self off, since you're so touchy, and slip into this heavenly Chinese robe, while I mix you a violet. Know what a violet is? It's pernod and vodka, mixed, on the rocks! —The strongest drink ever made. —That's why it's called a violet, I reckon ...

KARL: I never been given a knock out that knocked me out before I knocked out the bitch that give it to me. —Keep that in mind! Don't forget it ...

CANDY: Ha ha ha ...

KARL: —Shit ...

CANDY: I recognized your type the instant I met you. Big roughtalking two hundred pounds of lonely, lost little boy.

KARL: —I recognized your type *before* I met you.

CANDY: I have no secrets! Do I?

KARL: I don't care what you have besides crabs and cash.

[*He comes out in a magnificent Chinese robe.* CANDY *is mixing violets at a bamboo bar in a corner.*]

Aw.

[*Finding ivory white French phone, lifts phone and dials a number.*]

CANDY: Who you callin', baby?

KARL: Where's my drink?

CANDY: Here, Sugar.

KARL: [*Into phone, taking drink.*] I wanna speak to a lady whose first name is Alice. I can't remember the last name, a red-headed lady that drives a white '52 Cadillac with North Carolina plates on it.

CANDY: Oh, I know who *that* is. Alice "Blue" Jackson, we call her.

KARL: [*Into phone.*] Oh. Her last name is Jackson. Yeah, Jackson ...

POLITICAL STAGES

[Then to CANDY.]

Be careful what you say of her in front of me. Huh?

CANDY: I don't attack people's character when they're not present.

KARL: There's no woman as low as a faggot.

CANDY: You must've had some bad experiences with them.

KARL: I've had bad experiences with them and they've had worse experiences with me.

CANDY: You know, I think your bark is worse than your bite.

KARL: That's because —*Huh?*—[*Speaking into phone.*] Aw … Well, tell her to call this number. [*To* CANDY.] What's your number?

CANDY: Magnolia 0347.

KARL: [*Repeats number and adds.*] —Soon's she comes in … [*Hangs up. Drains glass.*]

CANDY: A violet ought to be sipped. You're going to like me. I know that you're going to like me. You already do. I can tell by your eyes when you look at me.

KARL: When I look at you I'm measuring you for a coffin.

CANDY: You're going to discover that Candy's your—

KARL: When did she say she'd get here?

CANDY: Nine-thirty.

KARL: What time's it now?

CANDY: Seven-fifteen.

KARL: Call me at nine. [*Goes to sleep in the next room.*]

Scene Three

[*Somewhat more than a week later: Sunday A.M., rain.* CANDY, *in drag, is having coffee and Knox gelatine in fruit juice at a daintily set breakfast-table on which is a pale blue Japanese vase of pussy-willows. In the next room, someone* [KARL] *is sleeping loudly. All of* CANDY's *motions and actions are muted so as not to disturb the loud sleeper. Presently another queen* [JERRY] *enters without knocking. This one is still under thirty, is handsome but with a pinched look and a humorous lisp.*]

JERRY: Good morning and happy birthday to you, Miss Delaney.

CANDY: Quiet, please. [*Indicates bedroom with sleeper.*]

Didn't I tell you he'd come back before Sunday.

[JERRY *starts towards bedroom.*]

Stay out of the bedroom.

JERRY: I'm just taking a peek. [*Thrusts head through curtains and whistles softly.*]

CANDY: Come back out of the bedroom.

JERRY: I'm not in the bedroom.

CANDY: Everything in my life has been messed up by bitches, and I am sick of it.

JERRY: I was going to give you a birthday present.

CANDY: Please don't bother. Just don't mess up the only important thing in my life right now.

JERRY: I hope it lasts, Mother.

CANDY: And don't use bitch-talk in here. It's not only common, it's also very old-fashioned, it places and dates you. My name is Candy Delaney.

JERRY: Miss Delaney to me.

CANDY: Then get out of here, will you?

—No. wait. —Sit down. I want to talk to you seriously a minute. Things have got to change here because I will not have my happiness jeopardized by two bitches under my roof that think to be homosexual means to be cheap and common. And do the bars every night, and only think of new tricks.

JERRY: That's fine coming from you, the mother of us all, on her 35th birthday.

CANDY: Yes, I'm not young anymore. The queen-world is full of excitement for young queens only. For me it's *passée*, and *finit*. I want to have some dignity in my life, and now I have found a person that I can live with on a *dignified* basis and on a *permanent* basis, who won't compromise me in my professional life, my career, and that I can give something to and who can give something to me, so that between us we can create a satisfactory new existence for both.

JERRY: You've got the birthday blues.

CANDY: I've never been so happy in my life.

JERRY: You've had a sad life, Mother.

CANDY: Will you please leave here and go to your own apartment and when your month is up I will appreciate it if you and that faggot you live with will please move out. Why don't you rent an apartment in the project?

JERRY: And I spent twenty bucks on your birthday present, Candy.

CANDY: Since I won't receive it it's safe for you to exaggerate what it cost you.

JERRY: —This is the last time you will ever insult me.

CANDY: I hope so.

[JERRY *exits, slamming door.* KARL *wakes with a groan and comes stumbling into the kitchen.*]

Baby, what d'ya want for breakfast?

KARL: You can mix me a violet.

CANDY: Baby, not for breakfast.

KARL: I know what I want for breakfast, don't try and tell me. Where's the Pernod bottle?

[CANDY *rises with a sigh and produces the pernod.*]

Where's the vodka?

412

[*Same business.*]

Get me some ice-cubes in a big glass.

[*Same business.*]

All right now. Drink your goddam coffee and leave me alone.

CANDY: [*Almost tearful.*] I hate to see you just flying into ruin, baby. You are too wonderful a person, and I love you.

KARL: When I'm at sea I go weeks without liquor.

CANDY: You are a wonderful, wonderful, beautiful person and you know I adore you?!

KARL: You're a slob.

CANDY: I don't think you mean that, baby.

KARL: Don't take any bets on it.

CANDY: Otherwise why would you be here?

[*Another queen* [ALVIN] *in her early twenties, very attractive, silently opens the door and stands in it, ignored by the pair at the table.*]

KARL: I run out of money.

CANDY: That's just an excuse that you make for coming back to me last night.

KARL: If you think so, just try to get out of paying me for last night, and I mean plenty. Plenty!

ALVIN: Candy, I want to speak to you.

CANDY: I told your room-mate not to come in this apartment without knocking at the door and that goes the same for you, Alvin.

ALVIN: You have hurt Jerry.

CANDY: I'm glad. If it made some impression.

ALVIN: What's gotten into you, Candy?

CANDY: I am fed up with bitches and bitch talk and bitch manners. Why do you think I did this apartment over?

413

[KARL *rises and starts to cross to a door.*]

Where are you going, baby?

KARL: The head.

[*Crosses to bathroom.*]

CANDY: [*To* ALVIN.] Sit down and have some coffee.

ALVIN: You have broke Jerry's heart.

CANDY: No, I haven't.

ALVIN: You have.

CANDY: I had to make it plain to him that from now on I want no tenants under my roof anymore that have no respect for what I am trying to do.

ALVIN: What are you trying to do? Ditch your old friends?

CANDY: There's nobody values old friends more than I do but I will not have them bitching my life up for me when I want to preserve the first true worth-while relationship I have found since I broke up with [Sidney].

ALVIN: If you're talking about Karl, just let me tell you something.

CANDY: You and Jerry cheat all the time on each other and can't stand to see me working out something decent.

[ALVIN *rises with an angry shrug and starts out.*]

CANDY: [*Rising.*] What were you going to tell me? I just want to know!

ALVIN: [*Turning at door.*] Karl was shacked up with a woman all last week while you were crying your heart out, and only returned to this place because she threw him out of her house on Saint Charles Street.

CANDY: A lie!

[ALVIN *starts out.*]

Who told you this story?

ALVIN: Nobody. I know it. I know the woman, and so do you. Alice Jackson.

CANDY: When Karl comes out of the bathroom I will ask him. Meanwhile I will appreciate it if you and Miss Johnson start packing. I will refund the rest of your rent for this month.

ALVIN: Jerry is packing already.

[*Goes out, slamming door.*]

CANDY: [*Rushing after him into hall, shouting.*] Remember I don't know you after this! Nowhere! On the street!

[*Shuts door: is visibly shaken.*]

[KARL *comes out of bathroom with towel in damp shorts and starts to dress.*]

KARL: What was that all about?

CANDY: I want to ask you a question. I've never lied to you, baby. I want you to tell me the truth. Have you had any connection with a woman this week?

KARL: Huh. What woman?

CANDY: A woman named Alice Jackson?

KARL: The answer is yes. What of it?

CANDY: Come over here and sit down at the table.

KARL: I'm dressing.

CANDY: You can dress later.

KARL: I can but I want to now. OK?

CANDY: You are risking a wonderful future between us by not treating me with respect which I deserve from you. I have spent over three hundred dollars on you in the past week, at a time when I am just getting established in my own business, after long plans and great efforts! Let me tell you what I plan for us. First of all, I'm throwing out Alvin and Jerry and am redecorating this building to attract the highest class tenants. I own three pieces of property in the quarter and I have my own decorating place on Saint Charles Street. Is it or is it not true that you have been shacking up with this woman while you were not here last week, and lied about it, and told me you'd been to Biloxi with shipmates?

KARL: Can you think of any good reason for me to lie to you, fruitcake?

CANDY: Yes. I can, Butcher boy. You're not too drunk or hungover to know that I am the one, only me, that offers you a sound future. Just, just let me tell you the plans I've made for our future life together! I need a partner in business. You will be it. I'm going, in one year's time, to be the most high-paid, fashionable decorator in town. Wait! My talent is recognized! I did the TV show for the "Two Americas Fair."

[KARL *crosses to him and starts snapping his fingers.*]

CANDY: [*Ignoring* KARL'*s gesture.*] Photographs of my interiors are going to be reproduced in *Southern Culture*'s next issue, *in color!—a full page spread!*

[KARL *continues snapping fingers closer to* CANDY'*s face.*]

Why are you snapping your fingers in my face?

KARL: The loot, give with the loot, I'm going.

CANDY: Where?

KARL: Alice's. We spent her month's allowance and that is why I come back here for one night only.

CANDY: You will stay *here* or get *nothing*!

KARL: You give the wrong answer, fruitcup.

[*Knocks him around, first lightly, then more severely:* CANDY'*s sobbing turns to stifled outcries.*]

Where do you keep it, where do you keep your loot, come on before I demolish you and the whole fucking pad!?

CANDY: [*At last.*] Tea-pot, the—silver teapot ....

[KARL *helps himself to a thick roll of greenbacks in the teapot and starts out.*]*

KARL: Fill it back up. I might drop in here again the next time I ship in this town.

---

* Williams's text provides no indication that Karl remembers that there was money in the teapot in Scene 1, or that if he had remembered he would have refrained from beating Candy. Directors could choose how they want to stage it.

[*Exits.* CANDY *has fallen to her knees but she crawls after* KARL *with surprising rapidity, shrieking his name over and over and louder and more piercingly each time:* JERRY *and* ALVIN *burst in just as* CANDY *topples lifelessly forward onto her face with a last strangulated outcry.*]

JERRY: Jesus, get her a drink.

[ALVIN *rushes to liquor cabinet as* JERRY *lifts* CANDY *from floor.*]

—Alvin? I think she's dead!

[ALVIN *freezes with cognac bottle in hand.*]

Help me get her on the godam bed for Crissake.

ALVIN: Make it look like she died natural, Jerry.

JERRY: Will you shut up and take her legs, you cunt?

ALVIN: [*Obeying.*] We warned her, she wouldn't listen.

JERRY: She isn't breathing, she's gone.

ALVIN: We got to get her out of drag before the cops come, anyhow.

JERRY: Who's going to call the police? It's even too late for a priest.

ALVIN: Who do we notify? Korngold?

JERRY: Who is Korngold?

ALVIN: Her husband: separated: the one that left her: He went to Texas: Houston.

JERRY: Alvin? She's breathing: the brandy!

[*Business: they pour brandy down her: she gags and retches. They laugh wildly.*]

ALVIN: Pull yourself together on your birthday!

CANDY: [*Sitting up slowly.*] —Oh, my God. —I'm old! —I've gotten old, I'm old ...

[JERRY *motions* ALVIN *to sit beside her.*]

[*A pause: it begins to rain.*]

JERRY: Now let us sit upon a rumpled bed
And tell sad stories of the deaths of queens...

[*They giggle,* ALVIN *and* JERRY: *finally even* CANDY *but her giggle turns to tears, as the scene dims out.*]

Not About Nightingales

TENNESSEE WILLIAMS

Edited by Allean Hale

———

Not About Nightingales *was given its world premiere on March 5, 1998, at the Royal National Theatre, London, England.* Nightingales *was directed by Trevor Nunn; set design was by Richard Hoover; costume design by Karyl Newman; lighting by Chris Parry, music arrangement by Steven Edis, and sound by Christopher Shutt. Production Manager was Jo Maund and Stage Manager, Courtney Bryant.*

OPENING

The action takes place in a large American prison during the summer of 1938. The conditions which the play presents are those of no particular prison but a composite picture of many.

LOUD-SPEAKER: Yeah, this is the Lorelei excursion steamer, All-day trip around Sandy Point. Leave 8 A.M., return at Midnight. Sight-seeing, dancing, entertainment with Lorelei Lou and her eight Lorelights! Got your ticket, lady? Got your ticket? Okay, that's all. We're shoving off now. Now we're leaving the boat dock, folks. We're out in the harbor. Magnificent skyline of the city against the early morning sunlight. It's still a little misty around the tops of the big towers downtown. Hear those bells ringing? That's St. Patrick's Cathedral. Finest chimes in America. It's eight o'clock sharp. Sun's bright as a dollar, swell day, bright, warm, makes you mighty proud to be alive, yes, Ma'am! There it is! You can see it now, folks. That's the Island. Sort of misty still. See them big stone walls. Dynamite-proof, escape-proof! Thirty-five hundred men in there, folks, and lots of 'em 'll never get out! Boy, oh, boy, I wonder how it feels t' be locked up in a place like that till doomsday? Oh, oh!! There goes the band, folks! Dancing on the Upper Deck! Dancing, folks! Lorelei Lou and her eight Lorelights! Dancing on the Upper Deck—dancing!—Dancing!— Dancing ... [*Fade.*]

> [*Flash forward to end of play. Light fades except for a spot on* EVA, *clutching* JIM'*s shoes.*]

LOUD-SPEAKER: Aw, there it is! You can see it now, folks. That's the Island! Sort of misty tonight. You'd see it better if there was a moon. Those walls are dynamite-proof, escape proof—Thirty-five hundred men in there—some won't get out till Doomsday.—There's the band!—Dancing on the Upper Deck, folks! Lorelei Lou and her eight Lorelights! Dancing—dancing—dancing ... [*Fade.*]

> [*Music comes up. The shoes fall from* EVA'*s hands, and she covers her face.*]

Blackout

ACT ONE

Episode One

ANNOUNCER: "Miss Crane Applies for a Job"

A spot lights the bench outside the WARDEN'*s office where* MRS. BRISTOL *is sitting.* MRS. B *is a worn matron in black, holding a napkin-covered basket on her lap.* EVA *enters the spot from the right and sits on the bench, nervously. She grips her pocketbook tensely and stares straight ahead.*

MRS. B: Your hat!

EVA: My hat?

MRS. B: Yes, look!

EVA: Oh, dear!

MRS. B: Here.

EVA: Thanks!

> [MRS. BRISTOL *removes a spot from* EVA'*s hat with tissue paper from her basket.*]

MRS. B: It's those pigeons, the little rascals!

EVA: Yes, they're much too casual about such things.

MRS. B: It's such a nice hat, too.

EVA: Oh, it's quite old. [*She puts the hat back on and drops her purse.*]

MRS. B: You're nervous.

EVA: So nervous I could scream!

MRS. B: Is it your husband?

EVA: Who?

MRS. B: That you're coming to see about?

EVA: Oh, no. No I'm coming to see about a job.

MRS. B: A job? Here?

EVA: Yes, here. I've heard there's a vacancy.

MRS. B: But wouldn't you find it an awfully depressing sort of place to work in?

EVA: I don't think so. It's not an ordinary prison.

MRS. B: Isn't it?

EVA: No, it's supposed to be a model institution.

MRS. B: A model institution!

EVA: Yes, everything's done scientifically they say. They've got experts—in psychology and sociology and things like that, you know!

MRS. B: Well!

EVA: The old idea used to be punishment of crime but nowadays it's—social rehabilitation!

MRS. B: Now just imagine! How did you come to know?

EVA: I read all about it in the *Sunday Supplement*!

[JIM *passes across the spot.*]

EVA: [*Jumping up.*] May I see the Warden?

JIM: Sorry. He's not back yet. [*He crosses into the door of the office.*]

EVA: Oh.

MRS. B: I've got a son in here. He used to be a sailor. Jack's his name.

EVA: A sailor?

MRS. B: Yes, he was one of Uncle Sam's Navy-boys. Till he got in trouble with some kind of woman.

EVA: What a shame!

MRS. B: Yes, wasn't it though—the common slut!—Excuse me but that's what she was. My Scott! [*She clutches her bosom.*]

EVA: What?

MRS. B: I've got the most awful palpitations!

EVA: [*Jumping up.*] You're sick? Let me get you some water!

MRS. B: No, thanks, dear. I'll just take one of my phenobarbital tablets, and I'll be all right in a jiffy. [*Stage business.*] I've been under such a strain lately with Jack on my mind all the time.

EVA: You shouldn't be worried. My landlady's brother-in-law is one of the guards—it was through him that I heard about this vacancy—and he says they have less serious trouble here than any penitentiary in the country. Mr. Whalen, the Warden, is very highly respected.

MRS. B: Well, I do hope you're right for Jack's sake. But I haven't gotten much comfort out of his letters. Especially the last one. It was that one which upset me so. It wasn't at all like those long marvelous letters that he used to write me when he was at sea. It was scribbled in such a bad hand and—well—it sounded sort of—*feverish* to me!—What is Klondike?

EVA: Klondike? Part of Alaska!

MRS. B: That's what I thought. But in Jack's letter he said he'd been sent down there and it was as hot as—well, I won't say it!

EVA: Possibly it's one of those colonization schemes.

MRS. B: No, I don't think so. In fact I'm positive it isn't. He said they wouldn't let him write me about it if they knew, so he was sneakin' the letter out by one of the boys.

EVA: How long does he have to stay here?

MRS. B: Five years!

EVA: Oh, that's not so long.

MRS. B: It seems like forever to me.

EVA: He'll probably come out a better and stronger boy than before he went in.

MRS. B: Oh no. They couldn't make a better and stronger boy than Jack was.

I don't understand all about it, but I know one thing—whatever happened it wasn't my boy's fault!—And that's what I'm going to say to the Warden soon as I get in to see him—I've been waiting here two days—he never has time!

EVA: [*Rising.*] I can't stand waiting. It makes me too nervous. I'm going right in and make that young fellow tell me when Mr. Whalen will be here.

MRS. B: Yes, do! Tell him how long I've been waiting! And ask him if Jack—

[EVA *has already entered office*—MRS. B *sinks slowly down, clutching her bosom.*]

Oh, dear. . .

[*The spot moves from the bench to the interior of the office.*]

EVA: [*At the door.*] I beg your pardon.

JIM: [*Giving her a long look.*] For what?

EVA: For intruding like this. But I couldn't sit still any longer. When can I see Mr. Whalen?

JIM: What about?

EVA: A job.

[JIM *is filing papers in a cabinet. He continues all the while.*]

JIM: He's out right now. Inspecting the grounds.

EVA: Oh. Will it take him long?

JIM: That depends on how much grounds he feels like inspecting.

EVA: Oh.

JIM: Sometimes inspecting the grounds doesn't mean inspecting the grounds. [*He gives her a brief smile.*]

EVA: Doesn't it?

JIM: No. [*He crumples a paper.*] Sometimes it's an idiomatic expression for having a couple of beers in the back room at Tony's which is a sort of unofficial clubhouse for the prison staff—Would you like to sit down?

EVA: About how long do you suppose I'd have to wait?

JIM: It's a hot afternoon. He might do a lot of ground inspection and then again he might not. His actions are pretty unpredictable. That's a good word.

EVA: What?

JIM: Unpredictable. Anything with five syllables is a good word.

EVA: You like long words?

JIM: They're my stock-in-trade. I'm supposed to use a lot of 'em to impress you with my erudition. There's another one right there!

EVA: Erudition?

JIM: Yes, only four but it's unusual. I get 'em all out of this big book.

EVA: Dictionary?

JIM: *Webster's Unabridged.* [*He slams the file cabinet shut and leans against it.*] Y'see I'm one of the exhibition pieces.

EVA: Are you really?

JIM: I'm supposed to tell you that when I came in here I was just an ordinary grifter. But look at me now. I'm reading Spengler's *Decline of the West* and I'm editor of the prison monthly. Ask me what is an archaeopteryx.

EVA: What is it?

JIM: An extinct species of reptile-bird. Here's our latest issue.

EVA: [*More and more confused.*] Of—what?

JIM: *The Archaeopteryx.* Our monthly publication.

EVA: Why do you call it that?

JIM: It sounds impressive. Do you know what an amaranth is?

EVA: No. What is it'?

JIM: A flower that never dies. [*He lifts a book.*] I came across it in here. One of the classical poets compares it to love. What's your opinion of that?

EVA: Well, I—what's yours?

JIM: I wouldn't know. I started my present career at the age of sixteen.

EVA: That early.

JIM: Yes, the usual case of bad influences. And at that age of course—love is something you dream about and blush when you look at yourself in the mirror next morning! [*He laughs.* EVA *looks away in slight confusion.*] Say, d'you know that song?

EVA: What song?

JIM: [*Giving a sour imitation.*] "Ah, tis love and love alone the world is seeking!" A guy sang it in chapel last night—Is that on the level?

EVA: Well, I—not exactly.

JIM: You're inclined to admit a few qualifications?

EVA: Yes. For instance what I'm seeking is a job. And a, new pair of stockings.

JIM: Those look good to me.

EVA: They're worn to shreds!

JIM: Well, perhaps I'm prejudiced.

[EVA *clears her throat.* JIM *clears his.*]

EVA: [*Picking up the newspaper.*] "Prison: The Door to Opportunity!"

JIM: Yes, that's one of my best editorials. It's been reproduced all over the country—I got ten years of copper for writing that.

EVA: Copper?

JIM: Not what they make pennies out of. In here copper means good time. Time off your sentence for good behavior. I've got about ten years of copper stashed away in the files and most of it's for extolling the inspirational quality of prison life—

[MRS. BRISTOL *enters timidly, clutching her basket.*]

JIM: Hello.

MRS. B: How do you do. Is Mr. Whalen in yet?

JIM: No, he's still out inspecting the grounds.

MRS. B: Oh, I do so want to see him this afternoon. I'm—I'm Jack Bristol's mother.

JIM: Sailor Jack?

MRS. B: [*Advancing a few steps.*] Yes—yes! You—know him?

JIM: Slightly.

MRS. B: [*Struggling to speak.*] How is my boy?

JIM: Sorry. I'm not allowed to give out information.

MRS. B: Oh.

JIM: You'd better talk to Mr. Whalen tomorrow morning.

MRS. B: What time, please?

JIM: Ten o'clock.

MRS. B: Ten o'clock. Could you give him these now? [*She places the basket carefully on the table.*] I'm afraid they'll get stale if they're kept any longer. They're for my boy. [*She turns slowly and goes out.*]

EVA: Couldn't you tell her something to relieve her mind?

JIM: Not about Sailor Jack!

EVA: Why not?

JIM: He's gone—stir bugs.

EVA: You mean?

JIM: [*Touching his forehead.*] Cracked up in here. It's sort of an occupational disease among convicts.

EVA: But they said in the *Sunday Supplement*—

JIM: I know. They interviewed me and the Warden.

EVA: You didn't tell them the truth?

JIM: What is it that Plato said about truth? Truth is—truth is—Funny I can't remember! Was it the *Sunday Supplement* that gave you the idea of getting a job in here?

EVA: That and my landlady. Her brother-in-law is Mr. McBurney, one of the prison guards.

JIM: Mac's a pretty good screw.

EVA: What?

JIM: That means a guard in here. Here's one of our sample menus. It shows what a connie gets to eat every day. You can see that it compares quite favorably with the bill-of-fare at any well-known boarding school. Everything's done scientifically here. We have an expert dietitian. Weighs everything by calories. Units of body heat—Hello, Mr. Whalen!

> [WHALEN *enters. He is a powerful man, rather stout, but with coarse good looks.*]

WARDEN: Hello, hello there! [*He removes his coat and tosses it to* JIM.] Breezy day, hot breezy day! [*He winks at* JIM, *then belches.*] Too much ground-inspection! [*He loosens his collar and tie.*] Excuse me, lady, I'm going to do a striptease! Yep, it's a mighty wind—feels like it comes out of an oven! Reminds me of those—[*He wipes his forehead.*]—those beautiful golden brown biscuits my mother used to bake! What's this? [*He removes the cover from the basket.*] Speak of biscuits and what turns up but a nice batch of homemade cookies! Have one, young lady—Jimmy boy!

> [JIM *takes two.*]

Uh-h, you've got an awful big paw, Jimmy! [*He laughs.*] Show the new Arkywhat's-it to Miss *Daily News*—or is it the *Morning Star*? Have a chair! I'll be right with you—[*He vanishes for a moment into the inner room.*] Sweat, sweat, sweat's all I do these hot breezy days!

JIM: [*Sotto voce.*] He thinks you're a newspaper woman.

WARDEN: [*Emerging.*] Turn on that fan. Well, now, let's see—

EVA: To begin with I'm not—

WARDEN: You've probably come here to question me about that ex-convict's story in that damned yellow sheet down there in Wilkes County—That stuff about getting pellagra in here—Jimmy, hand me that sample menu!

JIM: She's not a reporter.

WARDEN: Aw.—What *is* your business, young lady?

EVA: [*In breathless haste.*] I understand that there's a vacancy here. Mr. McBurney, my landlady's brother-in-law, told her that you were needing a new stenographer, and I'm sure that I can qualify for the position. I'm a college graduate, Mr. Whalen. I've had three years of business experience—references with me—but, oh—I've—I've had such abominable luck these last six months—the last place I worked—the business recession set in—they had to cut down on their salesforce—they gave me a wonderful letter—I've got it with me—[*She opens her purse and spills its contents on the floor.*] Oh, goodness! I've—broken my glasses!

WARDEN: [*Coldly.*] Yeah?

EVA: [*Rising slowly.*] Could you give me a job?—Please, I'm terribly nervous, I— if I don't get a job soon I'll—

WARDEN: What? Go off the deep end?

EVA: Yes, something like that! [*She smiles desperately.*]

WARDEN: Well, Miss—uh—

EVA: [*Eagerly.*] Crane! Eva Crane!

WARDEN: They call that window the "Quick Way Out"! It's the only one in the house without bars. I don't need bars. It's right over the bay. So if it's suicide you got in mind that window is at your disposal. No, Miss Crane. Next time you apply for a job don't pull a sob story. What your business executive is interested in is your potential value, not your—your personal misfortunes! [*He takes a cigar.*]

EVA: [*Turning away.*] I see. Then I—

WARDEN: Hold on a minute.

EVA: Yes?

WARDEN: [*Biting and spitting out the end of the cigar.*] There's just one prerequisite for a job in this office. Jimmy will explain that to you.

EVA: [*Turning to* JIM.] Yes?

JIM: The ability to keep your mouth shut except when you're given specific instructions to speak!

WARDEN: Think you could do that?

EVA: Yes.

JIM: The motorboat leaves the dock at seven forty-five in the morning.

EVA: Thanks—Yes, *thanks*! [*She turns quickly and goes out, blind with joy.*]

WARDEN: What do you think of her, Jimmy boy? Okay, huh?

JIM: Yes, Sir.

WARDEN: Yes, Siree! Dizzy as hell—But she's got a shape on her that would knock the bricks out of a Federal Pen! [*He erupts in sudden booming laughter.*]

Dim Out

Episode Two

ANNOUNCER: "Sailor Jack."

Musical theme up: "Auprès de ma Blonde." Fade.

There is a spot on a cell. Electric lights from the corridor throw the shadow of bars across floor. The cell is empty except for the figure of SAILOR JACK, *slumped on a stool with the shadow of bars thrown across him. His face has the vacant look of the schizophrenic, and he is mumbling inaudibly to himself. His voice rises—*

SAILOR JACK: Where? Port Said!—And not one of 'em but woulda done it 'emselves if they'd 'ad ha'f a chance. [*He begins to sing hoarsely.*]

Auprès de ma blonde
Il fait bon, fait bon, fait bon!
Auprès de ma blonde
qu'il fait bon dormir!

No chance for advancement, huh? What would you say if I told you that I was Admiral of the whole bitchin' navy? [*He laughs.*]

Je donnerai Versailles,
Paris et Saint Denis—

[*Sounds are heard: a shrill whistle in hall and the shuffle of feet: the door of the cell clangs open and* JOE, BUTCH, *and the* QUEEN *enter.*]

SCHULTZ: Lights out in five minutes.

BUTCH: Ahh, yuh fruit, go toot yuh goddam horn outa here. Mus' think they runnin' a stinkin' sweatshop, this workin' overtime stuff. Git yuh task done or come back after supper. Goddam machine got stuck. Delib'rate sabotage, he calls it. I'd like to sabotage his guts. [*To* QUEEN.] What happened to you this mornin'?

QUEEN: [*In a high tenor voice.*] I got an awful pain in the back of my neck and flipped out. When I come to I was in the hospital. They was stickin' a needle in my arm—Say! What does plus four mean?

JOE: Christ! It means—

BUTCH: Pocket yuh marbles!

QUEEN: Naw. Is it bad?

JOE: We're in swell sassiety, Butch. A lunatic an' a case of the syph!

QUEEN: The syph?

[*A whistle is heard: the lights dim in the corridor.*]

QUEEN: Naw! [*He tries to laugh.*] It don't mean that!

SAILOR: *Auprès de ma blonde*
   II fait bon, fait bon, fait bon!
   Auprès de ma blonde—

SCHULTZ: Cut the cackle in there! It's after lights.

BUTCH: God damn it, can't you see he's blown his top?

JOE: Yeah, get him out of here!

SCHULTZ: He's putting on an act.

SAILOR: *Je donnerai Versailles,*
   Paris et Saint Denis—

SCHULTZ: You take another trip to Klondike, Sailor, it won't be on a round-trip ticket!

BUTCH: It's Klondike that got him like this. He's been ravin' ever since you brung him upstairs. You must've cooked the brains out of him down there, Schultz.

SAILOR: *La Tour d'Eiffel aussi!*

SCHULTZ: [*Rapping the bars.*] Dummy up, the lot of you! One more squawk an' I'll call the strong-arm squad!

QUEEN: Mr. Schultz!

SCHULTZ: Yeah?

QUEEN: What does plus four mean?

[SCHULTZ *laughs and moves off.*]

BUTCH: If I wasn't scared of losin' all my copper I'd reach through and grab

433

that bastard. I'd rattle them pea-pod brains of his 'n roll 'em out on the floor like a pair of dice. The trouble is in here you gotta pick your man. If I rubbed out a screw I'd never git a chance at the boss.—What time is it?

JOE: Ten-thirty.

BUTCH: Mac comes on duty now.

JOE: You think he'll take the Sailor out?

BUTCH: I'll tell him to.

QUEEN: Naw. It's nothin' that serious or they woulda kept me in the hospital. It's just indigestion. That's what I told 'em, I said the food is no good. It don't set good on my stomach. Spaghetti, spaghetti, spaghetti! I said I'm sicka spaghetti!

SAILOR: *Auprès de ma blonde*
Il fait bon, fait bon, fait bon!
Auprès de ma blonde
qu 'il fair bon dormir!

[BUTCH *clips him with a fist.*]

JOE: What did you do that for?

BUTCH: You wanta tangle with the strong-arm squadron on account of him?

[*A whistle is heard: doors clang.*]

They're changin' now. [*He goes to the bars.*] Who's 'at? McBurney?

MAC: What do you want, Butch?

BUTCH: For Chrissakes git this kid outta here.

MAC: Which kid?

BUTCH: Sailor Jack. He's been stir-bugs since they brung him upstairs a week ago Tuesday.

MAC: [*At the door.*] What's he doing?

BUTCH: He's out right now. I had to conk him one.

MAC: What did they tell you about roughin' up the boys?

434

BUTCH: Roughin'? ME? Lissen!—Ask Joe, ask anybody, ask the Canary—the kid had blown his top—Schultz was gonna call the strong-arm squad an' have us all thrown in Klondike cause he wouldn't quit singin' them dirty French songs! Ain't that right, Joe?

JOE: Sure, Mac.

    [*Whistle.*]

MAC: Where's his stuff?

BUTCH: Here. I got it tied up nice.

MAC: Well, it's no put-in of mine. He should've done his task in the shop.

BUTCH: He done his task pretty good.

JOE: That boy worked hard.

MAC: Not hard enough to suit the Boss.

    [*Enter guards.*]

Awright, git him outta here. Put him in isolation tonight an' have him looked after tomorrow.

QUEEN: Mr. McBurney, what does plus four mean? Mr. McBurney—

    [MAC *goes out with guards carrying* SAILOR. *Bird calls are heard in the hall.*]

VOICE: [*In hall.*] Goodnight, Mac.

MAC: G'night, Jim.

BUTCH: Who's 'at? Allison?

JOE: Yeah. It's the Canary.

SAILOR: [*From down the hall.*] "*Auprès de ma blonde, Il fait bon, fait bon, fait bon!*"

    [*The sound fades.*]

BUTCH: Hey, Canary! Allison!

    [*The spot shifts to include* ALLISON's *cell.*]

JIM: What do you want, Butch? [*He is shown removing his shirt and shoes.*]

BUTCH: Next time you're in a huddle with the boss tell him the Angels in Hall C have put another black mark on his name for Sailor Jack.

JIM: I'll tell him that.

BUTCH: Tell him some day we're going to appoint a special committee of one to come down there an' settle up the score.—You hear me, Stool?

JIM: I hear you.

BUTCH: Just think—I used to be cell-mates with him. I lie awake at night regrettin' all the times I had a chance to split his guts—but didn't!

JOE: Why didn'tcha?

BUTCH: That was before he started workin' for the boss. But now he's number three on the Angel's Records. First Whalen, then Schultz, and then the Stool! You hear that, Stool?

JIM: Yes, I hear you, Butch. [*He rolls and lights a cigarette.*]

BUTCH: That's good. I'm glad you do.

JIM: I know you're glad.

JOE: What's he say?

BUTCH: He says he knows I'm glad.

JOE: He oughta know. Wonder he don't go stir-bugs, too. Nobody have nothin' to do with him but Ollie.

BUTCH: He'll blow his top sometime, if I don't git him first. You hear that, Stool? I said you'll blow your top sometime like Sailor Jack—I'm lookin' forward to it.

JOE: What's he say?

BUTCH: Nothin'. He's smokin' in there.

JOE: We oughta tip 'em off.

BUTCH: Naw, I never ratted on nobody. Not even that Stool.

QUEEN: Allison! Hey! Jim! What does plus four mean?

436

JIM: Who's got plus four?

QUEEN: I have. What does it mean, Jim?

JIM: It means your physical condition is four points above perfect.

QUEEN: [*Relieved.*] Aw. These bastards had me worried.

BUTCH: [*Climbing on a stool by the window.*] Foghorns. It's thick as soup outside— Lissen!

JOE: What?

BUTCH: Excursion steamer.

JOE: Which one?

BUTCH: The Lorelei.

JOE: Lookit them lights on her, will yuh. Red, white, green, yellow!

BUTCH: Hear that orchester?

JOE: What're they playin'?

BUTCH: "Roses a Picardy!"

JOE: That's an old one.

BUTCH: It come up the year I got sent up. Why, I remember dancin' to that piece. At the Princess Ballroom. With Goldie. She requested that number ev'ry time I took her out on the floor. We danced there the night they pinched me. On the way out—right at the turnstile—them six bulls met me—six of 'em— that's how many it took—they had the wagon waitin' at the curb.

JOE: Last time it was four bulls. You're gettin' less conservative, Butch.

BUTCH: "Roses a Picardy." I'd like to dance that number one more time. With Goldie.

JOE: Maybe it was her that put the finger on you.

BUTCH: Naw. Not Goldie. I bet that girl's still holdin' the torch for me.

JOE: Keep your illusions, Butch, if they're a comfort to yuh. But I bet if Goldie was still holdin' all the torches that she's held before an' after you got put in the stir she'd throw more light across the water than a third-alarm fire!

QUEEN: Where's my manicure set?

BUTCH: I wonder if a guy is any good at sixty?

JOE: What do you mean?

BUTCH: You know. With women.

JOE: I guess it depends on the guy.

BUTCH: I'll still be good. But twenty years is a lot of time to wait.

QUEEN: Has anybody seen my manicure set?

BUTCH: You know there's a window in Boss Whalen's office from which a guy could jump right into the Bay.

JOE: Yeah. The Quick Way Out.

BUTCH: I was thinkin' that it would be a good way to kill two birds with a stone. Rub him out an' jump through that window for the getaway. Providin' you could swim. But me I can't swim a goddam stroke. I wish that I'd learned how before I come in here.

JOE: Wouldn't do you no good. Nobody's ever swum it yet.

BUTCH: I'd like to try.—They say some people swim instinctive like a duck.

JOE: You'd take a chance on that?

BUTCH: Naw. I'm scared a water.

QUEEN: [*Excitedly.*] I put it here last night. Butch, did you see it?

BUTCH: What?

QUEEN: My manicure set.

BUTCH: It's gone out wit' the slop-bucket.

QUEEN: What did you do that for?

BUTCH: It stunk up the place. Smelt like rotten bananas—What's this on Sailor Jack's bunk?

JOE: A package a letters from his ole lady.

BUTCH: Aw.

438

JOE: She said she was comin' from Wisconsin to see him in the last one.

QUEEN: All my life I've been persecuted by people because I'm refined.

BUTCH: Somebody oughta told her how the Sailor is.

JOE: Well, she'll find out.

QUEEN: Because I'm sensitive I been persecuted all my life!

BUTCH: Yeah, she'll find out.

QUEEN: Sometimes I wish I was dead. Oh, Lord, Lord, Lord! I wish I was dead!

[*Musical theme up. Fade.*]

Blackout

Episode Three

ANNOUNCER: "The Prognosis"

A spot comes up on the WARDEN*'s office. He's looking at a racing form-sheet when* EVA CRANE, *his secretary, enters.*

WARDEN: [*Lifting the phone and dialing.*] How's the track, Bert? Fast? Okay. I want twenty bucks on Windy Blue to show. [*He hangs up.*] Anybody outside?

EVA: Yes. That woman.

WARDEN: What woman?

EVA: The one from Wisconsin. She's still waiting—

WARDEN: I told you I—

[SAILOR JACK*'s mother has quietly entered. She carries a neatly wrapped bundle in brown paper—she smiles diffidently at the* WARDEN.]

MRS. B: I beg your pardon, I—I took the liberty of coming in. I hope you won't mind. You see I'm Jack Bristol's mother and I've been wanting to have a talk with you so long about—about my boy!

WARDEN: Set down. I'm pretty short on time.

MRS. B: I won't take much. To begin with, Mr. Whalen, I never felt the jury did exactly right in giving Jack three years. But that's done now. I've got to look to the future.

WARDEN: Yes, the future—that's right.

MRS. B: I haven't heard from Jack lately. He'd been writing me once a week till just lately.

WARDEN: Lots of boys get careless about their correspondence.

MRS. B: For two years not a week passed without a letter. Then suddenly just a month ago they stopped coming. Naturally I felt rather anxious.

WARDEN: Jim!

JIM: Yes, sir?

WARDEN: Check on a boy named Bristol.

MRS. B: Thank you, I—I came all the way from Wisconsin.

WARDEN: Long trip, huh? Wisconsin's where they make all that fine cheese.

MRS. B: Yes, we're very proud of our dairy products up there.

> [*She looks anxiously after* JIM *who has gone slowly to the filecase as though stalling for time.*]

WARDEN: They manufacture the best cheese this side of Switzerland. Yes, Siree!

MRS. B: Jack's last letter was strange. I—I have it with me. It's not at all like Jack. He wasn't transferred to any other prison, was he? Because he kept complaining all through his letter about how terribly hot it was in a place called Klondike. His penmanship has always been quite irregular but this was so bad I could scarcely read it at all—I thought possibly he wasn't well when he wrote it—feverish, you know—he's very subject to colds especially this time of year. I—I brought this wool comforter with me. For Jack. I know it's not easy, Mr. Whalen, to make exceptions in an institution like this. But in Jack's case where there are so many, *many* considerations—so much that I regret *myself* when I look back at things—Mistakes that I made—

WARDEN: Mistakes, yes, we all make mistakes.

MRS. B: Such *grave* mistakes, Mr. Whalen. Our household was not an altogether happy one, you see. Jack's father—well, he was a Methodist minister and his views naturally differed quite a bit from most young boys'—

WARDEN: [*With a cynical smile.*] A preacher's son?

MRS. B: Yes! But there was a disagreement among the congregation not long ago and my husband was forced to retire.

WARDEN: [*Impatiently.*] I see. I'm very busy, I—[*To* JIM.] Have you found that card?

JIM: [*Stalling.*] Not yet.

MRS. B: He was so—so uncompromising, even with poor Jack. So Jack left home. Of course it was against my wishes but—[*She opens her bag and produces sheaf of letters.*] Oh, those long marvelous letters that he wrote! If you would only read them you'd see for yourself what an exceptional boy Jack was. Port Said,

Marseilles, Cairo, Shanghai, Bombay! "Oh, mother, it's so big, so terribly, terribly big," he kept on writing. As though he'd tried to squeeze it in his heart until the bigness of it made this heart crack open! Look! These envelopes! You see they're packed so full that he could hardly close them! Pictures of places, too! Elephants in India. They're used like pack-horses, he said, for common labor. Little Chinese junkets have square sails. They scoot about like dragonflies on top of the water. The bay at Rangoon. Here's where the sun comes up like thunder, he wrote on the back of this one! Kipling, you know—I wrote him constantly— "Jack, there's no advancement in it. A sailor's always a sailor. Get out of it, son. Get into the Civil Service!" He wrote me back— "I kept the middle watch last night. You see more stars down here than in the northern water. The Southern Cross is right above me now, but won't be long— because our course is changing—" I stopped opposing then, I thought that anything he loved as much as that would surely keep him safe. And then he didn't write a while—until this came. I still can't understand it! He mentioned a girl—He said it wasn't his fault, I know that it wasn't—If I could convince you of that!

WARDEN: It's no use ma'am! You might as well be talking to the moon. He's had his chance.

MRS. B: But in Jack's case—!

WARDEN: I know, I know. I've heard all that before. Jim, have you found that card?

JIM: [*Coming slowly forward with a card from files.*] You'd better look at it yourself.

WARDEN: Read it, read it! We running a social service bureau?

[JIM *looks uncertainly at* MRS. BRISTOL *who raises a clenched hand to her breast.*]

MRS. B: [*Softly.*] If anything's gone wrong I'd like to know.

JIM: [*Reading huskily.*] "Jack Bristol. Larceny. Convicted May, 1936. Sentenced three years." [*Looks up.*] He slacked his work. Spent three days in Klondike.

WARDEN: [*Sharply.*] Is that on the card?

JIM: No, but I wanted to explain to this lady what happened.

MRS. B: [*Rising slowly.*] What happened?

JIM: You see, ma'am—

WARDEN: [*Sharply.*] Read what's on the card, that's all!

JIM: "Came up before the lunacy commission, May 1938, transferred to the psychopathic ward. Violent. Delusions. Prognosis—Dementia Praecox"—

[*Pause.*]

MRS. B: That isn't—Jack—my boy!

WARDEN: Now see here—I—[*He motions to* JIM *to get her out.*] I know how you feel about this. I got all the sympathy in the world for you women that come in here, but this is a penal institution and we simply can't be taking time out from our routine business for things like this.

MRS. B: My boy, Jack, my boy! Not what you said! Anything but that! Say he's dead, say you killed him, killed him! But don't tell me that. I know, I know. I know how it was in here. He wrote me letters. The food not decent. I tried to send him food—he didn't get it—no, even that you took from him. That place you sent him three days. Klondike. I know—You tortured him there, that's what you did, you tortured him until you drove him—[*She turns slowly to* JIM.]—Crazy? Is that what you said?—Oh, my precious Jesus, oh, my God! [*She breaks down, sobbing wildly.*]

WARDEN: Get that woman out!

[JIM *assists her to the door.*]

Whew! [*He lights a cigar and picks up the form-sheet.*]

Blackout

Episode Four

ANNOUNCER: "Conversations at Midnight!"

The spot lights the two cells with a partition between. OLLIE *kneels praying by his bunk.* BUTCH *lounges, covertly smoking, on a bench along the wall. The others sit on their bunks.*

OLLIE: [*In an audible whisper.*] Oh, Lawd, de proteckter an preserbation ob all, remebuh dis nigguh. Remebuh his wife Susie an his six chillun, Rachel, Rebekah, Solomon, Moses, Ecclesiastics an' Deuteronomy Jackson. You look out fo' dem while Ise in jail. An ah'd git out fo de cole weathuh sets in cause Susie's gonna have another baby, Lawd,' an' she can't git aroun't' gatherin' kindlin' wood. God bless my ole Woman an' daddy an' Presiden' Roosevelt an' de W.P.A.* in Jesus Chris' name—Amen. [*He rises stiffly.*]

BUTCH: [*Grinning.*] Hey, Ollie, yuh better have 'em reverse the charges on that one!

OLLIE: It don' cos' nothin'.

BUTCH: It ain't worth nothin'.

OLLIE: De Lawd remembuhs who remembuhs Him.

BUTCH: Hawshit!

> [OLLIE *sits dejectedly on the edge of his bunk. There are derisive whistles and bird-calls in the hall as* JIM *enters.*]

JIM: Whatsamatter, Ollie?

OLLIE: [*Jerking his thumb at* BUTCH'*s cell.*] He says there ain't no God.

JIM: How's he know?

OLLIE: That's what I say.

> [JIM *removes his shirt and swabs sweat off his face and chest with it, then pitches it into the corner. He picks up a naked art magazine and fans himself with it.*]

---

* The Works Progress Administration (W.P.A) was a Depression-era agency created by President Franklin D. Roosevelt and the United States Congress in 1935 to give employment to persons on the relief rolls.

OLLIE: You think they is, don't you, Jim?

JIM: Somebody upstairs?—I dunno. I guess I'm what they call an agnostic.

OLLIE: You mean a Piscopalian?

JIM: Yeah. Rub my back for me, Ollie. I'm tired.

OLLIE: Awright. Liniment aw bacon grease?

JIM: Gimme the liniment.

BUTCH: Haven't you started seein' 'em yet, Canary?

JIM: [*As* OLLIE *starts to rub.*] Gawd, it burns good.

BUTCH: Them little blue devils, they're the first symptom.

JIM: It makes the air feel cool.

BUTCH: They crawl in through the bars an' sit on the end of yuh bunk an' make faces at yuh.

JIM: Rub harder on the left shoulder.

BUTCH: Yuh'd better start sleepin' with one eye open, Canary. Can yuh do that?

JIM: Never tried it, Butch.—Ah, that's good.

BUTCH: Well, yuh better, cause if they catch you off guard, Canary, they'll climb down yuh throat an' tie knots in yuh gizzard! [*He laughs delightedly at the prospect.*]

JIM: That's good, ah that's—swell.

OLLIE: How'd you get them purple scars, Jim?

JIM: From Dr. Jones.

OLLIE: Who's Dr. Jones?

BUTCH: Dr. Jones is the guy that gave Canary his singin' lessons! Remembuh when I found out that you'd grown feathers?

JIM: [*To* OLLIE.] That's enough. Thanks. [*He produces cigarettes.*] Have one?

OLLIE: Thanks, Jim.

BUTCH: It's lucky for you that I was interrupted—or you'd be readin' books witcha fingers instead of yer eyes! It's listed on th' record as unfinished business, to be took care of at some future date—I figure that ev'ry dog has his day an' mine's comin' pretty soon now.

OLLIE: Don't pay him no mind.

JIM: Naw. There's a wall between him an' me.

BUTCH: You bet there is. Or you'd be a dead Canary. There'd be yellow feathers floating all over Hall C!

JIM: [*Exhaling smoke as he speaks—à la Jules Garfield*.*] There's a wall like that around ev'ry man in here an' outside of here, Ollie.

OLLIE: Outside? Naw!

JIM: Sure there is. Ev'ry man living is walking around in a cage. He carries it with him wherever he goes and don't let it go till he's dead. Then the walls come to pieces and he stops being lonesome—

  [BUTCH *grins delightedly and nudges* JOE; *he describes a circle with his finger and points at* JIM's *cell. They both crouch grinning, listening, on the bench by the wall.*]

—Cause he's part of something bigger than him.

OLLIE: Bigger than him?

JIM: Yes.

OLLIE: What's that?

JIM: [*Blowing an enormous smoke ring and piercing it with his finger.*] The Universe!

  [BUTCH *erupts in hoarse derisive laughter.*]

JIM: [*Ignoring* BUTCH's *outburst.*] But, sometimes, I think, Ollie, a guy don't have to wait till he's dead to get outside of his cage.

OLLIE: Yuh mean he should bump himself off?

JIM: No. A guy can use his brain two ways. He can make it a wall to shut him

---

* John Garfield, actor, whose real name was Julius Garfinkle, was known as Jules Garfield on the stage. The 1938 film *Four Daughters* features him smoking, a cigarette dangling from his mouth.

in from the world or a great big door to let him out. [*He continues musingly.*] Intellectual emancipation!

OLLIE: Huh?

[BUTCH *gives a long whistle.*]

What's that?

JIM: Couple of words I came across in a book.

OLLIE: Sound like big words.

JIM: They are big words. So big that the *world* hangs on 'em. They can tell us what to read, what to say, what to do—But they can't tell us what to *think*! And as long as man can think as he pleases he's never exactly locked up anywhere. He can think himself outside of all their walls and boundaries and make the world his place to live in—It's a swell feeling, Ollie, when you've done that. It's like being alone on the top of a mountain at night with nothing around you but stars. Only you're not alone, though, cause you know that you're part of everything living and everything living is part of you. Then you get an idea of what God is. Not Mr. Santie Claus, Ollie, dropping answers to prayers down chimneys—

OLLIE: Naw?

JIM: No, not that. But something big and terrible as night is, and yet—

OLLIE: Huh?

JIM: And yet—as soft as a woman. Y'see what I mean?

BUTCH: I see whatcha mean—it's kind of a—*balmy* feeling! [BUTCH *and* JOE *laugh.* JIM *looks resentfully at wall.*]

JIM: You guys don't get what I'm talking about.

OLLIE: [*Musingly.*] Naw, but I do. Thinkin's like prayin', excep' that prayin' yuh feel like yuh've got some one on the other end a th' line ...

JIM: [*Smiling.*] Yeah.

[*The spot fades on* JIM's *cell and focuses on* BUTCH's.]

QUEEN: Be quiet, you *all*. I'm sick. I need my sleep. [*He mutters to himself.*]

447

[*A searchlight from river shines on the window.*]

JOE: Where's that light from?

BUTCH: [*At the window.*] Anudder boat load a goddam jitterbugs. Dey're trowin th' glims on us. Whaddaya think this is? Th' Municipal Zoo or something? Go to hell, yuh sons-a bitches, yuh lousy—

SCHULTZ: [*Rapping at the bars with a stick.*] After lights in there!

BUTCH: Someday it's gonna be permanuntly 'after lights' for that old screw.

JOE: [*Twisting on bed.*] Oooooo!

BUTCH: Bellyache?

JOE: Yeah, from them stinkin' meatballs. By God I'm gonna quit eatin' if they don't start puttin' in more digestable food.

BUTCH: [*Reflectively.*] Quit eating, huh?—I think yuh got something there.

JOE: Oooooo—*Christ*! [*He draws his knees up to his chin.*]

BUTCH: You ever heard of a hunger-strike, Joe?

JOE: Uh.

BUTCH: Sometimes it works. Gits in the papers. Starts investigations. They git better food,

JOE: Oooooooo! We'd git—*uh*!—Klondike!

BUTCH: Klondike won't hold thirty-five hundred men.

JOE: No. But Hall C would go first on account of our reputation.

BUTCH: Okay. We'll beat Klondike.

JOE: You talk too big sometimes. You ever been in Klondike?

BUTCH: Yeah. Once.

JOE: What's it like?

BUTCH: It's a little suburb of hell.

JOE: That's what I thought.

BUTCH: They got radiators all aroun' the walls an' there ain't no windows.

JOE: Christ Almighty!

BUTCH: Steam hisses outa the valves like this. [*He imitates the sound.*] Till it gits so thick you can't see nothing around you. It's like breathin' fire in yer lungs. The floor is so hot you can't stand on it, but there's no place else to stand—

JOE: How do yuh live?

BUTCH: There's an air hole about this size at the bottom of the wall. But when there's a bunch in Klondike they git panicky an' fight over the air hole an' the ones that ain't strong don't make it.

JOE: It kills 'em?

BUTCH: Sure. Unless the Boss takes 'em out. And when you beat Klondike you beat everything they've got to offer in here. It's their Ace of Spades!

QUEEN: [*Rising sleepily on his bunk.*] What's that about Klondike, Butch?

JOE: Nothing. He's talking in his sleep.

QUEEN: I dreamed about Klondike one night.

JOE: Did ja?

QUEEN: Sure. That was the night I woke up screaming. Re member?

JOE: Sure. I remember.—Oooooo! Uhhhhhh! Ahhhhhh! Jesus! [*He springs out of bed and crouches on the floor, clasping his stomach.*]

Blackout

Episode Five

ANNOUNCER: "Band Music!"

Theme up: Tchaikovsky, "1812 Overture," 2nd Theme. Fade.

A spot comes up on the office. JIM *is settled comfortably in a chair by the window, writing.* EVA *enters.*

EVA: [*Brightly.*] Good morning.

JIM: Hi.

EVA: [*Removing her hat, etc.*] I believe you spend more time here than the boss does.

JIM: I like it here. Especially when I'm alone.

EVA: Oh—well, excuse my intrusion.

JIM: I don't mean you. You don't bother me. [*His immediate tension at her entrance belies this.*]

EVA: Thanks.

JIM: [*Watching her as she removes the cover from the machine.*] As a matter of fact it's a rare and enviable privilege for a connie to get close to a member of the opposite sex.

EVA: Really?

JIM: Yes. Really and truly. I have to blink my eyes a couple of times to be sure you're not just one of them—visual and auditory hallucinations—that some fellows develop in stir.

EVA: [*Inserting a form-sheet in the typewriter.*] Wasn't there a girl working here before me?

JIM: There was. But she wasn't nearly such a strain upon one's—credulity.

EVA: How do you mean?

JIM: She was sort of a cow.

EVA: Oh.

JIM: Whalen's wife's second cousin. But he's a remarkable man.

EVA: [*Whose typing obscured the last phrase.*] He is or she is?

JIM: They both were. [*He laughs.*] Now you know why I'm called the Canary. I talk too much.

EVA: No. In what way?

JIM: [*Thumbing toward the inner room.*] He had her in there the first week.

EVA: What's in there?

JIM: He goes in there to relax after ground-inspection. She would go in there with him.—She died of an operation and Whalen bought his wife a mink coat. How do you like your new job?

EVA: Well!—Not so good now.

JIM: There's some features of life on the grounds that aren't mentioned in the *Sunday Supplement*.

EVA: Yes. I didn't sleep last night.

JIM: No?

EVA: From thinking about that boy's mother.

JIM: You'll get used to things like that.

EVA: I don't want to get used to them.

JIM: Why don't you quit, then?

EVA: Say! You don't know much about the unemployment situation.

JIM: No. I got here before the Depression.

EVA: You're lucky.

JIM: Think so?

EVA: There was a case in the paper where a man busted a plate-glass window so he could go to jail and get something to eat.

JIM: I bet he regretted it afterwards. Especially if he came here.

EVA: I don't know. The sample menu's okay.

JIM: Huh! We spill that stuff on everybody comes in the office to cover up what's actually going on.

EVA: [*Removing the form-sheet.*] What's that?

JIM: Starvation.

EVA: You're crazy!

JIM: Sure I am, crazy as a bedbug! But I've still got sense enough to recognize beans an' hamburger an' spaghetti when I see them six or seven times a week in slightly variegated combinations! You wonder why we make such a fuss about eating? Well, I'll tell you why. It's because eating's all we got. We got nothing else, no women to sleep with, no hammers, no shovels, no papers to write on, no automobiles, no golf—nothin' to do but eat—so eating's important to us. And when they make that so darned monotonous that you feel like puking at the sight of it—then they're putting the match to a keg of powder! [*He lights his cigarette.*] Ask me what is a pyrotechnical display!

EVA: I think I know.

JIM: You'll know better if you stick around. We're going to have the loveliest Fourth o'July you ever laid eyes on. Only it's going to come, maybe in the middle of August. Y'see I've got my ear to the ground—in here and in Hall C— This place, lady, is the practical equivalent of Mt. Vesuvius. Maybe a hundred years from now little woolly white lambs will be grazing peacefully on the slopes of an extinct volcano. But down at the bottom tourist guides will be pointing out the bones of people who didn't get out of Pompeii!

EVA: Too bad you won't be one of the guides. You make such good speeches.

JIM: Okay. Be funny about it.

        [*The sound of a brass band playing a martial air in the assembly hall is heard.*]*

EVA: [*Her face brightening.*] Band music!

---

* In the margin of his original typescript Williams has written: "Bells in the Burning City—1812 Overture—Tschaikovsky." This seems to relate to Jim's mention of fireworks and the 4th of July, Independence Day, when the Festival Overture is traditionally performed in the United States. The symphony's ending with the sound of canon fire is the signal for a fireworks display.

JIM: Yes. They're practicing for the Commissioner's banquet.

EVA: [*Rising.*] Sounds very gay!

JIM: Uh-huh. If you believed in brass bands you'd think the millennium was going to arrive at exactly 6 A.M. tomorrow.

EVA: [*Facing him with desperate gaiety.*] Why not? Maybe it will!—A brass band can sell me *anything*, Jim!

JIM: Can it sell you this? [*He catches her against him in a hard impulsive embrace.*]

EVA: [*Breaking away.*] Yes, it could even sell me that! [*Then she laughs.*]—But not in the Warden's office!

[*She goes quickly back to her typing*—JIM *stands motionless looking at her back his arms raised slowly—the hands clench into fists—they vibrate, outstretched, with a terrific intensity—then slowly fall to his sides.* EVA *whistles gaily to the band music.*]

Dim Out

Episode Six

ANNOUNCER: "Mister Olympics!"

A spot comes up on the cell. Men have just returned from supper.

JOE: Did you eat yours?

BUTCH: Eat that stuff? Naw. It made me sick to look at it.

JOE: Spaghetti four times a week!

BUTCH: That's nutten. I useta work in a spaghetti factory.

QUEEN: Really?

BUTCH: Yeah. I remember one time the spaghetti machines got out of control. We couldn't stop 'em. The whole place was full of spaghetti. It was spaghetti ev'rywhere, oozin' out of the floor an' the walls, an' the ceilin', spaghetti, spaghetti, blockin' up the windows an' the doors, a big suffocatin' mass of spaghetti.

QUEEN: Please!

BUTCH: So I says to the foreman, "For Chrissakes, how we gonna git outa this place wit' all this spaghetti sloppin' aroun' ev'rywhere?"—An' the boss says, "Boys—there's only one way to git out of here now!"—"How's that?" I ast him.—"Here!" he says—an' he han's me a big knife an' fork—"Yuh got to EAT yuh way out!"

QUEEN: Oh, for the love of nasturtiums!

[*The steel doors clang.*]

VOICE: Hello, new boy! [*Other greetings are given.*]

BUTCH: They're bringin' a new boy in.

[SCHULTZ *stops in front of the cell with* SWIFTY.]

SCHULTZ: Here's yer boudoir, Sonny.

SWIFTY: Here?

SCHULTZ: Yeah. Here. [*He shoves him roughly in and slams the door.*]

SWIFTY: What did he do that for? Shove me! I was going in, wasn't I?

JOE: Sure you was going in. He just wanted to help you.

SWIFTY: I don't like being pushed around like that.

JOE: I'd complain to the Governor.

SWIFTY: [*Pausing as he looks about.*] I've got an appeal coming before the Governor.

JOE: Have you now?

SWIFTY: Yes, I didn't get a fair trial. I was railroaded up here. My lawyer said so.

JOE: Your lawyer said so.

SWIFTY: Yes, he said—Hey, do we all stay in here together like this? Jeez, it's too small!

JOE: What's that your lawyer said?

SWIFTY: He said—What's that? A cockroach! Gosh—I don't like being cooped up like this!

JOE: What did your lawyer say?

SWIFTY: He said for me to sit tight. He'd have me out of here in two weeks, a month at the most.

JOE: A month at the most! What do you think of that, Butch?

BUTCH: I think it's a lot of what they use shovels to clean off the stable floor! [*He rises.*]—That's your new bunk, new boy. Get up there an' lissen to what I tell yuh.—Go on!

SWIFTY: Quit shoving!

BUTCH: Huh?

SWIFTY: I told you I don't like being pushed around!

BUTCH: [*Exhibiting his fists.*] When you talk back to me you're talking back to this!—Now git up there an' pay attention to what I say.

SWIFTY: Why should I take orders from you? You're not one of the officials around here.

BUTCH: Ain't I?

SWIFTY: No!

BUTCH: Lissen, buddy. In Spain, it's Mussolini.

JOE: You mean Italy it's Mussolini.

BUTCH: I mean wherever there's wops! An' in Germany it's that monkey wit' the trick mustache!—But in here it's Butch O'Fallon! And Butch O'Fallon is me! So now that we've been properly introduced I would like to repeat my polite invitation to remove your butt from my bunk an' git up in your own! [BUTCH *jerks* SWIFTY *up by the collar and hoists him by the seat of his pants to the upper bunk.*] What's yuh name?

SWIFTY: Jeremy Trout.

BUTCH: This yuh first stretch?

SWIFTY: Yes. What of it?

BUTCH: What's yuh rap?

SWIFTY: I was indicted for—stealing—money.

BUTCH: What from?

SWIFTY: Cash register in a chain store. I was cashier. But I didn't do it. I was framed by a couple of clerks.

BUTCH: I believe you. You don't look like you'd have gumption enough to crack a till. How much you got?

SWIFTY: On me? Nothing. They even took my cigarettes.

BUTCH: I mean your stretch. How long?

SWIFTY: Judge Eggleston gave me five years. But my lawyer says—

BUTCH: You'll do five years.

SWIFTY: In here? Why, I'd go crazy locked in here that long!

BUTCH: Pocket yuh marbles!

SWIFTY: I—I feel sick. The air in here's no good.

BUTCH: No?

SWIFTY: It smells. It's making me sick at the stomach.

BUTCH: There's the slop bucket.

SWIFTY: No!

BUTCH: It ain't been emptied yet. That's your job. The new man always empties.

SWIFTY: No—[*He sinks into his bunk*.]—Five years? I couldn't stand being cooped up that long. I got to have space around me. I get restless. That's why I didn't like working in the chain store. Kept me behind a counter all day, felt like I was tied up there.—At high school I was a runner.

BUTCH: A runner, huh?

QUEEN: That's what I said to myself. He looks athletic.

SWIFTY: Yes. I held the 220 state record for three years.

BUTCH: Fancy that.

SWIFTY: I like anything that's moving, that don't stay put. It's not an ordinary thing with me, it's kind of an obsession. I like to kill distance. See a straight track—get to the other end of it first, before anyone else—That's what I was made for—running—look at my legs!

JOE: Pips, huh?

SWIFTY: That's from training. If this hadn't happened I'd be on my way to the Olympics right now. I could still have a chance at the New York eliminations if my lawyer can spring me before the fifteenth. [*He flexes his legs*.]—But look at that! Getting loose already!—If I could get permission to run around the yard a few times—say, before breakfast or supper—why, I could keep in pretty good shape even in here. Even if I had to stay in here a year—that way I could keep in condition!

JOE: He'll go like Sailor Jack.

BUTCH: Pocket yuh marbles!—Buddy, I ain't sentimental—but I feel sorry for you.

SWIFTY: Why? Don't you think he'll let me?

BUTCH: Naw.

SWIFTY: Why not?

BUTCH: Because you're a con.

SWIFTY: But a con's a human being. He's got to be treated like one.

BUTCH: A con ain't a human being. A con's a con. [*The lights fade on the others and concentrate on* BUTCH.] He's stuck in here and the world's forgot him. As far as the world is concerned he don't exist anymore. What happens to him in here—them people outside don't know, they don't care. He's entrusted to the care of the State. The State? Hell! The State turns him over to a guy called a Warden and a bunch of other guys called guards. Who're they? Men who like to boss other men. Maybe they could've been truckdrivers or street cleaners or circus clowns. But they didn't wanta be none a them. Why? Cause they've got a natural instinck for swinging a shelailee! They like to crack heads, make sausage out of human flesh! And so they get to be guards. That sounds like 'gods'—which ain't so much a coincidence either, because the only difference between 'guards' an' 'gods' is that 'guards' has an 'r' in it an' the 'r' stands for 'rat'!—That's what a guard is accordin' to my definition— 'A rat who thinks that he's GOD!'—You better not forget that. Because, Sonny, you're not in high school no more. You ain't in the chain store, you're not at the Olympics— That's Part One of your education. Part Two is stay away from stool pigeons. Hey, Canary!—He ain't in yet but we got a little songbird in the next cage who sings real sweetly sometimes for the boss.—So don't be buddies wit him. Give 'im a cigarette, Joe.

JOE: Here, mister Olympics.

BUTCH: Keep it covered.—How's yuh stomach now?

SWIFTY: Some better.

BUTCH: Hungry?

SWIFTY: No.

BUTCH: That's good. Because we might quit eating.

QUEEN: Quit eating?

BUTCH: Yep. I been thinkin' over what we talked about las' night, Joe, an' I'm just about sold on it.

JOE: I'm still on the fence about that.

BUTCH: There ain't any fence to be on, Joe. When I say hunger strike in here it's going to be hunger strike.

QUEEN: Hunger strike!

SWIFTY: What's that?

BUTCH: Pocket yuh marbles. The Canary's comin' to roost.

[*Derisive whistles are heard in the hall.*]

Help me off wit' these shoes, Queenie. That's right. Here, hang up my shirt. Joe—

JOE: What the hell?

BUTCH: You fold my pants up nice an' lay 'em over the chair.—Hello, moon. [*He stands in a shaft of moonlight through the barred window.*]

JOE: You're going like Sailor Jack, saying hello to the moon!

BUTCH: She's big an' yellow tonight. Y'know me an' God have got something in common, Joe.

JOE: Yeah, what's that?

BUTCH: A weakness for blondes!

Blackout

Episode Seven

ANNOUNCER: "Butch Has A Dream."

Theme up: "Roses of Picardy." Fade.

GOLDIE: Hello, Butch.

BUTCH: [*Half-rising on his bunk.*] Goldie!

GOLDIE: Yes, it's me.

BUTCH: How didja get in here?

GOLDIE: Walls ain't thick enough to keep us apart always, Butch.

BUTCH: You mean you walked right through? They couldn't stop you?

GOLDIE: That's right, honey.

BUTCH: It's marvelous, marvelous!

GOLDIE: Sure. I never was an ordinary bim. There was always something unusual about me. You noticed that. How light I was on my feet and always laughing. A girl that danced like me, all night till they wrapped up the fiddles and covered the drums, that never got tired, that always wanted one more of whatever was offered, is something kind of special. You know that, Butch. You don't buy us two for a quarter at the corner drug.

BUTCH: Yeah, I know that, Goldie. I always had that special feeling about you, kid. Honey, I used to try to find words to tell yuh what you did to me nights when you opened your mouth against mine and give me your love ...

Room twenty-three! That was yours. Six flights up the narrow stairs with brass tacks in an old red carpet and bulbs at the end of the hall. Fire-escape. We used to sit out there summer nights and drink iced beer till all we could do was giggle and then go to bed.

Day used to come so slow and easy through the long white blinds. Maybe a little wind making the curtains stir. The milk wagons rattled along, and out on the East River the foghorns blew. I never slept, I lay and watched you sleeping. Your face was like the face of a little girl then. A girl no man ever touched.

I never told you about those time I watched you sleeping and how I felt toward you then. Because I wasn't good at making speeches. But I guess you knew.

GOLDIE: Of course I knew. I knew you loved me, Butch.

BUTCH: I wonder if your face still looks like that when you're sleeping.

GOLDIE: I haven't changed. You oughta know that, Butch.

BUTCH: You don't go out with other fellows, do you?

GOLDIE: No. You know I don't. I been as true as God to you, Butch.

BUTCH: But how do you live, how do you get along now, Goldie?

GOLDIE: As good as a girl can expect. I still work days over at the Imperial Dry Cleaners and nights I work at the Paradise, Butch.

BUTCH: I wanted you to quit the Paradise, Goldie.

GOLDIE: What for?

BUTCH: I don't like other guys dancin' witcha.

GOLDIE: They don't mean nothing. Just pasteboard tickets, that's all they are to me, Butch. I keep the stubs an' turn 'em in for cash. And that's as far as it goes.

BUTCH: But when they hold you close sometimes when the lights go out for the waltz—you don't ever close your eyes and blow your breath on their necks like you done for me, Goldie?

GOLDIE: No. Never.

BUTCH: You wouldn't lie to me, Goldie?

GOLDIE: Of course I wouldn't. Some of the girls say one man's as good as another. They're all the same. But I'm not made like that. I give myself, I give myself for keeps. And time don't change me none. I'm still the same.

BUTCH: The same old Goldie, huh?

GOLDIE: The same old kid. Running my dancing slippers down at the heels. But not forgetting your love. And going home nights alone. Sleeping alone in a big brass bed. Half of it empty, Butch. And waiting for you.

BUTCH: Waiting for me!

GOLDIE: Yes! Waiting for you! [*She begins to fade into the shadows.*]

BUTCH: [*Reaching toward her.*] Goldie!

GOLDIE: So long, Butch. So long …

BUTCH: [*Frantically.*] Goldie! Goldie! [*She has completely disappeared.*]

JOE: [*Sitting up on his bunk.*] What's the matter, Butch.

QUEEN: He's talkin' in his sleep again.

BUTCH: [*Slowly and with terrific emphasis.*] God—*damn*!

Blackout

Episode Eight

ANNOUNCER: "A Rubber Duck for the Baby!"

A spot comes up on the WARDEN's *office. The Boss is seated at his desk inflating a rubber duck.*

WARDEN: [*To* EVA *who lays papers on his desk.*] Look at this.

EVA: Yes.

WARDEN: It's a rubber duck for the baby.

EVA: I didn't know you had one.

WARDEN: You bet I got one. Cutest little baby doll you ever set eyes on!

EVA: Boy or girl?

WARDEN: Girl! Wouldn't have nothing else. Will she be tickled when she sees this!

   [*Eva starts to leave.*]

Wait! I'm gonna git her on the phone now! You wanta hear this, Eva? [*He dials.*] Hello, Mama? How's tricks? Yeah? Well, put the baby on, will yuh? [*To* EVA.] Now lissen to this! Puddikins? Popsy dust wanted to know if oo was bein' a dood little duff! Oo are? Dat's dood. Popsy'd dot somefin fo dood little durls! No. Not a stick-candies. Oo see when Popsy dets home, 'es oo will! Bye bye now! Bye-bye!—[*He hangs up with a chuckle.*] Cute's the dickens—looks just like Shirley Temple—don't she though? [*He shows a picture to* EVA.]

EVA: Yes, there is a resemblance.

   [JIM *enters.*]

WARDEN: [*Heartily.*] Hello, Jimmy boy! What's new?

JIM: Nothing new. Just the same old complaints about food. Only they're getting louder all the time, Boss.

WARDEN: What do they want? Caviar? Cream puffs? Charlotte Russes? Do they want us to have printed menus so they can order their meals *à la carte*? Stick these medical reports in the file case, Eva.

JIM: If you look those reports over you'll see there was seven cases of ptomaine poisoning after the Wednesday night supper. Those meatballs were worse on the stomach than they were on the nose!

WARDEN: What do you mean? They weren't good?

JIM: I think they were meant for the buzzards out at the zoo. Got mixed up at the market or something and came over here by mistake.

WARDEN: Look here, Jim. You're talking too uppity. Showing off for Miss Crane, I guess—'s at it?

JIM: No, Sir. If I didn't give you my honest opinion what good would I be?

WARDEN: [*Slowly, studying* JIM's *face.*] Okay. Yeah, you're a good boy, Jim.

JIM: Thanks.

WARDEN: [*Leaning back.*] I like you, Jim. Why? Cause you got a face that looks like it was cut outa rock. Turn sideways, Jim—Eva?

EVA: [*At the files.*] Yes, Sir?

WARDEN: Ever seen a cleaner cut profile than that? Like it was carved in stone, huh? Them jaws, the nose, the mouth? I tried to break that when Jim first come in here. Never did. It stayed like it is—stone face! Never got it to change, not even when I give him fifty stripes with a rubber hose ev'ry morning for fourteen days.—Remember that, Jim?

JIM: [*His face barely tightening.*] Yes, Sir.

WARDEN: When I seen I couldn't break him I said to myself, "Hey, Bert, here's a man you could use!" So I did. Jim's a trusty, now, a stool pigeon—Canary Jim—that's what the other cons all call him. Ain't that so, Jim?

JIM: Yes, Sir.

WARDEN: Keeps me posted on conditions among the men. He don't come gum-shoeing, whispering like the other stool pigeons I got in here—he comes straight out and says what he thinks!—That's what makes him valuable to me!—But the men don't like him. They hate your guts, don't they, Jim?

JIM: Yes, Sir. [*He speaks in almost a whisper.*]

WARDEN: Jim's on my side, all right. I couldn't break him so I made him useful. Take off your shirt, Jim—show Eva your back.

JIM: Yes, Sir. [*He obeys with curious, machine-like precision. Diagonally across his
shoulder down to the waist are long scars which ten years could not obliterate.*]

WARDEN: See them scars, Eva? He got them ten years ago. Pretty sight he was
then. Raw meat. The skin hung down from his back like pieces of red tissue
paper! The flesh was all pulpy, beat up, the blood squirted out like juice from
a ripe tomato ev'ry time I brung the whip down on him. "Had enough, Jim?'
Ready to go back to that embossing machine?"—"Naw," says Jim,— "Not till
it's fixed!"—He defied me like that for fourteen days.—I seen I'd either have
to kill him or I'd have to admit that he had me licked.—I says to him, "Jim,
you win! You don't go back to that embossing machine, you stay right here in
the office an' work for me because you're a man that's made out of stuff that
I like!" Stone face! Huh, Jim?

JIM: Yes, Sir.

[*The papers have already slipped from* EVA'S *hands. She utters a slight
breathless cry and grips the edge of the desk.*]

WARDEN: Thunderation! What's wrong?

JIM: I think she's fainting. [*He catches* EVA.]

WARDEN: Let go of that girl—get your shirt on and get out.—Tell the boys in
Hall C I'm tired a complaints about food.—Well, young lady?

EVA: I'm all right now.

WARDEN: Awright, I've got her.—Get your shirt back on, Jim—I want you to
have a little talk with Butch O'Fallon tonight.—Tell him I'm tired a complaints
in Hall C, and if he wants trouble I'm the baby that can dish it out!—Go on,
get on out!

JIM: Yes, Sir. [*He exits slowly.*]

WARDEN: [*To* EVA *who has sunk in her chair.*] Well, young lady?

EVA: I'm all right now.

WARDEN: Sorry. I didn't mean to make it that strong. Jim's a good boy, but it
don't hurt to remind him once in a while of his old friend Dr. Jones.

[EVA *averts her face.*]

You think I'm brutal, dontcha? You got to realize the position I'm in. I got thirty-five hundred men here, men that would knife their own mothers for the price of a beer. It takes a mighty firm hand.—Yes, Siree! [*He picks up the rubber duck inflates it some more*.] Cute, huh?—She'll make a fuss over this!

Dim Out

Episode Nine

ANNOUNCER: "Explosion!"

The spot comes up on the cell. We should feel a definite increase of tension over the preceding cell scenes. BUTCH *paces restlessly. The others sit sullenly on their bunks, the* QUEEN *with an old movie magazine,* SWIFTY *anxiously flexing his legs.*

JOE: [*Entering from the hall and removing the jacket.*] Save your shoe leather.

BUTCH: What for?

JOE: You might want to eat it tonight instead of cold beans.

BUTCH: Beans, huh?

SWIFTY: [*With a letter.*] It's from my lawyer.

QUEEN: What's he say, honey?

SWIFTY: He says for me to sit tight.

QUEEN: Goodness!—My nails are in awful condition.

SWIFTY: Sit tight! What does he think I've been doing since I got here? Sit tight— sit tight! Don't he know I've got to be moving around?

BUTCH: Take it easy, Mister Olympics!—Who toleja cold beans?

JOE: Boy that works in the kitchen.

SWIFTY: I don't trust that lawyer. This time he says six months.

QUEEN: I don't trust no man, honey. No further'n I could kick Grant's Tomb with a fractured toe! [*He giggles.*]

BUTCH: He oughta know.

SWIFTY: My lawyer?

BUTCH: Your lawyer! Naw—the kitchen boy.

JOE: Maybe our friend the Canary forgot to spill.

BUTCH: He'd never forget to spill anything.

JOE: Then maybe the Boss don't care how we feel about cold beans for supper.

BUTCH: He wants to call our hand.

JOE: Sure. He's got an ace in the hole.—Klondike!

BUTCH: We've got one, too.

JOE: Hunger strike?

BUTCH: You named it, Brother.

JOE: Two guys can't hold the ace of spades.

BUTCH: Once I sat in a game where that was the situation.

JOE: How didja solve it?

BUTCH: [*Producing his razor.*] Wit' this.

JOE: You better quit flashin' that thing.

BUTCH: Ev'rybody knows I got tough whiskers. [*He laughs and replaces razor in his belt.*] "Fawchun's always hiding—I looked ev'rywhere!"

[*Bird calls are heard from the hall.*]

Here it comes, it's th' Canary. [*He gives a shrill whistle.*] Hello, Canary. How's them solo flights you been makin? You know—out there on the mountain tops wit' nothing around ja but the stars?

[*He and* JOE *laugh.*]

OLLIE: [*From next cell.*] Don't pay 'em no mind, Jim.

JIM: Never mind about that. I got something to tell you.

BUTCH: Tell us about Goldilocks and the bears.

JOE: I like Goody-Two-Shoes.

JIM: Come outside for a minute.

BUTCH: You wanta fight?

JIM: No, I wanta talk.

468

BUTCH: You allus wanta talk, that's your trouble. If you got something to spill come in here.

JIM: I know what happened last time I got in a cage with you, Butch.

BUTCH: I'm glad I made that good an impression.

JIM: Are you coming out?

BUTCH: Naw. Are you coming in?

JIM: Yeah. I will. Soon as they douse the glims.

QUEEN: Better not, honey. Butch has got tough whiskers.

JIM: Yeah, I know what he cuts 'em with.

BUTCH: Why dontcha spill it, then?

JIM: I never deliberately ratted on nobody, Butch.

[*A whistle sounds. The lights dim.*]

Okay. I'm coming in now. [*He unlocks the cell and enters.*]

QUEEN: Now, Butch—

JOE: Watch, yourself. It's not worth getting jerked to Jesus for.

BUTCH: Naw, Canary, my respect for you is increased two hundred percent. I never thought you'd have what it takes to step inside here.

JIM: It's like what I was telling Ollie last night. We've all got walls around ourselves, Butch, that we can't see through—that's why we make so many mistakes about each other. Have a smoke?

BUTCH: Naw. Just say what you got to say and then take a double powder. I don't wanta lose control.

JIM: I know what you've got in mind.

BUTCH: What?

JIM: Hunger strike.

BUTCH: What of it?

JIM: I don't recommend it, Butch.

BUTCH: Did Whalen tell you to say that?

JIM: Naw, this is on the level, Butch.

BUTCH: Yeah, about as level as the Adirondacks.

JIM: I'll admit I've made myself useful to him. But I haven't forgotten two weeks we spent in the Hole together, and those visits he paid every morning to inquire about our health. He was even more solicitous about mine than yours, Butch. Things like that can make a common bond between men that nothing afterwards can ever—

BUTCH: Come to the point!

JIM: All right. I'm coming up for parole next month.

BUTCH: [*Rising.*] You are, huh?

JIM: There's a chance I might get it. And if I do I'm going to justify my reputation as a brilliant vocalist, Butch. I'm going to sing so loud and so high that the echo will knock these walls down! I know plenty from working in the office. I know all the pet grafts. I know all about the intimidation of employees and torture of convicts; I know about the Hole, about the water cure, about the overcoat—about Klondike!—And I know about the kind of food—or slop, rather!—that we been eating! You wait a month! That's all! When I get through Whalen will be where he belongs—in the psychopathic ward with Sailor Jack! And I promise you things will change in here—look here's an article about the Industrial Reformatory in Chillicothe!—that's the kind of a place this'll be!

BUTCH: [*Throwing the paper aside.*] I don't want no articles!—Allison, you're full of shit.

JOE: Take it easy, Butch. [*To* JIM.] So you don't want us to go on hunger strike?

JIM: No. It won't do any good. The Boss'll throw the bunch of you in Klondike. Do yourself a favor. Work with me. We can case this jug. But not if we keep on going opposite ways.—Give me your hand on it, Butch.

BUTCH: Fuck you!

JIM: It's no dice, huh? What do you say, Joe? Swifty?

BUTCH: They say what I say! Now git out before I lose my last ounce a restric-

470

tion!

JIM: Okay. [*He goes out.*]

JOE: Maybe he *was* on the level.

BUTCH: He will be on the level when he's laid out straight under ground. [*He slaps* SWIFTY's *rump.*] Git up! It's supper time!

SWIFTY: [*His face buried in the pillow.*] Leave me alone. I'm sick. I'm not hungry.

BUTCH: You're coming along anyhow. We need you to help make some noise in case the kitchen boy was right about supper.

JOE: Noise?

BUTCH: Yep, *plenty* of noise!

[*The bell rings in the hall.*]

BUTCH: Come along, youse! [*He shoves* QUEEN *and jerks* SWIFTY *to his feet.*] Hell's bells are ringin'! Come on, boys! Before them biscuits git cold! T-bone steaks for supper! Smothered in mushrooms! Come and git it!

[*A whistle is heard and the lights dim out. Theme up: "1812 Overture."*
Fade.]

Blackout

Episode Ten

ANNOUNCER: "Hell—an Expressionistic Interlude"

The following scene takes place on a dark stage. The shuffling of feet is heard and continues for several moments. A whistle sounds.

VOICE: TAKE PLACES AT TABLES!

[*More shuffling is heard.*]

Set down!

[*Now we hear the scrape of chairs or benches as the men sit.*]

Start eating!

[*A low yammering commences.*]

Start eating, I said! You heard me! Start eating!

[*Very softly, in a whisper, voices begin to be heard, transmitting a message from table to table with rising intensity.*]

VOICE: Quit eating—quit eating—quit eating—quit eating—don't eat no more a dis slop—trow it back in deir faces—quit eating—quit eating—we don't eat crap—we're human—quit eating—QUIT EATING—

[*The chorus grows louder, more hysterical, becomes like the roaring of animals. As the yammering swells there is a clatter of tin cups. The lights come up on BUTCH and others seated on benches at a table. Each has a tin cup and plate with which he beats time to the chorus of the Chant led by OLLIE, who stands, stage forward, in the spotlight.*]

OLLIE: Devil come to meet us an' he rang on a bell,
Twenty-five men got a ticket to hell!

CHORUS: Turn on the heat, turn on the heat,
They're gonna give us hell when they turn on the heat.
Turn on the heat, turn on the heat,
They're gonna give us hell when they turn on the heat.

OLLIE: Down in Mizzoura where I was born
           I worked all day in a field of corn,
           Got pretty hot but at night it was nice
           'Cause we kept our beer in a bucket of ice.

CHORUS: Turn on the heat, turn on the heat,
           They're gonna give us hell when they turn on the heat.
           Turn on the heat, turn on the heat,
           They're gonna give us hell when they turn on the heat.

BUTCH: There's one rap that a connie can't beat
           When the Warden says, Boys, we gonna turn on the heat!

CHORUS: Turn on the heat, turn on the heat,
           They're gonna give us hell when they turn on the heat.

OLLIE: Devil come to meet us an' he rang on a bell,
           Twenty-five men got a ticket to HELL!

CHORUS: Turn on the heat, turn on the heat,
           They're gonna give us hell when they turn on the heat.
           Turn on the heat, turn on the heat,
           They're gonna give us hell when they turn on the heat.

[*The lights fade. There is a loud ringing of bells: a whistle sounds; then
a sudden dead silence. The lights fade and come up on* SCHULTZ *and
the guards, entering cellblock. The prisoners are back in their cells.*]

SCHULTZ: Now you boys are gonna learn a good lesson about makin' distur-
bances in mess hall! Git one out of each cell! Keep 'em covered!

JOE: [*To* BUTCH.] You started something all right.

QUEEN: Oh, Lord!

SCHULTZ: Ollie! Shapiro! Come on out, you're elected! Mex!

SHAPIRO: What for! Distoibance? I make no distoibance!

MEX: [*He protests volubly in Spanish.*]

OLLIE: What you want me fo', Mistuh Schultz?

SCHULTZ: [*At the door of* BUTCH's *cell.*] Stand back there, Butch. [*He prods him
with a gun.*] Who's in here with you? Joe? Queenie?

473

BUTCH: I started the noise.

SCHULTZ: I know you started the noise. But we're saving you, Butch. You're too good to waste on the Hole.

QUEEN: I didn't make any noise, Mr. Schultz. I was perfectly quiet the whole time.

SCHULTZ: Who's that on the bunk? Aw, the new boy. Playing Puss-in-the-Corner! Come on out.

QUEEN: He didn't make noise, Mr. Schultz.

SCHULTZ: Come out, boy!

SWIFTY: [*Shaking.*] I didn't make any noise. I was sick. I didn't want any supper. I've been sick ever since I come here.

SCHULTZ: Yes, I've heard you squawking! Git in line there.

SWIFTY: I wanta see the Warden. It makes me sick being shut up without exercise.

SCHULTZ: We'll exercise you! [*He blows a whistle.*]

SWIFTY: [*Wildly.*] The Hole? No! No!

SCHULTZ: [*Prodding him roughly with a billy.*] Git moving! Krause! Alberts! Awright, that's all! Two weeks in the hole, bread an' water—maybe we'll finish off with a Turkish bath.—Step on it, Mex!

MEX: [*He swears in Spanish.*]

SHAPIRO: Distoibance? Not me. Naw.

SCHULTZ: Hep, hep, hep—

[*A slow shuffling is heard as the lights begin to dim.*]

JOE: Christ!

QUEEN: Swifty won't make it! They'll kill him down there!

[*The whistle is heard, then the distant clang of steel.*]

BUTCH: [*Whistles a few bars then sings out.*]

They fly so high, nearly reach the sky
Then like my dreams they fade an' die!
Fawchun's always hiding—I looked ev'rywhere!

[*Theme up and dim out.*]

MEX: [*He protests in Spanish.*]

SCHULTZ: Fall in line! March! Hep, hep, hep—

[*The voice diminishes as they move, heads bent, shoulders sagging, shuffling down the corridor.*]

Blackout Slowly

Episode Eleven

ANNOUNCER: "Hunger Strike!"

A spot comes up on the office. EVA *enters.*

WARDEN: Had your supper?

EVA: Yes.

WARDEN: [*Watching her as she crosses downstage.*] Hate to keep you overtime like this—but with the boys in Hall C kicking up such a rumpus, we got to have all our books in perfect shape—just in case the professional snoopers git on our tails about something!

EVA: Yes Sir. [*She removes the cover from the typewriter.*]

WARDEN: [*Watching her closely.*] Hope working nights don't interfere too much with your social life.

EVA: [*Tiredly.*] I don't have any social life right now.

WARDEN: How come?

EVA: I've been so busy job hunting since I moved here that I haven't had much time to cultivate friends.

WARDEN: No boyfriends, huh?

EVA: Oh, I have a few that I correspond with.

WARDEN: Yeah, but there's a limit to what can be put in an envelope, huh?

EVA: I suppose there is.—Mr. Whalen, there seem to be quite a number of bad discrepancies in the commissary report.

WARDEN: You mean it don't add up right?

EVA: I failed to account for about six hundred dollars.

[*The* WARDEN *whistles.*]

What shall I do about it?

WARDEN: I'll git Jim to check it over with you. You know a lot can be done about things like that by a little manipulation of figures. Jim'll explain that to you.

EVA: I see.

WARDEN: How long have you been working here?

EVA: Two weeks.

WARDEN: Gin'rally I git shut of a girl in less time'n that if she don't measure up to the job.

EVA: [*Tensely.*] I hope that I've shown my efficiency.

WARDEN: Aw, efficiency! I don't look for efficiency in my girls.

EVA: What do you look for, Mr. Whalen?

WARDEN: Personality! You're in a position where you got to meet the public. Big men politically come in this office—you give 'em a smile, they feel good—what do they care about the tax-payers' money?—Those boobs that go aroun' checkin' over accounts, where did this nickel go, what's done with that dime—jitney bums*, I call 'em!—No, Siree, I got no respect for a man that wants a job where he's got to make note of ev'ry red copper that happens to slip through his hands!—Well—policy, that's what I'm after!—Being political about certain matters, it don't hurt *ever*, yuh see?

EVA: Yes, I think so.

WARDEN: [*Pausing.*] What color's that blouse you got on?

EVA: [*Nervously sensing his approach.*] Chartreuse.

WARDEN: [*Half-extending his hand.*] It's right Frenchy-looking.

EVA: Thank you. [*She types rapidly.*]

WARDEN: [*Opening the inner door and coughing uncertainly.*] Look here.

EVA: Yes?

WARDEN: Why don't you drop that formality stuff? [*He crosses to her.*] How do I look to you? Unromantic? Not so much like one of the movie stars?—Well, it might surprise you to know how well I go over with some of the girls! [*He*

---

* Jitney: an adjective meaning "cheap."

seats himself on corner of the desk.]—I had a date not so long ago—girl works over at the Cattle and Grain Market—'bout your age, build, ev'rything—[*He licks his lips.*]—When I got through loving her up she says to me—"Do it again, Papa do it again!"—[*He roars with laughter and slaps the desk.*]—Why? Because she *loved* it, that why! [*He rises and goes to the inner door.*] You ever been in here?

EVA: No.

WARDEN: [*Heartily.*] Come on in. I wanta show you how nice I got it fixed up.

EVA: No.

WARDEN: Why not?

EVA: [*Rising stiffly.*] You're married, Mr. Whalen. I'm not that kind of girl.

WARDEN: Aw, that act's been off the stage for years!

EVA: It's not an act, Mr. Whalen!

WARDEN: Naw, neither was *Uncle Tom's Cabin* when little Eva goes up to heaven in Act III on a bunch of steel wires! [*He slams the inner door angrily, then laughs.*] You're okay, sister. You keep right on pitching in there.

EVA: Now that you know me better, do I still have a job?

WARDEN: Why, you betcha life you still got a job!

> [*He laughs and grips her in a fumbling embrace which she rigidly endures.* JIM *enters.*]

JIM: Excuse me.

WARDEN: [*Still laughing.*] Come on in, Jimmy boy. Want you to check over this commissary report with Miss Crane. She says there's a few—what you call 'em? Discrepancies! You know how to fix that up!

JIM: Yes, Sir.

WARDEN: How's things in Hall C? Pretty quiet?

JIM: Too quiet.

WARDEN: How's that?

JIM: When they make a noise you know what's going on.

WARDEN: They're scared to let a peep out since I put that bunch in the Hole.

JIM: I don't think so. I got an idea they might quit eating tonight.

WARDEN: Quit eating? You mean—*hunger strike*? [*The word scares him a little.*]

JIM: Yes. They're tired of spaghetti.

WARDEN: Maybe a change of climate would improve their appetites!

JIM: Klondike?

WARDEN: Yeah.

JIM: Klondike won't hold thirty-five hundred men.

WARDEN: It would hold Hall C.

JIM: Yes, but Butch is in Hall C.

WARDEN: What of it?

JIM: He's got a lot of influence with the men.

WARDEN: He's a troublemaker an' I'm gonna sweat it out of him.

JIM: I wouldn't try that, Boss. Hunger makes men pretty desperate and if you tortured them on top of that there's no telling what might happen.

WARDEN: Hunger strike's something I won't put up with in here. Creates a sensation all over, the country. Then what? Cranks of ev'ry description start bitching about the brutal treatment of those goddamn mugs that would knife their own mothers for the price of a beer!

JIM: The easiest way to avoid it would be to improve the food.

WARDEN: Avoid it, hell. I'll bust it to pieces! Wait'll they see that gang we've got in the Hole—if that don't make sufficient impression I'll give 'em the heat! [*He leaves the office.*]

JIM: The man's a lunatic. Ask him who he is, he'd say, "Benito Mussolini!"

EVA: You're right about him. I suspected it last week when he made you show me those scars on your back. Just now—before you came in—he convinced me of it.

JIM: What happened?

EVA: He wanted me to go in that room with him.

JIM: You didn't?

EVA: No. I was sure he'd fire me but he only laughed and squeezed my arm— Look!

JIM: What?

EVA: I've got a blue mark on my arm where he pinched me.

JIM: When he was a boy I bet he got lots of fun drowning kittens and pulling the wings off butterflies.—Were you scared?

EVA: Terribly scared—and at the same time—something else.

JIM: What?

EVA: If I told you, you'd be disgusted with me.

JIM: Attracted?

EVA: Yes, in a way. I knew that if he touched me I wouldn't be able to move.

JIM: In the pulps they call it fascinated horror.

EVA: Yes. Or a horrible fascination.

JIM: So you're convinced it's no place for a lady?

EVA: I'm not going to quit. Not yet.

JIM: No? If you wait for a third alarm it might be too late.

EVA: I'm going to stay. I've got a favorite nightmare, Jim, about finding myself alone in a big empty house. And knowing that something or somebody was hidden behind one of the doors, waiting to grab me—But instead of running out of the house I always go searching through it; opening all of the closed doors—Even when I come to the last one, I don't stop, Jim—I open that one, too.

JIM: And what do you find?

EVA: I don't know. I always wake up just then.

JIM: So you're going to try the same thing here?

EVA: Something like that.

JIM: I guarantee you won't be disappointed. Gimme the commissary report—No, take that sheet out, we'll start over again—See how much spaghetti we can make out of a Packard Six. * Ten pounds of sodium fluoride. No, you better make it sixteen.

EVA: Sixteen pounds of sodium fluoride.

JIM: Sixteen pounds of—sodium fluoride.

EVA: You just gave me that.

JIM: Aw. Twenty bushels of—

EVA: Jim.

JIM: Yeah?

EVA: Why don't you ever open the door *you're* hiding behind?

JIM: What makes you think I'm hiding behind anything?

EVA: Your eyes, the way your hands shake sometimes.

JIM: Oh. That.

EVA: It would help to let go. I mean with the right person.

JIM: Who is that right person?

EVA: Me.

JIM: How do I know?

EVA: Because I tell you.

JIM: Lots of people tell lots of things and most of them are lies.

EVA: I'm not lying, Jim—I want you to trust me.

JIM: Okay.

EVA: Then tell me—what is it?

JIM: What?

---

* The Packard was an American luxury car of the period.

EVA: Your hands—why do they shake like this?

JIM: I thought I gave you a clear demonstration once.

EVA: When ?

JIM: That morning we heard the band music.

EVA: You mean it's—repression.

JIM: That's it. Something that's locked up and keeps getting more and more all the time. There's lots of men in here with fingers that shake like this. It's power. Outside it runs dynamos, lights up big cities. But in here the power's all gone to waste. It just feeds on itself, gets bigger, does nothing. Till something sets it off like a match does a keg of powder—and then you got an explosion!

EVA: Explosions are such a—waste—of power!

JIM: Yeah. But what's the alternative here?

EVA: Your writing!

JIM: Editorials for *The Archaeopteryx*?

EVA: No! You've got next month to think of, Jim.

JIM: Next month is still on the lap of the gods. Which is a complimentary way of referring to the Board of Pardons and Paroles.

EVA: I don't know why, but I feel so sure of it, Jim. These ten years of—of waiting—They've made you stronger than other men are—You've stored up so much in you that when you get it out, there's nothing could stand in your way—You'll push down all the ordinary walls and walk right over them, Jim—People will say, "Who is this man? Where did he come from?"—and I'll smile proudly because I'll know. —He's a man from another country, I'll say—He's a giant— He's got lightning in his right hand and thunder in his left—But I'll know— I'll know secrets about you—all the sweet, strange things that only a woman can know—and I can tell you—

    [WHALEN *enters*.]

How many pounds was that—of sodium fluoride?

JIM: Sixteen.

482

WARDEN: How you getting along with that report?

JIM: We haven't done much yet. We got to talking.

WARDEN: About what?

JIM: Fireworks.

WARDEN: Very appropriate. Schultz is bringing the Hole gang up for inspection. Get them chairs out of the way.

JIM: Yes, Sir.

WARDEN: You stand over by the window and look sharp! Eva—you wanta stay in here or go in the next room?

EVA: I'll stay.

[*A buzzer sounds.*]

WARDEN: Okay. March 'em in!

[*A file of haggard, ghostly figures shuffles into the room, their eyes blinking against the light, barely able to stand —some with heads bloody, others with clotted, shredded shirts. The* WARDEN *whistles.*]

SCHULTZ: Stand up against that wall!

WARDEN: Nice-lookin' bunch. Oughta make quite an impression when they go back to Hall C! [*To* SWIFTY.] How long have you been in the hole, Son?

[SWIFTY *cannot speak. His lips move and he staggers forward with a pleading gesture. The* WARDEN *raises the "billy" and continues.*]

Stand back there! Why don't you speak?

JIM: He can't talk.

WARDEN: Dumb?

EVA: No. Sick. He's had five days in a strait jacket.

WARDEN: I think he needs five more. [SWIFTY *falls to his knees.*]

JIM: I think Swifty's had enough, boss.

WARDEN: Who asked you?

JIM: Nobody.

WARDEN: Just volunteered the information?

JIM: Yes, Sir.

WARDEN: Maybe you'd like to take his place down there?

JIM: No, Sir.

WARDEN: Then you'd better cut the cackle. Ollie?

OLLIE: [*Faintly.*] Yes, Sir.

WARDEN: You look kind of all in.

OLLIE: [*His voice shaking.*] I is, suh. I neahly checked out las' night. Boss, ah didn' think ad'd live t' see day!

WARDEN: Think another night would just about fix you up?

OLLIE: Couldn't make it, Boss.

WARDEN: What do you think, Schultz?

SCHULTZ: I think another night would do that boy a world of good, Mr. Whalen.

OLLIE: [*Wildly.*] Please, God, Boss, ah cain't make it! Ah cain't make it!

WARDEN: Two nights!—One extra for squawking!

OLLIE: Oh, Laws, a mussy, please, oh, Jesus, please, a mussy—[*He continues this prayer in a sort of chant as they are led out the door.*]

WARDEN: Get 'em out! I'll check 'em over again tomorrow morning.

[*They shuffle out slowly,* OLLIE *chanting his prayer.* JIM *follows.*]

Ever heard such a squawk?

[EVA *sinks wearily into a chair.*]

You going to flip out again?

EVA: No. I'm all right. They looked so awful it made me a little sick.

WARDEN: Sure they looked awful. Maybe they'll appreciate good treatment after this—I'll wager there'll be no more kick about food.

[*From the hall comes the sound of a disturbance*—JIM *enters*.]

WARDEN: What's going on out there?

JIM: Ollie just—

WARDEN: Took a dive?

JIM: Yes. Butted his head against a wall and broke it.

WARDEN: Head or wall?

JIM: Head.

WARDEN: All right. Cart him over to the sick-house.

JIM: Not the sick-house.

WARDEN: Dead?

JIM: Yes.

WARDEN: Why dontcha watch out? You coulda prevented that—Give Eva one of them cards—Naw, outa the top drawer. Fill that out. Name—What was that smoke's name?

JIM: Oliver. Oliver Jackson.

WARDEN: Special friend of yours?

JIM: All of the men liked Ollie.

WARDEN: Huh. How old?

JIM: Twenty-six.

WARDEN: Color—black! Sentence—

JIM: Three years.

WARDEN: Charge?

JIM: [*Slowly.*] Stole a crate of canned goods off a truck to feed his family.

WARDEN: Larceny!—Cause of death?—What's his Wasserman?

JIM: Negative.

WARDEN: Hmmm. Put this down, Eva. Stomach Ulcers. Severe hemorrhages.

JIM: That's what you gave the boy last week.

WARDEN: Well, make it a bad cold—complications—pneumonia!

[*The sounds of yammering begin to penetrate the office.*]

[*The* WARDEN *is unnerved for a moment but continues.*] What's that?

JIM: They're making a noise.

WARDEN: [*Instinctively seizing his whip.*] Where's it from? Hall C?

JIM: Naw. Halls A, B, C, D, E, and F!

WARDEN: [*Shakily.*] What are they bitching about now?

JIM: They must have heard about Ollie. They like him pretty good.

WARDEN: Aw—[*He looks frightened.*] —Schultz? [*He seizes the phone.*] Schultz? How's the pipes in Klondike? Git them radiators tested an' ready for action.

[*There is a sudden complete darkness on stage.*]

WHISPERS: [*Gradually rising in volume and pitch.*]   Somebody got hurt down-stairs—Who was it?—Ollie!—Ollie?—Yeah, they killed Ollie—Ollie's dead.—They killed Ollie—Ollie's dead—They KILLED OLLIE—THEY KILLED OLLIE—OLLIE'S DEAD!

[*A spot comes up on the cell.* BUTCH *is bending to the wall. He suddenly rises.*]

BUTCH: Ollie's dead—THEY KILLED OLLIE! [*He shouts through the bars.*]

CHORUS: Ollie's dead! They killed Ollie!

JOE: What are we going to do about it?

BUTCH: Quit eating! [*He shouts through the bars.*] QUIT EATING!

CHORUS: Quit eating! Quit eating!

[*Blackout.*]

WHISPERS: What does Butch say?—Butch says quit eating—hunger strike?—Yeah, hunger strike!—Butch says HUNGER STRIKE!—Hunger strike—

quit eating—Quit eating—HUNGER STRIKE!

VOICE: The men in Hall C have quit eating!

SECOND VOICE: Hunger strike in Hall C!

NEWSBOY: *Morning Star*! Paper! *Morning Star*! Paper! Read about the big hunger strike!

WOMAN'S VOICE: It is reported that some of the men in the state prison have gone on a hunger strike!

[*The click of a telegraph is heard.*]

VOICE: Associated Press Bulletin—Hunger strike at Monroe City Penitentiary! Men rebel against monotonous diet!

VOICE: United Press!

VOICE: Columbia Broadcasting System!

VOICE: Commissioners promise an investigation of alleged starvation in state penitentiary!

VOICE: Warden denies hunger strike!

VOICE: Hunger strike reported!

VOICE: Hunger strike denied!

VOICE: Hunger strike! HUNGER STRIKE!

[*Traffic noises, sirens, bells are heard. Theme up: "1812 Overture" theme reprise. Blackout. Fade.*]

END OF ACT ONE

ACT TWO

Episode One

ANNOUNCER: "Not About Nightingales!"

A spot comes up on the office. The hunger strike has been in effect for several days and a tense, electric atmosphere prevails as everyone waits for the inevitable explosion when nerves are stretched beyond the point of endurance. EVA *is seated alone as the scene opens. Her movements are jittery. The phone rings.*

EVA: Warden's office. *The Morning Star*? No, Mr. Whalen is not seeing any reporters. No, there is no serious trouble. No, you can't get on the Island without a special permit from Mr. Whalen. The rule has been in effect for about six days. No, not on account of a hunger strike! Yes, good-bye.

     [*During this the* CHAPLAIN *has entered.* EVA *is startled, then continues.*]

Oh!

CHAPLAIN: Nervous, young lady?

EVA: Terribly—terribly!

CHAPLAIN: I don't blame you. So am I. This thing has got to be stopped before something serious happens.

EVA: Oh, if it only could be!

CHAPLAIN: That's what I want to see Mr. Whalen about. It does no good trying to suppress all news of what's going on. We might as well face the music—and do something constructive to put a stop to it!

EVA: Yes. Something constructive.

CHAPLAIN: But in the meantime—couldn't you take a little vacation?

EVA: You think there's real—danger?

CHAPLAIN: Certainly there's danger. And it's aggravated by the fact that Mr.

Whalen apparently won't recognize it. I wish that I could reason with that man, but—Well—[*He glances at his watch*.]—I'll visit some boys in the hospital and be back here for a talk with the Boss in about twenty minutes.

EVA: All right.

[JIM *enters*.]

CHAPLAIN: Hello, Jim. How are things upstairs?

JIM: [*Showing a bloody arm in a torn sleeve*.] That's the answer!

EVA: [*Springing up*.] Jim!

JIM: [*Laughing grimly*.] I walked too close to one of the cages.

CHAPLAIN: Who did that?

JIM: [*Slowly shaking his head*.] I don't know.

CHAPLAIN: [*Patting his back*.] You've had ten bad years, Jim. I hope next month will be the end of it for you.

JIM: Thanks, Reverend.

[*The* CHAPLAIN *goes out*.]

EVA: Jim, I'll—I'll fix that up for you.

[*He sits down by desk*.]

JIM: They gave me this stuff to put on it down at the sickhouse. They were sore as hell because I wouldn't tell them who done it.

EVA: [*Painting his arm and applying a bandage*.] You shouldn't stay up there. It's not safe for you.

JIM: No place is safe in here. Aren't you finally convinced of that?

EVA: Why are you so anxious to get rid of me?

JIM: You know a lot you could tell.

EVA: Yes. I suppose I do.

JIM: Why don't you then?

EVA: I want to stay here a while longer. Maybe next month I'll go—we'll both go then.

JIM: They've been on a hunger strike six days and the Warden only gave them seven. Tonight may be the deadline. Tomorrow night at the latest.

EVA: Then what?

JIM: The boiler room is in perfect condition. The pipes have been reinforced.

EVA: I can't imagine anything as brutal as that—I don't believe it!

JIM: Well—I ought to spill it myself—but if I did it would cost my ticket-of-leave!—It's funny.

EVA: What?

JIM: Nothing has quite so much value as the skin our own guts are wrapped in. [*He takes a book and sits down at the window.*]

> [EVA *resumes typing.* JIM *suddenly tears a page out and throws it on the floor in disgust.*]

Christ!

EVA: What did you do that for?

JIM: I didn't like it.

EVA: What was it?

JIM: A little piece of verbal embroidery by a guy named Keats.

EVA: What's wrong with it?

JIM: It's sissy stuff—"Ode to a Nightingale!" Don't those literary punks know there's something more important to write about than that? They ought to spend a few years in stir before they select their subjects!

EVA: Why don't you show them, then?

JIM: I'd give my right arm for the chance.

EVA: You have the chance!

JIM: Not in here I don't. If I wrote what I wanted to write, I'd stay in here till Klondike becomes an ice-plant!—But maybe next month—

EVA: Yes. Next month—

JIM: Maybe then I'll start writing—but not about nightingales!

EVA: John Keats didn't have a very good time of it, Jim.

JIM: No?

EVA: No. He died at the age of twenty-six.

JIM: Smothered himself in lilies, I guess.

EVA: No. He wanted to live. Terribly. He was like you, he had a lot of things he
wanted to say but no chance to say them. He wrote another poem, Jim. A poem
you'd like. Give me the book—here it is! [*She reads the sonnet "When I have fears
that I may cease to be".*]:

> When I have fears that I may cease to be
> Before my pen has gleaned my teeming brain,
> Before high pilèd books, in charactry,
> Hold like rich garners the full-ripened grain;
> When I behold, upon the night's starred face,
> Huge cloudy symbols of high romance,
> And think that I may never live to trace
> Their shadows, with the magic hand of chance;
> And when I feel, fair creature of an hour!
> That I shall never look upon thee more,
> Never have relish in the faery power
> Of unreflecting love!—then on the shore
> Of the wide world I stand alone, and think
> Till Love and Fame to nothingness do sink.

You see he was like you, Jim. He got out of his prison by looking at the stars.
He wrote about beauty as a form of escape.

JIM: Escape, huh? That's not my kind of escape.

EVA: What is your form of escape?

JIM: Blowing things wide open!

EVA: Destruction, you mean?

JIM: Yes! Destruction!

EVA: I'm sorry to hear you say that.

JIM: Would you rather hear me warbling about nightingales?

EVA: No. But there are other things.

JIM: For instance?

EVA: There must be some things you love.

JIM: Love?

EVA: Yes.

JIM: Love is something nasty that's done in dark comers around this place.

EVA: I'm sorry you're so bitter.

JIM: Why should you be sorry about anything except the possible loss of your job?

EVA: Why should I? Because I like you, Jim.

JIM: Even after—after the last time we were in here together?

EVA: More than ever.

JIM: When you've been without women as long as I have, there's something mythological about them. You can't believe they're real, not even when you place your hands on them like this and—

EVA: Jim!

[*She breaks away as* WHALEN *enters.*]

WARDEN: What's the matter Jim?

JIM: Why?

WARDEN: You got a funny look on your face.

JIM: I'm just concentrating.

WARDEN: On what?

JIM: The new *Archaeopteryx*.

WARDEN: Aw, what are you going to write about, Jim?

JIM: [*Quietly.*] Not about—nightingales.

WARDEN: Huh? [*Absently fiddles with his papers.*] Aw, Jim—

JIM: Yes, Sir?

WARDEN: You might want to drop a word to the boys on hunger strike about the radiator test we made in Klondike. We got the temperature up to 150 degrees—You might mention that. You know a word to the wise is sufficient.

JIM: I'm afraid there's not much wisdom in Hall C. Good night.

    [JIM *goes out. The* CHAPLAIN *enters.*]

WARDEN: [*Lighting cigar.*] What do yuh want, Reverend?

CHAPLAIN: I want to talk to you about the death of Oliver Jackson.

WARDEN: What about it?

CHAPLAIN: I think it could have been avoided.

WARDEN: Sure it could. Nobody made that fool nigger take a dive.

CHAPLAIN: He was goaded to desperation.

WARDEN: Oh, you think so?

CHAPLAIN: There have been too many suicides, several drownings, hangings, so-called accidents, since I've been here. Now it appears that we're in danger of having a mass suicide in Hall C. The men have gone on hunger strike which I think is fully justified by the quality of food they've been getting.

WARDEN: Aw. Now I'm beginning to suspect who's responsible for the wild stories that have been leaking out to the public about things here. I'm afraid you're what the boys call a stool pigeon, Reverend.

CHAPLAIN: I'm a conscientious steward of Christ, and as such I protest against the inhuman treatment of convicts in this prison!

WARDEN: [*Jumping up.*] Who's running this prison, you or me?

CHAPLAIN: Mr. Whalen, the universe is like a set of blocks. The kind you had in kindergarten. A little one that fits into a big one, a bigger one over that, till you get on up to the very biggest of them all that fits on top of all the rest—

WARDEN: Yes?

CHAPLAIN: Yes, and that biggest block is the one I'm representing—the Kingdom of God. [*He rises with dignity.*]

WARDEN: Well, I'm afraid your work here has begun to interfere with your— your higher duties—I want you to climb up there on top of that great big block you're talkin' about an' stay up there. That's your place. You leave me alone down here on the little block—There's your notice, Reverend—You're free to go now.

CHAPLAIN: I could leave here gladly if it wasn't for what I have to take with me.

WARDEN: You're taking nothing with you but the clothes on your back.

CHAPLAIN: I'm taking much more than that.

WARDEN: Aw. Maybe I'd better have you frisked on the way out.

CHAPLAIN: You could strip me naked and I'd still have these.

WARDEN: These what?

CHAPLAIN: Memories—shadows—ghosts!

WARDEN: Ahhhh? [*He lifts phone.*] Git me Atwater 2770.

CHAPLAIN: Things I've seen that I can't forget. Men, tortured, twisted, driven mad. Death's the least of it. It's the *life* in here that's going to stay with me like an incurable sickness. And by God, Whalen, that's not profanity—by God, I won't rest easy till I've seen these walls torn down, stone by stone, and others put up in their place that let the air in! Good night!—[*He goes out quickly.*]

WARDEN: Hello. Reverend? This is Warden Whalen. Our chaplain's just resigned. I want you to come over and talk to me—might be a steady job in it for you. Yes, Siree! You be over here in time for Sunday service—[*He hangs up.*] Memories, shadows, ghosts! What a screwball! [*He pours himself a drink.*]

Dim Out

Episode Two

ANNOUNCER: "Sunday Morning in Hall C!"

A spot comes up on the cell JOE, QUEEN, *and* SWIFTY *are reading sections of a Sunday paper. From down the corridor comes* BUTCH's *voice—*

BUTCH: [*Approaching.*] "I'm forever BLOW-ing BUB-BLES !" [*He enters the cell with a straight razor, towel, and soap.*] Who gave you that paper?

JOE: Allison. The Canary.

BUTCH: Git it out of here!

JOE: What for?

BUTCH: It's contaminated.

JOE: Aw, take a look at t' comics.

BUTCH: Naw, gimme 'at pitcher section. Hey! Look at 'is!

JOE: What?

BUTCH: "A bow-ket of buds!"

JOE: Yeah. They're comin' out in sassiety.

BUTCH: "Miss Hortense Maxine Schultz, daughter of Mr. and Mrs. Max W. Schultz, 79 Willow Drive, will make her bow to society early this Fall. She is one of a group of young women who traveled through Europe this summer with Mrs. J. Mortimer Finchwell—"

JOE: So what?

BUTCH: "On her fadder's side Miss Schultz is directly descendant from William th' Conq'ror an' on her mudders from Ponce de Leon, Sir Isaac Newton an' George Washington's Aunt!"

JOE: Gosh; de're pikers! Why don't they throw in Benito Mussolini for good measure?

BUTCH: "Her grandfather was duh late Benjamin F. Schultz, President and founder of th' Schultz Bottling Works."

JOE: Lotsa mazooma, huh?

BUTCH: "In addition to her many udder accomplishments—!" Hey, listen to this!

JOE: Huh?

BUTCH: Down here at th' bottom they come right out an' admit that she ain't even human!

JOE: How's that?

BUTCH: It says here "In addition to her many udder accomplishments, Miss Schultz is an excellent *horse*-woman!"

JOE: Hell, you could tell that by lookin' at her pitcher.*

Blackout

---

* A Hunt Club was prestigious in St. Louis in 1936 when the Post Dispatch reported 1000 persons attending the Spring Horse Show. "Schultz Bottling Works" is doubtless the Anheuser Busch brewery. In this scene Williams satirizes St. Louis society, from which his family was excluded, as being dominated by *nouveau riche* beer barons.

Episode Three

ANNOUNCER: "Mr. Whalen Interviews the New Chaplain!"

A spot comes up on the office. WHALEN *and the* REVEREND HOOKER *have just returned from Sunday dinner. The* REVEREND HOOKER *is a nervous, precise little man with a prodigious anxiety to please.*

WARDEN: I got you up here on pretty short notice. You see me an' the old chaplain had a little disagreement last night, which resulted in him handing in his resignation right off the bat!—He made one fatal mistake, Reverend—He kind of forgot who was in charge of this institution.

REVEREND: I don't think I shall make that error, Mr. Whalen.

WARDEN: Naw, neither do I. First time I seen you I said to myself "Here's a man who looks like he could adjust himself to conditions."

REVEREND: I pride myself on being—adjustable!

WARDEN: Good. You'll find that's an asset around this place, a definite asset. What's your idea of the universe, Reverend?

REVEREND: I beg your pardon?

WARDEN: Suppose you give me a little word-picture of how you conceive of this great mysterious—[*He makes a sweeping gesture.*]

REVEREND: Cosmos?

WARDEN: Yes! In which we humans are little fluttering motes, so to speak. [*He makes a derisive fluttering gesture with hands.*]

REVEREND: Well—uh—of course there's the orthodox conception of the universe as consisting of three elements—

WARDEN: Yep?

REVEREND: Heaven, earth and the—uh—regions below.

WARDEN: We call that Klondike in here.

REVEREND: I beg your pardon?

WARDEN: Skip it, Reverend.

REVEREND: Hmmm. Of course there is some question as to the material existence of those—uh—nether regions—

WARDEN: There's no doubt about 'em here. Naw, Sir. But what I wanted to know, Reverend, is if you've got any theories about a set of blocks—with you occupying the one on top and me way down at the bottom—that's what got the last preacher in trouble with me.

REVEREND: Blocks? Oh, dear, no! That strikes me as rather—elementary to say the least!

WARDEN: Yeah, kindergarten stuff. Well, you'll do, Reverend. [*He glances at his ponderous gold watch.*] We got about five minutes till church takes up. Are you good at makin' up extemporaneous speeches?

REVEREND: Oh, yes, indeed, yes, indeed! I think I may safely say that I have never lacked words for any occasion, Mr. Whalen.

WARDEN: Well, your job depends on this one. I haven't got time to go into details, Reverend. But I want you to touch on three particular subjects. I don't care how you bring 'em in, just so you do and so you give 'em the right emphasis!

REVEREND: Three subjects!

WARDEN: Yes, Siree. You mark 'em down, Reverend—food!

REVEREND: Food?

WARDEN: That's the first one. Then—heat!

REVEREND: Heat?

WARDEN: Yep. And then—Klondike!

[*A bell sounds.*]

There goes the bell. I'm two minutes slow. Remember, now, food, heat, and Klondike!

REVEREND: What was the last one? Klondike? You mean—uh—missionary work in the far north? Among the Eskimos? I'm afraid the association of ideas is going to be a little difficult for me to grasp, Mr. Whalen—but—

[*Dim out; a spot comes up on the* REVEREND HOOKER *behind a small lectern.*]

REVEREND: Yes—uh—very good afternoon to you all. [*He clears his throat: then beams at the convicts.*] I hope that you enjoyed your dinner as much as I did mine—

VOICE: Hamburgers and spaghetti!

[*There is a chorus of booing. A warning whistle sounds, then silence.*]

REVEREND: Food is such a familiar blessing that—uh we sometimes forget to be properly grateful for it. But when I read about the horrible conditions in famine-stricken portions of Europe and Asia—tch, tch!—I feel that I am indeed very fortunate to have a full stomach!

[*Booing is heard; someone whistles.*]

When one thinks of food—uh—one also thinks by a natural association of ideas—about—uh—the marvelous blessing of—uh—*Heat!* Heat—uh—that makes food possible—wonderful *heat!* Heat of all kinds! The heat of the sun that warms the earth's atmosphere and permits the growth of the vegetables and the grains and the—uh—fruits—uh—the heat of the—uh—body—uh— [*He wipes his forehead.*] heat, universal heat—At this time of the year some of us find heat oppressive—uh—but that is ungrateful of us, extremely ungrateful—

[*There is a slow stomping of feet.*]

[*The preacher continues, raising his voice.*] For all living matter depends on the presence of heat—northward and southward from the Equator to the twin poles—even to far Alaska—even in *Klondike*—

[*The stomping grows louder.*]

What would Klondike be without heat? A frozen wasteland! [*He scrubs his forehead and glances nervously about.*] In Klondike our brave missionaries, risking their lives among savage tribes of war-painted Indians—

[*A hymnal is hurled: there is furious stomping.*]

Goodness!—As I was saying—in Klondike—!

[*He is bombarded with hymnals. A whistle blows; there is shouting; a siren sounds. Dim out. A mocking jazz interlude plays. A spot comes up on the office. The* REVEREND *rushes in clasping his handkerchief to his forehead.*]

REVEREND: Oh, mercy upon us!

WARDEN: [*At the phone.*] Schultz? All guards on duty! Find out who conked the Reverend with that song book. Whew! I give you my word, Reverend, I wasn't expecting no such a reaction as this! It come as a complete surprise!

REVEREND: Ohhhh! I'm afraid I shall have to receive some medical attention.

WARDEN: Yeah, well, I want you to take this fin, Reverend.

REVEREND: And the nervous shock, you know! Tch, Tch!

WARDEN: Yeah? Well—

REVEREND: Terrific, terrific! A shocking experience!

WARDEN: Here's another two bucks.

[*Theme up: jazz.*]

Blackout

Episode Four

ANNOUNCER: "Zero Hour!"

A spot comes up on the warden's office. EVA *is typing nervously.* JIM *enters. His chronic tension has now risen to the point of breaking. Even his movements are stiff like those of a mechanical man: his eyes are smoldering.*

EVA: [*Jumping up as he enters.*] Jim, you're not—?

JIM: Naw, I'm not locked up in Hall C.

EVA: I hadn't seen you. I was afraid—

JIM: You must have forgotten what a special value there is attached to my hide.

EVA: You look awfully tired, Jim.

JIM: Yes. How do *you* sleep at night?

EVA: Not well lately.

JIM: How do you sleep at all knowing what you know and keeping still?

EVA: What else can I do but keep still?

JIM: You could talk. You could tell the State Humane Society that thirty-five hundred animals are being starved to death and threatened with torture.

EVA: And lose my job?

JIM: Aw. Excuse me for being so impractical.

EVA: You don't understand. I was out of work six months before I got this job.

JIM: You told me that.

EVA: I got down to my last dime. Once a man followed along the street and I stood still, waiting for him to catch up with me. Yes, I'd gotten down that low, I was going to ask him for money—

JIM: Did you?

EVA: No. At the last moment I couldn't. I went hungry instead.

[JIM *looks at her.*]

Now you want me to go back to that? Times haven't improved. Now maybe I'd have more courage, or less decency, or maybe I'd be hungrier than I was before.

JIM: You'd better hold on to your job, Miss Crane—even if it does mean participating in a massacre!

EVA: It's not that bad.

JIM: It's going to be that bad. I'm going to talk myself now. Even if it means giving up my chance of parole.

EVA: No, you can't do that. Wait a while and see how things turn out.

JIM: This is the zero hour. Whalen has given instructions to put Hall C in Klondike tonight if they don't eat supper.

EVA: I know. I heard him.

[JIM *lifts the telephone receiver.*]

What are you going to do?

JIM: Blow the lid off this stinking hole!

EVA: [*Grabbing the phone.*] No, Jim! I'll do it, myself! I'll talk!

JIM: When?

EVA: [*Lowering her voice.*] Now. Tonight. I'll visit the newspaper on my way home.

JIM: You will, huh?

EVA: Yes!

JIM: No. Wait till tomorrow. We'll have more definite evidence then. With Hall C in Klondike.

[WHALEN *enters.*]

WARDEN: Well, Jim. What do the boys in Hall C think about the change in climate that I've arranged for them?

JIM: They haven't heard yet. Wilson is going to tell them when he brings the men up from the Hole.

WARDEN: They'll be eating supper tonight.

JIM: What have they got for supper?

WARDEN: The old perennial favorites, hamburger and spaghetti. I'm not going to mollycoddle those bastards.—Excuse me, Eva.

JIM: I don't think they'll eat.

WARDEN: You don't, huh? Well, I do! Eva—

EVA: [*Who has gotten her hat.*] Yes, Sir?

WARDEN: I'll want you back after supper. We've got to have things in perfect order in case the snoopers get busy.

EVA: All right.

WARDEN: You'd better catch the ferry at seven-fifteen.

EVA: Yes, Sir. [*She exits.*]

JIM: About my parole, Mr. Whalen—

WARDEN: Yes? What about it?

JIM: It's coming up next month.

WARDEN: [*Grunting.*] Humph.

JIM: I guess it pretty much hangs on your decision.

WARDEN: You've got a lot of brass.

JIM: Why do you say that?

WARDEN: Bothering me about your goddamn parole at a time like this!

JIM: It's important to me. I've been in here ten years and I've got ten years of copper. I'm due for a ticket-of-leave.

WARDEN: You'll get a ticket to Klondike if you got any more to say on that subject!

JIM: [*Starting forward.*] By God, I—

WARDEN: What?

JIM: [*With desperate control.*] Nothing.

WARDEN: [*Uneasily.*] I'm going out for supper. Be back about eight or eight-thirty. You watch things here.

JIM: Yes, Sir.

[WHALEN *exits.* JIM *covers his face, strangling a sob.*]

Blackout

Episode Five

Musical theme up: "I'm Forever Blowing Bubbles."

ANNOUNCER: "Hall C!" *Musical theme fade. A spot comes up on the cell. The dialogue is fairly light, but an undercurrent of desperation should be felt.*

BUTCH: [*Hoarsely.*] "I'm forever blow-ing BUBBLES!"

JOE: Quit croakin' that corny number. Why dontcha learn something new?

BUTCH: That was new last I heard it.

JOE: Before you got in stir?

BUTCH: It had just come out.

JOE: It's had time to grow whiskers since then.

BUTCH: It was Goldie's fav'rite.

JOE: I thought you said she liked *Dardanella.*

BUTCH: She liked that one, too.

JOE: What's become of her?

BUTCH: How should I know? She quit writing ten years ago.

JOE: Christ. She's probably died of the syph by now.

BUTCH: Naw, not Goldie.

QUEEN: I wish I was dead. I used to have nice fingernails. Look at 'em now. My teeth was nice, too. I had nice hair. Now when I look at myself I wish I was dead.

BUTCH: "Faw'chun's always hi-ding! I looked ev'ry where!"

     [*A mimic down the hall echoes the refrain.*]

BUTCH: [*Jumping to the bars.*] Who was that? You, Krause?—Anytime I want you small-time grifters to muscle in on my singin' I'll send you a special request.

QUEEN: Yes, I wish I was dead. I hope that I starve to death. And I will. I can

505

feel myself dying already.

BUTCH: "They fly so high, nearly reach the sky—" They used to turn out the light on that number. There was a sort of silver glass ball at the top of the ceilin' that would turn round and round an' throw little rainbow-colored reflections all over the floor an' the walls—God, it was lovely!

QUEEN: [*Rising.*] Honest to God, I can't hold out much longer, Butch!

BUTCH: Naw?

QUEEN: Naw, I got a weak constitution. I was in a nervous run-down condition before I got sent up here. Hell, it was a bum rap. I didn't sell any weeds. I used to smoke 'em but I never sold any!—Persecution, all my life, persecution! Now maybe they'll kill me down there in Klondike, I'll never git out, never—never git out!

BUTCH: Dummy up!

QUEEN: You ever been in Klondike, Joe?

JOE: Naw. Butch has.

QUEEN: What's it like, Butch?

BUTCH: [*Rising slowly and going to stage front.*] "Then like my dreams they fade an' die—"

QUEEN: They say it ain't the heat so much.

JOE: What is it? The humidity?

QUEEN: Naw, you can't breathe good. It's kind of—suffocating! [*He fingers his collar.*]

BUTCH: Fortune's always hiding—I looked ev'rywhere!
I'm forever blow-ing BUBBLES! [*He stops short.*]

[*A door clangs—the men rise simultaneously, tense. There is the sound of a wracking cough and delirious sobbing.*]

[BUTCH *continues softly.*] They're bringin' 'em up from the Hole.

SCHULTZ: Gwan, git a move on, it ain't no funeral march yet awhile!

[*The dull shuffling of feet is heard accompanied by coughing, sobbing.*

The heads of the men in the cells move slowly from left to right, mouths open, as though watching some awful procession.]

Halt! Face your cells!—You, too, Shapiro, do I have to speak Yiddish to make you understand?

[*A low yammering commences.* BUTCH *seizes his tin cup and holds it poised. A whistle sounds; the cell door opens.*]

March in! Git in there, Trout—Shapiro!

[SWIFTY *stumbles into the cell, unshaven, ghastly, sobbing.*]

Awright! Take a good look at 'em. An' remember this! The Hole is just a small dose compared to Klondike! Klondike's the big medicine and the Boss is all set to pour it out in double doses for any of you wise bastards that don't feel like eating supper tonight!

VOICE: [*Slowly and emphatically.*] Where's Ollie?

ANOTHER: [*Staccato.*] Yeah, where's Ollie?

CHORUS: Where's Ollie, where's Ollie, what did you do with Ollie?

[*Slight pause.*]

SCHULTZ: Who's responsible if some fool nigger takes a notion to butt his own brains out? [*There is a slight whine of fear in his voice.*]

[BUTCH *suddenly hammers the cell bar with his cup. Yammering commences. During the preceding speeches, from the point of his entrance,* SWIFTY *has stood dazed; then he sags slowly to his knees beside the bunk. The* QUEEN *comforts him awkwardly.* JOE *and* BUTCH *stand with attention fixed on* SCHULTZ. *A whistle sounds. The yammering subsides a little.*]

[SCHULTZ, *standing directly outside the open cell door, continues.*] You see this here thermometer? [*He extracts a large one from his pocket.*] See that little red mark there? That says Blood Heat. Now see this one up here twenty degrees more? It says Fever Heat. You think it's going to stop there? Not a chance! It's going to keep right on rising till it busts clean out of the top of the little doojigit! It's going to break all records. It's going to be the biggest heat wave in history. Now if you don't think I'm a good weather prophet, just one of you finicky lads leave a little spaghetti on his plate tonight an' see what happens!

VOICE: Spaghetti?

[*There is complete tense silence for a moment.*]

SCHULTZ: Yeah, spaghetti!

BUTCH: Spaghetti, huh?—We ain't gonna eat it tonight or no other time—not till Whalen cuts out the graft and feeds us something besides hog-slop!

SCHULTZ: Is 'at what you want me to tell him?

BUTCH: Yeah, tell him that, an' if he don't like it—

[*Yammering; a whistle; the door clangs shut; the yammering subsides.*]

VOICE: Klondike?

ANOTHER: Tonight?

ANOTHER: Yeah, if we don't eat!

VOICE: Klondike? No?

ANOTHER: Not if we go to Klondike!

VOICE: [*Shrill and despairing.*] We can't make it!!

[*A wracking-cough and delirious sobbing are heard. Mex prays in a hoarse strangled voice.*]

MEX: *Santa María—Madre de Dios*—etc.

[BUTCH *advances to the bars and raps commandingly.*]

VOICE: It's Butch!

ANOTHER: What does Butch say?

MEX: *Jesus—muerto por nuestros pecados*!

BUTCH: Cut the cackle all of yuz! That goes for you too, Mex. You got plenty of time for talking to Jesus when you git there! Lissen here now!—Anybody in Hall C that eats is gonna pay for his supper in Kangaroo Court. I'll assess the maximum fine, you know what!—You're scared of Klondike? I say let 'em throw us in Klondike!—Maybe some of you weak sisters will be melted down

508

to grease-chunks. But not all twenty-five of us! Some of us are gonna beat Klondike! And Klondike's dere las' trump card, when you got that licked, you've licked everything they've got to offer in here! You got 'em over the barrel for good! So then what happens? They come up to us and they say, "You win! What is it you want?" We say, "Boss Whalen is out! Git us a new Warden! Git us decent livin' conditions! No more overcrowdin', no more bunkin' up wit' contajus diseasus; fresh air in the cell-blocks, fumigation, an' most of all—WE WANT SOME FOOD THAT'S FIT TO PUT IN OUR BELLIES!

[*Applause.*]

No more hamburger an' spaghetti an' beans, and beans an' hamburger an' spaghetti till you feel like the whole fucking world was made of nothin' else but hamburger an' beans an' spaghetti—

[*Applause.*]

—Maybe when we git through house-cleaning this place'll be like the Industrial Reformatory they got at Chillicothe! A place where guys are learnt how to make a livin' after they git outa stir! Where they teach 'em trades an' improve their ejication! Not just lock 'em up in dirty holes an' hope to God they'll die so as to save the State some money!!

[*Fierce yammering.*]

Tonight we go to Klondike!—Dere's three compartments! One of 'em's little hell, one of 'em's middle sized hell an' one of 'em's BIG HELL!—You know which one Butch O'Fallon is gonna be in!—So if I ain't yellow, boys, don't you be neither! That's all I got to say.

VOICE: Okay, Butch.

ANOTHER: We're witcha!

CHORUS: We'll beat Klondike!—You bet we'll beat it!—Put Whalen over a barrel—

[*There is nervous laughter and applause. Their voices die abruptly under a shadow of fear.*]

MEX: [*Chanting.*] *Muerto—por nuestros pecados—rojo—de sangre es—el Sol!*

Blackout

Episode Six

ANNOUNCER: "Definition of Life!"

A spot comes up on the office. JIM, *facing downstage, leans against the desk, smoking.* EVA *enters.*

EVA: Hello, Jim.

JIM: Yeah.

EVA: Nice out. A little bit cooler.—What's wrong with you?

JIM: [*Grinning wryly.*] Ask me what life is, Eva.

[EVA *looks at him and crosses downstage.*]

Ask me what it is and I'll tell you.

EVA: [*Removing her hat.*] No, darling.

JIM: Why not?

EVA: It smells like a bad epigram.

JIM: [*Tossing away his cigarette.*] It's a gradual process of dying, that's what it is!

EVA: Worse than I expected.

JIM: That's what it is in here. Maybe it's something else on your side of the fence. I'd like to find out, but I guess I won't have the chance!

EVA: [*Seriously.*] Your parole?

[JIM *strikes a match, watches it burn.*]

Turned down?

JIM: Not yet but it will be. I was talking about it to Whalen.

EVA: Oh. You shouldn't have mentioned it now when he's all steamed up about the hunger strike.

JIM: I didn't mean to. It just popped somehow. I'm getting out of control— Butch named me for the right kind of bird. Canaries never get out of their cages, do they, Eva?

EVA: Jim! Don't be a fool.

JIM: Naw, they die in 'em—singin' sweetly till doomsday! God damn!

EVA: [*Brushing her hat.*] Speaking of birds—I wish the pigeons would be a little more careful! Don't you think it's a nice hat, Jim?

JIM: [*Without looking.*] Yes, colossal.

EVA: I bought it on the way home. I felt sort of gay and irresponsible—knowing tomorrow was the last day, I suppose! Jim!

   [*She catches his arm: he averts his face.*]

JIM: [*His fear visible.*] If I get turned down again this time, I'll never get another chance.

EVA: Why not?

JIM: Because I'll blow up!—Crack to pieces! I'm drawn as tight as I can get right now!

EVA: Don't be a damn fool, Jim.

JIM: You know what it's been like. Hated like poison for ten years by everybody but him. Working for him and all the time hating him so that it made me sick at the guts to look at him even! Ten years of being his stooge. Jimmy boy, do this, do that! Yes, Sir. Yes, Mr. Whalen!—My hands aching to catch that beefy red neck of his and choke the breath out of it! That's one reason why they shake so much—and here's another. Standing here at this window, looking out, seeing the streets, the buildings, the traffic moving, the lights going off and on, and me being pent up here, in these walls, locked in 'em so tight it's like I was buried under the earth in a coffin with a glass lid that I could see the world through! While I felt the worms crawling inside me ...

EVA: No. Don't be a fool. [*She crosses upstage to the window.*] It's nice out. Gotten cooler.

JIM: You said that before.

EVA: [*Smiling desperately.*] Well, it's still true. There's a carnival on South Bay. I ran in like a kid and took a ride on the zebra!

JIM: Yes?

EVA: There's two seats on the zebra, Jim. One in front, one in back—Next month we'll ride him together!

JIM: [*Suddenly breaking.*] Eva! Eva! [*He covers his face.*]

EVA: [*Running to him.*] I love you!

   [*Pause.*]

JIM: [*His voice choking.*] What is this place? What's it for? Why, why! The judges say guilty. But what is guilty? What does that word mean, anyhow? It's funny, but I don't know. [*He picks up the dictionary.*] Look it up in *Webster's Dictionary*. What's it say? "Responsible for the commission of crime." But why responsible? What's responsible mean? Who's ever been given a choice? When they mix up all the little molecules we're made out of, do they ask each one politely which he will be—rich man, poor man, beggar man, thief? God, no! It's all accidental. And yet the Judge says, "Jim, you're guilty!" [*He tosses the dictionary to the floor.*] This book's no good anymore. We need a new one with a brand new set of definitions.

EVA: Don't say any more—I won't let you! [*She kisses him.*]

JIM: How did this happen between you and me?

EVA: I don't know.

JIM: It's the dirtiest trick they've played on us yet.

EVA: Don't say that!

JIM: We can't have each other. We never can, Eva.

EVA: We can!

JIM: Where?

EVA: Somewhere.

JIM: How?

EVA: I don't know how.

JIM: Neither do I.

EVA: But next month—

JIM: There won't be any next month!

EVA: There will, oh, there will, there must be!

JIM: Why?—Why?

EVA: Because I love you so much that it's got to happen the way I want it to happen!

JIM: Why do you love me?

EVA: Why is anything on earth? I don't know why.

JIM: Neither do I—

[*They cling together in tortured ecstasy. Blackout. The lights come up as the phone rings.*]

JIM: Yes? I'll tell him. [*He hangs up.*]

EVA: What is it?

JIM: Schultz. They won't eat.

EVA: What's he going to do?

JIM: He's already got his instructions from Whalen. They'll be in Klondike at seven.

EVA: [*Pausing.*] I won't be down here tomorrow.

JIM: No?

EVA: I'll be in the newspaper offices. And at City Hall. Any place where people will listen!

JIM: You think they'll listen anywhere, Eva?

EVA: I'll make them listen!

JIM: And afterwards what will you do? With no job?

EVA: I'll only have to wait three weeks. And then I'll be *your* responsiblity, Jim!

JIM: I hope to God you're right.

EVA: I am! I know I am!

[WHALEN *enters.*]

WARDEN: Hello! Still here, Jim?

JIM: Yes, Sir. Schultz called. They wouldn't eat supper.

WARDEN: Well—he's got his instructions.

JIM: Yes, he said that he had.

WARDEN: [*Scribbling on a piece of paper.*] Take this down to the switchboard and have it posted there and sent to all stations.

JIM: Does this mean—?

WARDEN: Never mind what it means. Just take it down there. And step lively!

JIM: Yes, Sir.

[JIM *goes out.*]

WARDEN: [*To* EVA.] Back on the job, huh?

EVA: Yes.

WARDEN: [*Belching and removing his coat.*] I should have told you to bring some things with you.

EVA: What things?

WARDEN: Your little silk nightie and stuff.

EVA: What do you mean?

WARDEN: Quarantine! A bad epidemic's broken out! Twenty-five cases are going to be running a pretty high fever tonight so I've put this place under quarantine restrictions—nobody's gonna leave the grounds till the epidemic is over.

EVA: I can't stay here.

WARDEN: [*Busy with papers.*] Sure you can. My wife'll fix a room for you. You'll be very comfortable here.

EVA: No, I won't do it.

WARDEN: You've got no choice in the matter.

EVA: Haven't I?

WARDEN: Naw, I'm not running a risk on any outside interference while this trouble is going on. It's my business, I'm going to keep it my business. So just as a routine precaution I've ordered the boats to take no passengers on or off the island without my special permission.

EVA: I think you're exceeding your authority.

WARDEN: Naw, you're wrong there. Times of emergency I can do what I damn please. Say—what are you worried about?

EVA: [*Frightened.*] I—

WARDEN: I know. It's a nervous strain we've all been under these last few days. I got gas on the stomach myself. Here. [*He pours a shot of whiskey.*]

EVA: No, you've been drinking too much. I'm afraid it's affected your sense of judgment. You ought to know you can't get away with a thing like this!

WARDEN: Hey, now—look here!

EVA: [*Excitedly.*] I'm not a prisoner—I'm free to go and do as I please—you can't stop me!

WARDEN: Look here, now! [*She grasps the phone.*]

EVA: Riverside 3854 W! Riverside 3-8—[*She realizes the phone is cut off.*]

WARDEN: No out-going calls can get through. You're wasting your time.

EVA: Then I—I *am* a prisoner here!

WARDEN: You're temporarily detained on the island—might as well make the best of it! [*He pours another drink.*]

EVA: Oh!

WARDEN: Here, now, what's wrong with you?

EVA: I don't know why, but I'm terribly frightened.

WARDEN: [*Soothingly.*] You've gone and worked yourself up. There's nothing for you to be nervous about.

EVA: You! I'm afraid of you! [*She backs away from him.*]

WARDEN: Me? Why should you be scared of me?

EVA: I am, though. I'm scared to death of you. You've got to let me go, I can't stay with you any longer, Mr. Whalen.

WARDEN: Now, now.

EVA: No, don't touch me! Please don't.

WARDEN: You're hysterical, Eva.

EVA: Yes!

WARDEN: [*Purring.*] My wife gets spells like that, too—that "don't touch me" stuff!

EVA: [*Retreating.*] Yes!

WARDEN: I know a good treatment for it that always works. There, now little girl you just take it easy. Relax. You're all worked up over nothing. You're stiff, see? Your nerves and your muscles are all drawn up real tight.

EVA: Yes … [*She has nearly collapsed with nervous exhaustion—his purring voice has a hypnotic effect.*]

WARDEN: Mmm. Now when my wife gets like this, I—I rub my fingers along her throat—real, real gently—till all the stiffness goes out …

EVA: [*Her eyes falling shut.*] Yes …

WARDEN: [*Gazes at her lasciviously.*] … and then I—

[EVA *sighs as though asleep.*]

WARDEN: Eva?—Eva? [*He rises and opens the inner door, then hesitates.*]

[*The phone rings.*]

For Chrissakes, what is it now? Yeah? What? I'm coming right down there now!—[*He hangs up—purring drunkenly.*] You wait, li'l girl, I'll be right back in here! Yes, Siree … [*He fumbles into his coat and goes out.*]

[EVA *gasps as the door slams shut—she slowly rises. The outer door opens—* EVA *screams—*JIM *enters.*]

516

EVA: Jim! Jim!

[JIM *catches her in his arms.*]

Get me out of here, oh, please, *please*, get me out of here! [*She sobs wildly.*]

JIM: Hold on to yourself! [*He shakes her.*] Hold on to yourself!

EVA: I'm trying to, Jim.

JIM: Take a deep breath. Here—at the window.

EVA: Yes!

JIM: See those lights over there?

EVA: Yes!

JIM: That's the Lorelei on her way out. Be real quiet and you can hear the music.

[*She leans against him—faint music is heard.*]

Better now?

EVA: Yes. Thanks, Jim.

JIM: What happened? Just tell me real quietly and don't get excited about it.

EVA: He told me I—I'm a prisoner here! I can't leave! I don't know why, but it made me terribly frightened all of a sudden. His eyes, the way he looked at me, Jim—I had a feeling that something awful was going to happen—

JIM: Easy, now!

EVA: Yes. I guess I'm an awful a sissy.

JIM: No, you've got more guts than me.

EVA: He—he came real close to me—and his voice—sort of put me to sleep.

JIM: Did he—?

EVA: No! He only opened that door. And then a bell rang—I could hear it like it was a thousand miles off!

JIM: A bell?

EVA: They called him upstairs, I guess. He left the room and I—I would have jumped out the window if you hadn't come just then!

JIM: There's nothing but water out there.

EVA: I didn't care. I just wanted to get away somehow.

JIM: You'll get away.

EVA: With you, Jim? You'll take me?

JIM: Yes. In a while. Don't you feel the walls shaking? They can't hold up much longer. There's too much boiling inside them—hate, torture, madness, fury! They'll blow wide open in a little while and we'll be loose!

EVA: I want to be with you when that happens! I want you to hold me like this— so that when the walls start falling I won't be crushed down under them, Jim.

JIM: We'll be together.

EVA: Where?

JIM: Meet me tonight in the southwest corner of the yard.

EVA: Will we be safe there?

JIM: [*In a whisper.*] It's dark. Nobody could see us.

Blackout

END OF ACT TWO

ACT THREE

Episode One

ANNOUNCER: "Morning of August 15!"

A spot comes up on the office. The WARDEN *is at the phone. During the follow-ing episodes the theater is filled almost constantly with the soft hiss of live steam from the radiators—*

WARDEN: Schultz? How hot is it down there now? 125? What's the matter? Git it up to 130! You got Butch O'Fallon in No. 3 aintcha? Okay, give No. 3 135 and don't let up on it till you git instructions from me. Hey! Got them win-dows in the hall shut? Good. Keep 'em shut an' let 'em squawk their god-damn heads off!

> [*Blackout. A spot comes up on Klondike. The torture cell is seen through a scrim to give a misty or steam-clouded effect to the atmosphere. The men are sprawled on the floor, breathing heavily, their shirts off, skin shiny with sweat. A ceiling light glares relentlessly down on them. The walls are bare and glistening wet. Along them are radiators from which rise hissing clouds of live steam.*]

JOE: [*Coughing.*] W'at time is it?

BUTCH: How in hell would I know?

SWIFTY: [*Whimpering.*] Water—water.

JOE: I wonder if we been in here all night.

BUTCH: Sure we have. I can see daylight through the hole.

JOE: How long was you in that time?

BUTCH: Thirty-six hours.

JOE: Christ!

BUTCH: Yeah. And we've just done about eight.

SWIFTY: Water!

BUTCH: Hey! Y'know what—what the old maid said to the burglar when she— she found him trying to jimmy th' lock on th'—

JOE: Yeah. [*He coughs.*]

QUEEN: Swifty's sick. I am, too. Why don't somebody come here?

BUTCH: Aw, you heard that one?

JOE: Yeah. A long time ago, Butch. [*He coughs.*]

BUTCH: You oughta know some new ones.

JOE: Naw. Not any new ones, Butch.

BUTCH: Then tell some old ones, goddamn it!! Dontcha all lie there like you was ready to be laid under! Let's have some life in this party—Sing! Sing! You know some good songs, Queenie, you got a voice! C'mon you sons-of-guns! Put some pep in it! Sing it out, sing it out loud, boys! [*He sings wildly, hoarsely.*]

> Pack up your troubles in yuhr ole kit bag an'
> Smile, smile, smile!

[*The others join in feebly—.*]

Sing it out! Goddamit, sing it out loud!

> What's the use of worrying
> It never was worthwhile!

[JOE *tries to sing—he is suddenly bent double in a paroxysm of coughing.*]

SWIFTY: [*In a loud anguished cry.*] Water! Water! Water! [*He sobs.*]

[*There is a loud shrill hiss of steam from the radiators as more pressure is turned on.*]

QUEEN: [*In frantic horror.*] They're givin' us more! Oh, my God, why don't they stop now! Why don't they let us out! Oh, Jesus, Jesus, please, please, please! [*He sobs wildly and falls on the floor.*]

SWIFTY: [*Weakly.*] Water—water …

BUTCH: Yeah. They're givin' us more heat. Sure, they're givin' us more heat. Dontcha know you're in Klondike? Aw, w'at's a use, yer crybabies. Yuh wanta go on suckin' a sugar-tit all yer life? Gwan, sing it out—

> I'm forever blowing BUBBLES!
> Pretty bubbles in the—AIR!

SHAPIRO: There is nothing to be done about it, nothing at all. I come of a people that are used to suffer. It is not a new thing. I have it in my blood to suffer persecution, misery, starvation, death.

SWIFTY: Water.

SHAPIRO: [*Mumbles in Yiddish, then.*] My head is full, full. Aching in here. Broken already, perhaps. Rose? Rose? You know the property on South Maple Street— it's all in your name, my darling—be careful—don't make bad investments—

JOE: [*Coughing.*] Lemme at the air hole.

QUEEN: You're hoggin' it!

JOE: Cantcha see I'm choking to death? [*He coughs.*]

> [*The steam hisses louder.*]

BUTCH: [*Rising.*] We got to systematize this business. Quit fightin' over the air hole. The only air that's fit to breathe is comin' through there. We gotta take turns breathin' it. We done sixteen hours about. Maybe we'll do ten more, twenty more, thirty more.

JOE: Christ!

QUEEN: We can't make it!

BUTCH: We can if we organize. Keep close to the floor. Stay in a circle round the wall. Each guy take his turn. Fifteen seconds. Maybe later ten seconds or five seconds. I do the counting. And when a guy flips out—he's finished—he's through—push him outa the line—This ain't a first-aid station—this is Klondike—and by God—some of us are gonna beat it—Okay? Okay, Joe?

JOE: Yeah.

BUTCH: Well, git started then.

SWIFTY: Water!

BUTCH: Push the kid up here first.

> [*They shove* SWIFTY's *inert body to the air hole.*]

Breathe! Breathe! Breathe, goddamn you, breathe! [*He jerks* SWIFTY *up by the collar—stares at his face.*] Naw, it's no use. I guess he's beating a cinder track around the stars now!

QUEEN: He ain't dead! Not yet! He's unconscious, Butch! Give him a chance!

BUTCH: [*Inexorably.*] Push him outa the line.

> [*As the lights dim …*]

Okay—Shapiro—Joe—

> [*Theme up: "I'm Forever Blowing Bubbles." Fade.*]

Dim Out

Episode Two

ANNOUNCER: "Evening of August 15!"

A spot comes up on the office. WHALEN *is at the phone.*

WARDEN: You heard 'em what? Singin! Well, give 'em somthing to sing about! 140! Git it up to 145 in Butch's compartment! You bet I want 'em left in there all night. Naw, keep the windows shut. Water? Let 'em make their own water!

[*Blackout. A spot comes up on Klondike.* SWIFTY *lies dead in center, a shirt over his face. The voices are hoarse, breathing more labored.* JOE *coughs wrackingly. The radiators hiss loudly.*]

BUTCH: Here comes more! Keep down! Keep down!

[QUEEN *sobs wildly. Shapiro mumbles in Yiddish.*]

Joe! Look! I got it with me! [*He extracts a razor from his belt.*]

JOE: That's one way out.

BUTCH: Maybe the boss will come down here to look us over.

JOE: [*Coughing.*] Naw, he wouldn't.

BUTCH: Maybe Schultz will. Or the Canary. [*He rises.*] Schultz! Schultz! Naw, it's no dice, he's too yellow to stick his puss in here! But if he does ever—

[*A whistle sounds.*]

Hear that? It's the lock-up bell! We've done twenty-four hours, Joe. We only got twelve more to go!

JOE: How d'you know how long it will be?

BUTCH: They don't want to kill us!

JOE: Why don't they? [*He coughs.*]—Your turn, Butch.

BUTCH: Yeah, git moving, Queenie!

QUEEN: Naw! Lemme breathe!

[BUTCH *tears him away from air hole.* SHAPIRO *shouts something in Yiddish.* QUEEN *continues rising and staggering.*]

I got to get out of here! Lemme out, lemme out! [*He pounds at the wall, then staggers blindly towards the radiators.*]

BUTCH: Stay away from the radiators!

[QUEEN *staggers directly into the cloud of steam—screams—falls to the floor.*]

He's scalded himself.

[QUEEN *screams and sobs.*]

Stop it! Goddamn yuh—[*He grasps* QUEEN'*s collar and cracks his head against floor.*] There now!

JOE: Butch—you killed him.

BUTCH: Somebody shoulda done him that favor a long time ago.

[SHAPIRO *mumbles in Yiddish.*]

You heard that one about—the niggers in church? "—Rastus, she says—Naw, he says—Mandy—Mandy how long does the Preacher—"

[*Dim out. A spot comes up on the office.* WHALEN *is on the phone.*]

WARDEN: Schultz? How hot is it down there now in Butch's compartment? 150? Good! Keep it there till I give you further instructions—I'll be in my office till about midnight and if anything comes up—

[*Fade out. A spot comes up on Klondike.* SHAPIRO, QUEEN, *and* SWIFTY *are dead and lie in the center.* BUTCH *and* JOE, *gasping, crouch together by the air hole.*]

JOE: Butch—

BUTCH: Yeah.

JOE: Y'know that razor—

BUTCH: What about it?

JOE: Use it on me! Quick! I wanta get done with this!

524

BUTCH: Keep hold of yourself, Joe. You can make it.

JOE: Naw, I can't, Butch. I'm chokin' t' death. I can't stand it.

BUTCH: Breathe!

JOE: There ain't no air coming in now, Butch.

BUTCH: There's air—breathe it, Joe.

JOE: Naw ...

> [BUTCH *raises his face and shakes him.*]

BUTCH: [*Hoarsely.*] Goddamn yuh, don't chicken out! Stay with me, Joe! We can beat Klondike!

> [JOE *laughs deliriously.* BUTCH *continues, springing up.*]

Turn off them fucking radiators!! Turn the heat off, goddamn yuh, turn it off! [*He staggers toward the radiators.*] Stop it, y'hear me? Quit that SSSS! SSSS! [*He imitates the hissing sound.*] I'll turn yuh off, yuh suns-a-bitches! [*He springs on the radiators and grapples with them as though with a human adversary—he tries to throttle steam with his hands—he's scalded—screams with agony—backs away, his face contorted, wringing his hands.*] SSSSS! SSSSS! SSSSS! [*He is crazily imitating their noise.*]

JOE: Christ, Butch, it ain't no good that way. You've blown your top. What's the percentage? [BUTCH *staggers back to the air hole.*]

BUTCH: Joe! Hey, Joe! Swifty! You, Queen! Shapiro! [*He tugs at one of the bodies.*] Let's sing! Let's all sing something! Sing it out! Loud!

Fortune's always hiding!

Why don't you bastards sing something! Come on—sing! Sing!

I looked ev'rywhere—!

[*The lights dim as the music completes the final lines of "Bubbles".*]

Dim Out

Episode Three

ANNOUNCER: "The Southwest Corner of the Yard!"

Dark stage and complete silence for several moments. Then—

EVA: Jim!

JIM: Here!

EVA: I'm late. I couldn't help it.

JIM: Shhh!

EVA: [*Lowering her voice.*] His wife's not on the Island. She left this afternoon. I can't stay there in that place with him, Jim, I can't do it!

JIM: Shhh. Don't talk.

EVA: What am I going to do, Jim? What am I going to do?

JIM: *Don't talk*! It's not safe. They might hear us. Eva—

[*Pause. The beam of a searchlight moves over them.*]

EVA: Jim! They're moving the light!

JIM: Shhh! Keep it down!

[*The light disappears.*]

EVA: Oh. Thank God.

JIM: Now!

EVA: You've never even said that you loved me.

JIM: I love you. Now!

EVA: Oh, Jim—Jim!

[*A longer pause.*]

JIM: The light again!

[*It circles lower this time and pauses directly above them.*]

Christ! Keep down low!

EVA: Jim!

JIM: Crawl! No, that way! Quick!

> [*The light suddenly moves down and shines full upon* EVA's *face.* EVA *screams. A siren sounds. Blackout. A spot comes up on the office.* JIM *and* EVA *are there with a* GUARD. WHALEN *enters.*]

WARDEN: What is this?

GUARD: It looks like the Canary's turned into a lovebird, Mr. Whalen.

WARDEN: Aw!

GUARD: I heard a noise in the southwest corner of the yard. Sounded like a girl's voice. I dropped the light on—there they was!

WARDEN: Aw! Doing what?

GUARD: Well, they weren't picking daisies.

WARDEN: Aw! [*To* EVA.] You a while ago. Got hysterical in here. Objected because there wasn't no chaperone in the house. Then you run out there like a bitch in heat and—

JIM: [*Starting forward.*] Stop it!

WARDEN: Aw!

JIM: It's easy to say things like that when you've got a gun stuck in my back.

WARDEN: Put the gun down. [*He takes a rubber hose from the hall.*] It's disillusioning what happens when you put too much confidence in the wrong people. Take your coat off.

EVA: No, you can't do that to him. I won't stand for it. It wasn't his fault. I asked him to meet me out there. Because I was scared. Scared of you! Scared of this awful place you've got us locked up in! And now you let us out! You let us both out of here now! Before I scream! I'll let the whole world know what's going on here!

WARDEN: Take hold of that girl!

JIM: [*Springing toward them.*] Let her go!

527

[WHALEN *flails at him with the hose.* JIM *staggers to the floor covering his face.* EVA *screams and struggles.*]

WARDEN: Take him out of here!

GUARD: Where to?

WARDEN: Klondike! Throw him in there with Butch O'Fallon! They're real good friends! [*He laughs.*]

[*The guard goes out dragging* JIM.]

Well, Eva—

[EVA *turns her face sharply away.*]

I'm sorry about this whole thing. I mean it sincerely. What I just said—forget that! You probably don't stop to realize what a strain I've been under. It's not easy to be the head of an institution like this. I've handled it like I would handle anything else. The best I knew how. Sometimes—I'm telling you the truth, girl—I've been so sick at heart at things I've had to do and see done—that it hurt me to look into my own little girl's face and hear her call me—Daddy! [*He pours himself a drink.*] Here. You take one, too. [*He is breathing heavily and for the moment is perfectly in earnest.*] Maybe it's done something to me in here. [*He touches his head.*] Sometimes I don't feel quite the same anymore. Awful, awful! Men down there now being subjected to awful torture! But what can I do about it? I got to keep discipline—dealing with criminals—there's no other way—Take your drink.

EVA: Thank you. [*She takes it.*]

WARDEN: There's two ways I could look at this. It could be a serious business. By your own confession you—you remember what you said, you—had Jim meet you out in the yard—Now I'm inclined to be broad-minded about such things—these discrepancies in the commissary report—[*He shrugs and smiles.*]—things like that—serious sometimes—at least they can look that way—

EVA: What do you mean, Mr. Whalen? You mean you would—try to accuse me of—!

WARDEN: No, no, no! [*He smiles engagingly.*] Not unless you forced me to.

EVA: What do you want?

WARDEN: What does any man want? What did Jim want, what did you give him?—Sympathy!

EVA: Oh.

WARDEN: That way it could be very simple. We're all of us nervous, strained, overwrought!—Sympathy! All of us need it!

EVA: Oh. What will you do to Jim now?

WARDEN: Well—

EVA: I love him! You probably don't understand how it happened between us— He's coming up for parole next month.

WARDEN: Yes, I have the letter in my desk now.

EVA: What letter?

WARDEN: Recommending Jim's—release! Of course after this—

EVA: You won't send it?

WARDEN: Well—

EVA: Suppose I—I did sympathize—as you say—and—and kept my mouth shut and anything else that you want! Would you send the letter? Would Jim get his parole?

WARDEN: [Smiling.] Why not? [He laughs gently.] You see how easy it is to straighten things out!

EVA: Now? Would you send it now?

WARDEN: Now? It's—pretty late now—

EVA: The mailboat leaves at eleven-forty-five. You could have it sent over by that. Don't worry. I won't back out. I'm not afraid of you now. I like you—I'd like to show you how much!

[The WARDEN removes the letter from the drawer and rings the bell. A guard enters.]

WARDEN: Put this in the mail.

GUARD: Yes, Sir. [He goes out.]

WARDEN: My head aches, aches all the time—my wife's left me—the little girl, too—[*He opens the inner door.*] We're all of us nervous and tired, overwrought! Aren't we? Yes—[*He ushers* EVA *in as the light fades.*]

Dim Out

Episode Four

ANNOUNCER: "The Showdown"

A spot comes up on Klondike. BUTCH *lies by the air hole. The bodies of the others are heaped in the center—*BUTCH *is apparently unconscious. Voices are heard in the hall.* BUTCH *slowly raises his head, becomes tense.*

SCHULTZ: [*As the door opens.*]—makin' love to the Boss's secretary out in the yard—fancy that!

[BUTCH *rolls over quickly and feigns unconsciousness.*]

Whew! What a stink! Hey—Chick! C'mere! Steam's s' goddamn thick I can't see nothin'. Gimme that flash—

CHICK: Looks t' me like—Jeez! They're *stiffs*!

SCHULTZ: Stiffs! Y'mean—

CHICK: Roasted! Roasted alive! God Almighty! I didn't know nothin' like this was going on in here.

SCHULTZ: Shut up! How many are there?

[*During this* BUTCH *has slowly risen and poised himself for attack.*]

Gimme the flash! Shapiro, Joe—Swifty—The Queen—Where's Butch?

BUTCH: [*Springing.*] Here! Here! [*He clutches Schultz by the throat.*]

[JIM *attacks Chick. A shot is fired;* JIM *wrests the revolver from the guard.*]

JIM: Toss your mittens!

BUTCH: [*Slowly releasing* SCHULTZ.] Aw! You! The Canary!

SCHULTZ: [*Uncertainly.*] Good work, Jim!

JIM: I mean you, Schultz! Reach high! Butch—get them keys off him!

BUTCH: [*Slowly grinning.*] Aw—aw! [*He snatches the keys.*]

SCHULTZ: What is this?

JIM: Butch—let the boys out! We're going upstairs!

BUTCH: Yeah!

SCHULTZ: You'll get the hot seat for this! Every mother's bastard of you will! What are you going to do, Jim?

JIM: Get into something comfortable, Schultz! You're going to SWEAT!

> [JIM *backs out and slams the door.* SCHULTZ *rushes to it, pounds and screams. Blackout. The stage is dark for a moment. There is the long wail of a siren. A spot comes up in the* WARDEN's *office.* WHALEN *steps out of the inner room——he listens, tense with alarm.—The office door is thrown open—*JIM *enters.*]

WARDEN: Jim!

JIM: [*His clothes torn and bloody from the earlier beating.*] Yeah! Sometimes even hell breaks open and the damned get loose!

WARDEN: What's happened—downstairs? [*He edges back—pushes a buzzer.*]

JIM: No use pushing that. There's nobody on the other end of it.

WARDEN: They've broken out of—Klondike?

JIM: Yes. All of 'em but four. Four didn't break out cause they're dead—but they sent their regards to you, Boss, they want to be remembered!

WARDEN: How did you get that? [*He points to the revolver.*]

JIM: Raided the munitions!

WARDEN: What happened to Schultz?

JIM: He got in trouble downstairs, he's locked in Klondike, keeping the dead boys company down there—The other screws are locked up in the cellblock. Stand outa the way. [*He removes a revolver from the desk.*] Where's the girl?

WARDEN: She—left.

JIM: You're sure of that.

WARDEN: Yes—Why?

JIM: This ain't a safe place to be right now.

WARDEN: Look here, Jim—

JIM: What's the matter? You don't look good.

WARDEN: I'll make a deal with you—where are the—boys?

JIM: [*Jerking his thumb toward the door.*] Waiting out there at the gate. I wanted to make sure the girl wasn't here before I let 'em come in.

WARDEN: Naw! You can't do that!

JIM: Sure. I'm the reception committee. I've got the keys.

[*Men are heard shouting outside.* EVA *appears at the inner door.*]

JIM: Eva!

EVA: Jim, don't do it, Jim! It's no use—He's written a letter asking for your parole, he sent it already!

WARDEN: Yes, Jim. I done it just now, because she—

JIM: Because she—what? [*He looks at them both.*] Aw! Get back inside there, Eva.

[*The boss starts to follow.* JIM *jerks him back.*]

Naw, you stay out here!

EVA: Jim! [*He forces her inside and locks the door.*]

WARDEN: Jim, you wouldn't give up your parole for the chair?

JIM: Sure. It's worth it. I haven't forgotten.

WARDEN: Forgotten—what?

JIM: Twenty-one days in the Hole. Dr. Jones.

WARDEN: [*Following him to door.*] Afterwards I was your friend!

JIM: I wasn't yours!

WARDEN: [*Nearly screaming.*] I was good to you afterwards, Jim!

JIM: I still had your signature on my back! Now we've got a new whipping-boss waiting out there—Butch O'Fallon!

WARDEN: Naw! Jim! Jim!

[JIM *has gone out—the roar of the men rises as doors are opened. The* WARDEN *gasps and darts behind the desk—Men enter like a pack of wolves and circle about the walls.*]

BUTCH: [*Lunging through.*] Where is he?

WARDEN: Butch!

BUTCH: [*His eyes blinded.*] There! I've caught the smell of him now!

[*The two rulers face each other for the first time. Outside there is scattered gunfire, and a flickering light is thrown through the windows like the reflection of flames.*]

It's been you an' me a long time—you in here—me out there—But now it's—together at last—It's a pleasure, pig face, to make your acquaintance!

WARDEN: Look here now, boys—O'Fallon—Jim—I'll make a deal with you all—You've got to remember now—I've got the United States army in back of me!

BUTCH: [*Laughing and coming toward him.*] You've got that wall in back of you—Where's the Doctor?

CONVICT: Here! [*He snatches the rubber hose from the wall and hands it to* BUTCH.]

BUTCH: Yeah!

WARDEN: Naw! Think of the consequences! Don't be fools!

[BUTCH *strikes him with the hose.*]

WARDEN: [*Cowering to the floor.*] Stop! I'm a family man! I've got a wife! A daughter! A little—*girrrrl!*

[*The final word turns into a scream of anguish as* BUTCH *crouches over him with the whip beating him with demoniacal fury till he is senseless.*]

[*The siren of an approaching boat is heard.*]

CONVICT: What is it?

ANOTHER: Gunboat!

ANOTHER: Troopers!

ANOTHER: They're landing!

ANOTHER: Douse the glims!

> [*The room is plunged into total darkness except for the weird flickering of flame shadows on the walls—Men begin a panicky exodus from the room.*]

VOICES: Git down there—Fight 'em off—Troopers!—Not a chance—No chance anyhow!—You wanta go back to Klondike?—Fight!—Sure, fight!—We got nothing to lose! [*Names are shouted—gates clang—machine gun fire is heard.*]

> [*The noise becomes remote and dream-like—the room is almost quiet except for the distant, sad wail of the siren which continues endlessly (like the voice of damnation at the palace gates.)*]

JIM: What have you done to him?

BUTCH: Thrown his blubbering carcass out the window.

JIM: Into the water?

BUTCH: Yeah. Straight down.

JIM: Butch—we've got a chance that way.

BUTCH: Swim for it? Naw, not me. I don't know how to swim. Besides it's half a mile to shore and rough as hell.

JIM: What will you do?

BUTCH: Stay here and fight it out.

JIM: I think I'll take my chances with the water.

BUTCH: [*Slowly extending his hand.*] Good luck, I had you figured wrong.

JIM: Thanks.

BUTCH: [*Pulling off ring.*] Here. There used to be a girl named Goldie at the Paradise Dance Hall on Brook Street west of the Ferry. If you should ever meet her, give her this—And tell her that I—kept it—all this time.

JIM: Sure, Butch—I will if I make—

BUTCH: [*Going to the door.*] So long.

[*Rapid gunfire and distant shouting heard outside.* JIM *unlocks the inner door.*]

JIM: Eva.

[EVA *comes out slowly—she falls sobbing on his shoulder.*]

Don't cry!

EVA: No. I won't. There'd be no use in that. Jim, you were right about the pyrotechnical display!

JIM: Stand back from the window!

EVA: [*Hysterically gay.*] It's lovely, isn't it, Jim!

JIM: Yes, lovely as hell!

EVA: What did they do to him?—Whalen?

JIM: [*Thumb to window.*] The fish will have indigestion.

EVA: Jim! Have you thought what you'll get for this?

JIM: Nothing. They won't have a chance.

EVA: What are you going to do?

[*Sound cue: faint music.*]

JIM: There's water out that window. I can swim.

EVA: No, Jim, there's not a chance that way.

JIM: A chance? What's that? I never heard of it! [*On this speech he slowly approaches the window over the sea.*] Hear that? That music! It's—

EVA: The Lorelei!

JIM: The Lorelei—[*He tears off his coat.*] Now I retract those unkind things I said!

EVA: What will you do?

JIM: Swim out and catch a ride!

EVA: You couldn't, Jim—They'd bring you back—They wouldn't let you go!

JIM: They'll never see me.

EVA: Why?

JIM: Don't ask me why! There'll be a rope or something hanging over the side. Or if she doesn't ride too high I'll grab the rail! How! Don't ask me how! Now is the time for unexpected things, for miracles, for wild adventures like the storybooks!

EVA: Oh, Jim, there's not a chance that way!

JIM: Almost a chance! I've heard of people winning on a long shot. And if I don't— At least I'll be outside!

EVA: Oh, Jim I would have liked to live with you outside. We might have found a place where searchlights couldn't point their fingers at us when we kissed. I would have given you so much you've never had. Quick love is hard. It gives so little pleasure. We should have had long nights together with no walls. Or no *stone* walls—I know the place! A tourist camp beside a highway, Jim, with all night long the great trucks rumbling by—but only making shadows through the blinds! I'd touch the stone you're made of, Jim, and make you warm, so warm, so terribly warm your love would burn a scar upon my body that no length of time could heal! —Oh, Jim, if we could meet like that, at some appointed time, some place decided now, where we could love in secret and be warm, protected, not afraid of things—We could forget all this as something dreamed!— Where shall it be? When, Jim? Tell me before you go!

JIM: Quick! It's almost close enough! Get that shoe off!

EVA: [*Pulling off his shoes.*] Yes Jim! But tell me where?

JIM: [*Climbing to the sill.*] Watch the personal columns!

EVA: Jim!—Good-bye! [*He plunges from the window.*]—Good-bye ...

         [*Music from the Lorelei swells. Flame-shadows brighten on the walls. Shouting and footsteps are heard.* TROOPERS *rush in.*]

ONE: [*Switching on light.*] A girl—

TWO: The Warden's Secretary!

THREE: [*Crossing to her.*] You're all right, sister. [*To others.*] She's dazed, can't talk—Get her a drink, somebody.

ONE: What's that she's got?

THREE: A pair of—shoes!

ONE: Whose are they? What's she doing with them?

EVA: [*Facing the window with a faint smile.*] I picked them up somewhere. I can't remember.

> [*Light fades except for a spot on* EVA, *clutching* JIM's *shoes. Music from the Lorelei rises to a crescendo as a string of colored lights slides past the window. Dim out.*]

LOUD-SPEAKER: Aw there, it is! Y'can see it now, folks. That's the Island! Sort of misty tonight on account of the moon's gone under. Them walls are *escape-proof*, folks. Thirty-five hundred men locked in there an' some of them gonna stay there till Doomsday—

> [*Music.*]

—Ah, music again! Dancing on the upper deck, folks, dancing,—dancing …

> [*Musical theme up.*]

THE END

ANOTHER AMERICAN:
ASKING AND TELLING

MARC WOLF

Originally produced in New York by
The New Group in association with David Marshall Grant

Written and performed by Marc Wolf
Directed by Joe Mantello
Set Design by Robert Brill; Lighting Design by Brian MacDevitt;
Sound Design by David Van Tieghem

Another American: Asking and Telling *was presented as a workshop by the New York*
Stage and Film Company and The Powerhouse Theatre at Vassar in July, 1999.

This project was developed in the Resident Artists Program 1998 of
Mabou Mines/Suite, and at Provincetown Repertory Theatre in August, 1998.

INTRODUCTION
by Moises Kaufman

"The truth is not only stranger, but often more
entertaining and more dramatically effective than fiction."
—Hallie Flanagan.
Director, Federal Theatre

What is brilliant about what Marc Wolf has done in *Another American* is that he has subverted a national policy through theater, and by doing so, he has given voice to a population of American men and women who would have otherwise been silenced. When the "don't ask, don't tell" policy came into effect in 1993, a group of military personnel was silenced by law. They were required to "not tell" about their sexuality, about their identity, about themselves. But by conducting interviews and writing this play, Marc has given these men and women a voice.

"The people I interviewed love their country. And they love the military. That's why it's a complicated thing," Marc Wolf has said. In this play you hear of that love. But you also hear of their anger, and you hear of their fear. You hear their sense of duty and their sense of humor. You hear of their loves and their desires. The play becomes a *cri de coeur* for them.

They've been told to "not tell". Marc Wolf has asked them to tell. And he is a great listener in a culture where making noise is more valued. He has a great ear for both the poetry of the vernacular, and the intricacies of syntax. For the mistakes, the repetitions, the cadences of everyday language.

He is aware that it is in people's malapropisms, in their stutters, in their idiosyncratic turn of phrase that their individuality and their unique philosophies shine through. It is in the grammatical mistake, in the unnecessary repetitions, where truth lies. And because his writing reflects his listening, in this play we too learn to listen. A sentence captures a thought; a paragraph, an entire character.

Out of the hundreds of hours of interviews, Marc has crafted a piece that manages to flesh out both sides of the argument. With humor, insight and compassion he is able to bring out the humanity of all his characters — both the ones we see suffer at the hands of this policy as well as the ones who profoundly believe in its necessity. But in my opinion, that's not where the greatest power of this piece lies. Because after the argument itself is settled, after every side has had its say, long after this policy is overturned, the voices of those who suffered will remain.

The fact is that there have always been gays and lesbians in the military. And as one of the characters so beautifully puts it, "Don't ask, don't tell…Well, that's what it's been all along anyway." But by making it an official policy the State has done two things: it has publicly recognized the existence of gays and lesbians in the military, and endorsed silencing them.

The military is a societal institution and as such it only echoes what is being debated in the rest of the country. Laws like this point to our shortcomings as a society. They point to where we are stuck as a culture. And this play shows the personal cost we pay when our commitment to democracy and an egalitarian society falls short of the ideal.

The man who came up with the phrase "Don't ask, don't tell…" — Professor Charles Moskos — wants it inscribed on his gravestone. I find that a very appropriate metaphor. It should be on a gravestone. For in it lies the death of so much of our idea of what American democracy is about.

When in 1892 Queen Victoria was asked to sign a law banning "acts of gross indecency between male persons," she agreed to do so. When asked why the law didn't apply to women, Queen Victoria replied "Women don't do such things." Ignorance has worked for us in the past, but most often it works against us.

Another American addresses us as a nation. It questions our commitment to equality. And it is a record of its time.

In one of the most moving moments in the play, Edward Patrick Clayton Jr.'s father asks him to change his name after he learns that Clayton is HIV positive, so that he won't corrupt or stain the family name. Many of the characters in this play use pseudonyms because they have to hide, they have to deny their identity. This is the price they have to pay. Marc Wolf, however, has given identities to these nameless men and women: he has spoken their words.

Any actor in America can pick up this play, and with very little else, perform it. It doesn't need extensive sets or costumes. All he (or she) needs is an empty space and an audience. In this way, Marc Wolf is ensuring that their words will be heard.

This play will move you, it will make you laugh, and it will enrage you. But above all, it will allow you to hear these people, in their own words, tell you what it is like to be silenced in a country that otherwise believes in telling. Marc has said please tell. Please tell me. Please tell us. We need to hear. Let this obscurantism not win. Let your voices be heard.

Their stories and their words will survive the struggle. Their words will survive and resonate in every theater where this beautiful play is performed.

Let us not forget these words. Let us not forget these individuals. These men and women who so loved their country, and so had to suffer for it.

Foreword

Sometime in 1996, I realized that the "Don't Ask, Don't Tell, Don't Pursue" law, which bans gays and lesbians from military service, had effectively silenced a group of Americans that had been very vocal during the 1993 debate. The gays in the military had either gone back into hiding or had been discharged from the military. The brutal history of the twentieth century has taught that silencing a community can lead to disastrous consequences, and I consider "Don't Ask, Don't Tell" a dangerous formula for the continued gagging and stereotyping of the gay and lesbian community. If I could give a dramatic voice to people who had been silenced, maybe I could add to the country's exploration of this very sensitive issue. At the same time, I knew it would be important to find people who could persuasively argue the military's point of view.

With that motivation, I started asking questions of people who had some connection with the issue of gays in the military, and I started to learn what it was like for people to live with "Don't Ask, Don't Tell."

From all of these questions, I have amassed a wealth of material in the form of stories. I have interviewed straight, gay, and lesbian military personnel, veterans from WWII to Desert Storm, civil rights lawyers, federal judges, politicians, activists, and professors of sociology, constitutional law and military history. The interviews have been tape-recorded, transcribed, and then edited into monologues using the interviewees' own words to construct the text for the play.

My goal has been to collect interviews that represent a wide variety of viewpoints, experiences, and deeply held beliefs. Some of the interviewees are gagged and only spoke to me anonymously — usually because of a career in the military or in professions where coming out would jeopardize them. Some demanded anonymity for fear of losing custody of their children. Interviews were conducted in person due to the performance aspect of this project: to portray these people honestly and specifically, it was important that I be with them to get a sense of their physicality and their world.

I hope that the voices heard in the play will help to encourage a more constructive national dialogue and a more politicized theatre audience.

– Marc Wolf

Thank You to the approximately two hundred people I interviewed who bared their souls in the hopes of bettering their country. Thank You to the following for help in developing the project:

INDIVIDUALS: Anonymous, Mitchell Anderson, Mary Bailey, David Barnathan, Seth Barrish, Michelle Benecke, Jim Darby & Patrick Bova, Betsy Breitenbach, Chuck Brown, Paul Camacho, John Capps, Chiqui Cartanega, Jamie Cesa, Jeff Cleghorn, Laura Clement, Richard Cohen/Conquette, Subrata De, Dennis Delaney, Tessa Derfner, Tristan DiVincenzo, Beatrice Dohrn, Johnna Doty, Kevin Duggan, Kate Dyer, James Ellis, Eilhys England, David Eppel, Lara Fetsco, Bill Goodman, David Marshall Grant, Bruce Greenwood, Alec Harrington, Mickey Harrison, Ken Hoyt, Robin Hubbard, Jack Hyman, Sarah Jarkow, Jim Jones, Stephanie Klapper, Marcia Kuntz, Rebecca Laibson, Cale Lehman, Whitney Lockhart, Julie Lynch, Ken Maldonado, Ruth Maleczech, Joe Mantello, Bruce & Maureen McKenna, John Moll, Robert Murphy, Mari Nakachi, Terry O'Reilly, Dixon Osburn, Liz Page, Robert Jess Roth, Trish Santini, Wayne Scherzer, Mark Sendroff, Ronn Smith, Joseph Steffan, Gerry Studds & Dean Hara, Jean Ward, Chandler Warren, William Waybourn, Carl White, Jeff Wolf, Meredith Messinger & Larry Wolf, Amy Wolf, Ralph Wolf, Gerald & Audrey Wolf, Evan Wolfson, and, of course, Robert Westfield.

ORGANIZATIONS: Gay Lesbian Bi-Sexual Veterans of America, Gay Lesbian Bi-Sexual Veterans of Greater New York, Servicemembers Legal Defense Network, William Joiner Center for the Study of War and Social Consequences, Lambda Legal Defense and Education Fund, Volunteer Lawyers for the Arts, The Actors Studio, The Barrow Group, Dixon Place, Urban Stages.

Another American: Asking and Telling is a sponsored project of the New York Foundation for the Arts with funding provided by: Michael Palm Foundation, Manhattan Community Arts Fund; Barbara Bell & Stephen Remen, Andrew Blatter, Luceil & John Carroll, James Cottrell & Joseph Lovett, John DaSilva, Michael Dively, Guillermo Fernandez, Rudy & Judy Froeschle, Corinne & Rolf Hoexter, Marie & Jim Karanfilian, Anita & Jay Kaufman, Ruth & Peter Laibson, Renee & Henry Lerner, Stephen Lindenmuth, Ronald MacDonald & Steven Schor, Olin Corporation Charitable Trust, June Panick, Watson Seaman, Eric Smith, Richard & Holly Stover, Randall Sturges, Gregory Taylor, Richard Willett, Debra & Ellis Wolf, Audrey & Gerald Wolf.

Additional funding provided by: James Ellis, Ted Snowdon, Andrew Tobias & Charles Nolan.

Notes:

- The text of *Another American: Asking and Telling* is based on transcripts of interviews conducted over a three year period. The monologues are created from the interviewees' actual words. Where appropriate, names and places have been changed.

- When parentheses are used within a word of a monologue, they denote that the word was unfinished by the speaker.

- A double or triple space between words indicates a very short pause.

- Numbers after a person's introductory name denote that the person appears more than once.

- Though some props are noted, the play could be performed without props.

Under Article 31 of the Uniform Code of Military Justice (UCMJ), you have the right to remain silent and to consult with a defense attorney if you are investigated. SAY NOTHING, SIGN NOTHING, GET LEGAL HELP. Call Servicemembers Legal Defense Network at (202) 328-FAIR for confidential legal counseling.

Act One

Prologue
Voice-over with young anonymous officer, US Air Force Reserve

Fatal Attraction
Anonymous young Lieutenant, US Army

Don't Ask Don't Tell
"Hannah & Anna Mae" - #1

Boot Camp
Edward Clayton, former Corporal, US Marine Corps - #1

In God We Trust
Al Portes, Petty Officer Second Class, US Navy

Picture of a Dog
"Hannah & Anna Mae" - #2

Gotta
Anonymous Colonel, US Army (Retired) - #1

Lesbian Social Club
Bridget Wilson, activist lawyer and former enlisted, US Army

The Midget
"Brendan," anonymous former Sergeant, US Marine Corps

Fix the Bullet Hole
Anonymous young enlisted soldier, US Army

The Kiss
"Hannah & Anna Mae" - #3

Good Guy/Bad Guy
Edward Clayton - #2

Sergeant Miriam Ben Shalom
Miriam Ben Shalom, former Staff Sergeant, US Army Reserve - #1

In the Beginning
Edward Clayton - #3

Act Two

Leavenworth
Ed Modesto, former Colonel, US Army

Two Cheers for Hypocrisy
Charles Moskos, sociologist and former draftee, US Army

The Constitution
Anonymous Major, US Army Reserve

Golden Armor
Anonymous Colonel, US Army (Retired) - #2

Mary Alice
J. Harris, former private, US Army

Mom
Dorothy Hajdys-Holman

Traitor
Frank Kameny, WWII combat veteran and long-time activist

Can You Fight?
Major General Vance Coleman, US Army (Retired)

Anger
Miriam Ben Shalom - #2

The Wall
Don MacIver, former Sergeant First Class, US Army

ACT ONE

Prologue

VOICED-OVER dialogue from actual interview tape:

MARC: Ok, I'll just put this tape recorder right in front of you, and it's very good so you don't have to feel like you have to talk right into it or anything.

WOMAN: [*Coughs.*] I'll try not to cough into it.

MARC: Whatever. And we can wander, you know don't don't feel like —

WOMAN: don't feel like there's a structure to it.

MARC: Right. And I'm really, I probably will use what you say, like I'll use your text verbatim...

WOMAN: Right

MARC: and I'll I'll probably use your words, um 'cause I'm I'm looking for....

WOMAN: personal stories.

MARC: Personal stories and I'm traveling all over the country and I'm talking to straight people and gay people and people who are parents of people who are in the military, and I'm coming at it from all sorts of viewpoints —

WOMAN: Well let me start off first.

MARC: and also if you want it's definitely gonna be completely anonymous, but I can be your voice.

WOMAN: Ok, well let me start off first. Right the anonymity, but I have to do something paranoid. Just to cover my ass. Are you....do you work for the government?

MARC: No.

WOMAN: Are you a police officer?

MARC: No.

WOMAN: Are you in the military?

MARC: No.

WOMAN: Are you FBI or CIA?

MARC: No.

WOMAN: Alright you're fine then.

Fatal Attraction

Anonymous young Lieutenant, US Army

In a vehicle, he's giving Marc a tour of his base...

Have you seen the Fort at all?
We'll just kind o' drive around I'll point out some ... hot spots to ya.

This is, this is a ... historic building.
It's it's pretty impressive.
You can see on the map,
       kind of the shape of it.
This used to just be kind of training sites and that kind of thing —

I have to tell you, I've had a bad experience recently —
       —and this is our chapel—
I met someone that was a neighbor,
       a gay man [*Clears throat.*]
and it was probably the first respectable relationship I'd had with a gay man
                                                      that I knew of —
                                                      really uhm —

       you know that wasn't dark and dirty and ahm
we ended up being together for about a year and a ha ... half,
aaaand, ahhm I broke off the relationship it was kind of –
       it was messy –
eeehhh he's kind of one of these – not –
       it's not a fatal attraction necessarily
              but, he just wouldn't let me go
              and called
              and would come and show up at my house
              I'd go out on a date and he'd show up
              that kind of thing.....

well [*Exhale.*] um —
  he's threatened to go to the command to talk to my boss about me,
            and y'know to out me …

Oh I just –
  I was just … sick I was just sick
    I have to tell you I was … literally sick for about 3 days –
      I got in a car accident, that day,
        ahm I had no business being on the road I was a wreck
        I was a wreck when he said that.
'cause I messed up my car big time   [*Big exhale.*]

That's my boss's house, right there.
— he's a brigadier general, a one star.
I know what I'm gonna say,
  when the General calls me into his office
    and the first thing I would say is –
      "he's out of his mind.
      I don't know what he's talking about"
And I would lie through my teeth …
  umm and I wouldn't feel bad about it
    and I'm not one to lie.
  I mean that's not that's not my nature
      but what I'm saying is I …
        I just don't feel like it's ummmm
  that's something –
    I'd be willing to lie.…

552

Don't Ask Don't Tell

Anonymous, "Hannah and Anna Mae" - #1

HANNAH *drinks from a long-neck Coors,* ANNA MAE *smokes.*
Sound of FIGHTER JET passing low overhead.

ANNA MAE: Would we have let you interviewed us five years ago? No — absolutely
                                                                     not.
              Do we feel totally safe with what you're gonna do with this?

HANNAH: Probly…. Yeah, I do.

ANNA MAE: Moresooo — I'm a little hesitant. I'm sittin' here thinking "what are
              we doing here? spilling our guts to this guy we don't even <u>know</u>?"

HANNAH: what I told Anna Mae ….

ANNA MAE: Don't say the name.

HANNAH: [*Refers to tape recorder.*] bleep, bleep….
              What I told <u>her</u> when you come out —
                    I said you know he could be a spook from the …
                        spook shop or something come down here to find out …
                          something about us so …
              you could be part of the old time witch-hunt people.

ANNA MAE: 'cause I wanna quit, if you are, let's get this over with right quick,
              go ahead and get me out of this. [*Giggles.*]
              [*Pause.*]
                    Maybe it'll help …
                        in some way … help somebody,
              it it probly won't help us … because we're not gonna change.

HANNAH: Maybe it'll help a youngster realize
                    she doesn't have to be such a bandwaver all the time,
          some of the kids are gonna get in trouble advancing in their ranks,
                  in their career if they don't keep their mouth shut
                          about who they sleep with.
                    and I can guarantee you that the military is just ……

I thought it was stupid …
>President Clinton to do anything to do with the military,
>>he's a draft dodger.

Now if you want [*Laughs.*] anything else about something he's done…
I think it's inappropriate for a draft dodger to take on a military question,
>especially when the draft dodger is in charge of the military.

Where was he in Vietnam?
I saw young men come back without legs and he was sitting in England.
So and I really have strong feelings about that,
>and I'm sure the young men that don't have legs anymore
>>have strong feelings too.

I didn't think the military would change,
>regardless of what happened to the ban.
and I know w.. with or without a ban
>>I would not have changed anything I did.
uh so I think it was – to me it was an irrelevant gesture.

ANNA MAE: Even if they didn't … lift it … and and

HANNAH: did did they? they did lift it didn't they?

ANNA MAE: no it's not … uh…

HANNAH: oh that's right, you —

ANNA MAE: there are still a lot of gay peo-

HANNAH: you can be on active duty —
>oh it's no … tell, no a(sk) —

ANNA MAE: no ask —

HANNAH: don't —

ANNA MAE: no tell

HANNAH: don't ask no tell.

ANNA MAE: don't ask don't tell.

HANNAH: OK, OK,   that's what it is ……
>Well that's what it's been all along anyway.

Boot Camp

Ed Clayton, former Corporal, US Marine Corps - #1

One of my recruiters knew …
        uh that I was gay —
                after I signed my contracts it was about a quarter to five
                        and he said "well I'm going to take off early today."
we walked two blocks down the road to the Gizmo
        which was the most infamous gay bar in the city.
apparently he was quite a regular customer at the bar there
        cause we walked in and everybody went "Bob"
        you know it's like Norm walking into "Cheers" you know.
had a drink …

he never came out to me and said I am gay uhhh
he n.. never made any sexual advances or things like that
        but just through um uh body language
                                and our conversation
                                        and then of course going to the Gizmo
and having a drink you know uh
he didn't really have to confess so.....

so um I joined and uh off I went to boot camp.
I just knew for sure it was a life of celibacy,
        y'know there goes,
                my sex life's over,
                        I'll I'll be blind and buried with hairy palms by the time I'm 25.

Well,
        there was one afternoon when the platoon
                when I think they were out at the confidence course or something
and I had been left behind as fire watch,
        it was my turn.
so a drill instructor or an assistant drill instructor

said that he was gettin' in the shower
and uh he says, "while I'm in here you you clean the duty hut."
    so I mean I did —
he was this big strong masculine you know
       hunky marine with arms like this you know
          very light mulatto skin
             which I've always had an affinity for –
And it was an instant hint to me because he left the bathroom door open
he even left the shower door open y'know
and made it a point to soap very well like in plain view.

I was sweeping up y'know
      I was looking up and smiling....
Of course it's always possible that someone from another platoon
      or one of the OICs or something
walk in and knock on the door
but y'know the flies were closed
      the curtains were drawn
        the shades were pulled and....
I … I went in.....
    Yeah …
        oh I love to shower.

He was nearly twice my size
y'know I'm I'm a small man as far as American men go ummm
but he was very big, very muscular
I mean when he picked me up out of the shower
he literally just picked me up like a baby
     and took me into the duty hut to the rack um
and you know that's
he he seemed kind of shocked –
      it was – you know it was like
"this is my first time," I said
      "to be on the bottom, I don't mean to have sex with a guy — to be on the
                        bottom."
so you know he was
     he was he was very —
I was surprised cause he was just so gentle.

556

and he was the first marine that I ever kissed —
Most marines won't kiss —
        fuck 'em all night long but don't dare kiss 'em.
I don't know why…
uhh the thing I always found amazing about marines is uhh
you you can have any kind of kinky raunchy whatever sex you want
        but don't kiss 'em.
            the only thing you can't do is kiss 'em.
but oh when you find a marine that likes to kiss there's nothing better.

I don't want people to get the idea that the marine corps is rampant with
                                            homosexual activity

but it is.

In God We Trust

Petty Officer Second Class Al Portes, US Navy
Senate Armed Services Committee Hearing: May 10, 1993

Mr. Chairman and honorable members of this committee, my name is Al Portes. I am a storekeeper second class petty officer with almost 6 years of active duty in the Navy.

From 1990, I swore as a US citizen. I adopted this country as my country for one simple reason. I hold a coin here, a quarter dollar coin that says, In God We Trust. And I did not come to this country because I was attracted to economic opportunities, but because I believe that this country offers me the chance to express myself in a way that I believe.

Now we come before this committee today, Mr. Chairman, and to those of us who have had to endure the confinement, isolation, and lack of privacy that deployment in the military should entitle, when you are sometimes deployed and navigated for extended periods of time at one particular time. And you have, like in my case, I live aboard a ship. And in my berthing, I have to share a berthing that is probably roughly the size of twice probably the size of a normal house living room, I have to share it with 60 other guys.

Now there are some that have tried to put this issue on a discrimination level, on a remember the blacks, remember the women. Well, I am a minority myself. I was born in the Dominican Republic, you know, and yes, I am Hispanic. And I still have to listen to the jokes about being a chili bean, or when they forget my name, calling me Juan Valdez, and all that. This is perfectly acceptable.

But this issue comes to the moral fiber of all of us, like me, believe in a God and believe that we are going to be judged, and you ask me to express my views, well I want to do that. Because yes, I find it morally, morally incorrect. This is an act of rebellion. This is an act of rebelling against the God I believe in. And I am sorry I cannot divorce myself of who I am as of this day or what I believe.

Now I came into this service because yes I was not lied to, and I knew that there were no gays, openly, allowed in the military. Now to throw something that attacks people like me, you know, right in my inner being, in my deepest thoughts, in who Al Portes is, well, I find it unacceptable.

Mr. Chairman, I am proud of being a military man in the US Armed Forces. But I will testify in front of this committee today, and this is not a call to mutiny or to massive disobedience, that Al Portes will refuse to serve with gays in the military. Now, when the incidents like the Iowa accident and the other mishaps that we had in the Navy, happen because of lack of trained personnel, please do not come blaming me.

Picture of a Dog

"Hannah and Anna Mae" - #2

HANNAH: She's the windiest one so let her answer.

ANNA MAE: I think just because you had an acquaintanceship with another female,
    you never thought of yourself as being gay or lesbian or queer uh
you just –
    it it ne(ver) — it wasn't talked about, you didn't see it on TV…

HANNAH: I didn't even know what it was.
In fact I don't even know if they had it on —
    you were asking her about the box when I …
        that security checklist thing,
            I don't know if that was even a question.
I just checked everything "no" cause I didn't belong to anything.
I don't remember if it –
    was it a question in the 60s?

ANNA MAE: Oh yeah. "have you ever participated in a homosexual activity?"
or some some words to that … [*Cough.*]
    on the enlistment [*Cough cough.*] on the enlistment contract.
I I really thought for someone to answer "yes" to that
            it was kind of like being ahhhh

HANNAH: communist.

ANNA MAE: uh no a … prostitute,
    that you went out every night an'
        had sex with different women every night of the week,
I mean I never thought ….uh …
I would I would not classify myself with that so I said y'know…
I didn't feel I was lying …
It's bothersome to have to be worried
    or have to think
        oh somebody's gonna say something
           or think something or …

I had nothing in the office
             that would indicate any sexual preference whatsoever.
I think you should be able to but unfortunately uh I would not do it,
I would not put a picture of my partner in my office.

HANNAH: I never had a picture of anybody on my desk
             other than the Chief of the Army Nurse Corps.
I think it's inappropriate.
I told my bosses it was inappropriate,
             I said, "is that a picture of your wife?
                          why do you have it in the office?"
They should have pictures of their superiors,
             the commanding general.
um their their their wife is not working there.
             They're working there as a role model for young people.
             They're not working there as uh married to this
                                                individual.

I had a picture of a dog in my office.

Gotta

Anonymous Colonel, US Army (Retired) - #1

A lot of people said I blew it —
            and I threw away a whole bunch of stars,
you know — youngest colonel in the Army,
            most decorated guy, and all that stuff —
but I couldn't stomach the waste … in Vietnam anymore,
      so I sounded off to the press.…
I'd seen so many young guys get blown away,
      because of dumb captains, dumb colonels, dumb generals, dumb politicians
            and it, the the death wheel just keeps turning –
But we don't learn from the past,
      that's why we make the same mistakes.
Where do you get judgment?
      You get judgment from experience.
well it's it's a very good segue —
                        gays in the military.
I … from my experience …
      my individual judgment, based on my experience with gays in the military.
my first experience …
I was a young corporal
      so I was like … eighteen,
            uh squad leader,
responsible for ten guys,
      first — any uh responsibility,
            so a big deal for me …
                  and uh —
            I had uh reconnaissance squad, in Italy,
and I had a soldier named Gotta, Pfc. Gotta.
Gotta uh was a good soldier and uh
      he uh…
and remember I'm a dumb kid so I don't I don't really –
      I'm not that smart about what's going on, uh …

But – I always noticed that he's banged up.
      OK?
and it ends up that …
            Gotta was … uh blowing everybody in the squad. OK?
      and   but   th … then they'd get –
            they would b … start drinking and they beat up on Gotta.
Now I never could understand why Gotta   behaved,
                        why he got beat … beaten up like he did,
and uhhh … and I never could get the squad —
      and I'd been trained under good sergeants
                  and I knew the proper   ways of leadership and so on
      but it was always conflict in my squad,
      I and I didn't know what the conflict was,
                        well now looking back,
      uh the conflict was that uh …
            these guys got it on with Gotta,
                  then felt guilty about it,
                        got a few beers in them,
                        and used him as a punching bag,
but for me as a leader –
      this broke up any cohesion that I'm trying to develop,
and what battles and and getting small unit from a squad to a an army is cohesion,
                                    team work.

Well when I went to my sergeant I said "look this Gotta is blowing all these guys,"
my sergeant said [*Claps hands.*] he's gone, he was on the next boat.
      That's the way it was treated.
and he was a leper
      he was gone, taken out of my squad, disappeared, somebody,
            somewhere in the company on the ship gone —
      and that was the end of it. then my squad got together,
and they became very effective and I didn't have any   problems and so on.

so uh lesson learned for me ......
      that gays are bad,
            cause they cause trouble
                  and it broke up my squad
                        and I didn't get it to where I wanted to get it,
                           in the time frame.

Lesbian Social Club

Bridget Wilson, activist lawyer and former enlisted, US Army

We're at a coffeehouse.

Darlin', it used to be virtually a lesbian social club because,
                              they kept the straight women out.

uh, because for one thing until the
        until the '70s you couldn't be married or be pregnant and stay in the military.
'was 1972 —
        before they stopped throwing women out who got pregnant.
And not all that long prior to that in the '60s
        before they decided that you couldn't throw a woman out of the military
                              because she got married.
OK?
so you wouldn't let women marry,
        and they couldn't get pregnant,
              and then they're sitting around going
                              "where'd all these dykes come from?"
                                                Right?

The Midget

"Brendan," anonymous former Sergeant, US Marine Corps

At a restaurant, eating dinner

I'm a bookmaker right.
I just today I had to drop off a very large amount of money for somebody
then I had to go to an office you know illegal bookmaking office
and do all these deals and transactions
and now I'm sitting in a restaurant discussing gays in the military.
this is what my life is today
it's just it's just everything
      it's it's there's no limit
          it's just I'm open.
what would my buddies from the neighborhood say about that now.
the guys that I grew up with were on a tear.
I'll give you an example
There was a guy named Micky Slade —
he was a midget
he was a child molester
      but I thought he was gay
he used to –
he was a midget right?
he used to go into the Woolworth's —
      stand on the little stool in the booth where you take the pictures,
          pull his pants down,
             take pictures of his dick
               and then show it to us.
you know he never touched us
he never did anything like that
he just and we were curious kids looking at a man's dick y'know.

so uh one time I was walking down Highland Street
and he he he called me into the pizza shop
so I go in and he buys me a slice

so now I take the slice and I'm walking down the street
I'm about eight years old he's about twenty-three but he's a midget
and we're eating the slice —

Two teenagers come walking down the street
I walk into my courtyard where I live
they're eighteen years old ... seventeen, eighteen years old
        Brian Walsh and Billy Sullivan.
"What are you doing?" they said to Micky Slade.
he's older than them but he's a lot smaller he's a midget.
"What are you doing, what are you doing with him? ...
        [*Then to Brendan— .*] Brendan, what's he— what the fuck are <u>you</u> doing?"

"Nothin' he bought me a slice a pizza."

"What are you doing with —
        [*Then back to Micky Slade— .*] "What the fuck are you doing with him, come
                                                                                    here."
They grab him they got him up against the wall,
"what are you doing with him?" they were saying to the midget Micky Slade.
"What are you doing with Brendan? what are you.... "
        cause they knew he was a pedophile.

He said "I'm not doing anything I bought the kid a slice of pizza."

"Brendan, what he do to you?"

I says "He didn't do anything."
so they kept fucking—
        kept badgering me.
I said "I didn't he didn't do anything he bought me a slice of pizza."
I started crying.
Well if he's crying..... <u>he</u> must have done something....
They beat this guy from one end of the street to the other
they beat him
there was blood everywhere
they really fucked him up bad.
and uh he had to go the hospital and shit.

but ever since then
you see I didn't understand it then,
after after that I always said
I'll always
I always remembered that
and I always swore that I would do that for little kids
and when I ended up in the Bronx I used to tell little kids
"you see us down there? you see where we are? anybody bothers you like that
you come down there and you get me."
so with that mentality that we actually talked to kids about it "you gotta watch
                                                                these queers"

he's a pedophile —
to us that's gay. We didn't know the difference.
so everybody became, everybody that —
that was a faggot — that's a fag. he's a faggot,
that's what it was,
so when we grew up everything was a faggot
so when we got old enough to kick people's asses,
when you saw a faggot you fucking..... [*Gesture with fist.*] you know what I'm
                                                                saying.

you're assuming that this guy
if if he had control over me would fuck me
he'd try to fuck me...—

Now you take a guy coming out of that neighborhood
and you put him in the military
I went into the marine corps
and you tell him there's we're allowing gays in —
he's thinking about the guy, dada-dadada, now they're taking a shower in boot
                                                                camp
there's seventy fucking guys in the shower
        thirty five guys at a time shower
well it's gonna cause serious problems because of the —

I'm a grown man who's willing to change and listen and try to grow.
I had thanksgiving dinner with my girlfriend and a gay man.
I just thought about that now.

but I think about all those things
I think about me being in the shower at 18
and I think wow fuck oh shit.
I mean you you know my friend that I'm having thanksgiving dinner with —
if he's standing next to me in the shower
I I feel I don't know how to feel.
I don't know ...
I'm told that that's — you know what I mean
and I learned that that's a fucked up thing.
I mean how does how does anyone feel naked with someone looking at ...
it's like a woman being naked in front of a man
she knows what men are like.
and men have this.....you know
it's like a woman fearing rape.

but you know what — so what —
I survived the fucking pedophiles in my neighborhood
what is a a gay man in the shower gonna do to me?
I'm gay I mean straight —
there I go Freudian slip "I'm gay" —
fucking Marc what have you done.
"I'm gay" you got me all screwed up now —
I'm fucking finding out at 39.
my girlfriend's gonna be furious.

[*Refers over his shoulder.*] this woman's listening to everything I'm saying.
so I don't —
but the thing is —
if you if you know and the and the guy knows that you're straight
I don't have a problem with it.
the guy knows I'm straight
        like we're not in the shower for any other reason than to wash our dirty asses
that's it.
y'know what I'm saying we're sh ... we're gay we're —
now there I go again —
we're in the shower, we're men — <u>you're</u> gay <u>I'm</u> heterosexual —
so what —
I'm washing myself OK.

you know and this guy might be washing himself.
Maybe — you know what — maybe I'm not good looking enough for the guy,
maybe he don't want to look at me, maybe....—
you know what I'm saying.

[*To waiter.*] no I'm almost finished thanks.
[*Looks over his shoulder again and says to eavesdropping woman:*]
I had heterosexual food.
[*Turns back and addresses "Marc" again.*]
That's what they serve in the military —
if you know any gay guys that wanna join they're gonna have to eat chicken
sandwiches –

This is what we heterosexuals eat.

He takes a big bite of sandwich.

Fix the Bullet Hole

Anonymous young enlisted soldier, US Army

This is just for uh all future parties,
　　I understand that I will remain anonymous
　　　　and my contributions anonymous to this entire uh interview.

If we walk down the street now and you know,
　　stop ten people and you ask them some question about the military,
　　　　and you you're gonna you're gonna get ten different responses
　　　　or you're gonna get ten stupid looks,
　　　　　　because they don't know but ...
you know when somebody calls up on the phone and they're doing the opinion poll
　　that's all that matters to the guy in charge cause he's gotta be –
　　　　he's gotta constantly be worrying about handling damage
　　　　　　　　　　　　　　　　　control.
because you know ... it's ...... country's run by opinion polls...
　　and the people that you know bitch moan and gripe are the ones
　　　　　　　　　　　　that have never been,
　　　　have never worn the uniform,
and people are like ah you know –
　　very Hollywood kind of view of it, and it's like ...
you know that that rankles with me big time too
　　cause my mother's like that,
　　　　you know very CNN mom like
　　　　　　"oh I saw it on TV so ..."
you know and anytime a statement starts like that,
　　I automatically turn you off
　　or I get pissed in a heartbeat, whichever –
　　　　depending on which mood I'm in at the moment, but it's like ...
Who the hell cares whether or not — what somebody's sexual orientation is,
It's irrelevant,
OK right now we have a whole bunch of people that are like not trained to fight,
　　we have equipment that's so friggin old that I had trucks

that still have bullet holes from Panama,
Panama was ten years ago,
        you'd think somewhere in ten years
            we would have come up with the money to fix the bullet hole.
There's nobody to fix the bullet hole.
I went to the range to fire actual live ammunition, like 3 times —
                                                a year.
                I'm in the infantry.
                    you pay me to jump out of airplanes.
I'm supposed to be the first one that they drop in front of everybody else and
                                be like "OK now stop."
That's great,
        but that issue will never be addressed because you know what?
It's not up there,
        and it doesn't work for you know you can't do a glitzy little cool slide show
                                    about…. whatever.
I mean everything from everything from
        y'know hey they need they need
            you know you gotta get cold weather jackets to people or
                you gotta get,
                    you gotta come up with a better you know standard boot
                        that you're gonna issue to people —
                            whatever the case may be,
Those are little things and
you know you don't grab a head(line) –
        you don't have like a 6 o'clock headline news about
            "the army today issued new boots,"
you know but if today the army
        you know discovered another you know drill sergeant sex ring somewhere
                                            well,
                you know that's gonna be on *Hard Copy, Inside Edition*, everything else,
umm so if if one day the headline is
        "today the army lifted the ban on –
            you know or destroyed —
                got rid of the don't ask don't tell policy,
                    and homosexuals are now freely accepted and admitted into
                                    the armed forces" …

You would start a firestorm of debate,
     and ... all the attention is gonna be focused on that
         and everything else is gonna be — get put to the side
           and ... now what have you gained?
And it's unfortunate but there's gonna be a quicker response to that
     and more resources dedicated to that
         than to like oh yeah we forgot the ...
           you know send bullets to Kosovo,
              so right now they're just standing there like doing nothing....
                            but ...

No. do I have a problem with it? no.
Is it gonna cause more grief than it's worth?
     there's a definite chance.
You know ...
     And it sounds harsh and inconsiderate and and whatnot,
         but I would hope that they would focus on something more relevant.

The Kiss

"Hannah and Anna Mae" - #3

HANNAH *speaks*, ANNA MAE *looks on.*

HANNAH:
All the men in my family were in the military.
So, it was the thing to doo.
um my father died when I was a baby
     and I grew up as –
        I was literally raised as a as a boy I guess,
                   uh in terms of how little girls are raised.
My older sister was raised very feminine,
             in skirts
       and I was raised   as the little helper,
          the provider
              the … the mother's little man in coveralls.
       probly   for Sunday go to meetin' kind of stuff I wore a dress
             but other than that I was always in   coveralls,
               at a time when women didn't wear britches.
I grew up   very sheltered in terms of knowing
             that there was anything in life other than hes and shes.
I was in the Army for about —
     probly fifteen years before I had my first experience
            and all I did was kiss a woman on the lips.
When I kissed that woman,
    it was such a tremendous event,
       I started calling all my close friends
           to tell 'em how wonderful it was,
and thank goodness I called this one girl that was … was —
    I was a major then
      and I called her and she says,
        "hav… who have you—
        have you called anybody else in the military,
        have you called anybody that you work with?"

"No, you're the first —"

        she says
        "don't call anybody come over and let's talk."
and that's when I found out about –
        that you don't talk about these things.
Cause I really didn't know
        I was that stupid that you didn't –
        cause I thought it was so neat that everybody should know about it,
and I thought (what the —) hell I mean that was the greatest event of my life [*Laughs.*]
because I, I wasn't   nuts
        I wasn't uh   cuckooo.
        I thought I was you know something was wrong with me.
I thought I was the en …
        only woman in the entire world that loved other women the way I did.
I never …
        it never dawned on me
        that there were other people like me….
        or that you could do anything with it.
        you could
            you know I just thought
            it was just
            I had to grow up spinster or something.
that's what   people did where I came from—
        if you didn't get married, you just became a spinster.
but at that time,
when the kiss occurred,
        we went back to Denver   and went to bed
        and I didn't really know what to do when we got to bed …
cause the kiss was so wonderful —
        it was a kiss on the lips.
It was so wonderful….
        and that's when she says –
        told me that I was a butch,
        and I thought oh well …
        I need to figure out what to do about that.

Good Guy/Bad Guy

Ed Clayton - #2

Two MPs took me,
        slammed me down on the ground busted my nose
            and I had six stitches up here in my head –
                whipped the handcuffs out — handcuffed me
                        and hauled me off to the brig.
I set in a cell for about thirteen hours uhh
        no food no water no sleep no you know just I'd be sitting there asleep
            and just about the time I.. I'd fall off to sleep,
                one of the guards come by with a billy club
                      and bang on the the rack or something you know —
so at the end of thirteen hours I was
        I was emotionally just drained,
        but that's when NIS likes to get hold of you.
So they they took me in …
        They were playing good guy bad guy…
            but alll they wanted was —-
                "who else do you know that's queer?"

um they said that they had notified my father
        and my father –
            has had mmmmajor,
                it it's a miracle the man's still alive,
                he's had major heart trouble for the   for the past 30 years, uh
but you know you know
        "your father's your your father just couldn't take it you know
            we called and told him and all of a sudden the line went dead
                we finally found out you know he's in the hospital
                    and and they don't expect him to live
      you know you just sign this paper
            and and give us the names and we'll let you go home."
Four days I was held by NIS.

I would just refuse to answer their questions you know:
    "where do the gay people hang out?
    what bars are the gay bars?"
you know "I don't know of any gay bars in Japan."
um and and you know when they asked me for for names
        to give them specific names
            I just said,
                "I am not going to give you names of other people that I know are gay
                                                    I absolutely refuse."
oh the the goo ... the good guy was like you know
    "we understand but you know you're going to jail for a long time,
        we're talking probably if you were convicted of all these charges,
            we're talking probably 25, 30 years in prison,
                you could make it easier on yourself" —
and I'd say yeah make it easy on myself by putting somebody else through this crap
        by ruining someone else's life,
            no thank you,
                you know throw you can throw me in jail for 30 years,
        and I I actually told 'em at one point I —
            it was the one shining moment of interrogation
                                        when I got under their skin.
                "send me to jail I don't care I'll have all the men I want then."
                    you know [*Chuckle*.] and that <u>really</u> got under their skin.

I was shipped to to Camp Pendleton
    where nobody knew me
        you know nobody knew of my outstanding service records and awards
                                        and everything I had done.
        all they knew is "hey we got a queer coming in tonight boys."
um and that night I –
        is is the only time while I was waiting discharge
            that I l.. literally feared for my life.
ummmm I was chased out a window I spent half the night on a roof, um –
my seabags were dumped out
uh were defecated and urinated on
uh during the night

uhm finally
  there were a group of about 4 of 'em that were were chasing me down the street
   and I ran out in front of an MP car
    which almost hit me
     but he was able to stop
and um y'know I explained to him what was going on
  but of course — I had come out of the woods and onto the road
   and just as soon as the guys chasing me —
    you know —
 first thing I said to the MP is,
  "There they are, get 'em"
 and they're like
  "NO - you stand still."
   you know they had drawn their guns –
 so y'know I said
  "These guys are chasing me,"
  you know well
   "try — they threatened to kill me."
"Well why?"
well you know I had to say it,
  "because I'm awaiting discharge."
"Well why do they want to kill you just because you're getting discharged?"
"Because I'm being discharged because I'm gay."

They took me down to um
 to the um
  to the poli ... to the MP headquarters, police station
   to try and figure out what to do
    because obviously I couldn't go back to the marine house.
uhm so they decided to
 uh to keep me
  uh in jail over night –
um sometime during the night someone came into my cell –
 uhm how I was —
  they put me in a cell by myself
   which was good thinking

if they'd only remembered to lock the door,
                              or not give this guy a key or whatever ——
so um he ... he ... assaulted.... me....
[*Pause.*]
        I — he was bigger and stronger than me —
                there was a, there was a good fight,
                        which is another reason I think maybe
                                he paid one of the guards to turn their backs?
                        because there was so much noise coming from that cell,
                                I don't know how it could not have attracted the attention
                                                of one of the guards.
it — first me screaming for help,
        trying to avoid a fight,
                calling for the guard,
and there was no answer.
and then once the fight actually got in process I mean
        you know, I hurt him as much as he hurt me
                um uh we were both bleeding and bloody....
I'm I mean I'm I'm I'm a pretty good fighter
        but you know when when I'm outweighed and outsized umm....
ehhh — he won.
[*Long pause.*]

The next day though –
over to the to the medical call,
        and I was tended to —
and he was he was there with his papers
        and and I found out –
                what what I did was I saw his his record
                you know the military uses all these little color coded little round dots
well there was this   big —
        like a three inch orange dot
                right in the middle of the front of his uh
                        of one of the records he was carrying around, his medical record –
and um you know I was asking the doctor about my chart
        I said you know,
                "what's this what's this blue sticker on mine
                        and what's this red sticker on mine mean?"

and you know he was telling me what all the different things meant.
and I said "well y'know I've noticed someone round here with a great big ol'
orange spot,

what do they —"
he said "stay away from those — those are the guys that have AIDS."

After that I was put out at the back gate
and this is what infuriated the me the most.
the back gate at Camp Pendleton is fourteen miles from the nearest pay phone
anywhere
and I was put out at the back gate
with nothing but the clothes on my back,
and uh told "hasta la vista," you know.

um I I finally walked –
it took me a few hours but I walked to uh uh a pay phone
and eh found out where the nearest bus stop was
and actually got a bus into downtown Los Angeles —
which was a <u>scary</u> experience....
um I lived on the streets of downtown Los Angeles for four days.

And finally I
the the the thing that made me   think about calling um
was I I saw a billboard on the side of a bus,
for the uh Gay and Lesbian Community Center of Los Angeles
with a phone number on the side,
so I called 'em and they gave me a number for a woman veteran ...
Sergeant Miriam Ben Shalom.

Sergeant Miriam Ben Shalom

Miriam Ben Shalom, former Staff Sergeant, US Army Reserve - #1

The problem started when Leonard Matlovich was on the cover of *Newsweek* —
                                                   1975—
and I said "why are they kicking him out?"
you know um and "well," I said "well who cares?"

And and so what happened was I guess I started asking too many questions
and I got called in and was asked "Sergeant Ben Shalom are you a homosexual?"
and I said yes although I I don't like that term —
        homosexual is an adjective. .....
They proceeded to to y'know find me...
        that I was going to be considered for discharge.
and they recommended that I take a psychiatric evaluation
        and I asked if it was a direct order
                and they said no they're recommending it
                        and I said I refuse to do so. I am a lesbian I am not sick....
                                There's a difference.
and inside of myself I said
        well this really   stinks except I used another word...
and if I were not speaking into a tape recorder I might use much stronger language.
and I went public with it.

um you know it it wasn't fun
        because there were darned few of us who were public in those days
        and to be a Jewish lesbian from the midwest was even a rarer thing.

I've had my brake lines cut.
I also had the the lug nuts on the drive wheel of the vehicle I owned at the time
                                        loosened -
the wheel did come off —
        if it had come off at expressway speeds the ...
        it probably would have rolled
                I probably would have been killed. [*Pause.*]

I was a vocal gay activist and I was fair game back then.
and um oh yeah y'know the good old days weren't exactly the good old days.
I mean um lots of phone calls in the middle of the night
      people threatening to kill me, to disembowel me, to shoot me,
you know people screaming at me —
I remember one time one black lady called me the antichrist
      which is hilarious because I'm a Jew and I told her as much
I said I can't be.
y'know I am not the antichrist
      um hello Jewish person here you know.

I had the same thing down um in '93 in Clearwater Tampa
there's a bunch o' yahoos down there I I kid you not in pointy white hats and
                                          white sheets
— I'm a northern girl I had never seen this before OK first I was —
my joke is I was o-ffended because their shoes didn't match their dresses OK.
um but I watched fifteen hundred gay people freeze
      because the KKK and Aryan Nation
these young punks in black you know fatigues
      with their shaven heads
         were over there
and I I stood there and I faced them and I said my name my rank my serial number
      and said "here I am what will you do?"
and when they didn't do anything I deliberately turned my back on them and
walked away
yes my shoulder blades were twitching
      but it is the only thing you can do
      in the face of things like that
      because it takes away their power.
and we've digressed from the '70s — I apologize
would you like me to go back?

In 1978, or excuse me May of —
      I beg pardon wrong date
in May of 1980
um the Eastern Federal District Court, Judge Terence Evans of Wisconsin
ordered a writ of mandamus
and had ordered me immediately to be reinstated

the Army ignored that writ of mandamus for seven years.
and I actually had to go back to court
        to inform the Court that their writ of mandamus had never been enforced —
The Army promptly sent me a check for fifteen hundred dollars
                saying this is my back pay and I never cashed it.
I gave it to my attorney and said this is this is the wrong amount of pay anyhow
        um but that's not the point here
        I want my job back I was ordered reinstated.
and so I waited and I waited and I waited.
well I had to go back to court and notify the Court....

so finally.... I went back in in 1987.

Yeah I was the first openly gay person in the history of this country
        to go back in and serve under court order.

and I went back in.
        and —
interestingly enough it was the black troops who sat down and ate chow with me
I was sitting at this table — all by myself...
nobody would look at me
        nobody would sit with me
                I didn't say anything
and it was and it was black enlisted people came and sat down with me.

um they would not allow me to re-enlist
so that began a second case which I eventually lost
        under the um silly Seventh's uh ruling of uh speech equals conduct?
which I always found very interesting
that because I I refused to lie
                and therefore self identified by virtue of telling the truth
                        that somewhere somehow I would do something.
Whatever happened to the Constitution?
and it's the same —
        I mean I think it's hilarious.

it's the same issue that's being argued in most of the cases this day
it's the speech issue: "Don't Ask, Don't Tell, Don't Pursue"
     <u>SPEECH</u>.   Speech.
the simple ability to talk about what your life is
    and people do all the time.
       speech.
I mean we aren't talking about sashaying down the main drag of the military base
    while wearing lavender fatigues,
         we aren't talking about misbehaving you know
            or or bad conduct here.
We're talking about speech.

In the Beginning

Ed Clayton - #3

In the beginning the reason I wanted to be   a a marine
      was because   my father was one.
I come from a family of marines,
      my father was a marine,
         and his father,
            and his father uh back seven generations.
"My daddy was a marine."
And I can just remember …
      when when I was eight years old we were down in the basement –
        my brothers and I playing around –
          we came across this big old green chest,
and it had an old –
      it was a Marine Corps footlocker –
and it had a lock on it
      and over the months we managed to get the lock –
        you know take the hasp off and get into it,
and I just remember seeing that Essential Subjects textbook,
      which I immediately took
        so I could memorize the General Orders –
          I mean I knew my General Orders by the time I was ten years old.
uh and this shiny Marine Corps uniform –
      he had dress blue uniforms that was folded in there,
        with his … all of his memorabilia,
          mess kit and y'know all –
            everything from his days in in the Marine Corps.

My father would let me stay with him,
      up until the —
        up until he found out that I   was infected with HIV.

I di ...
      I didn't know that he knew   uhh,
          but my sister had had told him.
uh which I don't
      I don't hold against her –
          she had the best of intentions.
but that night at the dinner,
      I sat down at the dinner table and I noticed ...
            I've got a styrofoam plate
                  and plastic silverware and paper napkins
                      and a styrofoam cup.
I looked up and I said,
      "so I take it you know something."
        you know
           and he said ... "yeah" –
              and then he got up and left the table.

So I –
      my father and I haven't spokennnn in about two years now.
um a(s)... as much as I would like to, you know –
um he just –
      he he wishes –
        he said I would speak –
         he tells my sister,
            "I'd I'd speak to him again if he –
               if he'd just do the one thing I ask him,"
    which was to change my name,
        because I'm Junior. —
          Edward Patrick Clayton Junior.

End of Act One

ACT TWO

Leavenworth

Ed Modesto, former Colonel, US Army
A SPEECH to the members of Gay Lesbian Bisexual Veterans of America

Actor enters at end of intermission and addresses audience directly.
House lights remain up.

OK, my name's Ed Modesto. I was a colonel in the US Army.

In the middle of Fort Carson there's a park called Ironhorse Park
and a person who I knew had left his phone number in the bathroom in Ironhorse
                                                                      Park
      for a good time call Steve,
         and left a number.
The CID people called this number
    and set up a date with him
        and as soon as they were together
           he was arrested
             for making a move on the CID agent.
As an agreement not to be court martialed or have it proceed any further,
    he agreed to turn in other people that he knew were gay.
He turned in twelve of us,
    um   one of the people committed suicide,
        I was court martialed
           I believe there was another court martial
             and the rest of the people were dishonorably discharged.

I have to tell you a little bit about my ex lover was …
      uhm the exact opposite of me —
          very very flamboyant,
              he was a drag queen,
                  who performed almost weekly,
                       in Colorado Springs and in Denver.
     Actually he did very well too,
        made more money at that than he did at his regular job.

ahh but we lived
     we lived off post in on in Colorado Springs.

OK, I had to bring that part up because
     when I was,
        that day that I was arrested
           the MPs took me down to the house where
                   where I lived off post.
We get there and,
     as I said James was a drag queen –
well they found   oh at least a hundred dresses,
     and wigs, makeup,
        panty hose, bras and um –
           not mine,
              but anyway they were there.
And so all these things were inventoried uhm …
I meant to bring the list of inventory because it was like about 300 different items,
     that they found um …
When I look back –
     when I was looking back through it last week or the week before,
        some of 'em are actually kinda   ridiculous at this point.
        One of the things that they they took
              as evidence of homosexual activity
     I play the piano,
        was a vocal scorebook of *La Cage aux Folles*…
so I mean,
     if you have that book in your house or the music,
        you better get rid of it.

Uh ....
>   In Colorado Springs there is a AIDS house called the Lambda House?
>   and we both did volunteer work at this Lambda House.
And I told you that James was a drag queen
>   and that we used –
>   he used to do benefit shows for for the Lambda House a lot.
And so one time I said I'll do it ...
That was not a good idea
>   because that happened to be one of the days that the CID people came.
I've done drag maybe once in my entire life
>   and I'll never ever do it again.
First of all I was very ugly,
>   but also ...
>   I got charged with impersonating a female as conducting unbecoming,
>   and that charge is the one that probably was ...
>   was broadcast the most,
>   because then afterwards, there would be headlines in the newspaper:
>   "transvestite colonel arrested,"
and I was –
I made it into *Star Magazine* and *National Enquirer* ...
>   uh there's a cartoon that appeared in the *Washington Post*
>   that shows the backdrop of the Hide 'n Seek
>   and it has two military police dragging this   woman out of there
>   saying come along whatever,
>   and   the woman is saying "that's sir to you"
>   and it has my name on it.

I was sentenced to nine months at Fort Leavenworth.
And so uh...
>   got to Fort Leavenworth in –
>   that was around the first part of October of that year,
>   and I was there until the following May.
Uh –
>   That part is not very pleasant –
>   I still have a difficult time talking about that.
I was discharged from prison on May 7th, 1991.

Uh I had not come out to my family that I was gay,
    until this horrible horrible thing –
Oh by the way Mom and Dad
    I'm gay and I'm in jail.
And my parents –
    my parents were both born in Mexico
        and I don't and honestly I don't think my mother to the day I got out
            ever understood what – what I was trying to tell her,
    My dad did,
        but my mother just couldn't. I also have three children,
    who I had not told I was gay.
And uh …
if anything came good of this is that I really came close to them.
I I I know now that,
    before this I was really growing far apart from them,
        just because I thought "I can never tell 'em I'm gay
            because then they'll never speak to me again,
                my my family would disown me"
                    and it it turned out to be the opposite –
        if I –
            you know if I if I had to find a good thing
                it has to be that I became close with my family,
    although there's alot easier ways to come out to your family,
        a lot easier.
uh and there we are.....
[*Applause.*]
Thank you.

Two Cheers For Hypocrisy

Professor Charles Moskos, sociologist and former draftee, US Army

In a Greek restaurant. GREEK MUSIC is playing.

So you wanna talk to Professor Moskos — "Mr. Don't Ask Don't Tell."
y'know for some I'm the Great Satan.
I came up with the idea and I wrote it first to Sam Nunn,
and and I got a "don't ask don't tell don't seek don't … flaunt."
Later the Defense Department changed it — "don't ask don't tell don't pursue."
I preferred "seek" because I like to keep it anglo saxon words,
      throw in that Latin made stuff y'know –
          I thought it ruined the uh … the resonance.
[*He looks up at approaching waiter.*]
Ohhhh that's our appetizer huh, [*Chuckle.*]
we'll put that in the middle here
      this is your water I guess,
          Did you eat? uhh I hope you haven't eaten…..

I believe –I believe I got the idea…
I remember like a little   y'know light bulb went up like in a cartoon.
I was at the water cooler [*Chuckle.*]
      and I was thinking about other stuff and
          "I think I got it, don't ask don't tell."
And it came to me like in a flash,
      almost a divine inspiration,
          put that on there. [*Laughs and points to tape recorder.*]

I really wanted to ss … get –
      I thought this was killing the Clinton administration,
Clinton also came with some other baggage as you know
          he wasn't the most popular guy with the military to begin with,
so he starts off with a handicap then he comes off with one of his first initiatives
          was lifting the gay ban ……

and his, his popularity began to plummet.
so the question was......
    how to get him off the hook ...
In my world of druthers,
    I sort of looked at the – the inform(al) – ...
      like I — with my days in the Army,
        don't make an issue out of it,
but I am not for open gays in the military.
And if you say well that's not fair that's toughfff.

Privacy ...
uh my argument is basically uh   the privacy argument,
    and it's sort of wink wink   nod nod,
      but   why not have women and men then
        share intimate quarters together?
well, we do it for reasons of modesty,
    rightly or wrongly,
      I think rightly,
        I'm a prude,
          so there's a s ... element of prudishism.

[*Waves over to people leaving restaurant.*]
Efaristo para poli.
    efaristo mea.... take care....
[*Back to* MARC.]
Runs a fruit produce stand.
uhhh I also write about Greek Americans,
I think that's sold more than any of my other books. [*Laughs.*]

so a little ... my my argument is two cheers for hypocrisy.
You have to be a little bit hyp hypocritical about this.
They have showered,
    and if I –
      it's like a peeping Tom,
        I'm — if there's a peeping Tom and I don't know it,
          no harm done you might say,

but if you tell me I'm peeping,
        then there's …
                so don't tell me.
Not that they're gonna look at me, particularly, but uh.…
[*Sucking on his straw.*]
You don't know my sexual orientation either.
        Remember it's always don't ask don't tell.
I won't announce my sexual orientation –
        who knows? [*Chuckle.*]
It's my business.

It's – gonna put in my epitaph by the way, I've asked them …
On my epitaph on my tombstone they're gonna put "don't ask don't tell,"
        I think it's a good epitaph.

The Constitution

Anonymous Major, US Army Reserve
A LECTURE

The framers of the Constitution believed,
    that the military was the most dangerous government power,
and that it of all powers should be most closely subject to constitutional scrutiny.
and yet ironically,
    we have exactly the opposite.
We have the institution most dangerous to liberty
    that is least governed by constitutional principles.
It's a complete turnaround from framers' original intent.

Time and again the Federalists argue that these institutions are constitutionally
                                    controlled,
    you don't have to fear them,
and on top of that,
    there will be no modeling of the militia –
        primarily because they installed the second amendment to prevent that–
What they're talking about by modeling
    is they're talking about selecting certain people to serve in the military
        as opposed to others.
    It's like modeling clay,
        it's like taking something and turning it into the form that you want.
Once you do that,
    you eliminate what they perceive to be the militia's great strength,
        and that is that it was of the people,
            that it would be broadly defined,
                that citizens from all classes would participate.

Well the problem is right now that's not what we have,
    we have the worst of all possible worlds
        according to the words of the framers themselves,
you can look this stuff up in the records of the debates,

you don't have to trust me for it.
we have a standing army,
        which is highly professional
                and it is also modeled –
                        at least right now against gay people.
It was against African Americans, and Japanese Americans at one time,
                when they rounded up Japanese citizens in World War Two –
                        now these are citizens, US citizens –
I mean it happened fifty years ago, it shouldn't be beyond the imagination.

It's modeled and,
        it isn't controlled by the Constitution because ... the Courts don't require it
                                                                        to be
                because the the Courts are claiming that they they ...
They they're claiming that they can't really tell field commanders how to do their
                                                                        business,
        that justices can't tell people who are out fighting in the field ...
        how to take a machine gun nest.
Now I think that everyone would agree that rogue justices
        should not be telling captains and colonels in the field
                how to organize their troops to take a machine gun nest,
but we're not talking about that here,
we're talking about constitutional principles
        and the military is not IS NOT the vehicle for deciding constitutional
                                                                        issues.

and when we go before the Courts
        and we say this is an an issue involving freedom of expression, and speech,
                or involving uh equal protection or due process,
we're not asking them about how to take a machine gun nest,
we're asking them to interpret the Constitution...
        which in this case they won't do to the military.

"Don't Tell" quite literally is so broad that in telling my mother I'm gay,
        that could lead the military effectively to subpoena her,
                if they wanted to discharge me,

and frankly they all think that's OK that's hunky-dorey
 'cause we're in the military and it's all legitimized
  based on the fact that we've gotta have this separate culture.

Well I think you can have this separate culture and still obey the Constitution.

Golden Armor

Anonymous Colonel, US Army (Retired) – #2 (also "Gotta," Act I.)

Envision living in a situation tw — [*Quick cough.*]
    twenty-four hours a day,
        sixty ... minutes an hour,
            sixty seconds a minute
                uh with somebody with a ...
                    aiming a rifle at you [*Aims imaginary rifle at Marc.*]
And I and I haven't –
    and as a young kid,
        'til I was able to block it all,
            uhhhh   I'd be going along
                and I I'd see me, in my head,
                  and I'd see a North Korean
                      looking at me like that [*Aims rifle.*]
                    me with it ...
                        I'm in his sights?
And I would start going [*Laughs.*]
    "Why, why why,"
        I swear to God 'cause I knew he was up in that tree.
Or another terrible thing I had was I saw a an enemy mortar gunner turning the
                                          wheel,
    and a guy standing behind him putting putting a shell down the tube.
And I had to eh –
    you go crazy if you maintain that stuff in your brain,
        so I had to dismiss that.
Most of the soldiers are –
    that are, that are in infantry,
        that are in marines,
            that do that dying stuff...

Most of the people that are dying age
        and and do the dying business,
                are far from the people in the air force operating their computer,
                        flying around in their airplane,
                                don.. don't really get into the the killing stuff....
Uh they they have gotta bel ...
        they're they've gotta believe that they're bullet proof ...
                there's a thing of machoism,
                        that they gotta swagger
                                they gotta be tough,
                                        and they gotta think they're bullet proof
        and they gotta think that they –
                they wear Golden Armor
                                        no bullet can ever hit 'em
                                                and if you don't have that mentality,
                        that it ain't gonna happen to me,
                                there's no bullet around here that's got my name on it,
uh if you don't have that then you're gonna crack up,
        you just couldn't go through. [*Snaps fingers*.]
So...
        so if you in any way remove this Golden Armor –
                this machoism
                        then you fuck with a guy's head
                                and when you fuck with a guy's head it's all over...
uh because   the most important aspect in battle,
        is not that F-22,
                it's not that Abrams tank,
                        it's not that eh AEGIS cruiser,
The most important thing is man,
        and the most important thing in combat
                the kind of combat we were we just talked about
                is uhh the spirit of man,
and if you fuck with his spirit in any way, you destroy him. [*Snaps fingers*.]

So the thing that you don't want to ever   change,
        in the American fighting man ...

Don't tamper with that spirit.
and don't tamper with that w.. warrior ethic,
     which the two come together,
         "I'm a warrior I can do a hundred fifty, five hundred pushups and so on."
And uh,
And I think that trying to force feed gays into combat units,
     would would disrupt that spirit,
        and it could put the nation in jeopardy,
           the national defense of the of the United States in jeopardy.

Mary Alice

J. Harris, former private, US Army

I was one of the lucky ones pulled through,
      thank GOD I did, UGH
you know you pass them on the street
      and I go man,
           I can see how it — how they lost it.
I mean really
      y'know cause
          and I mean
             for me <u>being</u> there
      and I see these people out on the street and I go mmaann…
I can see how they lost it.
and it only takes a couple seconds,
      to be in that whole war zone to see all that around ya,
                    to lose it.
                    and I go damn [*Chuckling.*]
Mary Alice pulled through you bastard,
      which was my nickname but that's a whole 'nother story in Vietnam Mary Alice
             my nickname over there for ten and a half months,
                yeah,
          how they gave me <u>that</u> nickname.
Well some days it was a hundred and thirty degrees in Vietnam,
      a hundred and thirty.
          and when you came back from out in the fields every day from fighting,
             you're exhausted, you are hot …
             I mean more than hot, see a hundred and thirty is —
             MMMANN …
And then in that
      and then plus with the steel pot on my head –
          I said that's why I still have headaches that goddam steel pot on my head
                for ten and a half months
                you'd have a headache too.
and then with the jungle boots on and all that ammunition and grenades hanging
                    on ya.…

Anyway when you come back from   fighting out in the fields,
     you just want to let,
         just take that steel pot off …
           and look up and go thank God that you made it another day …
[*Pause.*]
I was.…
I'll just stop and take a little break,
     I'll be OK in a couple of seconds,
         sometimes I get choked up but that's OK.

But they put me in a –
     well I'll have to wait a couple of seconds.
[*Very long pause.*]
I was in the Mekong Delta it was the worst booby trapped   area in Vietnam —
     all of Vietnam,
         it was the worst booby trapped area.
They take you by helicopter.…
     and they drop you off into an area
         out in the rice paddies where there are suspected VC, Viet Cong.
and those helicopters didn't land right on the ground and you just step out
               like you're walking down a red rug.
NNNoooooo –
     you jump out that helicopter like John Wayne
             there I am with a goddam   rifle up like this,
          and you jump in the rice paddies,
          you got water up to here,
             oooohhhh mmmannn.
uh — every day.
And the –
     at the end of the day,
         you come back   with not all your friends …
     and some days you come back with   all your friends.
Yeah.
the days you don't come back with your friends,
     you   are   a messss.

and I'm not sayin' friend friends,
    but your –
        just like if three of us go out and you go …
           we didn't bring one back.

Where am I? I got a steel pot on my head I got a headache again, you bastard.

Anyway I …. took my jungle fatigues,
    and I would cut them off.
and it was sort of like the real macho guy you know they cut 'em off down to their
                                    knees,
    I had mine cut off where the cheeks of my ass was hanging out,
        it's haaaahhhht.
        you don't cut 'em off down to here, be fucking pullin' 'em up anyway.
So — and anyway I cut them off and there I am
    like eighty pounds …
        real skinny …
           with these goddam jungle fatigues on…
              with my   cheeks of my ass hanging out.
And there I am with the jungle boots on
    and of course there I am walkin' …
        and I never really had no full masculine walk …
        they're always like stuck together –
and I'm walking
    I'm walking around –
        not thinking anything   lady like about my way I'm walking ….
and before you know it they go "well check Mary Alice out."
So they started calling me Mary Alice …
    and that was my whole nickname for Vietnam for ten and a half months
        and it was OK to call Mary Alice,
           I — it didn't bother me at awllllll.
They go "well check him out — Mary Alice."
I picked the morale right up,
    as Mary Alice, [*Laughs.*]
Oh man.
I played house in the bunker,
    y'know tidied it up,
        could I have it lookin' like this?

I tidied it up I made a screen dooor
            and we had screen all around the top,
                        a little fancy sis touch to the bunker.
There was eleven of us, and …..
            oh wait a second [*Chokes up.*]

Eleven guys were in my bunker? …
and they all pulled through,
            all eleven.

And I – I just said
            I just think it was me that pulled 'em all through.
            I really do yeah,
                        I kept 'em all laughing —
                                    and we cried together too
                                    and that's OK
uh. a big part —
            how I pulled through was because I …
            I think cause I laughed and cried –
            lot of people don't cry –
                        I did, [*Laughs.*]
                                    goddam nerves no wonder I cried, man …
but alot of people hold it all in
            they really do,
                        uh I cried and laughed the whole time.

Mom

Dorothy Hajdys-Holman

I knew that he hated it — and ... that ship.
and he wasn't —
matter of fact when he was home I think he really wanted to go AWOL
but he really didn't want to get into trouble either
and now I wish I wouldn't never let him go to the airport....
[*Long pause.*]
the night before Allen was killed
      he called me to tell me that his paperwork was was gonna be there any day
                                          now

        and he'd be discharged
        and he'd be home before Christmas for good.
and then 24 hours later they were at the door knocking at the door telling me he
                                    was dead.

matter of fact, I had on one of those long night shirts?
it was only 7:15 and I was home alone
      and I didn't expect nobody to come over so when I came home after I ate
I just went and took my clothes off and put it on
and was watching TV and they came to the door
and any mother who has somebody in the service
      knows that if two guys come in dress blues that's something bad —
and um
they told me that Allen had been assaulted in the park in Japan and that he was dead
and I sat here for about 45 minutes before I even realized I didn't have any clothes
                                        on.
I was hysterical that night but compared to the night when they called me from
                                    California
and told me I wouldn't want the coffin open? — that was the worst.
until then I had no idea how he was killed you know I didn't know if he was shot
      or stabbed or um at first I didn't even know it was Americans who killed
                                      him —

shipmates. they were shipmates on the same ship —
The Navy did not tell me.
every time I would ask 'em they said they were looking into it.
The Navy wouldn't tell me —
They would never admit Allen was killed because he was gay.
they they don't know why he was killed.
      just that Terry Helvey was drunk.
Terry Helvey kept giving different statements
      every time the wind blew he gave a different statement
         so they didn't know what to believe
      and Charles Vins just kept his mouth shut he wouldn't say nothing
         so he said that he would tell the truth if they would make a deal with
                                       him
      and not charge him with murder.
so that— after they made the deal … he told them you know what did happen.
it wasn't until after the deal was made that he also told them that he also kil —
      kicked Allen three times. that he was an accomplice.
I mean he served 72 days.
you know I I cannot understand how someone can watch somebody get killed,
      even if he hadn't done anything —
how he could stand there and watch happen what happened to Allen and do
                            nothing —
and then just be charged with failure to report a crime.

Terry Helvey's shoeprint was embedded in my son's face.

The whole time I waited for his body to return,
I thought that um I would be able to hold him and I would be able to kiss him
                            good-bye
and then they told me that there was nothing that they could do to make him
                            presentable
and that I really should never open the coffin.
My minister begged me not to open the coffin cause he had seen it
      and not to go in there and look at him but
         there was nothing that was going to stop me from going to see him.
and I went in there and — and I couldn't hold that body
I mean it looked nothing like my Allen. it was nothing like my Allen.

and then they closed the coffin
>and the whole day I thought how do I know it's him?
I mean sure the hat's there
>and the uniform's there and it has his pin on it that says Schindler
but how do I know it's him?
and the next day during the wake that we had for him it just kept going through
>>my mind
I'm gonna have to open that coffin again. and I'm going I r(eally) I don't think I
>>can do it.
and um just before the wake was over I went out in the hallway
>and I talked to my daughter Kathy
and it was really funny cause she wanted to talk to me
>the same time I wanted to talk to her and we both wanted to say the same
>>thing.
she wanted to say, "Mom, how do we know that's Allen?"
and so she agreed — her husband and her,
that when everybody left they would reopen the coffin
>and they would roll up the sleeve and see if his tattoo was there.
[*Approaching TRAIN WHISTLE in distance.*]
He had um he had a shark on one arm and he had a tiger on the arm — other arm
>and he had the emblem of the USS Midway the ship that he loved on his arm.
but uh I was upset when he got the tattoo —
you know, disformed his beautiful body you know
but if it wasn't for that tattoo
to this day I would not know that's him in that coffin....

[*TRAIN rushes past, shaking house. Long pause.*]

If somebody could show me in the Bible where Jesus says — [*Cough.*]
I don't mean Paul or anybody else
but where Jesus says that I'm not to have anything to do with homosexuals,
where I'm to condemn 'em because they're worthless
and I mean that's the way I feel
>that a lot of these ministers make it seem like they're worthless.
um there's people out there like Jerry Farwell (*sic.*)
I think if I could ever [*Breath.*] stand as close as I am to you with Jerry Farwell
>I would slap him in the face I mean he just preaches so much hatred.

um I don't know if you've seen Oprah Monday
    but on Oprah Monday
    um next week on —
        when Ellen comes out
           Oprah plays her therapist and I guess Oprah tells her it's OK to be gay
               you know to be a lesbian
and um everyone on her show Monday in the audience was condemning her,
    telling her telling Oprah
               that she's gonna go to Hell because she's defending them.
well my opinion is the those people that are condemning it
    are probably going to be the first ones in Hell.
Allen's up in Heaven.

no matter what … those evangelical Christians think, I think Allen's in Heaven.

d'you wanna hear something really weird?
OK   I have a a a nephew who's —
    he's seven years old now
           so like he was only two and a half, three when Allen was killed
    so he really doesn't remember Allen that much
        I mean he remembers a little bit about him.
    and then he, you know, from being on the news and everything like that ….
but um he believes that when he —
    if he has a balloon or something and it and and it goes off up into the air
        then Allen catches it.
so a couple couple of weeks ago was my grandson's birthday
and we had bought some helium balloons and there was some — two purple ones
    and Allen's favorite color was purple
and so um James was kind of acting up
so I said "well James why don't we go get the purple balloons
    and then we'll release them up and let Allen catch 'em up in heaven."
and it was real windy out and we went outside
and we —
    him and my grandson were gonna release the balloons up in the —
    up into the air [Breath.]
and they went flying off so far cause it was so windy
they went really way up
and finally they got to the point that we couldn't see 'em

and the minute we couldn't see 'em like a storm came
and I mean it came down like buckets just like that
and it only lasted for a couple minutes and then it was gone.
Anybody'd think I'm really crazy but it was like Allen saying "I caught it Mom."

Traitor

Frank Kameny, WWII combat veteran and long-time activist

You have to get nasty with these people.
One of the problems with our whole gay movement,
    is that the opposition throw rocks at us
      and we throw mushballs back,
You do not win wars
      wi(th) … um uh by fighting ro.. er rocks with mushballs,
and our people haven't learned to throw rocks back yet in a lot of different
                                  contexts.

We should be hitting them hard.
uhhh if word gets around that any commanding officer,
    who starts one of these cases,
      is gonna be awakened at 3 o'clock in the morning by bullhorns
        in front of his eh in front of his house denouncing him as a traitor,
    and that his name –
      by name –
        you can't be
         you can't say
you can't use nice little uhhh official titles and departments,
    the Department of the Army has done this,
    and the Secretary of Defense, ex-officio, has done that.
You go out after Captain John Jones of the hundred and second infantry in Camp
                                    Hood
    whose address is such and so
      and whose telephone number is such and so
        has started this case –
          Start phoning him.
           He is a traitor.
and you send that out over the Internet
and you denounce them and you ridicule them in the media
    from one end of the country to the other
      you make their lives a living hell

um uh an ongoing never ending nightmare 24 hours a day seven days a week
                                        and it doesn't stop,
            and you go after them –
                that way once the word gets around you'll se..
                    you'll see them stop bringing some of those cases.
        And the argument,
            um the treason argument is a very simple one.
Uh studies have shown,
        that collectively and statistically,
            servicemembers — gay servicemembers — do better than the average...
Therefore if you're going to to throw uh gay service pe(ople) ... uh members out,
        you are uh impairing and and and diminishing the quality of our armed
                                                services –
            to diminish the quality of our armed services
                is to give aid and comfort to the enemy...
        Article 3 Section 3 of the Constitution defines aid –
                    defines treason ...
                        as giving aid and comfort to the enemy...
        Therefore anyone who is in any way involved
            in one of these discharges of a gay person at any level whatsoever...
                is a traitor ...
                and should be indicted,
                        prosecuted,
                            tried,
and hanged for treason and I will be delighted to provide the hangman's rope out
                                    of my own pocket.

Can You Fight?

Major General Vance Coleman, US Army (Retired.)

One of my commanders once told me an organization … mirrors its leadership.
And that's true — from the lowest level of command all the way up.
It's what <u>you</u> are is what your unit is.
If you -— toleratte negative behavior toward individuals,
        it's gonna happen —
                if ya don't it won't.
I enlisted, uhh 1947,   —   yeah a long time ago, [*Laughs.*] yeah.
We were very poor and I probably joined for economic reasons,
        I would suspect at that time,
And it was segregated then.
so … and some of the same arguments,
parents will <u>not</u> accept their sons and daughters –
        or their sons at that point –
ah in an integrates barr barracks sleeping with blacks, [*Knocking finger on table.*]
parents will not acccpt their sons and daughters sleeping with lesbians and gays.
ah and and the – you know the one about what having to build separate bathrooms
                                    … my God.
I've been there, I'm black don't give me that … horseshit.
uhh what … you know essentially what happens in the in in the military
        is that, we took young men and women …
        and brainwashed them really
                and retrained them, you know, just wash …
                        washed them clean and retrained them –
and what they were taught is that you're here to fight
        and when you fight you fight to win.
So the question was …
        who do I want beside me when I fight,
nothing to do with with whether you're sss … uh straight or gay,
but can you fight?
My life depended on it.

I was the commander of the unit Ben Shalom was assigned to that –
    when she was reinstated.
and I said to some of my peers,
      that uh y'know one day she's the best soldier in the unit
        and suddenly she says "I'm gay" and she's the worst?

Anger

Miriam Ben Shalom - #2

I guess my biggest problem if I had to –
     to come down to it all,
i.. is it's something.…
     I wish somebody could teach me –
          I don't know how to stop bein' angry .…
Day in and day out I have to listen to remarks
     "oh that's so gay
          you fag
               you mother fucker fag
                    asshole fag"
     you know, amongst the kids
               and then you turn to the administration —
                    the people who are supposed to be in charge
                         and they don't even listen.
In the course of your w … play, you wanna say what I do,
     you may say that I teach for Milwaukee public schools,
          and Milwaukee Area Technical College,
               and if you find a way to do so –
                    please do.
[*Pause.*]
um y'know because it's time for them to realize there are gay teachers.
Does it matter whether it's the Pentagon or the principal of my school or whatever,
and I don't know how to quit bein' angry,
     and and it gets to me because I really don't like being angry all the time,
          but I don't know what else to do.
huh [*Sighs.*]

I have better things to do than talk with you on a Sunday afternoon –
     I could be in bed making love with my partner right now,
          I could be fishing .…
               but you're important.

You know and part of the reason I talk to you is because I am angry,
     may … maybe that's a good way to to to deal with it,
         but – I don't know.
[*Pause.*]
Although there's a part of me that would like to shoot Jesse Helms between the
                          eyes.…
     um I don't think violence is the way
         um and one of the things I decided to do when I got out of the Army was
                        except in self defense
                 to not engage in violence,
           it was a very conscious decision on my part.
um I mean if I stop to think about what I've been trained to do …
     pause a moment and cogitate on that –
         I mean yes I'm old I'm 49 but some things never go away,
and … getting arrested in front of the White House was the only –
     one of the few things that I knew how to do to express my anger
                  in a non violent way.
huh [*Sigh.*]
It was planned of course it is –
     you talk to people about it,
but to have somebody take my shoelaces out,
     take my ribbons off,
         um to strip my uniform bare,
            and to handcuff me with my hands behind my back ….
um huh [*Sigh.*] –
     I would do it again,
         um I still have that uniform in exactly the same condition it was then.
um, it's a shameful thing when American veterans have to protest so,
     and get arrested that way,
         to try and make a point.
I mean, [*Starts to fight back tears.*]
     I'd like to think that because I was born here?
         um — that I'm an American citizen
            and it really brought home to me that day that I am not.
And it was so humiliating
     in front of the White House — my –
            in front of the home of my Commander in Chief.

That was an act of anger on my part.
And it's just…. but it hurts –
                    my own country man.

Sorry. [*Apologizing for having begun to cry during above.*]
It's just extremely painful …
         to be handled so.
[*Pause. Recovers herself.*]
I can't say that I felt proud I was arrested I felt ashamed,
         but … it wasn't that I was ashamed for what I was doing –
              I was ashamed for my country ….
I'm ashamed of President Clinton
He said he was going to end the ban and he didn't.
         He gave us his word and he broke it.
I feel ashamed that this country is letting wonderful wonderful people go to waste.

You don't … engage in a dialogue with the military –
         You give them an order …
              And they do it.
                   And Clinton didn't get it.
I just I just feel so betrayed at at at all the money –
I mean they spend half a billion dollars a year on ferreting out queers from the
                                                      military.

Give me one percent of that half a billion dollars a year as a teacher –
                        I could commit miracles,
                             in terms of education   you know.
     There's so much that could be done with that amount of money.
     Oh yeah.
         Oh yeah.

The Wall

Don MacIver, former Sergeant First Class, US Army
At the Vietnam Veterans War Memorial, Washington, D.C.

I told Boyd and Dennis that if they ever have to make an AIDS quilt for me, I
want it to say Don MacIver, the Gay Green Beret.
[*Pause.*]
I turned around to the White House and I thought –
      "oh my God here I am sitting [*Chuckles.*] in front of the White House
      in full military uniform
      protesting don't ask don't tell,"
and it was –
      y'know it w … — it was
            it was a very hu humbling experience,
but at the same time it was very empowering
      y'know I I felt I felt very powerful at that moment,
and it was also very interesting because
      the park police who guard the   perimeter   of the White House,
they wear uh blue shirts light light blue sh…short sleeve shirts they were wearing
                                        I think
and then dark dark pants
and over their right pocket –
      if they were in the military,
            they can wear a badge – designating the unit they were in.
and there were like four or five of them
      who had been Special Forces they were wearing a badge that indicated they
                                    were Special Forces.
And so here now, they were looking at a brother [*Laughs.*],
            I mean a real — a a real brother.
and um it was it was kind of interesting because there were two cops standing on
                                      the curb
      looking at me and the guy was pointing out   different things on my uniform,
and I mean when you –
      when you have   ll.. like three rows of ribbons …..
your whole military history is written up there … your —

well …
        like the Bronze Star,
        the Air Medal,
        the Army Commendation Medal,
        uh Combat Medic Badge for treating people in combat,
        Jump Wings,
        um y'know all kinds of service ribbons,
        unit decorations,
        Vietnamese Jump Wings,
I mean y'know there was alot of [*Laughs.*] shit on there you know,
and I mean no(t) not to brag but I mean you know the thing is that —
        that I did, I did what I was asked to of my country.
Sent me off to fight a dirty little war that they had no intention of ever winning
        you know
and uh
        y'know I'm I'm just as proud as I can be to be a veteran of this country
                and especially to be a veteran of th'United States Army Special Forces,
because uhh
        that took everything I had to give to get … to get it.
but it was something that I put my mind to that I was gonna do
        and I did it.
And I fought the war.

The day after I was arrested
        at the White House
I came down to the Wall, I put my uniform back on
        and I came down here.
and there's a troop of boy scouts out there
        seeing the Wall,
[*Pause.*]
and   these two boys are walking by
        and one of them
out of the corner of his eye, he he caught this image of whatever I was —
        and he looked up at me and his eyes got big as saucers
and he says "are you a Green Beret?"
and I smiled and I said "yes,"
and he says, "can I take your picture?" [*Laughs.*]

Flash - a photograph of Don MacIver appears. As he continues to speak, more photos flash up — the interviewed veterans and active duty men and women, regular people in or out of uniform, some whose identity is concealed. The photos appear slowly at first, and then rapidly cascade, filling the stage.

Anyway,
       but it's just …
              it's stuff that'll never –
None of this all …
       will ever leave me.

Photos continue to appear, and overwhelm the stage.

END OF PLAY.

CONTRIBUTORS

JON ROBIN BAITZ's plays include *Ten Unknowns, Mizlansky/Zilinsky or Schmucks, A Fair Country, The Film Society, The Substance of Fire, The End of the Day*, and *Three Hotels*. Screenplays include *The Substance of Fire* and the soon to be released *People I Know*.

KIM BENSTON is Professor of English at Haverford College. His is the author of *Baraka: The Renegade and the Mask* and, most recently, *Performing Blackness*, and has also edited books on Amiri Baraka, Ralph Ellison, and Larry Neal.

MICHAEL CADDEN is the Director of Princeton University's Program ing Theater and Dance. For over twenty years, he has taught regularly at the Bread Loaf School of English (Vermont, Alaska, New Mexico, Oxford). He is co-editor of *Engendering Men: The Question of Male Feminist Criticism* (Routledge) and a CD-ROM study of Henrik Ibsen's *A Doll House* (Annenberg/CPB).

OSKAR EUSTIS is Artistic Director of Trinity Repertory Company in Providence, Rhode Island, Professor of Theatre at Brown University, and Chair of the new professional training program initiated by Brown and Trinity. He has received Honorary Doctorates from Rhode Island College and Brown University, and has commissioned and developed many new plays, including Emily Mann's *Execution of Justice*, Tony Kushner's *Angels in America*, and Anna Deavere Smith's *Twilight: Los Angeles, 1992*.

SUSAN GLASPELL (1876-1948) was a founding member of the Provincetown Players and a playwright whose work, along with that of Eugene O'Neill, established the company as an influential writer's theatre. She wrote several plays for the Provincetown Players, including *Trifles* (1916), *The Inheritors*, and *The Verge*. Glaspell won the 1931 Pulitzer Prize for *Alison's House*, loosely based on the life of Emily Dickinson.

LANGSTON HUGHES (1902-1967) gained fame as a poet with the publication of his first book of verse, *The Weary Blues*, in 1925. He was one of the leading African American writers, whose contributions to poetry, fiction, and drama were central to the emergence of black literature in the United States. He was active in civil rights and social causes, and often voiced the aspirations of minorities and the dispossessed. All of his verse, and short stories, as well as his novel *Not Without Laughter*, are still in print.

LEROI JONES (AMIRI BARAKA) was born in 1934 in Newark, New Jersey. After attending Howard University in Washington, D. C., he served in the United States Air Force. In the late fifties he settled in New York's Greenwich Village, where he was a central figure of that bohemian scene. He became nationally prominent in 1964, with the New York production of his Obie Award-winning play, *Dutchman*. After the death of Malcolm X he became a Black Nationalist, moving first to Harlem and then back home to Newark. In the mid-1970s, abandoning Cultural Nationalism, he became a Third World Marxist-Leninist. In 1999, after teaching for twenty years in the Department of Africana Studies at SUNY-Stony Brook, he retired. However, in retirement he is as active and productive as an artist and intellectual as he has ever been in his career. Currently he lives with his wife, the poet Amina Baraka, in Newark

MICHAEL KAHN is the creative heart of The Shakespeare Theatre in Washington D.C., dubbed " … the nation's foremost Shakespeare company," by *The Wall Street Journal*. In addition, he is the Director of the Drama Division at Julliard, and founded the Academy for Classical Acting at George Washington University. Mr. Kahn knew and worked closely with Tennessee Williams — they spent the summer of 1975 together as Williams rewrote *Cat on a Hot Tin Roof*. Kahn would direct the acclaimed Broadway production of the newly rewritten masterpiece featuring Elizabeth Ashley. Williams asked Kahn to direct *Sweet Bird of Youth*, which he did in 1998 at The Shakespeare Theatre, reuniting with Ashley. Williams told Kahn that *Camino Real* was his personal favorite; Kahn would bring the rarely performed work to the Shakespeare Theatre stage in 2000.

MOISES KAUFMAN is an award winning playwright and director. His two most recent plays, *Gross Indecency: The Three Trials of Oscar Wilde* and *The Laramie Project*,. have been performed around the world. He is currently finishing the movie adaptation of *The Laramie Project*, which he wrote and directed for HBO.

ADRIENNE KENNEDY was born in Pittsburgh and now makes her home in New York City. Her best known plays are *Funnyhouse of a Negro*, *A Movie Star Has to Star in Black and White*, and *The Owl Answers*. She received a 1996 Obie Award for *June and Jean in Concert* and, with her son, Adam Kennedy, received the 1996 Obie Award for Best Play for *Sleep Deprivation Chamber*. It premiered at New York's Public Theater and was produced by Signature Theatre Company, which devoted an entire year-long season to Ms. Kennedy's work. Her plays are taught in colleges throughout this country, Europe, India, and Africa, and she has been a visiting lecturer at New York University, University of California at Berkeley, and Harvard. She has received numerous awards including a Guggenheim award, the Lila Wallace Readers Digest Award, and the American

Academy of Arts and Letters Award for Literature. Her published works include, *In One Act*, *Alexander Plays*, and *Deadly Triplets*, all published by University of Minnesota Press,;and *People Who Led to My Plays*, a memoir, published by Theatre Communications Group. A study of her work, *Intersecting Boundaries: Theatre of Adrienne Kennedy* has also been published by University of Minnesota Press.

TONY KUSHNER is the author of *Angels in America, Part One: Millennium Approaches* and *Part Two: Perestroika*, each of which received the Tony Award for Best Play in their respective years of production, among numerous other prizes and awards; *Millennium Approaches* also received the Pulitzer Prize. Kushner's other works for the stage, which include *Slavs!*, *A Bright Room Called Day*, and *The Illusion*, a free adaptation of Pierre Corneille's comedy, have been produced frequently throughout the country and the world.

SHIRLEY LAURO is probably best known for her Tony nominated Broadway drama, *Open Admissions*, named to The New York Times "Ten Best Plays of the Year" List and recipient of the prestigious Dramatist Guild Hull-Warriner Award, two Drama Desk nominations, a Theatre World Award, and a Samuel French Playwriting Award. She subsequently adapted the play for a CBS TV Special starring Jane Alexander. Ms. Lauro's work has been produced extensively both here and abroad. Her works include: *The Last Trial Of Clarence Darrow*, *Margaret And Kit*, *Pearls On The Moon*, *The Coal Diamond*, *Nothing Immediate*, *I Don't Know Where You're Coming From At aAll!*, *Sunday Go To Meetin'*, *Railin It Uptown*, *Out Of Time*, and her latest play, *Speckled Birds*. Her novel, *The Edge*, published by Doubleday, and Veidenfeld & Nocolson in Great Britain, where it was a Literary Guild Alternate. A Guggenheim Fellow, Ms. Lauro is proud to serve on the Steering Committee of the Dramatists Guild Council. Other affiliations include PEN, Writers Guild East, The Woman's Project, Ensemble Studio Theatre, and the League of Professional Theatre Women/NY. She is Adj. Professor in the Dramatic Writing Program at NYU's Tisch School of the Arts.

ROMULUS LINNEY is the author of three novels, essays, short fiction, and over thirty plays, produced throughout the United States and abroad. He has received many awards and is a member of the American Academy of Arts and Sciences.

EMILY MANN has been artistic director of McCarter Theatre since 1990. Her McCarter directing credits include *Romeo and Juliet*, *Because He Can*, *The Cherry Orchard* (also adapted), *Betrayal*, *The Mai*, *A Doll House*, *The Perfectionist*, *Miss Julie* (also adapted), *Cat on a Hot Tin Roof*, *Three Sisters*, *Betsey Brown* (co-author), *The Glass Menagerie*, *The Matchmaker* and *Twilight: Los Angeles, 1992*. She is also the author of *Greensboro (A Requiem)*, *Execution of Justice*, *Still Life* (winner of six Obie Awards, including Distinguished Playwriting and Distinguished Directing), and *Annulla, An Autobiography*. Ms. Mann wrote and directed the world premiere of *Having Our Say* at McCarter before it moved to Broadway, where it received three Tony nominations, including Best Play and Best Direction. A winner of the prestigious Hull-Warriner Award, Ms. Mann is a member of the Dramatists Guild and serves on its Council. Ms Mann also wrote the screenplay for the Peabody Award-winning television movie of *Having Our Say* that aired on CBS. A collection of her plays, *Testimonies: Four Plays*, is available through Theatre Communications Group, Inc.

NICHOLAS MOSCHOVAKIS has recently co-edited *The Collected Poems of Tennessee Williams* with David Roessel for New Directions, and is now planning an edition of several unpublished one-act plays that Williams conceived in the late 1930's and early 1940's as parts of his *American Blues* cycle. He taught English for three and a half years at the University of the South in Sewanee, Tennessee, which owns the rights to Williams's works.

CLIFFORD ODETS (1906-1963) joined the famed Group Theatre in 1931, and the six plays that he wrote for that troupe between 1935 and 1938, *Waiting for Lefty*, *Awake and Sing!*, *Till the Day I Die*, *Paradise Lost*, *Golden Boy*, and *Rocket to the Moon*, have all become part of the repertoire of twentieth-century American drama and are among the most famous and most authentic works about the Great Depression. In his later years he worked as a screenwriter in Hollywood.

JANICE PARAN is a New Jersey-based writer and the resident dramaturg and director of play development at the McCarter Theatre in Princeton, where she has worked closely with numerous writers, including Emily Mann, Nilo Cruz, Dael Orlandersmith, Eric Bogosian, writer/composer Polly Pen, and writer/director Stephen Wadsworth. She is a frequent contributor to *American Theatre* magazine.

ARNOLD RAMPERSAD is the Sara Hart Kimball Professor of English at Stanford University. He is the author of the two-volume *Life of Langston Hughes* (1986, 1988) and editor, with David Roessel, of *Collected Poems of Langston Hughes* (1994) and the forthcoming *Selected Letters of Langston Hughes*. He is currently working on a biography of Ralph Ellison.

DAVID ROESSEL is the co-editor of *The Collected Poems of Tennessee Williams*, the Associate Editor of *The Collected Poems of Langston Hughes*, and the author of *In Byron's Shadow: Modern Greece in the English and American Imagination*. He is currently working on a biography of Mike Gold.

DANIEL SULLIVAN (Director) has directed in theatres both nationally and abroad. On Broadway, Dan directed the current production of *Proof* and the recent productions of *Major Barbara* and *A Moon for the Misbegotten*. He also directed *The Heidi Chronicles, Conversations with my Father, I'm Not Rappaport* (also London and National tour), and Lincoln Center's *Ah! Wilderness, The Sisters Rosensweig*, and *An American Daughter*. His most recent Off-Broadway credits include *Ten Unknowns, Spinning Into Butter, Dinner With Friends* (also Geffen Playhouse), *Proof, Far East, Psychopathia Sexualis, A Fair Country, The Sisters Rosensweig, The Substance of Fire* (also Los Angeles), and *London Suite*. From 1981 to 1997, Mr. Sullivan served as Artistic Director of Seattle Repertory Theatre, where he directed more than 60 productions including *Uncle Vanya, Caucasian Chalk Circle, She Stoops To Conquer, Inspecting Carol, The Mandrake, The Wedding, As You Like It*, and *Major Barbara*, among many others. He established Seattle Rep's new play program, developing new works by Jon Robin Baitz, Herb Gardner, A.R. Gurney, Arthur Miller, Wendy Wasserstein, Charlayne Woodard, and William Mastrosimone, among others. Mr. Sullivan's film and television credits include *The Substance of Fire* and the forthcoming PBS presentation of *Far East*. Mr. Sullivan teaches in the theatre department at the University of Illinois, Champaign-Urbana and serves as Associate Director at Lincoln Center Theatre.

ALAN WALD is Director of the Program in American Culture and Professor of English at the University of Michigan. He is the author of six books on U.S. literary radicalism, including *The Revolutionary Imagination* (1983), *The New York Intellectuals* (1987), *Writing From the Left* (1994), and the forthcoming *Exiles From a Future Time* (2002).

TENNESSEE WILLIAMS (1911-1983) spent his early childhood in Mississippi, his adolescent years in St. Louis, and the rest of his life living between many different locales: Iowa, Chicago, New York City, Provincetown, Taos, Mexico, Santa Monica, Key West, and the most influential of all, New Orleans (probably where he first fully encountered and explored the lives available to a homosexual man at that time). Having lived through the 1930's as a desultory student and struggling writer of poetry, fiction, and drama, Williams drew the attention of Broadway theatrical circles in 1939 by winning an award for several one-act plays he called *American Blues*. Though a few productions of full-length plays by Williams were staged during the late 1930's and early 1940's, in Missouri and in Boston (the latter a failure), it was only the success of *The Glass Menagerie* in Chicago and then in New York in 1945 that made his reputation as a playwright. He went on to become widely celebrated for his works *A Streetcar Named Desire* (1947), *Summer and Smoke* (1948), *The Rose Tattoo* (1951), *Camino Real* (1953), *Cat on a Hot Tin Roof* (1955), *Suddenly Last Summer* (1958), *Sweet Bird of Youth* (1959), and *The Night of the Iguana* (1961), as well as many others.

MARC WOLF (writer/performer) received an Obie and was nominated for the Drama Desk and Outer Critics Circle Awards for his Off-Broadway performance of *Another American: Asking and Telling* at The New Group at the Theatre at St. Clements, directed by Joe Mantello. He has also presented the play at the McCarter Theatre; The Mark Taper Forum (Garland Award); Seattle Repertory Theatre; Trinity Repertory Company; The Studio Theatre, Washington D.C. (Helen Hayes Award, GLAAD Award); Center Stage, Baltimore; About Face Theatre; New Conservatory Theatre (San Francisco Bay Area Theatre Critics Circle Award); Henlopen Theatre Project. He has presented developing stages of *Another American: Asking and Telling* at New York Stage & Film at Vassar College, the Provincetown Repertory Theatre, Dixon Place and Mabou Mines, where he was a 1998 Resident Artist. Other New York appearances include Max in *Bent* at HERE, Platonov in *Wild Honey* at Synchronicity Space, and, on television, Brent Lawrence/Marian Crane on *Guiding Light*. He is a graduate of Williams College. Marc has been commissioned by the McCarter Theatre to create a new play.